PRAISE FOR
THE GOAL: A BUSINESS GRAPHIC NOVEL

"*The Goal* is the #1 business book of all time and the graphic adaptation makes this timeless classic and its powerful ideas even more accessible. If you only read one business book, it should be this one."

—Verne Harnish, Founder Entrepreneurs' Organization (EO)
and author of *Scaling Up (Rockefeller Habits 2.0)*

"A compelling adaptation of Eli's seminal work. This book should be required reading for CIOs, CTOs and technologists the world over."

—Kevin Behr, Chief Science Officer at PraxisFlow
and co-author of *The Phoenix Project*

"*The Goal* has never been more relevant for organizations that rely on technology. The original is a must-read, and now the graphic novel is another path to understanding the Theory of Constraints. I'll be adding this to my recommendations list!"

—Dr. Nicole Forsgren, CEO and Chief Scientist at
DevOps Research and Assessment (DORA)

"Prior to reading *The Goal*, I worked for three governors and ran large organizations, budgets, and enterprises across almost every area of government. I tested seemingly endless improvement methodologies with little success. However, once I began applying the principles taught in *The Goal*, I began to see enormous jumps in my organization's performance—not just once—but time after time."

—Kris Cox, Executive Director, Utah Governor's Office
of Management and Budget

"An illustrated and abbreviated version of Dr. Goldratt's revolutionary thought process may seem counterintuitive, but the visual representations bring the basic concepts of Theory of Constraints to life."

—*Gary Adams, Director*, Delta Connection TechOps
at Delta Airlines

Alex Rogo is a harried plant manager who has been given 90 days to save his failing factory. If he doesn't improve the plant's performance, corporate headquarters will close it down and hundreds of workers will lose their jobs. It takes a chance meeting with Jonah, a former professor, to help him break out of his conventional thinking and figure out what needs to be done. As Alex identifies the plant's problems and works with his team to find solutions, the reader gains an understanding of the fundamental concepts behind the Theory of Constraints.

Visual and fun to read, *The Goal: A Business Graphic Novel* offers an accessible introduction to the Theory of Constraints concepts presented in *The Goal*, the business novel on which it was based.

The Goal is widely considered to be one of the most influential business books of all time. A bestseller since it was first published in 1984, the business novel has sold over 7 million copies, been translated into 32 languages and is taught in colleges, universities, and business schools around the world. Named to *Time* magazine's list of the 25 Most Influential Business Management Books, it is frequently cited by executives as a favorite or must-read title.

- Red Hat CEO Jim Whitehurst, who cites *The Goal* as one of the four books that most influenced his career, says that the concepts Goldratt developed for manufacturing are now being applied to the development of software products and services.

- Jeremy Roche, founding CEO of the cloud-based applications company FinancialForce, assigns *The Goal* to his management team to get them thinking about running a business as an interconnected set of processes.

Eliyahu M. Goldratt's Theory of Constraints (TOC) is a process of ongoing improvement that continuously identifies and leverages a system's constraints in order to achieve its goals. TOC revolutionized the factory floor in the 1980s and '90s and has been taught in business schools and MBA programs around the world ever since. Adopted by government agencies, the military, and businesses large and small, it is used in supply chain management, healthcare, retail, sales, marketing and project management. Its influence in software development is evident in Kanban methodology, Lean and Agile practices, and DevOps. The TOC-derived Logical Thinking Processes are also applied in areas such as education and personal development.

Dr Goldratt was once asked if he could summarize the Theory of Constraints in five sentences. He responded by saying that he didn't need five sentences, he only needed one word: Focus. He claimed that if we deal with symptoms, no matter how motivated we are or how hard we work, we shouldn't be surprised that we reach only limited results. Thus, when attempting to significantly improve our outcome in any area, we should strive to reveal the core problem and challenge the underlying assumptions in order to construct breakthrough solutions, solutions that will lead to quantum leaps in results rather than incremental improvements.

TOC novels by Eliyahu M. Goldratt

The Goal: A Process of Ongoing Improvement

It's Not Luck (sequel to The Goal)

Critical Chain

Necessary But Not Sufficient

Isn't it Obvious?

ELIYAHU M. GOLDRATT'S
THE GOAL
A BUSINESS GRAPHIC NOVEL

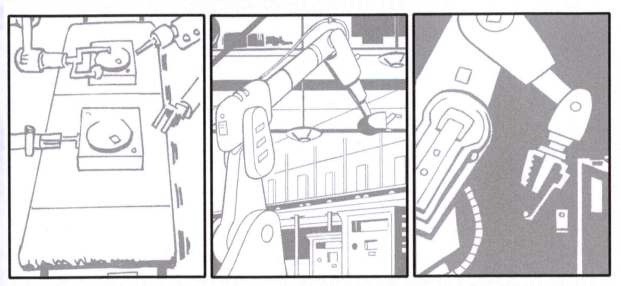

BASED ON THE BUSINESS NOVEL,
THE GOAL: A PROCESS OF ONGOING IMPROVEMENT
BY ELIYAHU M. GOLDRATT
AND JEFF COX

North River Press

First published 2018
by Routledge
2 Park Square, Milton Park, Abingdon, Oxon OX14 4RN

and by Routledge
711 Third Avenue, New York, NY 10017

Routledge is an imprint of the Taylor & Francis Group, an informa business

© 2018 Goldratt, Ltd., and The North River Press Publishing Corporation Based on the business novel, The Goal: A Process of Ongoing Improvement by Eliyahu M. Goldratt and Jeff Cox, Copyright © 2014.

British Library Cataloguing in Publication Data
A catalogue record for this book is available from the British Library

Library of Congress Cataloging in Publication Data
A catalog record for this book has been requested

ISBN: 978-0-815-38512-7 (hbk)
ISBN: 978-0-815-38513-4 (pbk)
ISBN: 978-1-351-20235-0 (ebk)

Publisher's Note
This book has been prepared from camera-ready copy provided by The North River Press Publishing Corporation.

Script by Dwight Jon Zimmerman
Interior art and design by Dean Motter
Cover Illustration by Dean Motter
Graphic Assistance by Courtney Remillared
Edited by Howard Zimmerman

Printed and bound by CPI Group (UK) Ltd, Croydon, CR0 4YY

AN INTRODUCTION TO THE THEORY OF CONSTRAINTS

ADAPTED BY DWIGHT JON ZIMMERMAN

ILLUSTRATED BY DEAN MOTTER

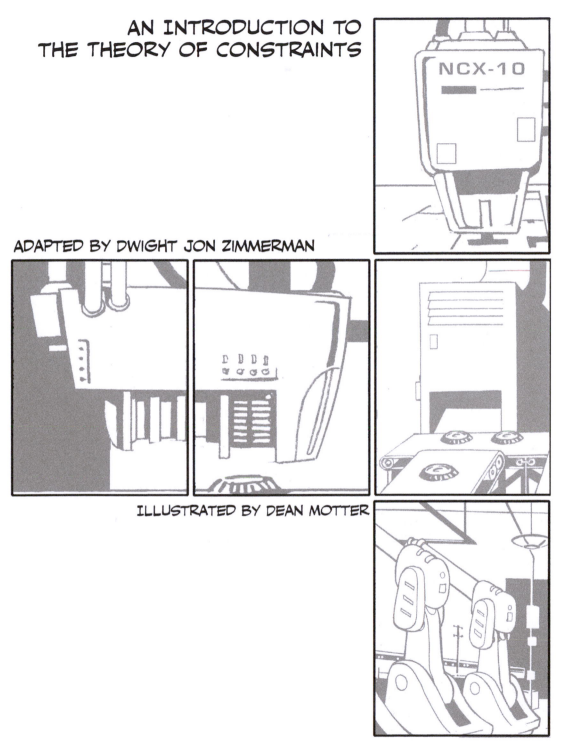

DEVELOPED AND EDITED BY HOWARD ZIMMERMAN

ABOUT ELIYAHU M. GOLDRATT

ELIYAHU M. GOLDRATT was an Israeli physicist and the father of the Theory of Constraints (TOC). He has been heralded as a "guru to industry" by *Fortune Magazine* and called "a genius" by *Business Week*. His first business novel, *The Goal*, has been a bestseller since 1984. With more than 7 million copies sold worldwide, it is recognized as one of the best-selling business books of all time. He authored many other books, including the business novels, *It's Not Luck* (the sequel to *The Goal*), *Critical Chain*, *Necessary but Not Sufficient* and *Isn't It Obvious?*. Dr. Goldratt was the founder of Goldratt Consulting (www.goldrattconsulting.com) and TOC for Education, a nonprofit organization dedicated to bringing TOC Thinking and TOC tools to teachers and their students (www.tocforeducation.com).

ABOUT THE SCRIPTER

DWIGHT JON ZIMMERMAN is a New York Times bestselling author and editor. He has written more than a dozen books, including *Lincoln's Last Days*, the New York Times bestselling adaptation of *Killing Lincoln*. He has written more than 300 articles on military history, as well as comic book stories for Marvel Comics and other comic book publishers.

ABOUT THE ARTIST

As art director and designer for CBS Records, Byron Preiss Visual Publications and DC Comics, illustrator DEAN MOTTER has created a plethora of award-winning book and record jackets. As a graphic novelist he is best known for *Terminal City*, *The Prisoner*, *Batman: Nine Lives* and his seminal creation, *Mister X*. He has illustrated nonfiction comic books for the Davis S. Wyman Institute and the Los Angeles Holocaust Museum, including *The Book Hitler Didn't Want You to Read* and *Karski's Mission: To Stop the Holocaust*.

INTRODUCTION

When my father, Dr. Eli Goldratt, started developing the Theory of Constraints, he decided to use a book to introduce its first application. He knew that many people didn't like reading boring management books. He thought he had an answer, he would write a story, a business novel or as some say a teaching novel. He was confident that publishers would welcome his book with open arms, but to his surprise, he got one rejection after another. One publisher was kind enough to explain: "If you want to write a novel, write a novel, if you want to write a business book, write a business book. But a business book that is written as a novel? We wouldn't even know what shelf to put it on." The tenth publisher he approached was Larry Gadd from The North River Press. Larry was an established publisher who published only books he believed in. He recognized the potential in the book and regardless of the fact that, at that time, there were no other business novels, he thought the risk was worth it. "People will enjoy a good story that they can also learn from," he said. The millions of copies *The Goal* sold, proved he got it right. That was over 30 years ago. I was just a kid.

Nowadays, more and more people don't like to read books at all. They have become accustomed to absorbing information in fast paced bits and bytes and reading is just too slow. *The Goal* is as relevant a book as it was decades ago, but the text format may discourage many from reading it. As the person in charge of my father's books I thought I may have a solution he would have been happy with. How about turning *The Goal* into a graphic novel? People raised an eyebrow. They said that if I want to publish comics, I should write comics but a business novel that is transformed to comics? Speaking of déjà vu... I turned to The North River Press, my father's long time publisher. Once again, Larry Gadd was enthusiastic. He recognized a new and greater potential for the still successful book he has been publishing for over thirty years, and regardless of the fact that there aren't many other business graphic novels around, he thought the risk was worth it. "You know, people will enjoy a story that they can also learn from." Larry accepted the challenge. He put together a team and we got to work. Did we get it right? You will be the judge of that.

Efrat Goldratt-Ashlag

THE GOAL

A BUSINESS GRAPHIC NOVEL

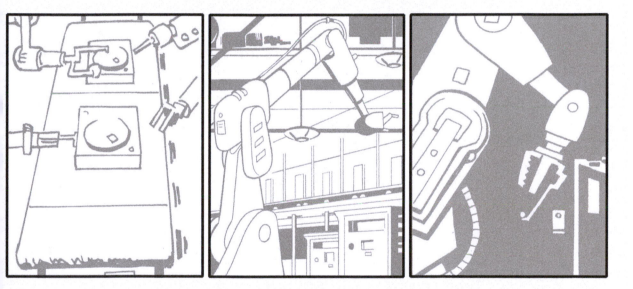

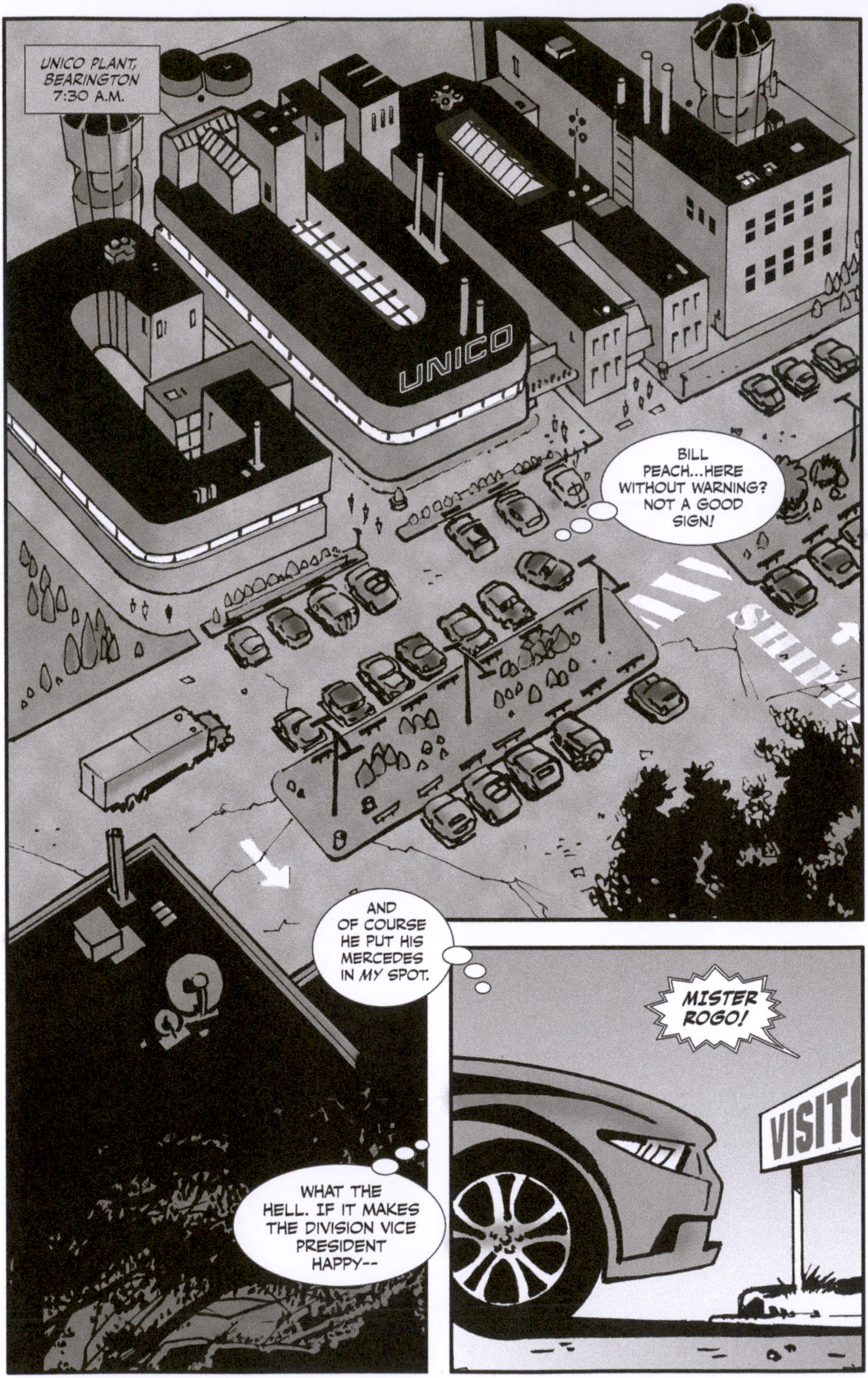
UNICO PLANT, BEARINGTON 7:30 A.M.
UNICO
BILL PEACH...HERE WITHOUT WARNING? NOT A GOOD SIGN!
AND OF COURSE HE PUT HIS MERCEDES IN MY SPOT.
WHAT THE HELL. IF IT MAKES THE DIVISION VICE PRESIDENT HAPPY--
MISTER ROGO!

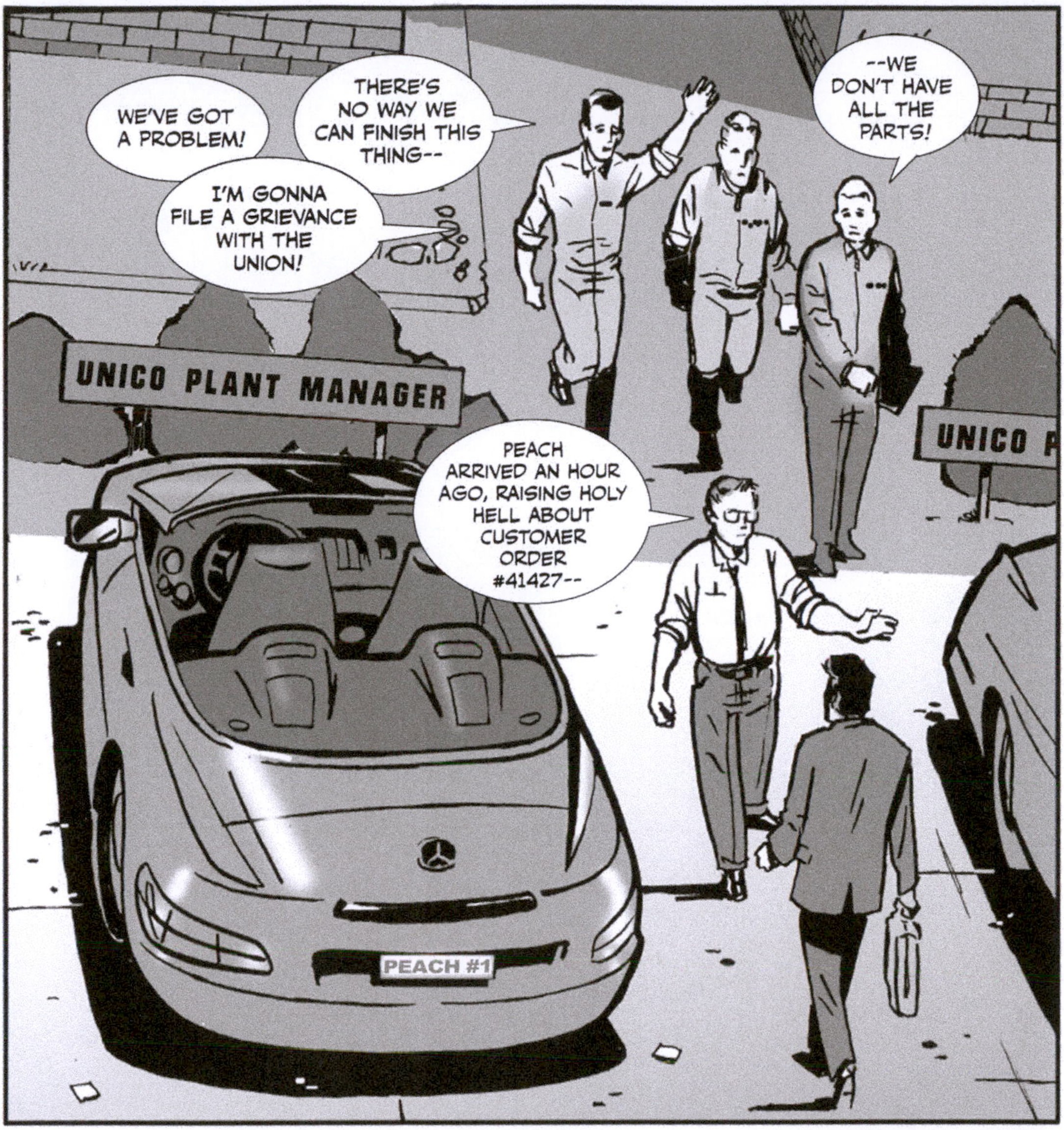
WE'VE GOT A PROBLEM!
THERE'S NO WAY WE CAN FINISH THIS THING--
--WE DON'T HAVE ALL THE PARTS!
I'M GONNA FILE A GRIEVANCE WITH THE UNION!
UNICO PLANT MANAGER
UNICO
PEACH ARRIVED AN HOUR AGO, RAISING HOLY HELL ABOUT CUSTOMER ORDER #41427--
PEACH #1

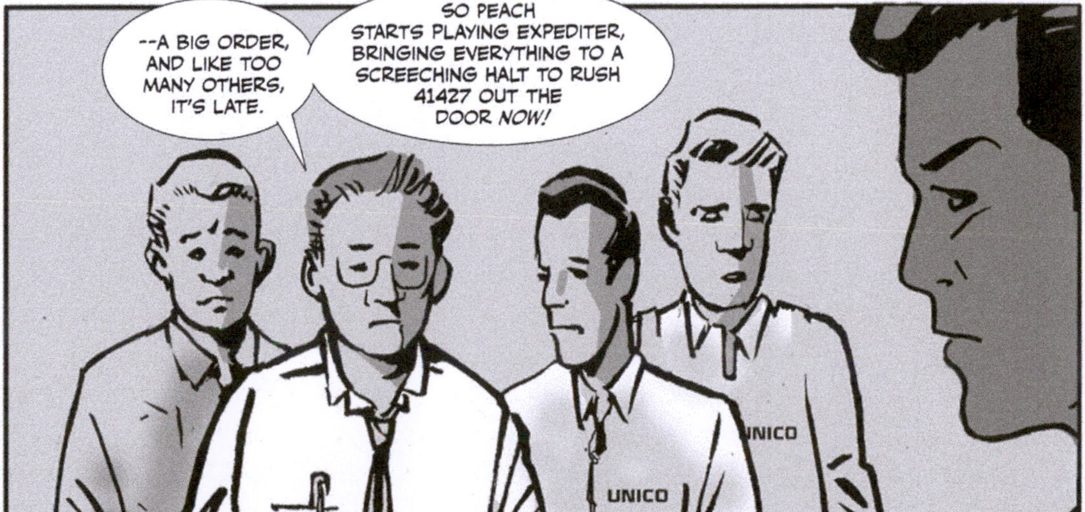
--A BIG ORDER, AND LIKE TOO MANY OTHERS, IT'S LATE.
SO PEACH STARTS PLAYING EXPEDITER, BRINGING EVERYTHING TO A SCREECHING HALT TO RUSH 41427 OUT THE DOOR *NOW!*
UNICO
NICO

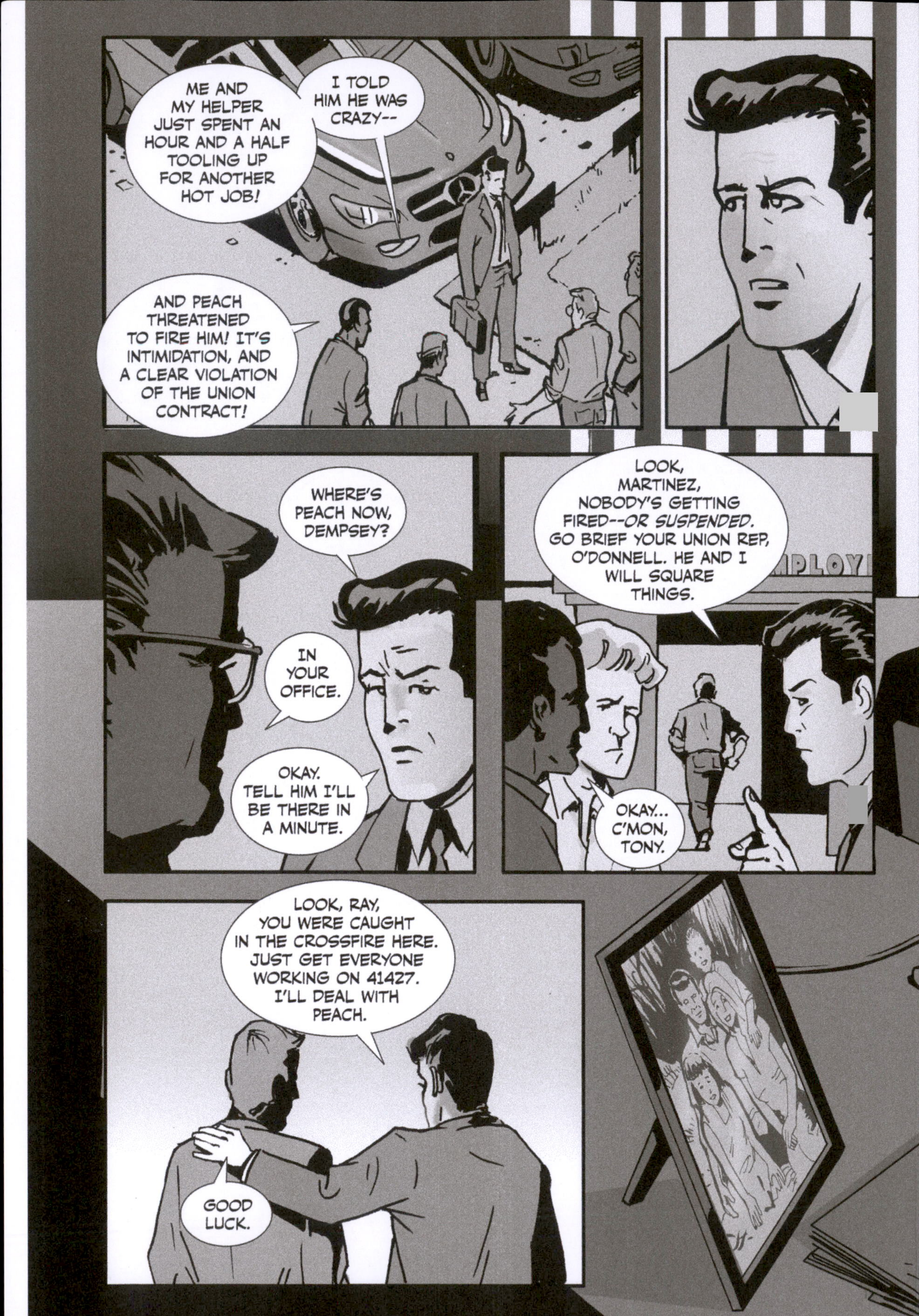
ME AND MY HELPER JUST SPENT AN HOUR AND A HALF TOOLING UP FOR ANOTHER HOT JOB!
I TOLD HIM HE WAS CRAZY--
AND PEACH THREATENED TO FIRE HIM! IT'S INTIMIDATION, AND A CLEAR VIOLATION OF THE UNION CONTRACT!
WHERE'S PEACH NOW, DEMPSEY?
IN YOUR OFFICE.
OKAY. TELL HIM I'LL BE THERE IN A MINUTE.
LOOK, MARTINEZ, NOBODY'S GETTING FIRED--*OR SUSPENDED.* GO BRIEF YOUR UNION REP, O'DONNELL. HE AND I WILL SQUARE THINGS.
OKAY... C'MON, TONY.
LOOK, RAY, YOU WERE CAUGHT IN THE CROSSFIRE HERE. JUST GET EVERYONE WORKING ON 41427. I'LL DEAL WITH PEACH.
GOOD LUCK.

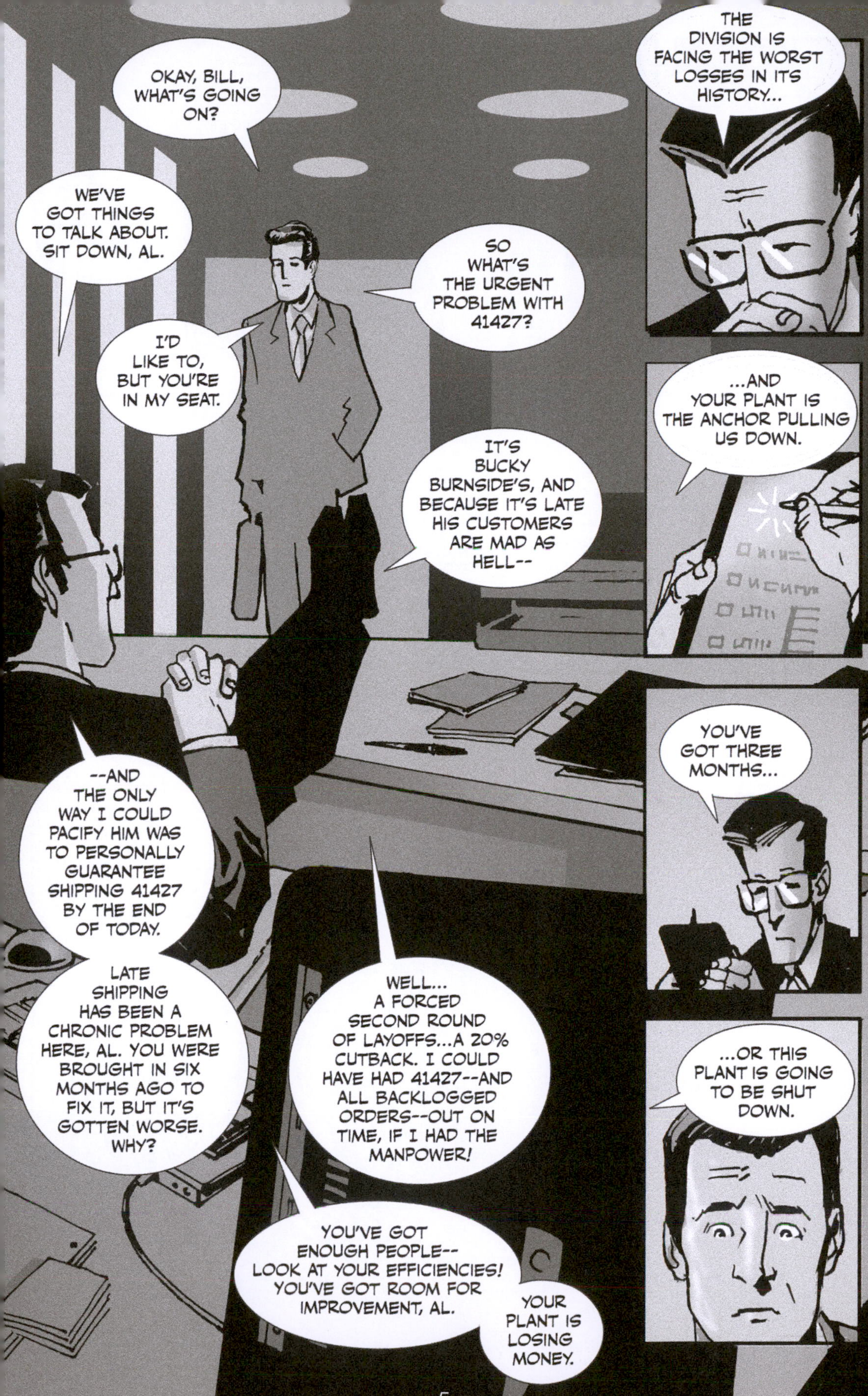
OKAY, BILL, WHAT'S GOING ON?
WE'VE GOT THINGS TO TALK ABOUT. SIT DOWN, AL.
I'D LIKE TO, BUT YOU'RE IN MY SEAT.
SO WHAT'S THE URGENT PROBLEM WITH 41427?
IT'S BUCKY BURNSIDE'S, AND BECAUSE IT'S LATE HIS CUSTOMERS ARE MAD AS HELL--
--AND THE ONLY WAY I COULD PACIFY HIM WAS TO PERSONALLY GUARANTEE SHIPPING 41427 BY THE END OF TODAY.
LATE SHIPPING HAS BEEN A CHRONIC PROBLEM HERE, AL. YOU WERE BROUGHT IN SIX MONTHS AGO TO FIX IT, BUT IT'S GOTTEN WORSE. WHY?
WELL... A FORCED SECOND ROUND OF LAYOFFS...A 20% CUTBACK. I COULD HAVE HAD 41427--AND ALL BACKLOGGED ORDERS--OUT ON TIME, IF I HAD THE MANPOWER!
YOU'VE GOT ENOUGH PEOPLE-- LOOK AT YOUR EFFICIENCIES! YOU'VE GOT ROOM FOR IMPROVEMENT, AL.
YOUR PLANT IS LOSING MONEY.
THE DIVISION IS FACING THE WORST LOSSES IN ITS HISTORY...
...AND YOUR PLANT IS THE ANCHOR PULLING US DOWN.
YOU'VE GOT THREE MONTHS...
...OR THIS PLANT IS GOING TO BE SHUT DOWN.

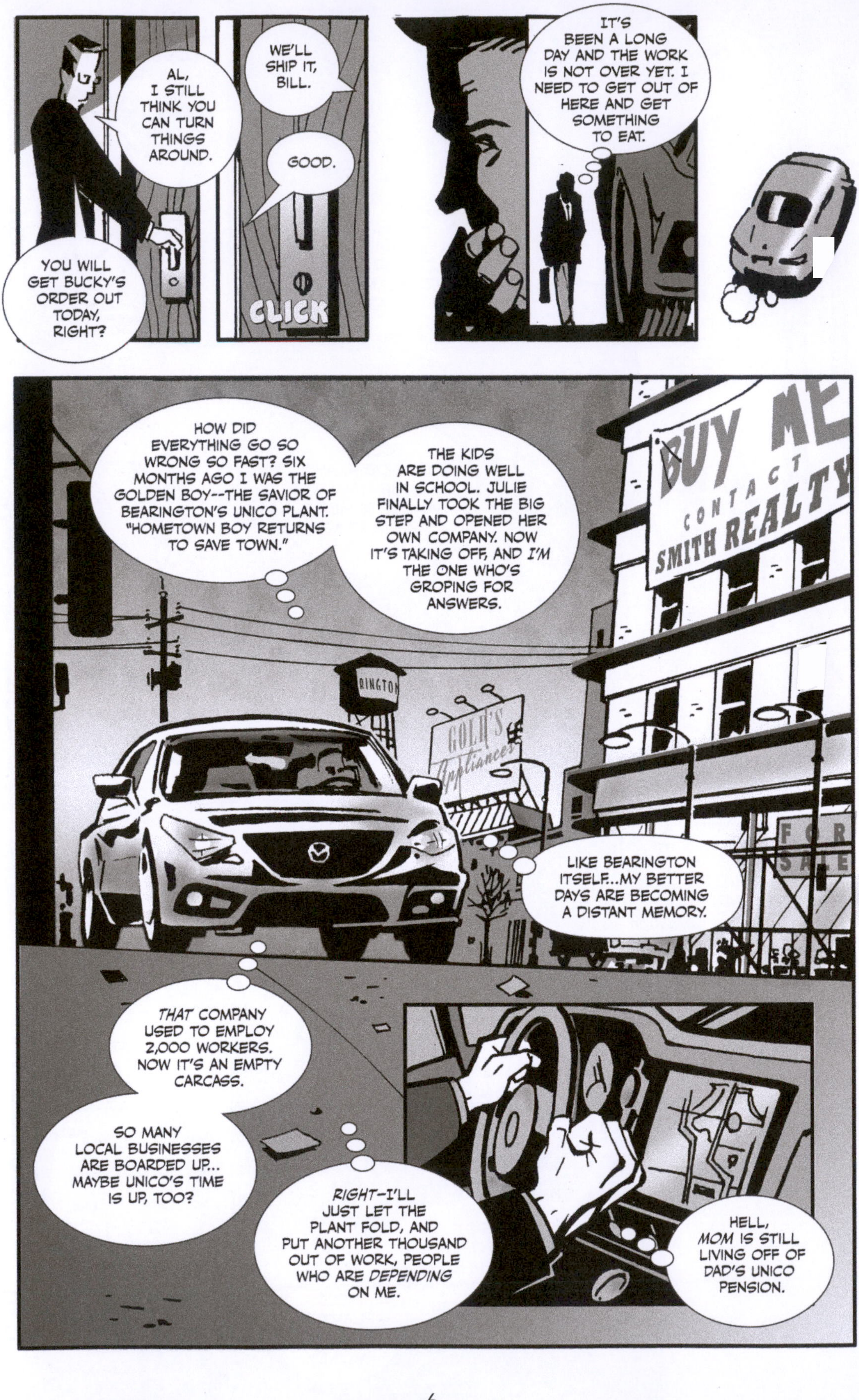

AL, I STILL THINK YOU CAN TURN THINGS AROUND.
YOU WILL GET BUCKY'S ORDER OUT TODAY, RIGHT?
WE'LL SHIP IT, BILL.
GOOD.
CLICK
IT'S BEEN A LONG DAY AND THE WORK IS NOT OVER YET. I NEED TO GET OUT OF HERE AND GET SOMETHING TO EAT.
HOW DID EVERYTHING GO SO WRONG SO FAST? SIX MONTHS AGO I WAS THE GOLDEN BOY--THE SAVIOR OF BEARINGTON'S UNICO PLANT. "HOMETOWN BOY RETURNS TO SAVE TOWN."
THE KIDS ARE DOING WELL IN SCHOOL. JULIE FINALLY TOOK THE BIG STEP AND OPENED HER OWN COMPANY. NOW IT'S TAKING OFF, AND *I'M* THE ONE WHO'S GROPING FOR ANSWERS.
BUY ME
CONTACT
SMITH REALTY
GOLD'S
Appliances
LIKE BEARINGTON ITSELF...MY BETTER DAYS ARE BECOMING A DISTANT MEMORY.
THAT COMPANY USED TO EMPLOY 2,000 WORKERS. NOW IT'S AN EMPTY CARCASS.
SO MANY LOCAL BUSINESSES ARE BOARDED UP... MAYBE UNICO'S TIME IS UP, TOO?
RIGHT–I'LL JUST LET THE PLANT FOLD, AND PUT ANOTHER THOUSAND OUT OF WORK, PEOPLE WHO ARE *DEPENDING* ON ME.
HELL, *MOM* IS STILL LIVING OFF OF DAD'S UNICO PENSION.

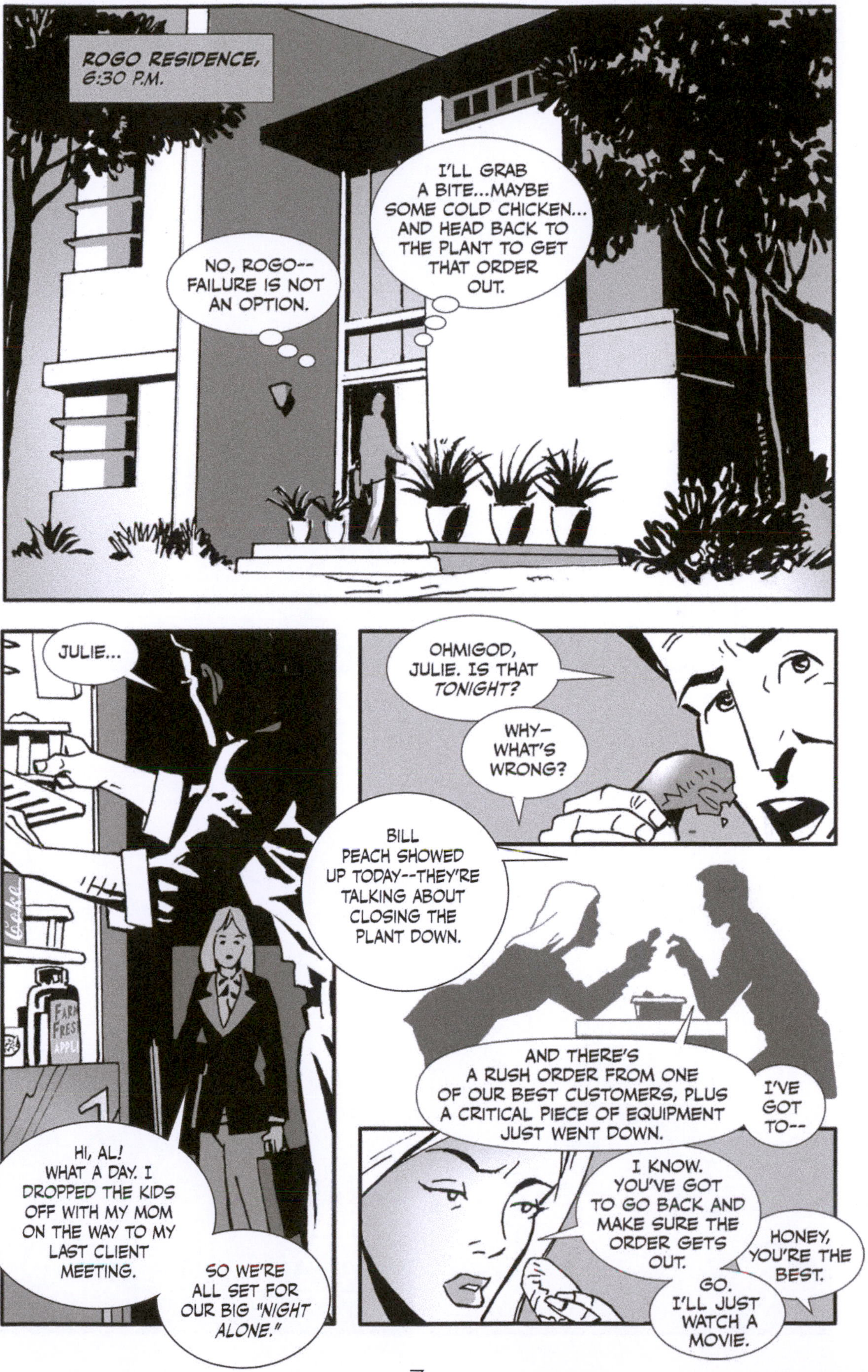
ROGO RESIDENCE, 6:30 P.M.
I'LL GRAB A BITE...MAYBE SOME COLD CHICKEN... AND HEAD BACK TO THE PLANT TO GET THAT ORDER OUT.
NO, ROGO-- FAILURE IS NOT AN OPTION.
JULIE...
HI, AL! WHAT A DAY. I DROPPED THE KIDS OFF WITH MY MOM ON THE WAY TO MY LAST CLIENT MEETING.
SO WE'RE ALL SET FOR OUR BIG *"NIGHT ALONE."*
OHMIGOD, JULIE. IS THAT *TONIGHT?*
WHY— WHAT'S WRONG?
BILL PEACH SHOWED UP TODAY--THEY'RE TALKING ABOUT CLOSING THE PLANT DOWN.
AND THERE'S A RUSH ORDER FROM ONE OF OUR BEST CUSTOMERS, PLUS A CRITICAL PIECE OF EQUIPMENT JUST WENT DOWN.
I'VE GOT TO--
I KNOW. YOU'VE GOT TO GO BACK AND MAKE SURE THE ORDER GETS OUT.
GO. I'LL JUST WATCH A MOVIE.
HONEY, YOU'RE THE BEST.

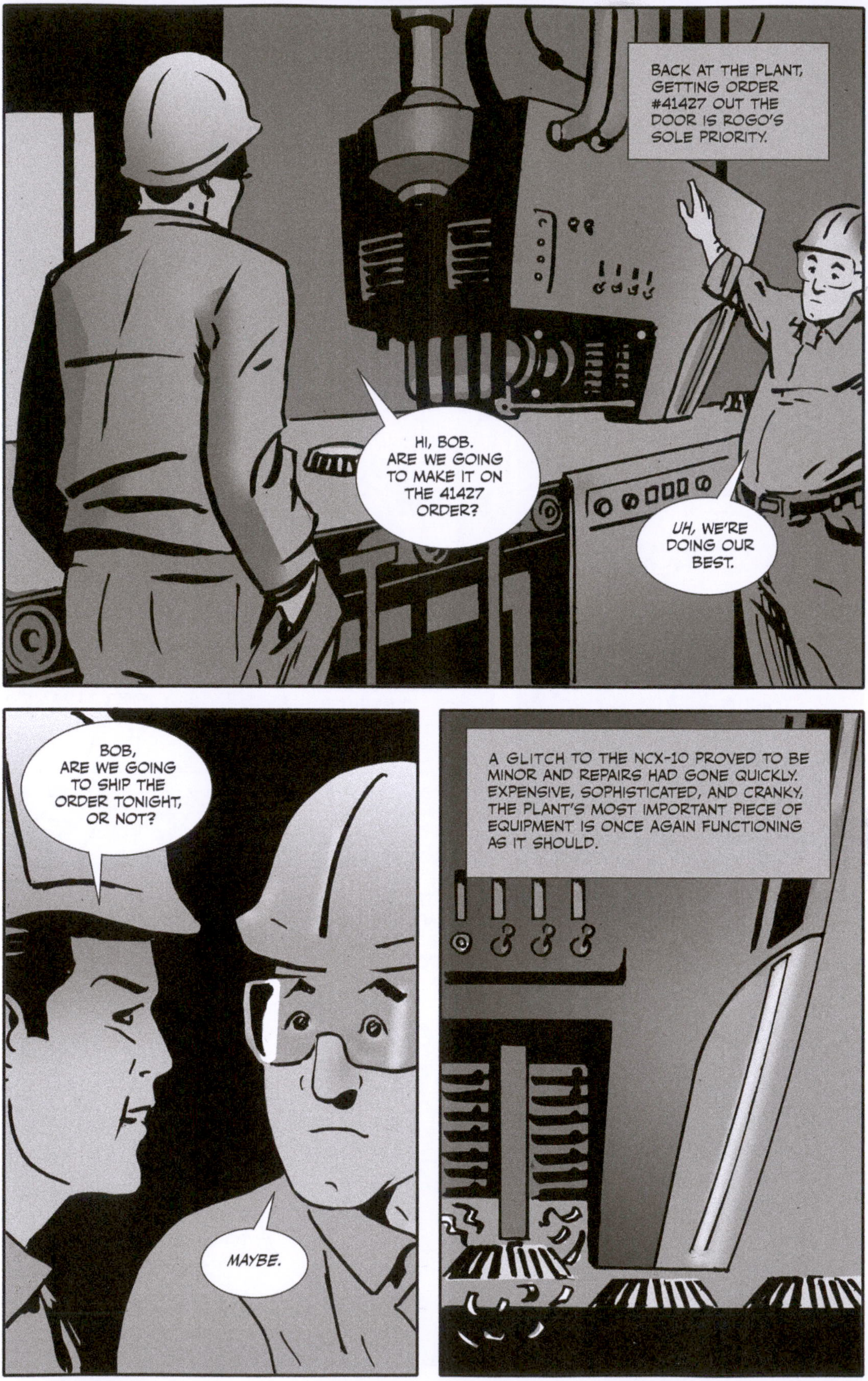

BACK AT THE PLANT, GETTING ORDER #41427 OUT THE DOOR IS ROGO'S SOLE PRIORITY.
HI, BOB. ARE WE GOING TO MAKE IT ON THE 41427 ORDER?
UH, WE'RE DOING OUR BEST.
BOB, ARE WE GOING TO SHIP THE ORDER TONIGHT, OR NOT?
MAYBE.
A GLITCH TO THE NCX-10 PROVED TO BE MINOR AND REPAIRS HAD GONE QUICKLY. EXPENSIVE, SOPHISTICATED, AND CRANKY, THE PLANT'S MOST IMPORTANT PIECE OF EQUIPMENT IS ONCE AGAIN FUNCTIONING AS IT SHOULD.

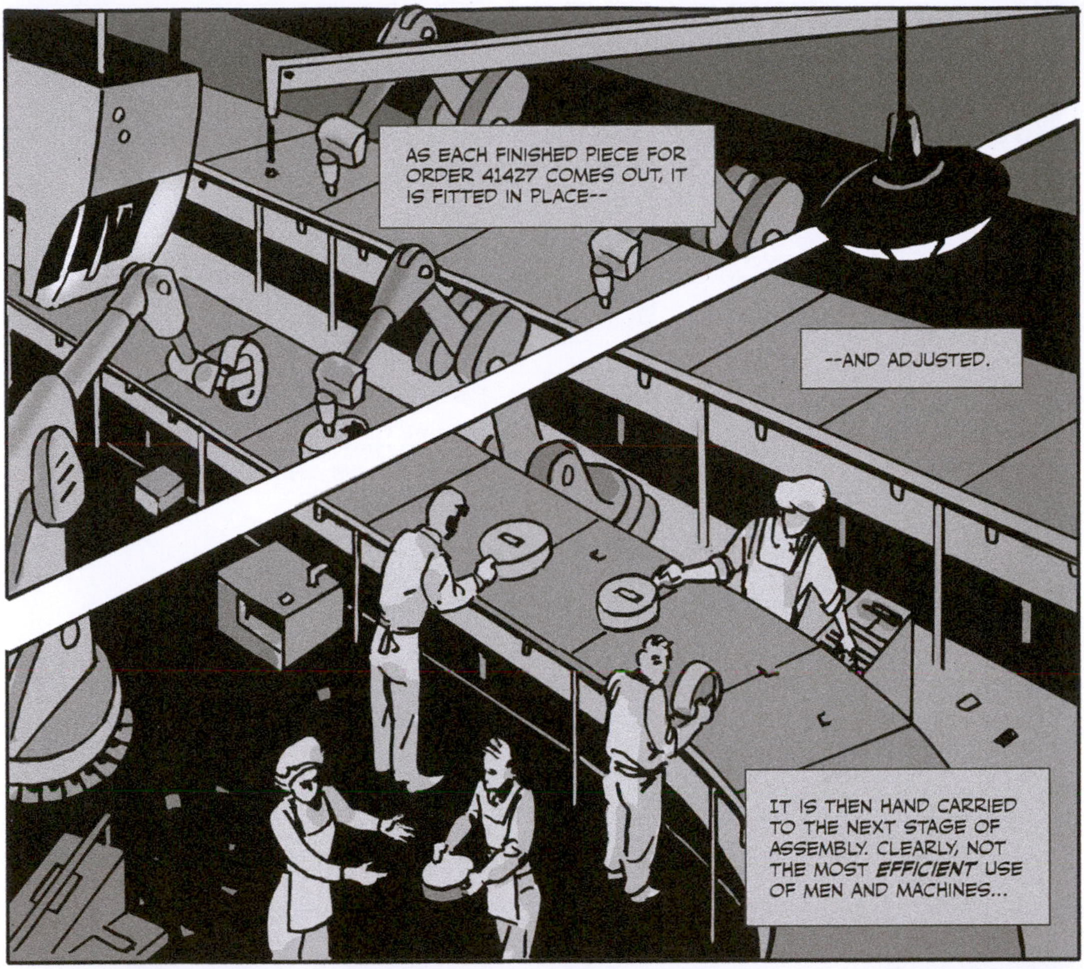
AS EACH FINISHED PIECE FOR ORDER 41427 COMES OUT, IT IS FITTED IN PLACE--
--AND ADJUSTED.
IT IS THEN HAND CARRIED TO THE NEXT STAGE OF ASSEMBLY. CLEARLY, NOT THE MOST *EFFICIENT* USE OF MEN AND MACHINES...

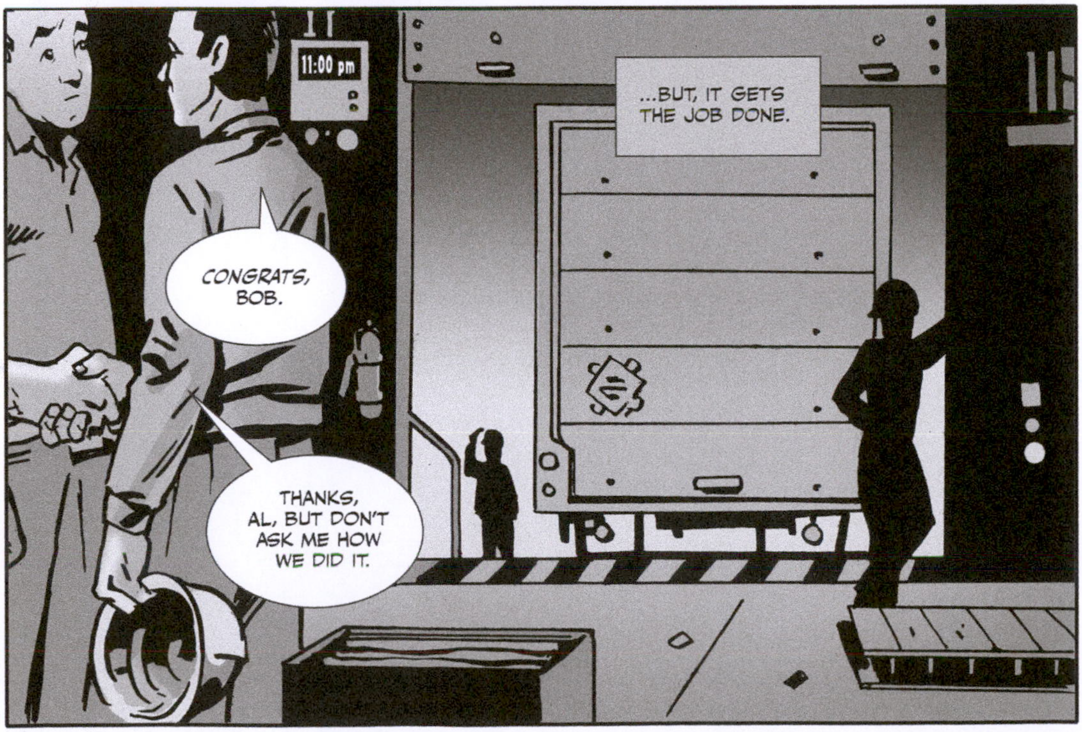
11:00 pm
...BUT, IT GETS THE JOB DONE.
CONGRATS, BOB.
THANKS, AL, BUT DON'T ASK ME HOW WE DID IT.

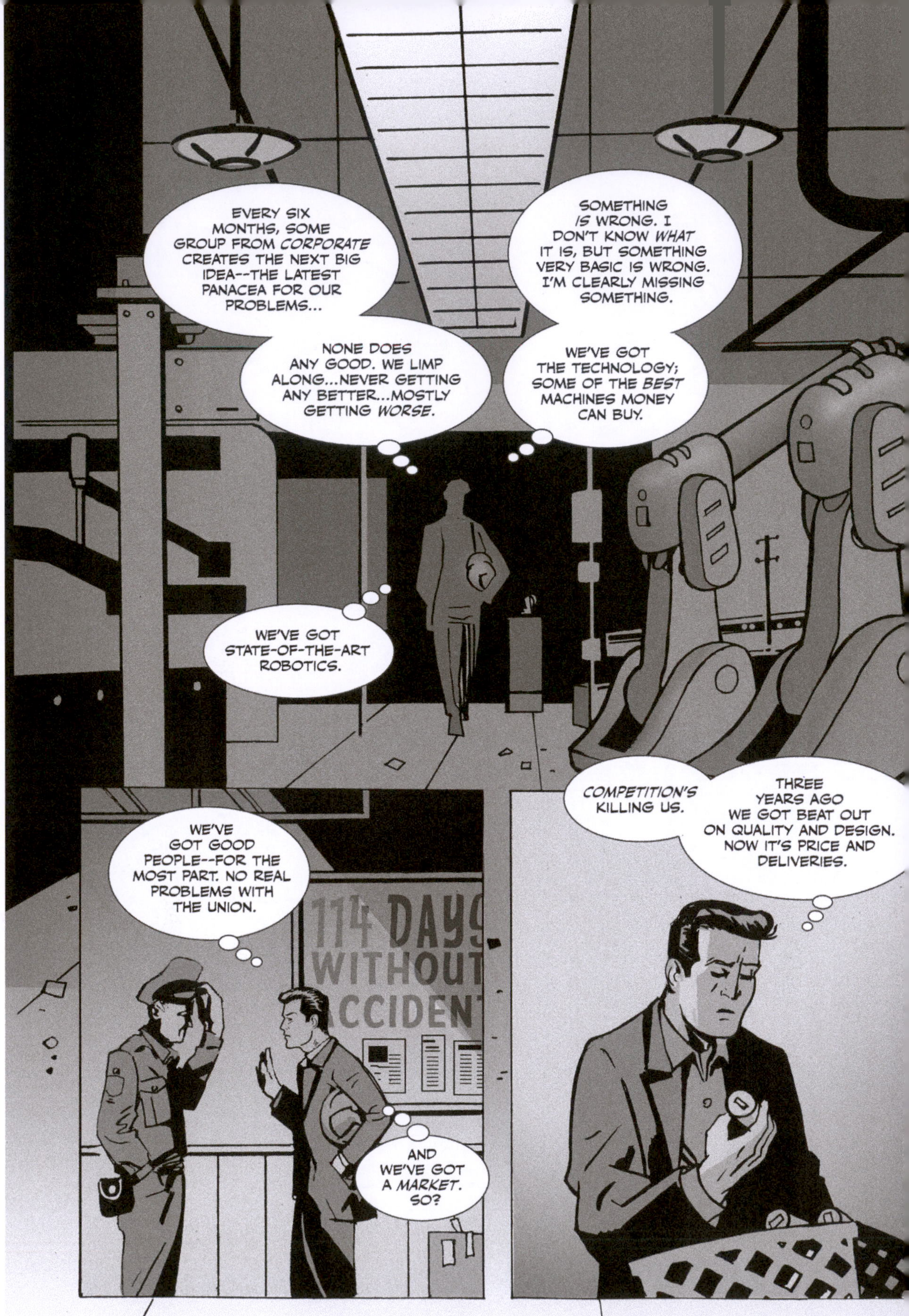
EVERY SIX MONTHS, SOME GROUP FROM CORPORATE CREATES THE NEXT BIG IDEA--THE LATEST PANACEA FOR OUR PROBLEMS...
NONE DOES ANY GOOD. WE LIMP ALONG...NEVER GETTING ANY BETTER...MOSTLY GETTING WORSE.
SOMETHING IS WRONG. I DON'T KNOW WHAT IT IS, BUT SOMETHING VERY BASIC IS WRONG. I'M CLEARLY MISSING SOMETHING.
WE'VE GOT THE TECHNOLOGY; SOME OF THE BEST MACHINES MONEY CAN BUY.
WE'VE GOT STATE-OF-THE-ART ROBOTICS.
WE'VE GOT GOOD PEOPLE--FOR THE MOST PART. NO REAL PROBLEMS WITH THE UNION.
114 DAYS WITHOUT ACCIDENT
AND WE'VE GOT A MARKET. SO?
COMPETITION'S KILLING US.
THREE YEARS AGO WE GOT BEAT OUT ON QUALITY AND DESIGN. NOW IT'S PRICE AND DELIVERIES.

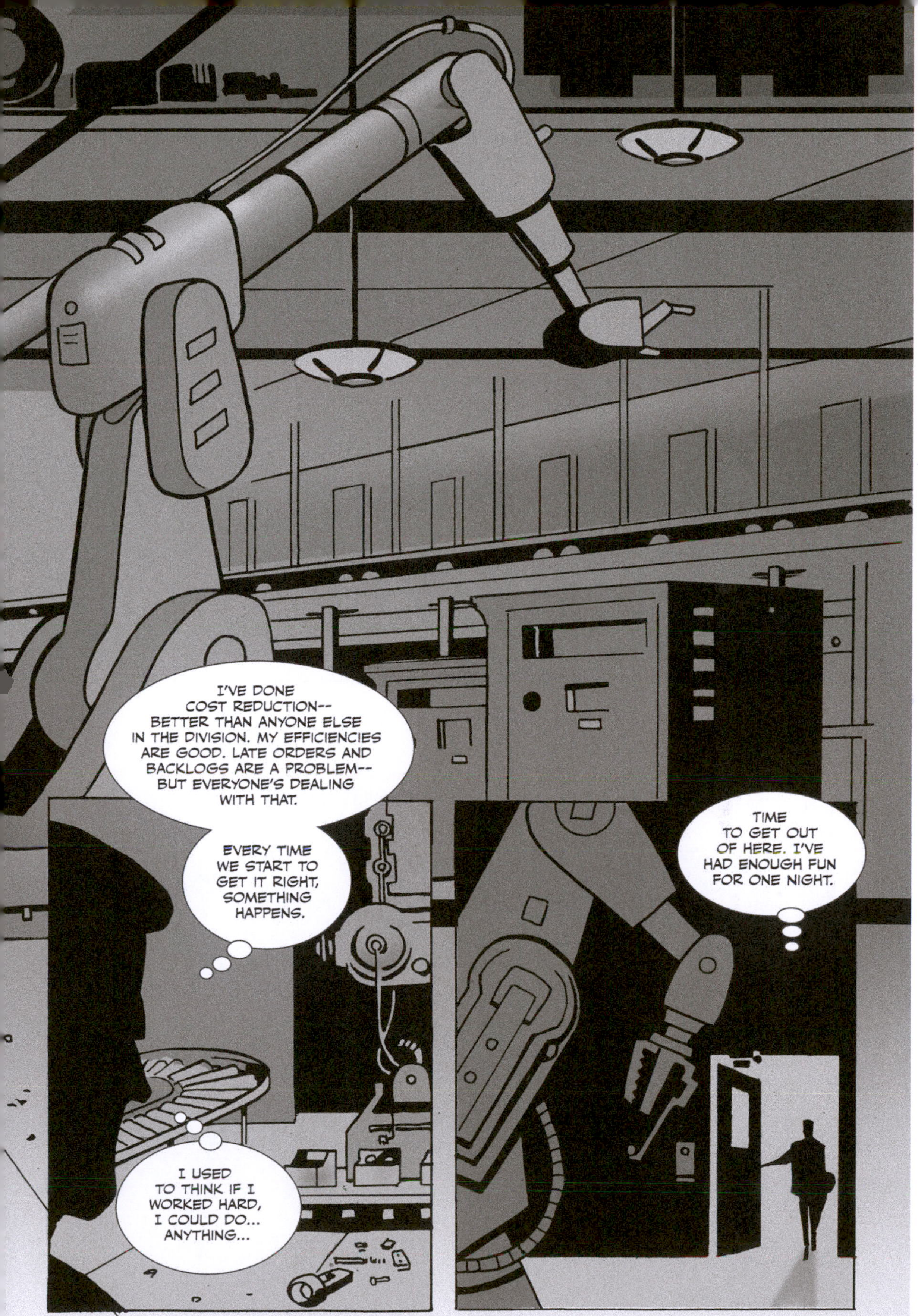
I'VE DONE COST REDUCTION-- BETTER THAN ANYONE ELSE IN THE DIVISION. MY EFFICIENCIES ARE GOOD. LATE ORDERS AND BACKLOGS ARE A PROBLEM-- BUT EVERYONE'S DEALING WITH THAT.
EVERY TIME WE START TO GET IT RIGHT, SOMETHING HAPPENS.
I USED TO THINK IF I WORKED HARD, I COULD DO... ANYTHING...
TIME TO GET OUT OF HERE. I'VE HAD ENOUGH FUN FOR ONE NIGHT.

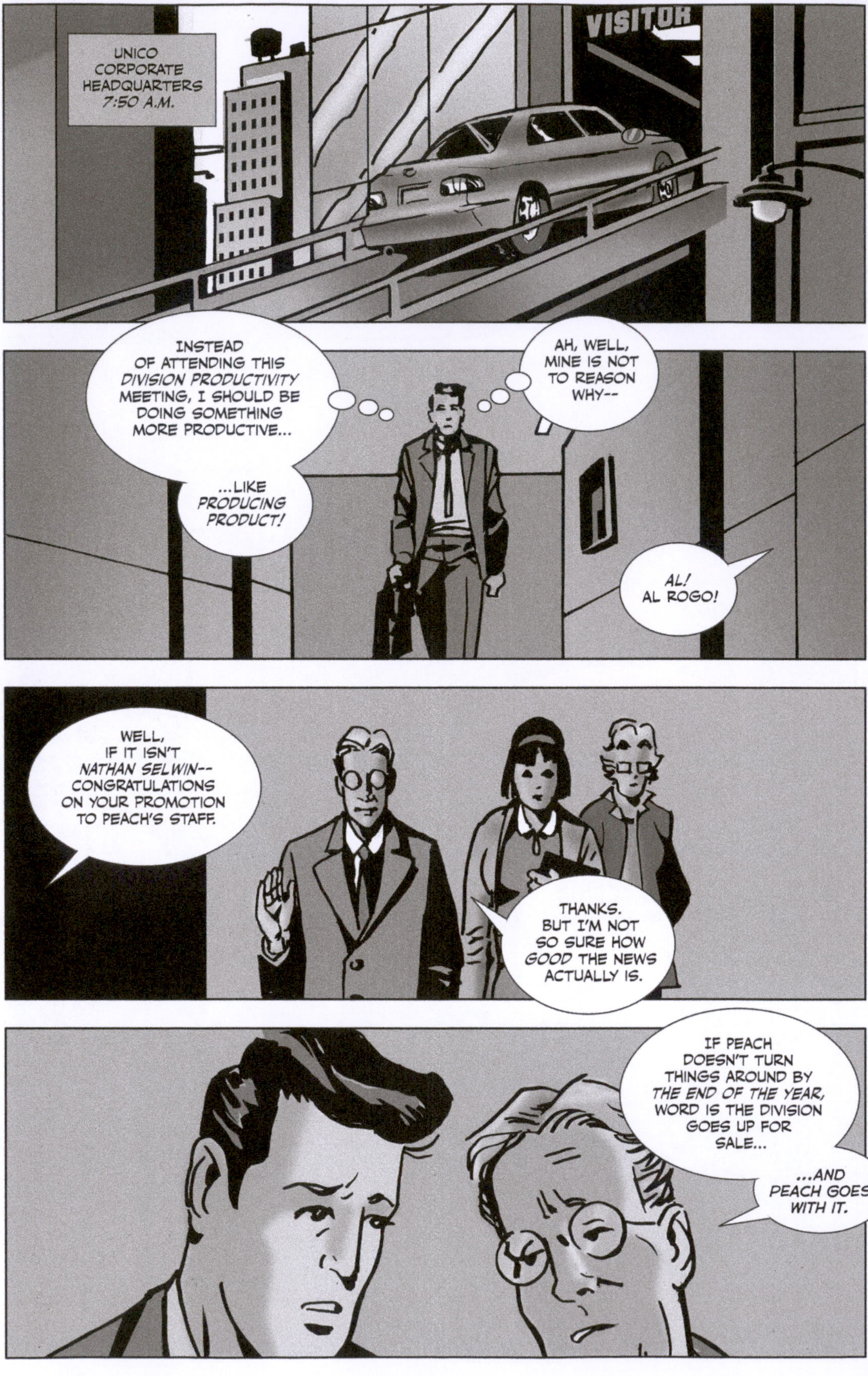
UNICO CORPORATE HEADQUARTERS 7:50 A.M.
VISITOR
INSTEAD OF ATTENDING THIS *DIVISION PRODUCTIVITY* MEETING, I SHOULD BE DOING SOMETHING MORE PRODUCTIVE...
...LIKE *PRODUCING PRODUCT!*
AH, WELL, MINE IS NOT TO REASON WHY--
AL! AL ROGO!
WELL, IF IT ISN'T *NATHAN SELWIN*-- CONGRATULATIONS ON YOUR PROMOTION TO PEACH'S STAFF.
THANKS. BUT I'M NOT SO SURE HOW *GOOD* THE NEWS ACTUALLY IS.
IF PEACH DOESN'T TURN THINGS AROUND BY *THE END OF THE YEAR,* WORD IS THE DIVISION GOES UP FOR SALE...
...AND PEACH GOES WITH IT.

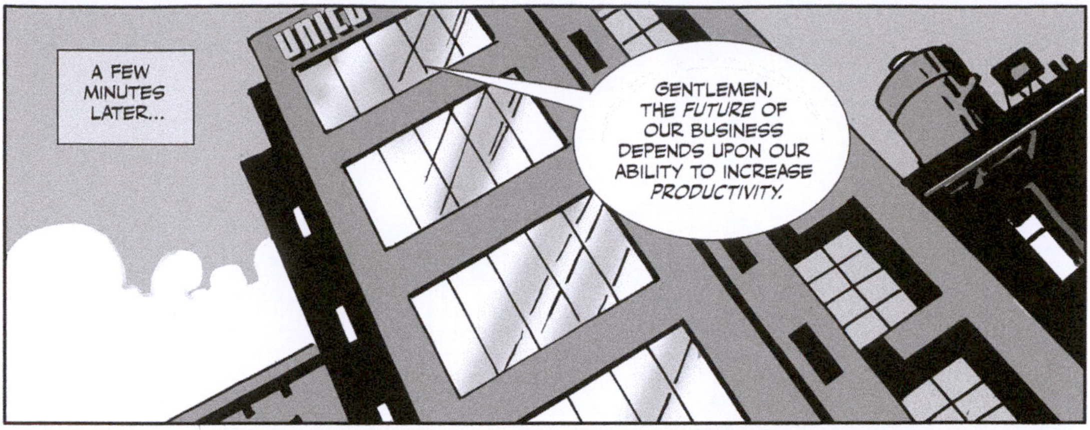
A FEW MINUTES LATER...
GENTLEMEN, THE *FUTURE* OF OUR BUSINESS DEPENDS UPON OUR ABILITY TO INCREASE *PRODUCTIVITY.*

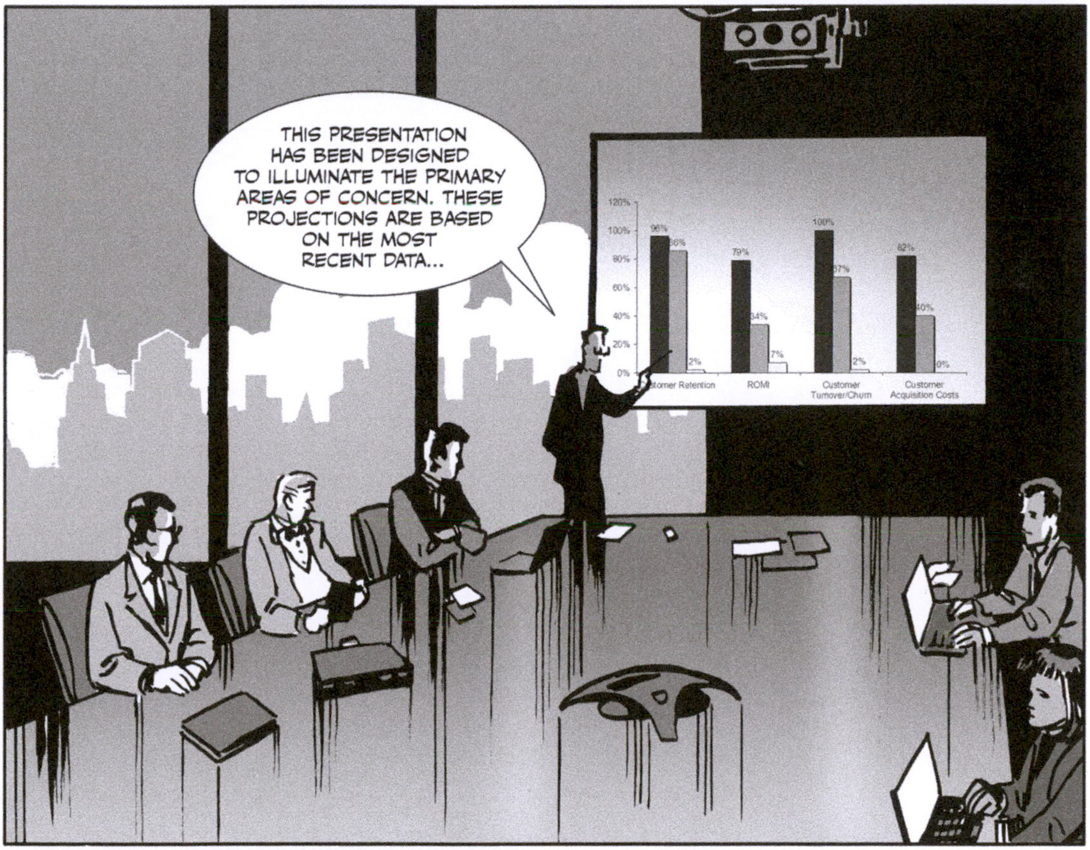
THIS PRESENTATION HAS BEEN DESIGNED TO ILLUMINATE THE PRIMARY AREAS OF CONCERN. THESE PROJECTIONS ARE BASED ON THE MOST RECENT DATA...
ROMI
Customer Turnover/Churn
Customer Acquisition Costs

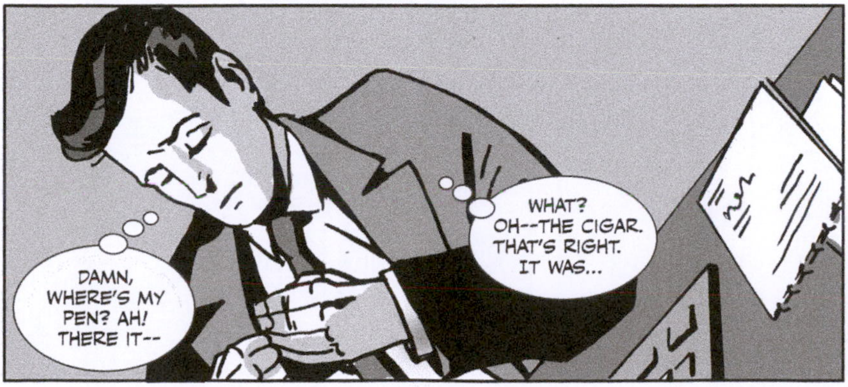
DAMN, WHERE'S MY PEN? AH! THERE IT--
WHAT? OH--THE CIGAR. THAT'S RIGHT. IT WAS...

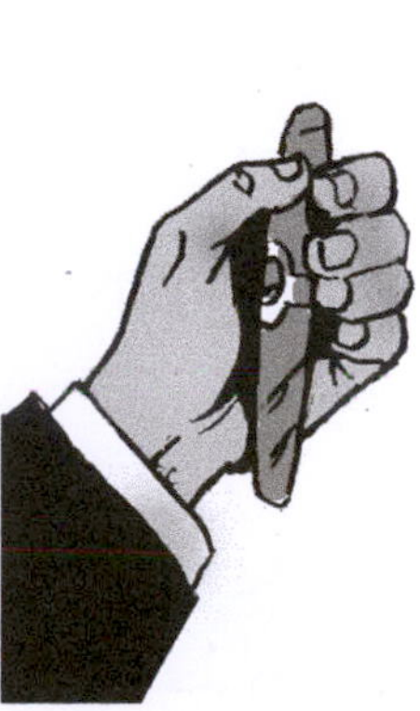

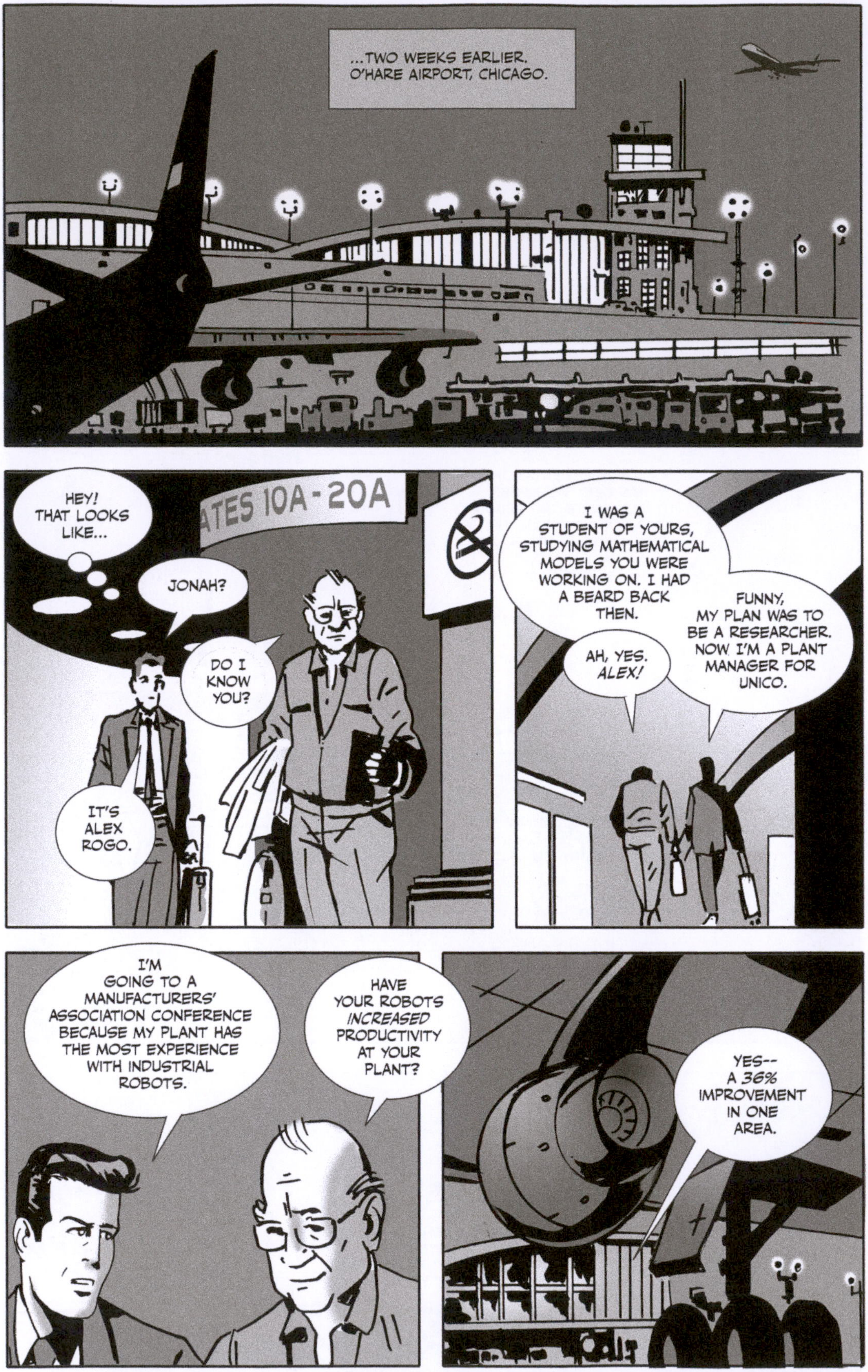
...TWO WEEKS EARLIER. O'HARE AIRPORT, CHICAGO.
ATES 10A - 20A
HEY! THAT LOOKS LIKE...
JONAH?
DO I KNOW YOU?
IT'S ALEX ROGO.
I WAS A STUDENT OF YOURS, STUDYING MATHEMATICAL MODELS YOU WERE WORKING ON. I HAD A BEARD BACK THEN.
AH, YES. *ALEX!*
FUNNY, MY PLAN WAS TO BE A RESEARCHER. NOW I'M A PLANT MANAGER FOR UNICO.
I'M GOING TO A MANUFACTURERS' ASSOCIATION CONFERENCE BECAUSE MY PLANT HAS THE MOST EXPERIENCE WITH INDUSTRIAL ROBOTS.
HAVE YOUR ROBOTS *INCREASED* PRODUCTIVITY AT YOUR PLANT?
YES-- A *36%* IMPROVEMENT IN ONE AREA.

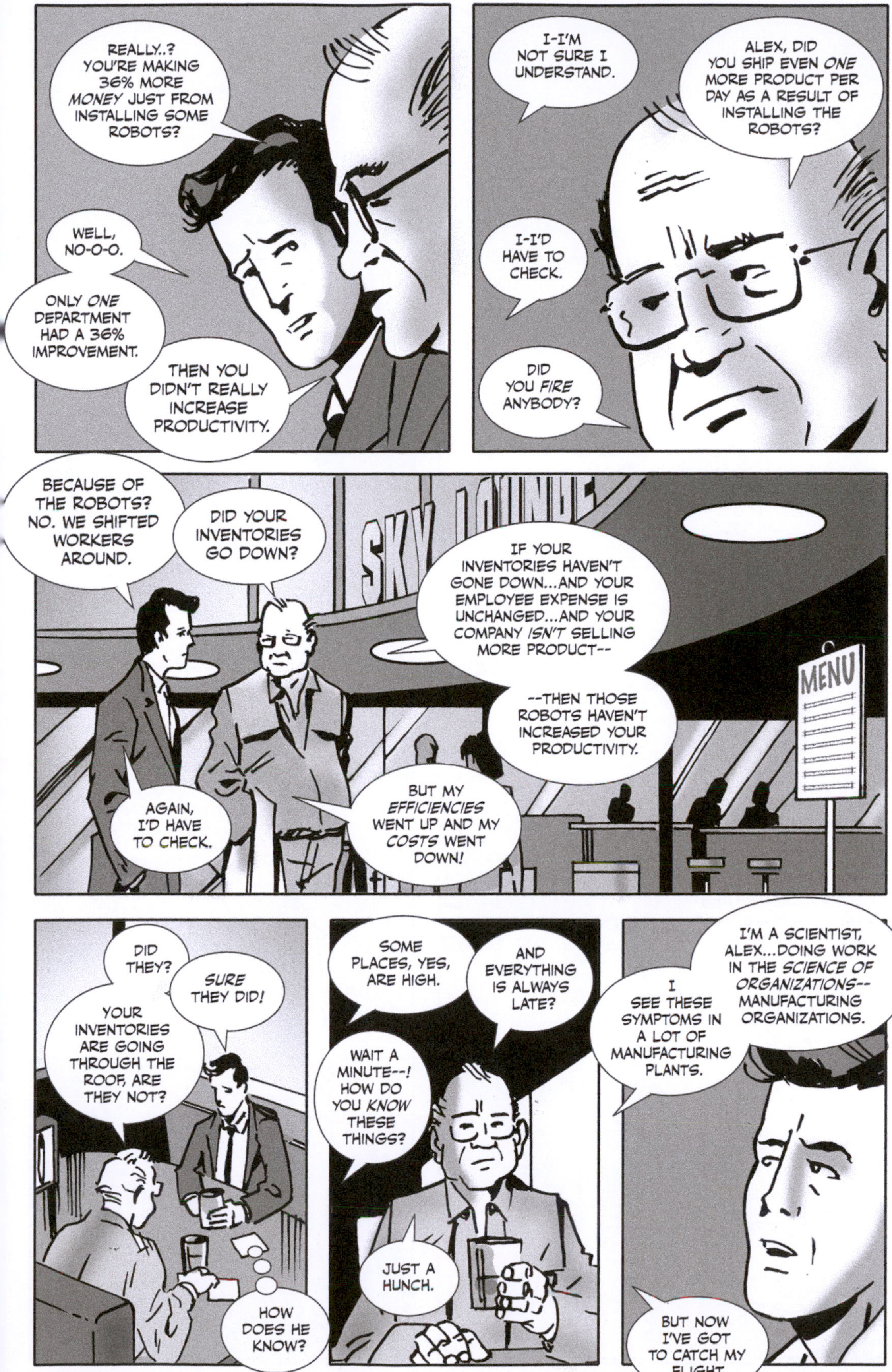
REALLY..? YOU'RE MAKING 36% MORE *MONEY* JUST FROM INSTALLING SOME ROBOTS?
WELL, NO-O-O.
ONLY *ONE* DEPARTMENT HAD A 36% IMPROVEMENT.
THEN YOU DIDN'T REALLY INCREASE PRODUCTIVITY.
I-I'M NOT SURE I UNDERSTAND.
ALEX, DID YOU SHIP EVEN *ONE* MORE PRODUCT PER DAY AS A RESULT OF INSTALLING THE ROBOTS?
I-I'D HAVE TO CHECK.
DID YOU *FIRE* ANYBODY?
BECAUSE OF THE ROBOTS? NO. WE SHIFTED WORKERS AROUND.
DID YOUR INVENTORIES GO DOWN?
SKY LOUNGE
IF YOUR INVENTORIES HAVEN'T GONE DOWN...AND YOUR EMPLOYEE EXPENSE IS UNCHANGED...AND YOUR COMPANY *ISN'T* SELLING MORE PRODUCT--
--THEN THOSE ROBOTS HAVEN'T INCREASED YOUR PRODUCTIVITY.
MENU
AGAIN, I'D HAVE TO CHECK.
BUT MY *EFFICIENCIES* WENT UP AND MY *COSTS* WENT DOWN!
DID THEY?
SURE THEY DID!
YOUR INVENTORIES ARE GOING THROUGH THE ROOF, ARE THEY NOT?
HOW DOES HE KNOW?
SOME PLACES, YES, ARE HIGH.
AND EVERYTHING IS ALWAYS LATE?
WAIT A MINUTE--! HOW DO YOU *KNOW* THESE THINGS?
JUST A HUNCH.
I'M A SCIENTIST, ALEX...DOING WORK IN THE *SCIENCE OF ORGANIZATIONS*-- MANUFACTURING ORGANIZATIONS.
I SEE THESE SYMPTOMS IN A LOT OF MANUFACTURING PLANTS.
BUT NOW I'VE GOT TO CATCH MY FLIGHT.

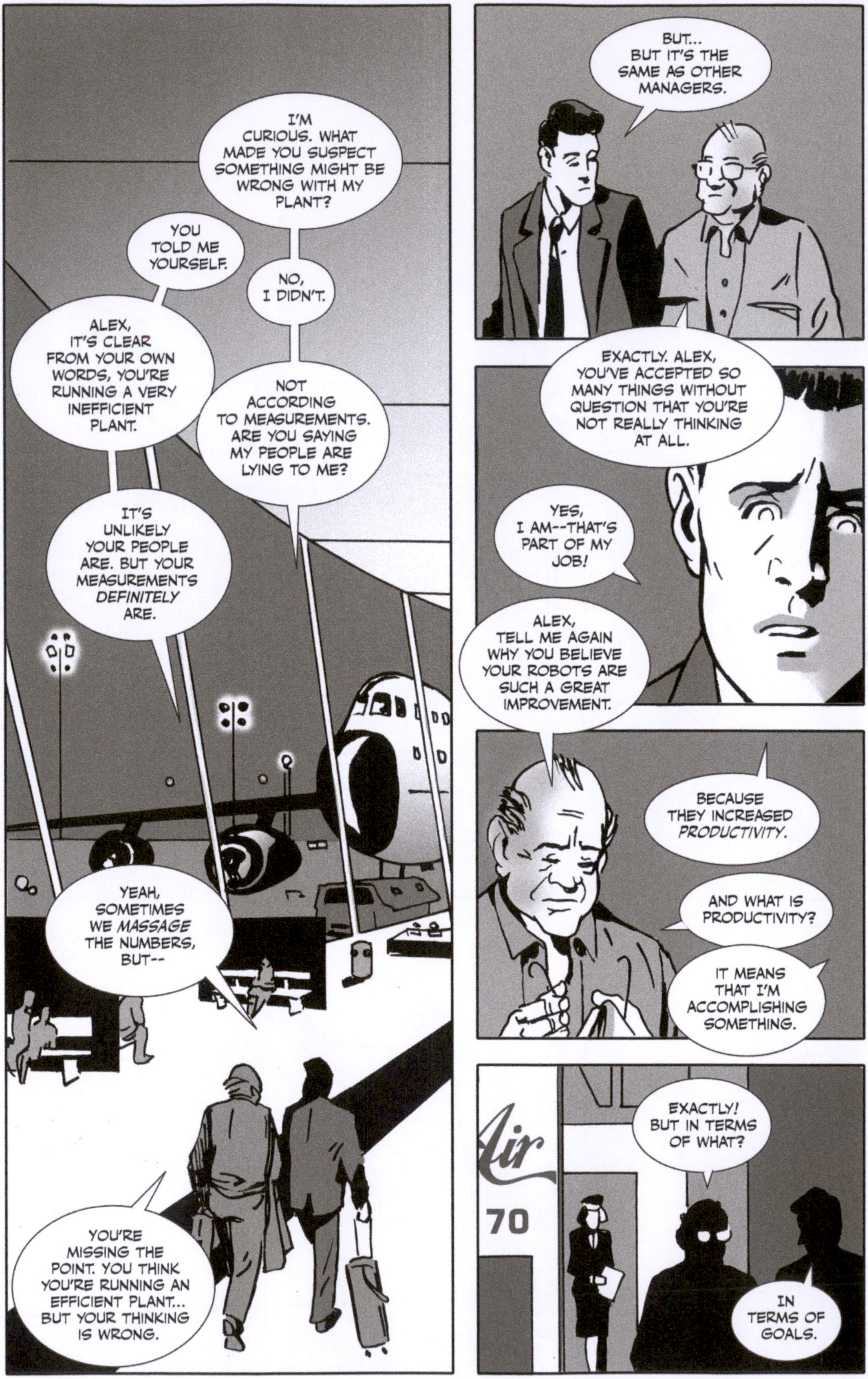
I'M CURIOUS. WHAT MADE YOU SUSPECT SOMETHING MIGHT BE WRONG WITH MY PLANT?
YOU TOLD ME YOURSELF.
NO, I DIDN'T.
ALEX, IT'S CLEAR FROM YOUR OWN WORDS, YOU'RE RUNNING A VERY INEFFICIENT PLANT.
NOT ACCORDING TO MEASUREMENTS. ARE YOU SAYING MY PEOPLE ARE LYING TO ME?
IT'S UNLIKELY YOUR PEOPLE ARE. BUT YOUR MEASUREMENTS *DEFINITELY* ARE.
YEAH, SOMETIMES WE *MASSAGE* THE NUMBERS, BUT--
YOU'RE MISSING THE POINT. YOU THINK YOU'RE RUNNING AN EFFICIENT PLANT... BUT YOUR THINKING IS WRONG.
BUT... BUT IT'S THE SAME AS OTHER MANAGERS.
EXACTLY. ALEX, YOU'VE ACCEPTED SO MANY THINGS WITHOUT QUESTION THAT YOU'RE NOT REALLY THINKING AT ALL.
YES, I AM--THAT'S PART OF MY JOB!
ALEX, TELL ME AGAIN WHY YOU BELIEVE YOUR ROBOTS ARE SUCH A GREAT IMPROVEMENT.
BECAUSE THEY INCREASED *PRODUCTIVITY*.
AND WHAT IS PRODUCTIVITY?
IT MEANS THAT I'M ACCOMPLISHING SOMETHING.
Air
70
EXACTLY! BUT IN TERMS OF WHAT?
IN TERMS OF GOALS.

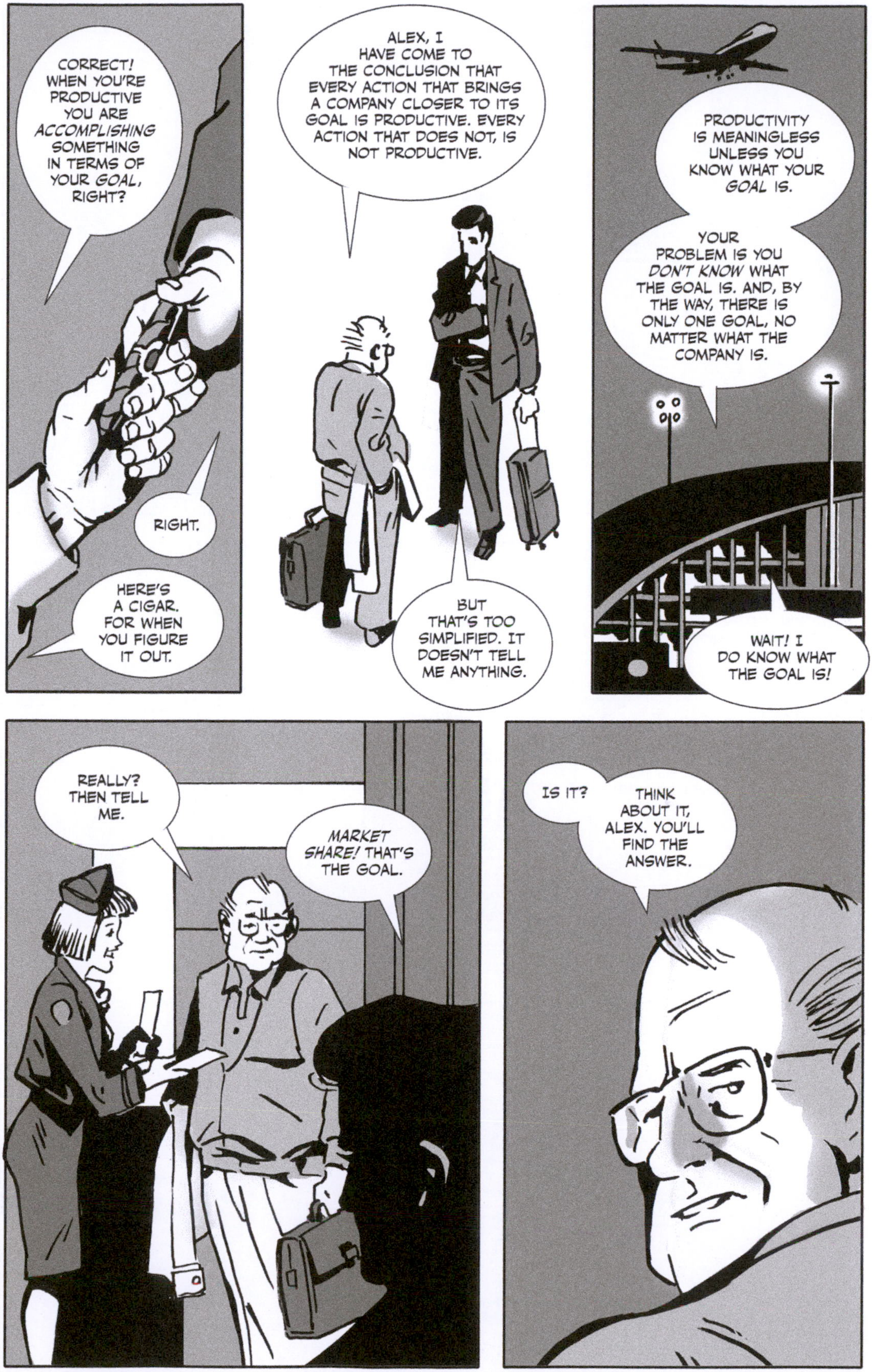
CORRECT! WHEN YOU'RE PRODUCTIVE YOU ARE ACCOMPLISHING SOMETHING IN TERMS OF YOUR GOAL, RIGHT?
RIGHT.
HERE'S A CIGAR. FOR WHEN YOU FIGURE IT OUT.
ALEX, I HAVE COME TO THE CONCLUSION THAT EVERY ACTION THAT BRINGS A COMPANY CLOSER TO ITS GOAL IS PRODUCTIVE. EVERY ACTION THAT DOES NOT, IS NOT PRODUCTIVE.
BUT THAT'S TOO SIMPLIFIED. IT DOESN'T TELL ME ANYTHING.
PRODUCTIVITY IS MEANINGLESS UNLESS YOU KNOW WHAT YOUR GOAL IS.
YOUR PROBLEM IS YOU DON'T KNOW WHAT THE GOAL IS. AND, BY THE WAY, THERE IS ONLY ONE GOAL, NO MATTER WHAT THE COMPANY IS.
WAIT! I DO KNOW WHAT THE GOAL IS!
REALLY? THEN TELL ME.
MARKET SHARE! THAT'S THE GOAL.
IS IT?
THINK ABOUT IT, ALEX. YOU'LL FIND THE ANSWER.

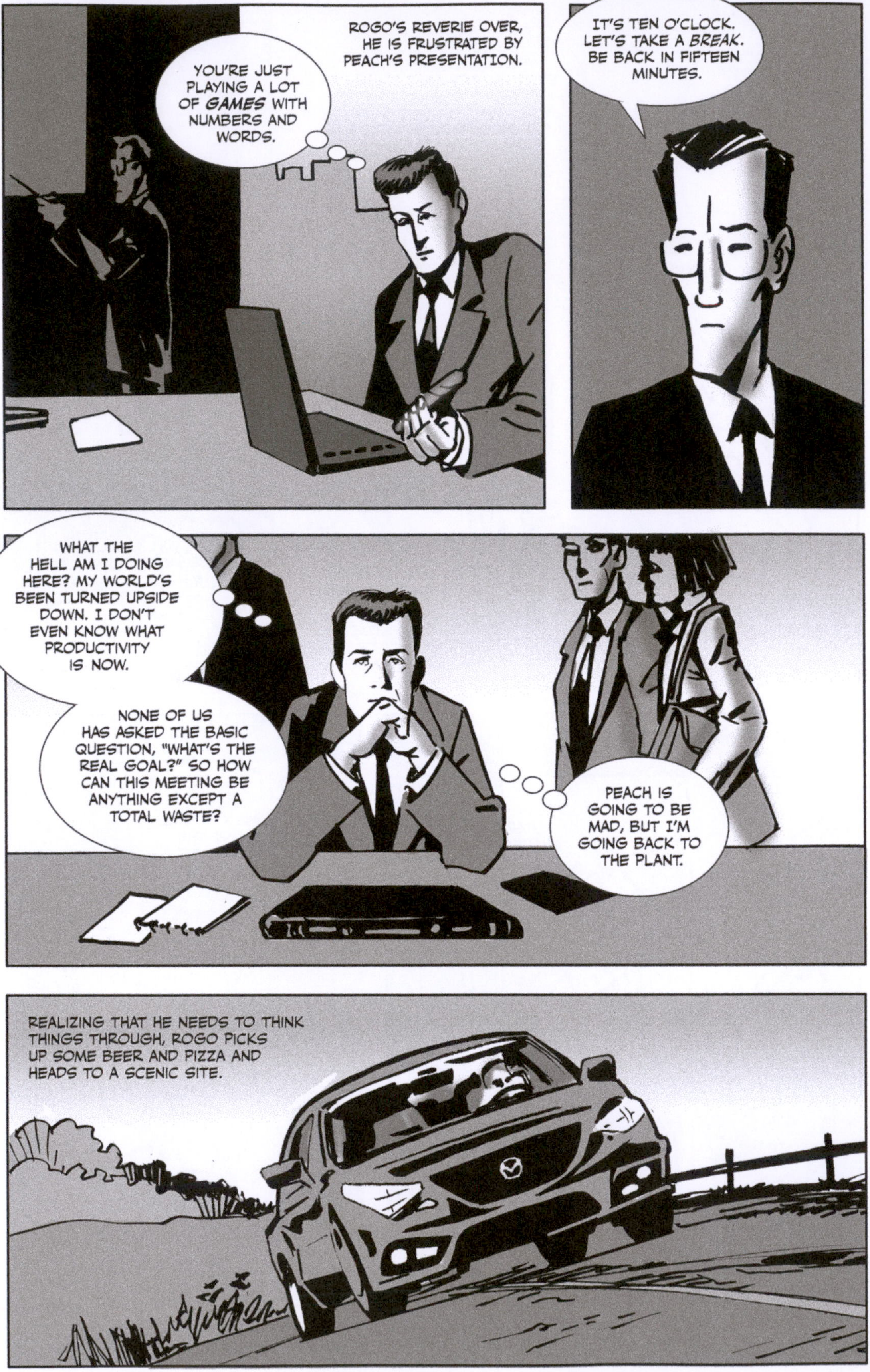
ROGO'S REVERIE OVER, HE IS FRUSTRATED BY PEACH'S PRESENTATION.
YOU'RE JUST PLAYING A LOT OF *GAMES* WITH NUMBERS AND WORDS.
IT'S TEN O'CLOCK. LET'S TAKE A *BREAK*. BE BACK IN FIFTEEN MINUTES.
WHAT THE HELL AM I DOING HERE? MY WORLD'S BEEN TURNED UPSIDE DOWN. I DON'T EVEN KNOW WHAT PRODUCTIVITY IS NOW.
NONE OF US HAS ASKED THE BASIC QUESTION, "WHAT'S THE REAL GOAL?" SO HOW CAN THIS MEETING BE ANYTHING EXCEPT A TOTAL WASTE?
PEACH IS GOING TO BE MAD, BUT I'M GOING BACK TO THE PLANT.
REALIZING THAT HE NEEDS TO THINK THINGS THROUGH, ROGO PICKS UP SOME BEER AND PIZZA AND HEADS TO A SCENIC SITE.

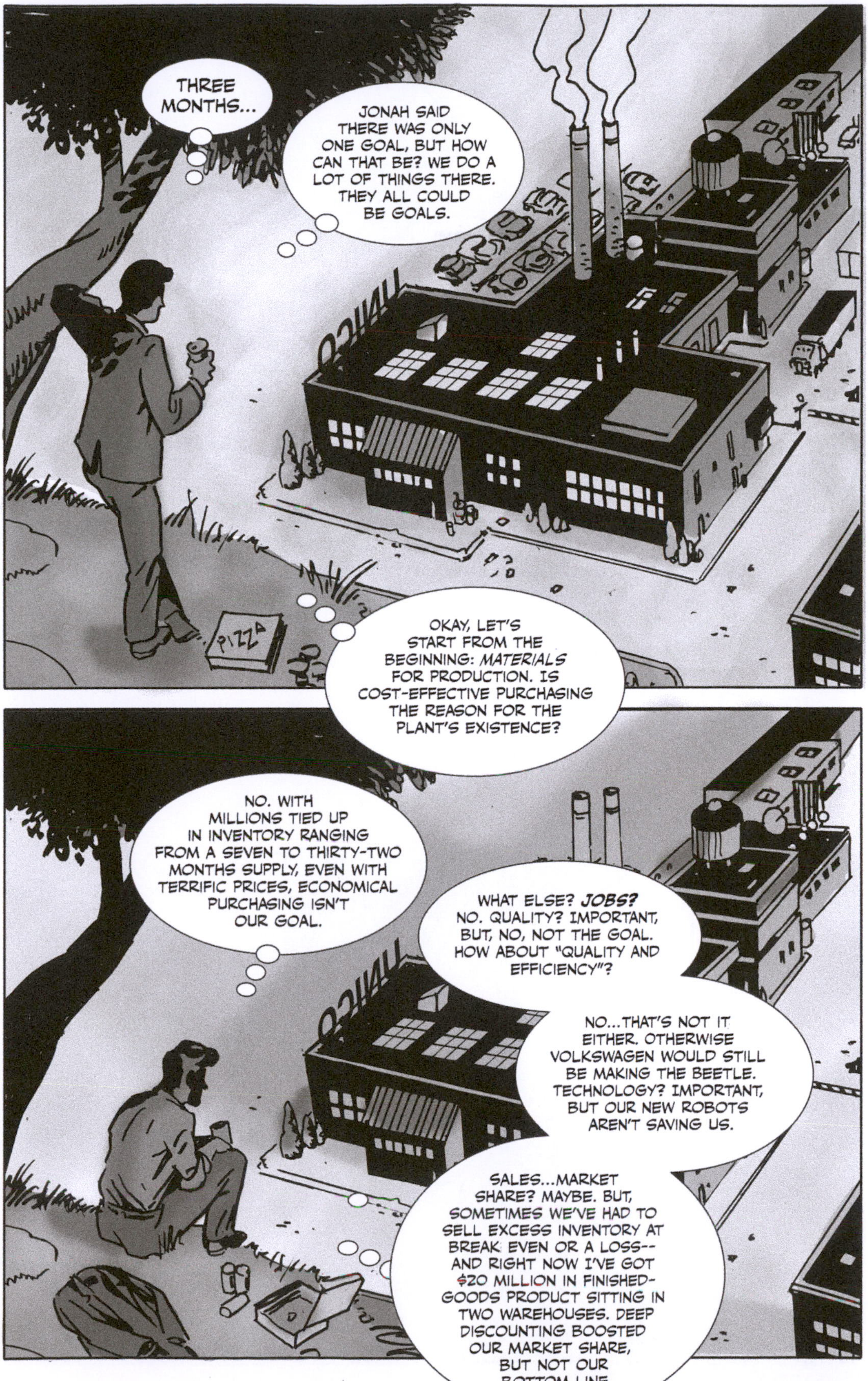
THREE MONTHS...
JONAH SAID THERE WAS ONLY ONE GOAL, BUT HOW CAN THAT BE? WE DO A LOT OF THINGS THERE. THEY ALL COULD BE GOALS.
PIZZA
OKAY, LET'S START FROM THE BEGINNING: *MATERIALS* FOR PRODUCTION. IS COST-EFFECTIVE PURCHASING THE REASON FOR THE PLANT'S EXISTENCE?
NO. WITH MILLIONS TIED UP IN INVENTORY RANGING FROM A SEVEN TO THIRTY-TWO MONTHS SUPPLY, EVEN WITH TERRIFIC PRICES, ECONOMICAL PURCHASING ISN'T OUR GOAL.
WHAT ELSE? ***JOBS?*** NO. QUALITY? IMPORTANT, BUT, NO, NOT THE GOAL. HOW ABOUT "QUALITY AND EFFICIENCY"?
NO...THAT'S NOT IT EITHER. OTHERWISE VOLKSWAGEN WOULD STILL BE MAKING THE BEETLE. TECHNOLOGY? IMPORTANT, BUT OUR NEW ROBOTS AREN'T SAVING US.
SALES...MARKET SHARE? MAYBE. BUT, SOMETIMES WE'VE HAD TO SELL EXCESS INVENTORY AT BREAK EVEN OR A LOSS--AND RIGHT NOW I'VE GOT $20 MILLION IN FINISHED-GOODS PRODUCT SITTING IN TWO WAREHOUSES. DEEP DISCOUNTING BOOSTED OUR MARKET SHARE, BUT NOT OUR BOTTOM LINE.

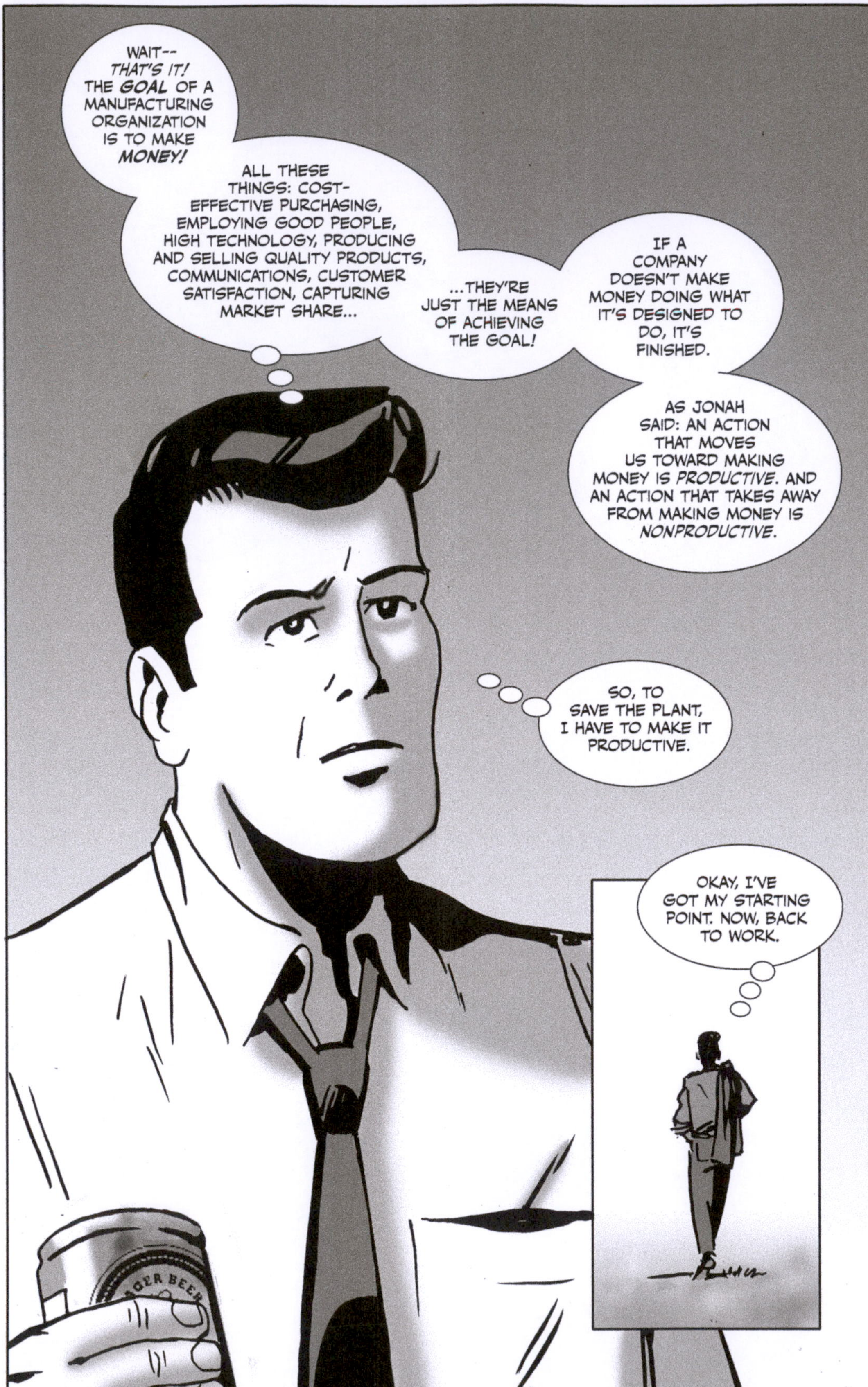
WAIT-- THAT'S IT! THE GOAL OF A MANUFACTURING ORGANIZATION IS TO MAKE MONEY!
ALL THESE THINGS: COST-EFFECTIVE PURCHASING, EMPLOYING GOOD PEOPLE, HIGH TECHNOLOGY, PRODUCING AND SELLING QUALITY PRODUCTS, COMMUNICATIONS, CUSTOMER SATISFACTION, CAPTURING MARKET SHARE...
...THEY'RE JUST THE MEANS OF ACHIEVING THE GOAL!
IF A COMPANY DOESN'T MAKE MONEY DOING WHAT IT'S DESIGNED TO DO, IT'S FINISHED.
AS JONAH SAID: AN ACTION THAT MOVES US TOWARD MAKING MONEY IS PRODUCTIVE. AND AN ACTION THAT TAKES AWAY FROM MAKING MONEY IS NONPRODUCTIVE.
SO, TO SAVE THE PLANT, I HAVE TO MAKE IT PRODUCTIVE.
OKAY, I'VE GOT MY STARTING POINT. NOW, BACK TO WORK.

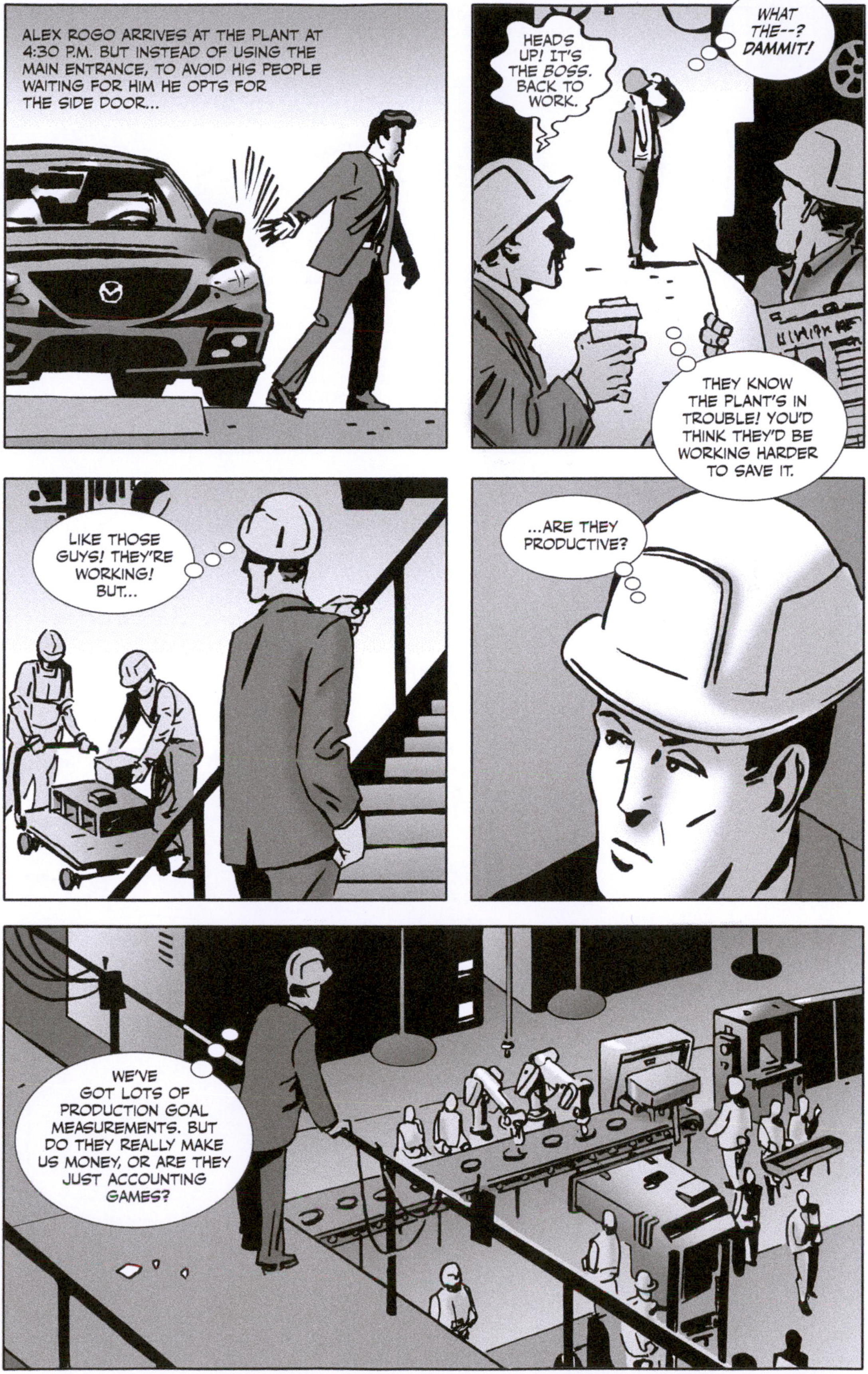
ALEX ROGO ARRIVES AT THE PLANT AT 4:30 P.M. BUT INSTEAD OF USING THE MAIN ENTRANCE, TO AVOID HIS PEOPLE WAITING FOR HIM HE OPTS FOR THE SIDE DOOR...
HEADS UP! IT'S THE *BOSS*. BACK TO WORK.
WHAT THE--? DAMMIT!
THEY KNOW THE PLANT'S IN TROUBLE! YOU'D THINK THEY'D BE WORKING HARDER TO SAVE IT.
LIKE THOSE GUYS! THEY'RE WORKING! BUT...
...ARE THEY PRODUCTIVE?
WE'VE GOT LOTS OF PRODUCTION GOAL MEASUREMENTS. BUT DO THEY REALLY MAKE US MONEY, OR ARE THEY JUST ACCOUNTING GAMES?

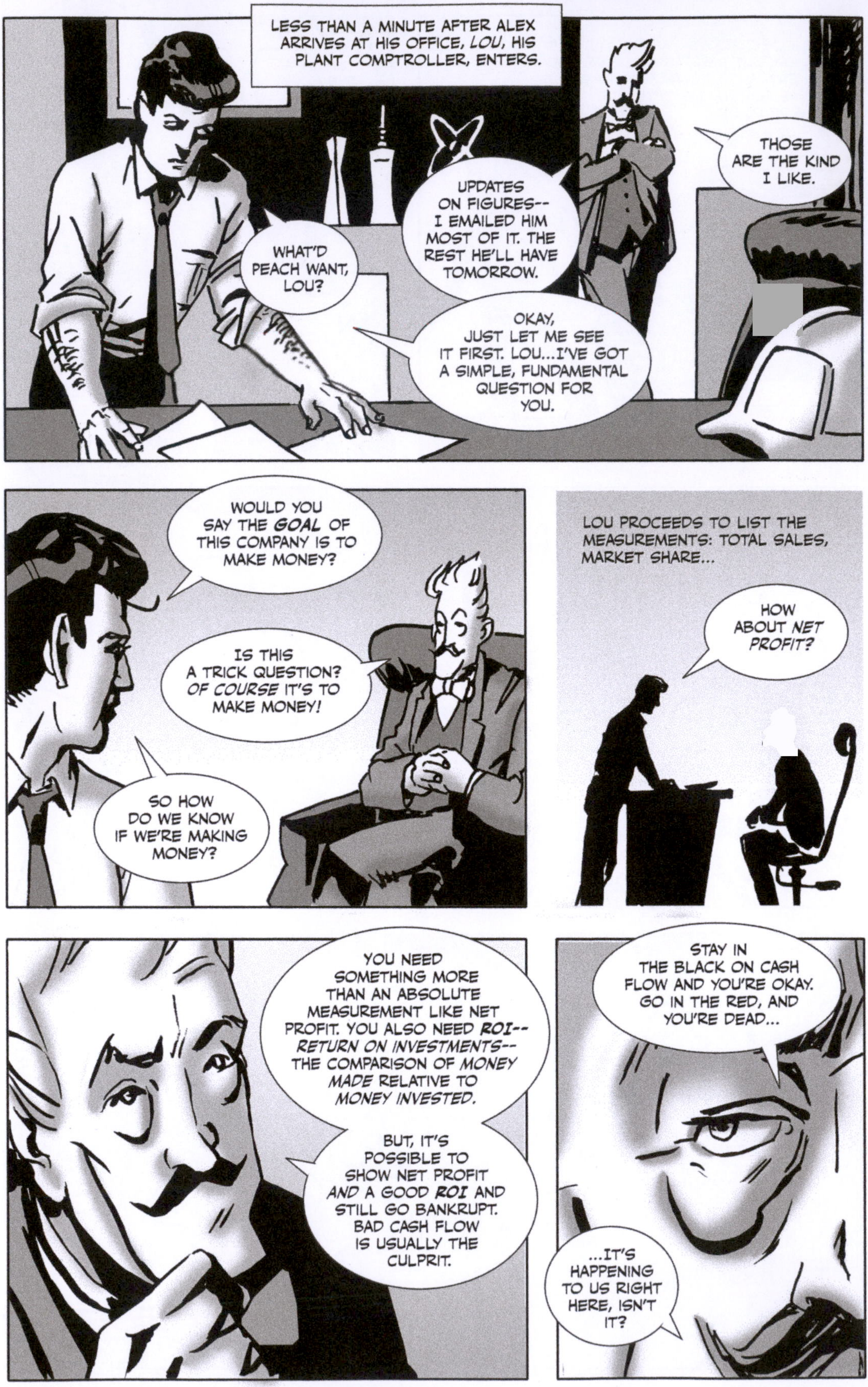
LESS THAN A MINUTE AFTER ALEX ARRIVES AT HIS OFFICE, *LOU*, HIS PLANT COMPTROLLER, ENTERS.
WHAT'D PEACH WANT, LOU?
UPDATES ON FIGURES-- I EMAILED HIM MOST OF IT. THE REST HE'LL HAVE TOMORROW.
THOSE ARE THE KIND I LIKE.
OKAY, JUST LET ME SEE IT FIRST. LOU...I'VE GOT A SIMPLE, FUNDAMENTAL QUESTION FOR YOU.
WOULD YOU SAY THE ***GOAL*** OF THIS COMPANY IS TO MAKE MONEY?
IS THIS A TRICK QUESTION? *OF COURSE* IT'S TO MAKE MONEY!
SO HOW DO WE KNOW IF WE'RE MAKING MONEY?
LOU PROCEEDS TO LIST THE MEASUREMENTS: TOTAL SALES, MARKET SHARE...
HOW ABOUT *NET PROFIT?*
YOU NEED SOMETHING MORE THAN AN ABSOLUTE MEASUREMENT LIKE NET PROFIT. YOU ALSO NEED ***ROI***-- *RETURN ON INVESTMENTS*-- THE COMPARISON OF *MONEY MADE* RELATIVE TO *MONEY INVESTED.*
BUT, IT'S POSSIBLE TO SHOW NET PROFIT *AND* A GOOD ***ROI*** AND STILL GO BANKRUPT. BAD CASH FLOW IS USUALLY THE CULPRIT.
STAY IN THE BLACK ON CASH FLOW AND YOU'RE OKAY. GO IN THE RED, AND YOU'RE DEAD...
...IT'S HAPPENING TO US RIGHT HERE, ISN'T IT?

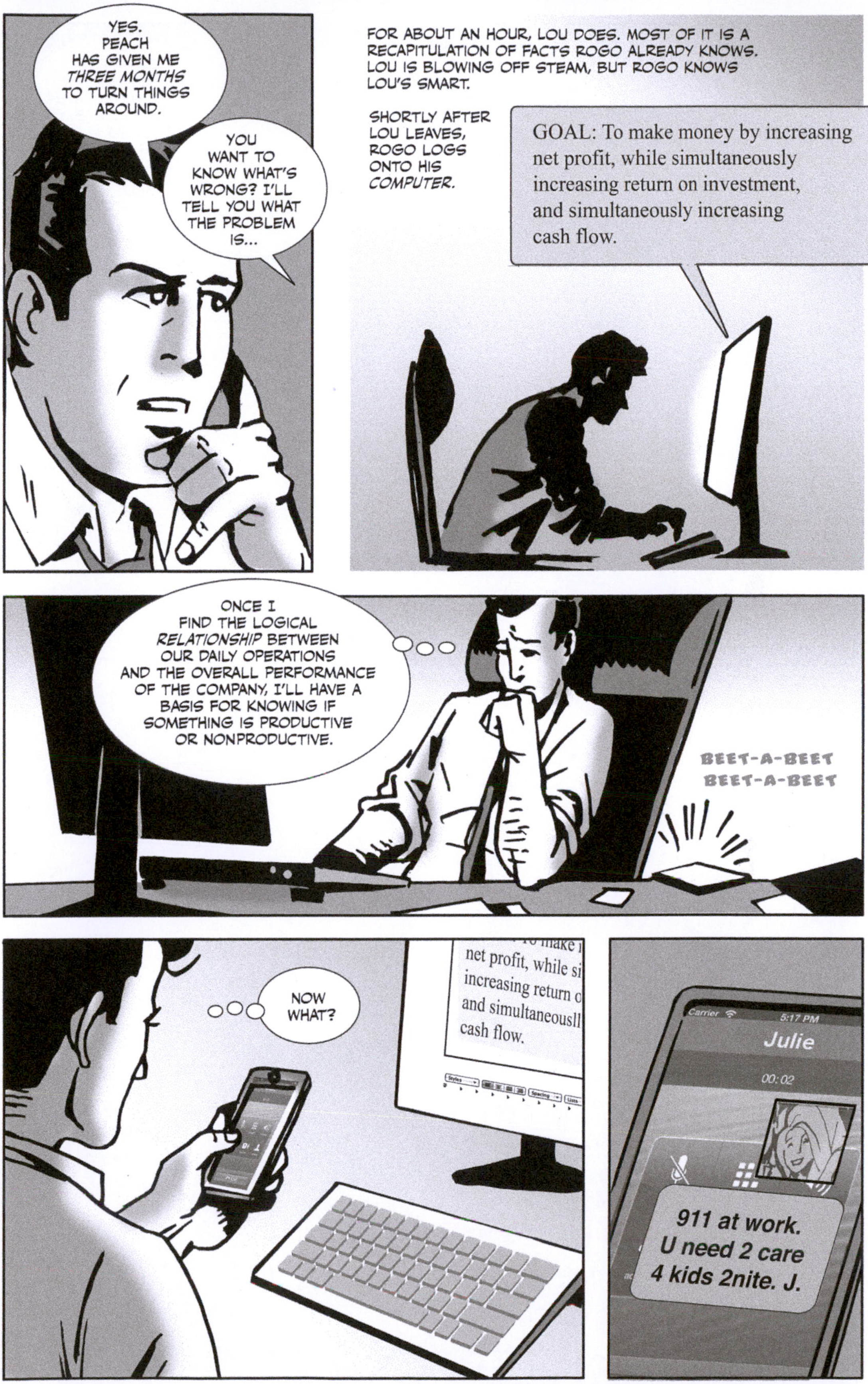
YES. PEACH HAS GIVEN ME *THREE MONTHS* TO TURN THINGS AROUND.
YOU WANT TO KNOW WHAT'S WRONG? I'LL TELL YOU WHAT THE PROBLEM IS...
FOR ABOUT AN HOUR, LOU DOES. MOST OF IT IS A RECAPITULATION OF FACTS ROGO ALREADY KNOWS. LOU IS BLOWING OFF STEAM, BUT ROGO KNOWS LOU'S SMART.
SHORTLY AFTER LOU LEAVES, ROGO LOGS ONTO HIS *COMPUTER*.
GOAL: To make money by increasing net profit, while simultaneously increasing return on investment, and simultaneously increasing cash flow.
ONCE I FIND THE LOGICAL *RELATIONSHIP* BETWEEN OUR DAILY OPERATIONS AND THE OVERALL PERFORMANCE OF THE COMPANY, I'LL HAVE A BASIS FOR KNOWING IF SOMETHING IS PRODUCTIVE OR NONPRODUCTIVE.
BEET-A-BEET
BEET-A-BEET
NOW WHAT?
Carrier
5:17 PM
Julie
00:02
911 at work. U need 2 care 4 kids 2nite. J.

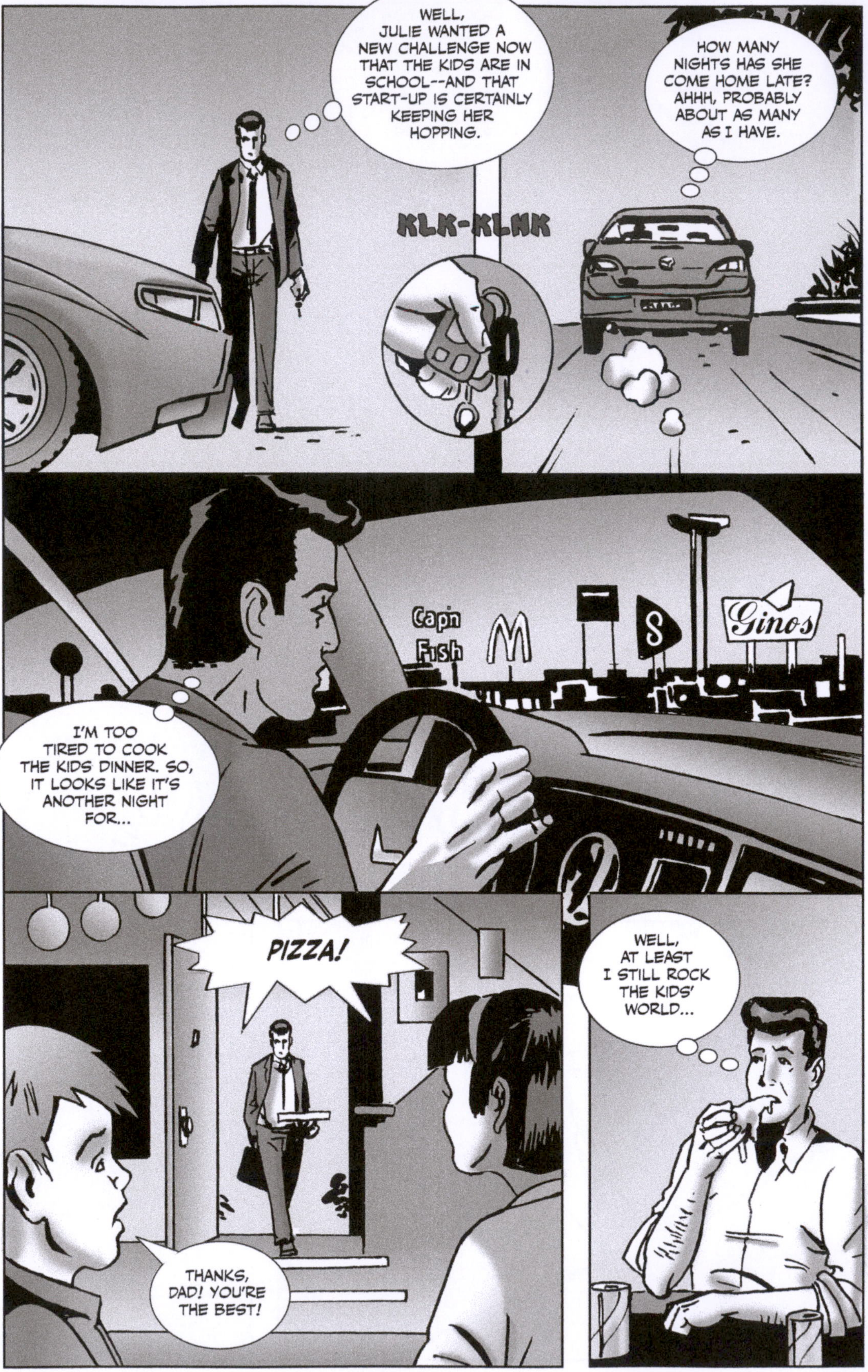
WELL, JULIE WANTED A NEW CHALLENGE NOW THAT THE KIDS ARE IN SCHOOL--AND THAT START-UP IS CERTAINLY KEEPING HER HOPPING.
HOW MANY NIGHTS HAS SHE COME HOME LATE? AHHH, PROBABLY ABOUT AS MANY AS I HAVE.
KLK-KLNK
Capn Fish
Ginos
I'M TOO TIRED TO COOK THE KIDS DINNER. SO, IT LOOKS LIKE IT'S ANOTHER NIGHT FOR...
PIZZA!
THANKS, DAD! YOU'RE THE BEST!
WELL, AT LEAST I STILL ROCK THE KIDS' WORLD...

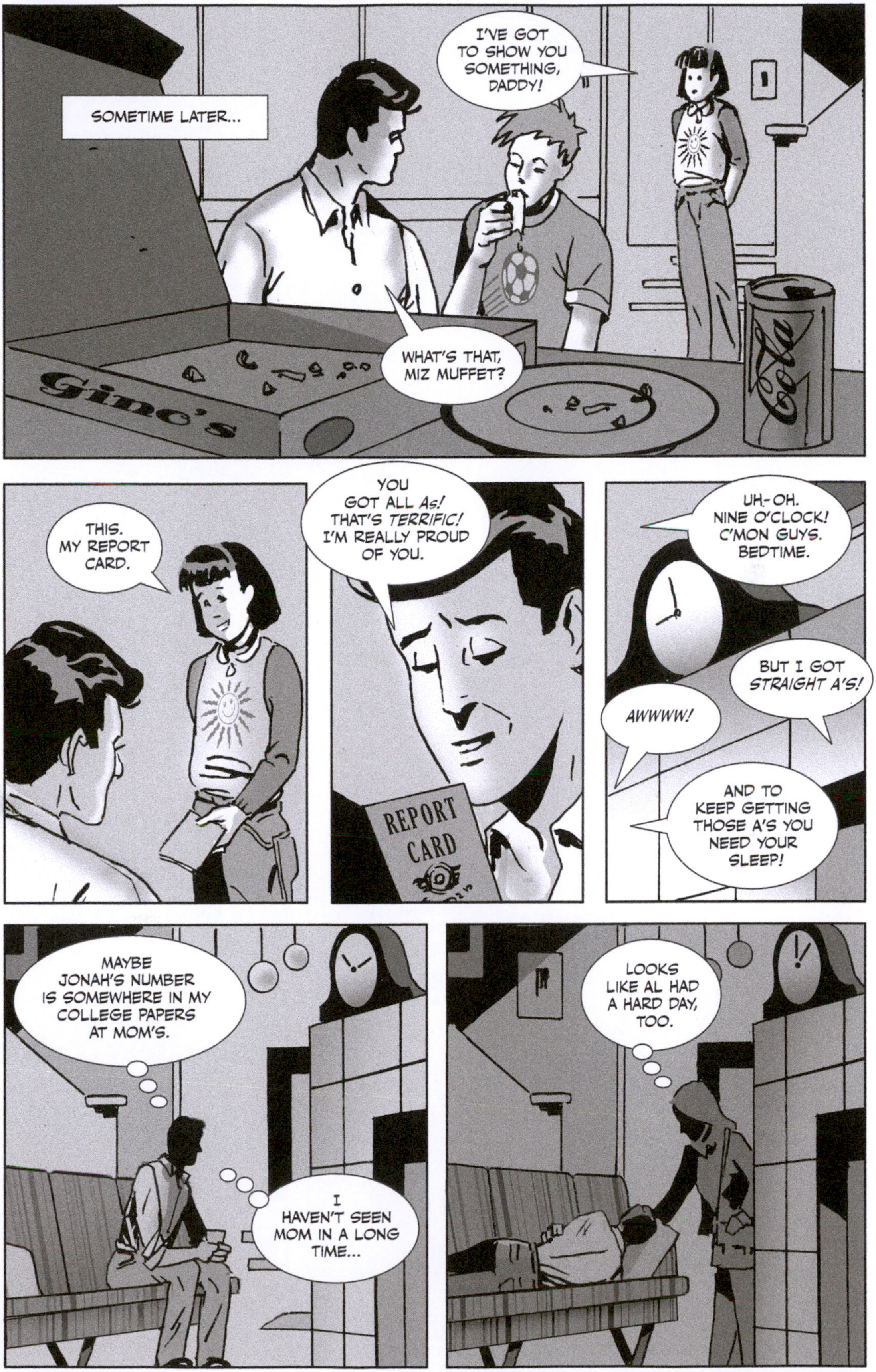
SOMETIME LATER...
I'VE GOT TO SHOW YOU SOMETHING, DADDY!
WHAT'S THAT, MIZ MUFFET?
Gino's
Cola
THIS. MY REPORT CARD.
YOU GOT ALL *As!* THAT'S *TERRIFIC!* I'M REALLY PROUD OF YOU.
REPORT CARD
UH-OH. NINE O'CLOCK! C'MON GUYS. BEDTIME.
AWWWW!
BUT I GOT *STRAIGHT A'S!*
AND TO KEEP GETTING THOSE A'S YOU NEED YOUR SLEEP!
MAYBE JONAH'S NUMBER IS SOMEWHERE IN MY COLLEGE PAPERS AT MOM'S.
I HAVEN'T SEEN MOM IN A LONG TIME...
LOOKS LIKE AL HAD A HARD DAY, TOO.

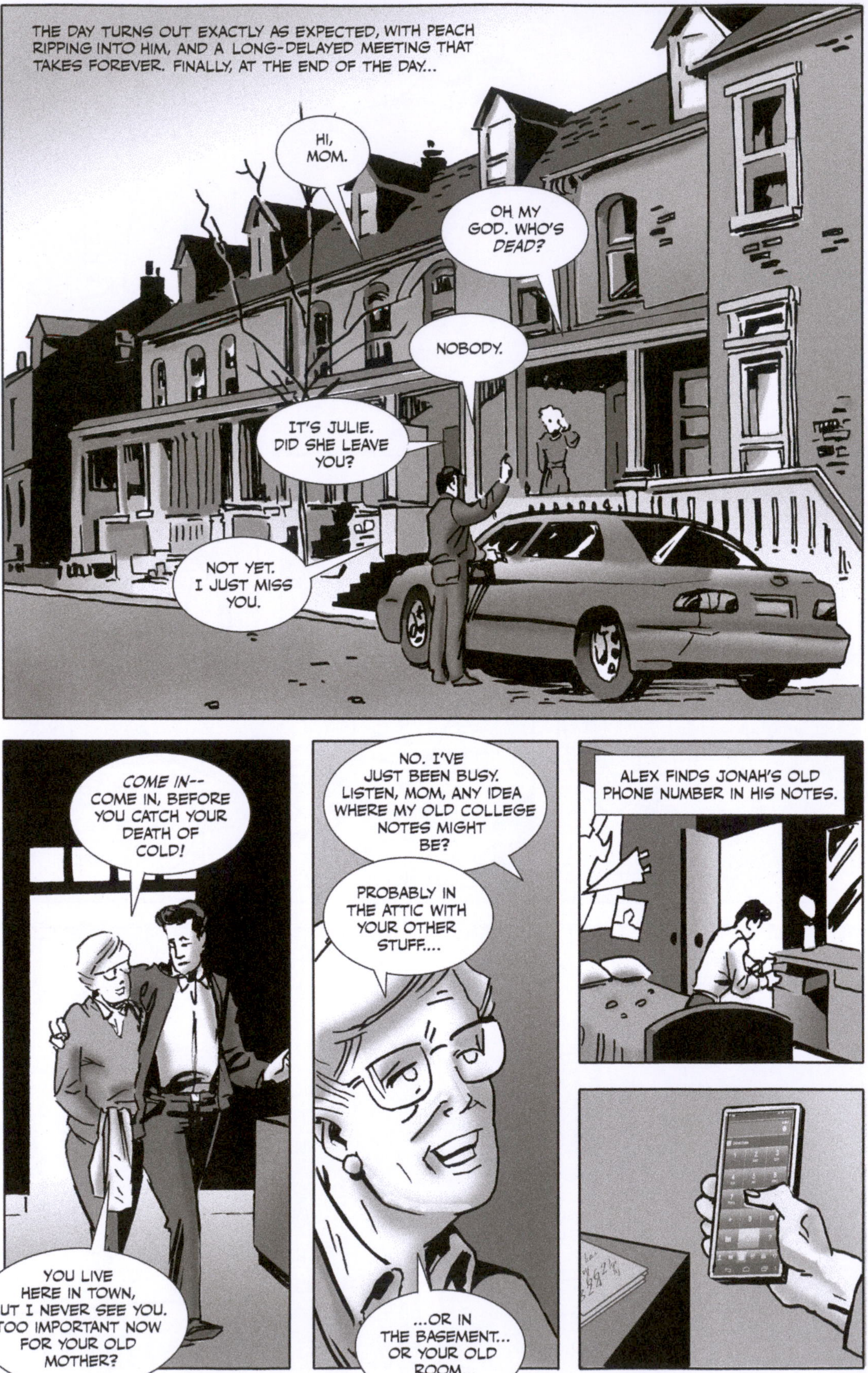
THE DAY TURNS OUT EXACTLY AS EXPECTED, WITH PEACH RIPPING INTO HIM, AND A LONG-DELAYED MEETING THAT TAKES FOREVER. FINALLY, AT THE END OF THE DAY...
HI, MOM.
OH MY GOD. WHO'S *DEAD?*
NOBODY.
IT'S JULIE. DID SHE LEAVE YOU?
NOT YET. I JUST MISS YOU.
COME IN-- COME IN, BEFORE YOU CATCH YOUR DEATH OF COLD!
YOU LIVE HERE IN TOWN, BUT I NEVER SEE YOU. TOO IMPORTANT NOW FOR YOUR OLD MOTHER?
NO. I'VE JUST BEEN BUSY. LISTEN, MOM, ANY IDEA WHERE MY OLD COLLEGE NOTES MIGHT BE?
PROBABLY IN THE ATTIC WITH YOUR OTHER STUFF...
...OR IN THE BASEMENT... OR YOUR OLD ROOM...
ALEX FINDS JONAH'S OLD PHONE NUMBER IN HIS NOTES.

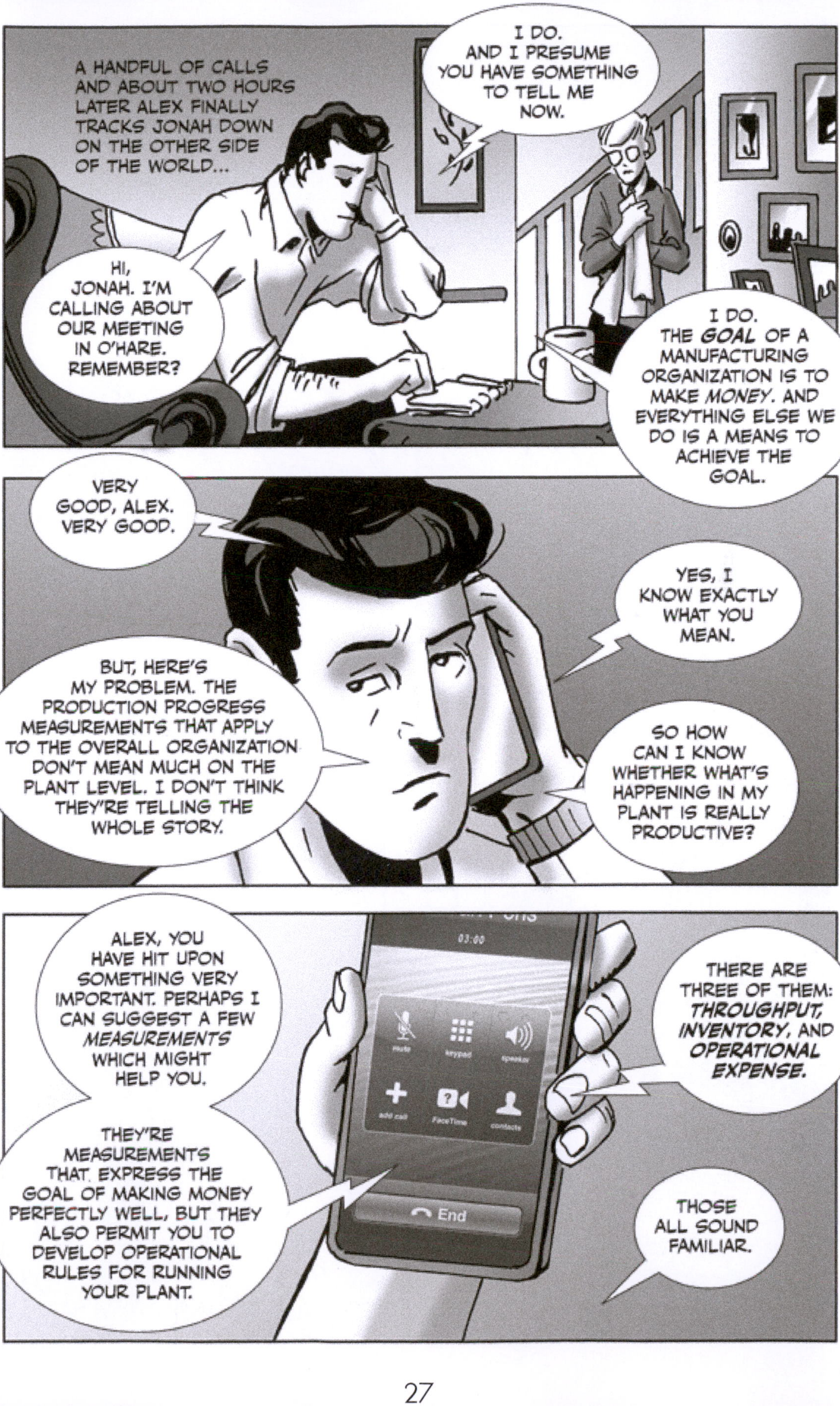
A HANDFUL OF CALLS AND ABOUT TWO HOURS LATER ALEX FINALLY TRACKS JONAH DOWN ON THE OTHER SIDE OF THE WORLD...
HI, JONAH. I'M CALLING ABOUT OUR MEETING IN O'HARE. REMEMBER?
I DO. AND I PRESUME YOU HAVE SOMETHING TO TELL ME NOW.
I DO. THE *GOAL* OF A MANUFACTURING ORGANIZATION IS TO MAKE *MONEY*. AND EVERYTHING ELSE WE DO IS A MEANS TO ACHIEVE THE GOAL.
VERY GOOD, ALEX. VERY GOOD.
YES, I KNOW EXACTLY WHAT YOU MEAN.
BUT, HERE'S MY PROBLEM. THE PRODUCTION PROGRESS MEASUREMENTS THAT APPLY TO THE OVERALL ORGANIZATION DON'T MEAN MUCH ON THE PLANT LEVEL. I DON'T THINK THEY'RE TELLING THE WHOLE STORY.
SO HOW CAN I KNOW WHETHER WHAT'S HAPPENING IN MY PLANT IS REALLY PRODUCTIVE?
ALEX, YOU HAVE HIT UPON SOMETHING VERY IMPORTANT. PERHAPS I CAN SUGGEST A FEW *MEASUREMENTS* WHICH MIGHT HELP YOU.
THERE ARE THREE OF THEM: ***THROUGHPUT, INVENTORY***, AND ***OPERATIONAL EXPENSE.***
THEY'RE MEASUREMENTS THAT EXPRESS THE GOAL OF MAKING MONEY PERFECTLY WELL, BUT THEY ALSO PERMIT YOU TO DEVELOP OPERATIONAL RULES FOR RUNNING YOUR PLANT.
THOSE ALL SOUND FAMILIAR.
End

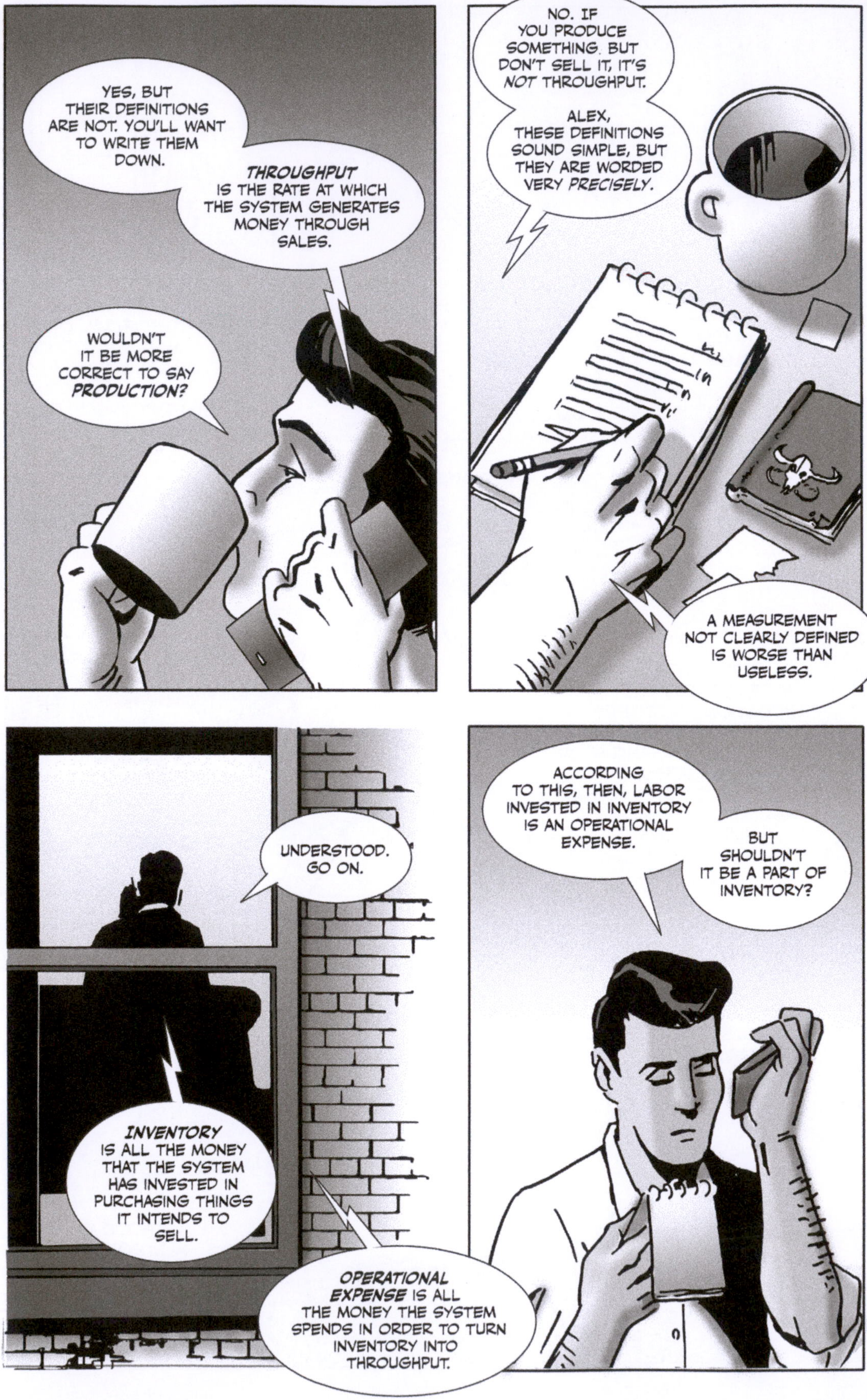
YES, BUT THEIR DEFINITIONS ARE NOT. YOU'LL WANT TO WRITE THEM DOWN.
THROUGHPUT IS THE RATE AT WHICH THE SYSTEM GENERATES MONEY THROUGH SALES.
WOULDN'T IT BE MORE CORRECT TO SAY PRODUCTION?
NO. IF YOU PRODUCE SOMETHING, BUT DON'T SELL IT, IT'S NOT THROUGHPUT.
ALEX, THESE DEFINITIONS SOUND SIMPLE, BUT THEY ARE WORDED VERY PRECISELY.
A MEASUREMENT NOT CLEARLY DEFINED IS WORSE THAN USELESS.
UNDERSTOOD. GO ON.
INVENTORY IS ALL THE MONEY THAT THE SYSTEM HAS INVESTED IN PURCHASING THINGS IT INTENDS TO SELL.
OPERATIONAL EXPENSE IS ALL THE MONEY THE SYSTEM SPENDS IN ORDER TO TURN INVENTORY INTO THROUGHPUT.
ACCORDING TO THIS, THEN, LABOR INVESTED IN INVENTORY IS AN OPERATIONAL EXPENSE.
BUT SHOULDN'T IT BE A PART OF INVENTORY?

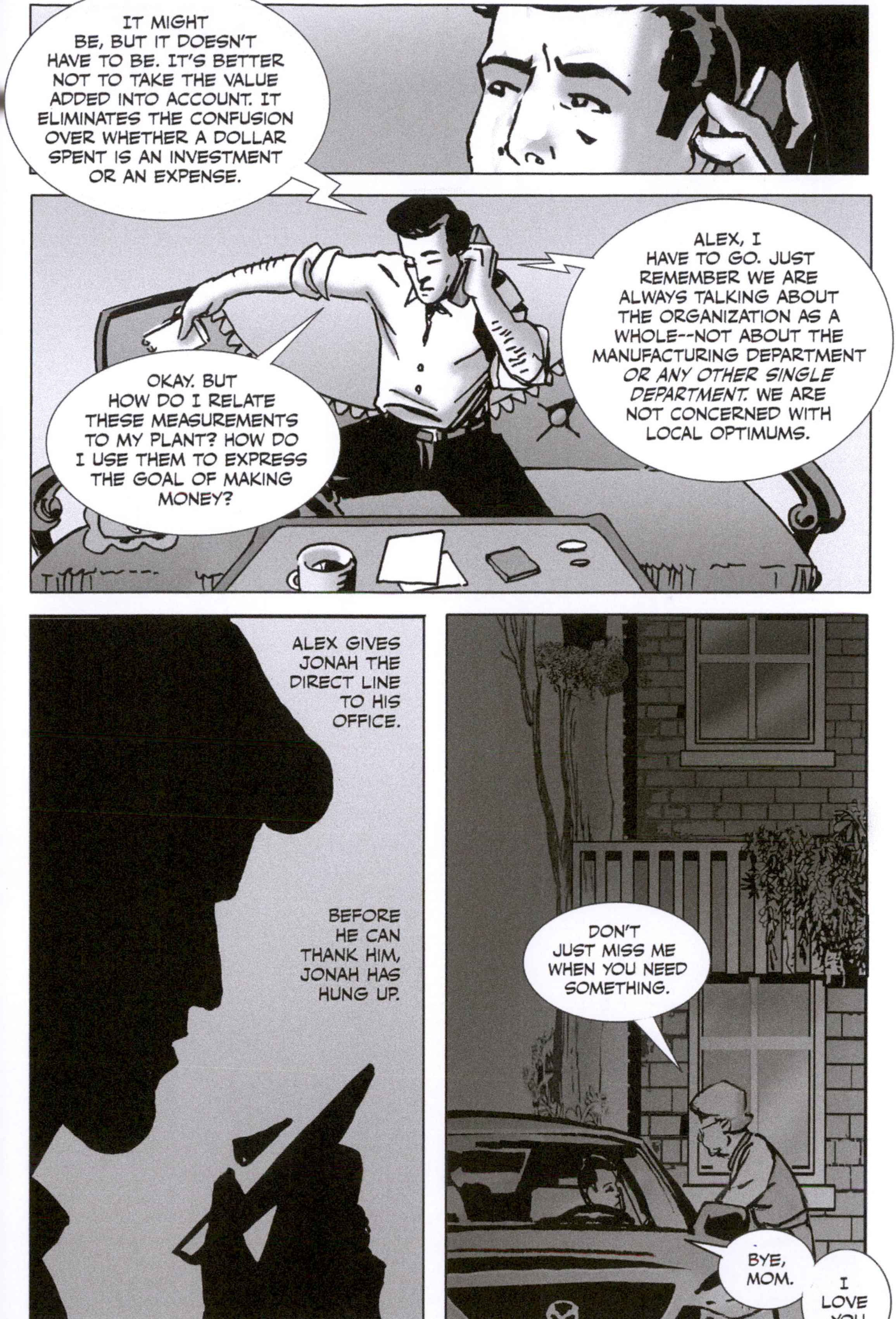
IT MIGHT BE, BUT IT DOESN'T HAVE TO BE. IT'S BETTER NOT TO TAKE THE VALUE ADDED INTO ACCOUNT. IT ELIMINATES THE CONFUSION OVER WHETHER A DOLLAR SPENT IS AN INVESTMENT OR AN EXPENSE.
OKAY. BUT HOW DO I RELATE THESE MEASUREMENTS TO MY PLANT? HOW DO I USE THEM TO EXPRESS THE GOAL OF MAKING MONEY?
ALEX, I HAVE TO GO. JUST REMEMBER WE ARE ALWAYS TALKING ABOUT THE ORGANIZATION AS A WHOLE--NOT ABOUT THE MANUFACTURING DEPARTMENT *OR ANY OTHER SINGLE DEPARTMENT.* WE ARE NOT CONCERNED WITH LOCAL OPTIMUMS.
ALEX GIVES JONAH THE DIRECT LINE TO HIS OFFICE.
BEFORE HE CAN THANK HIM, JONAH HAS HUNG UP.
DON'T JUST MISS ME WHEN YOU NEED SOMETHING.
BYE, MOM.
I LOVE YOU.

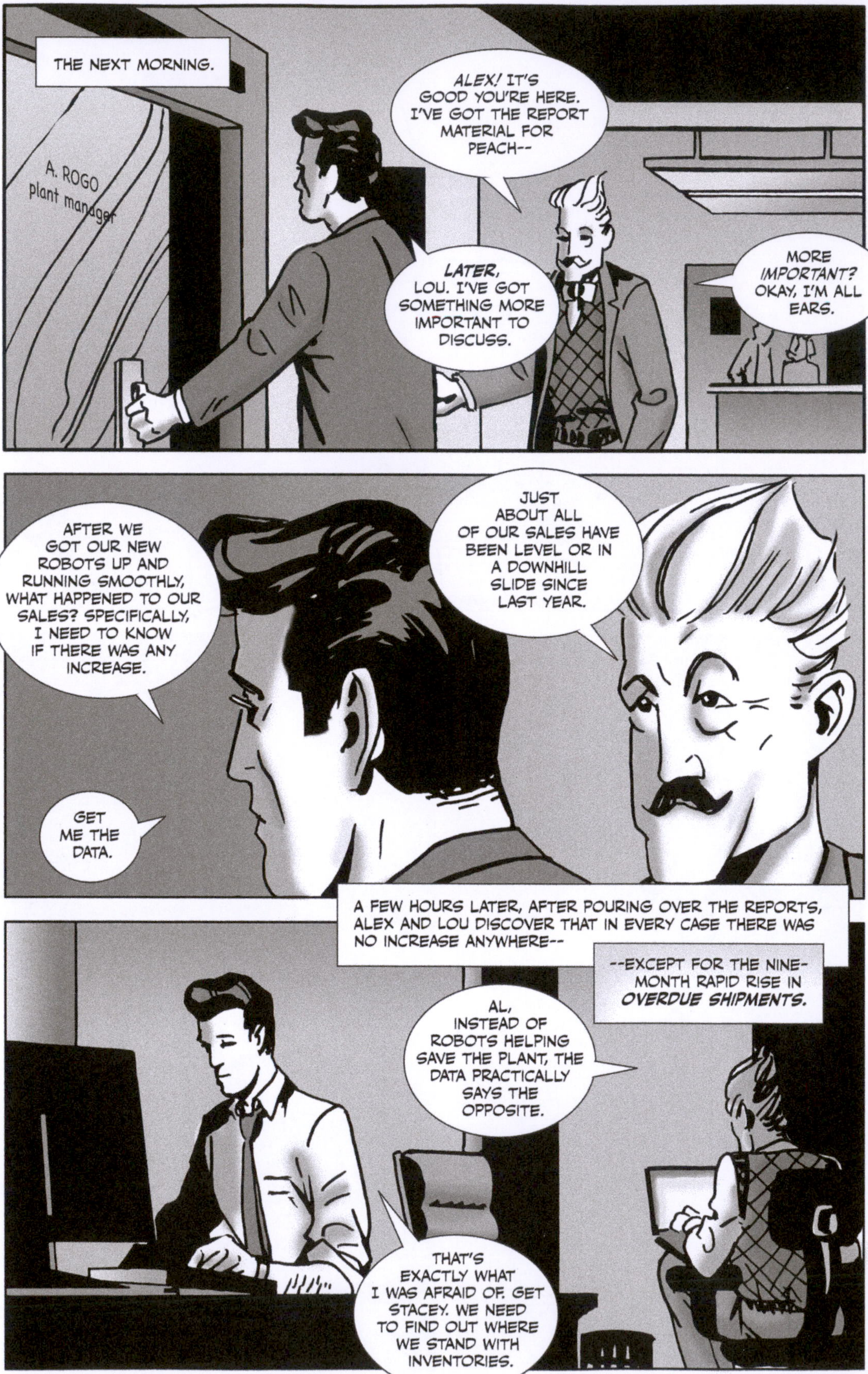

THE NEXT MORNING.
A. ROGO plant manager
ALEX! IT'S GOOD YOU'RE HERE. I'VE GOT THE REPORT MATERIAL FOR PEACH--
LATER, LOU. I'VE GOT SOMETHING MORE IMPORTANT TO DISCUSS.
MORE IMPORTANT? OKAY, I'M ALL EARS.
AFTER WE GOT OUR NEW ROBOTS UP AND RUNNING SMOOTHLY, WHAT HAPPENED TO OUR SALES? SPECIFICALLY, I NEED TO KNOW IF THERE WAS ANY INCREASE.
JUST ABOUT ALL OF OUR SALES HAVE BEEN LEVEL OR IN A DOWNHILL SLIDE SINCE LAST YEAR.
GET ME THE DATA.
A FEW HOURS LATER, AFTER POURING OVER THE REPORTS, ALEX AND LOU DISCOVER THAT IN EVERY CASE THERE WAS NO INCREASE ANYWHERE--
--EXCEPT FOR THE NINE-MONTH RAPID RISE IN OVERDUE SHIPMENTS.
AL, INSTEAD OF ROBOTS HELPING SAVE THE PLANT, THE DATA PRACTICALLY SAYS THE OPPOSITE.
THAT'S EXACTLY WHAT I WAS AFRAID OF. GET STACEY. WE NEED TO FIND OUT WHERE WE STAND WITH INVENTORIES.

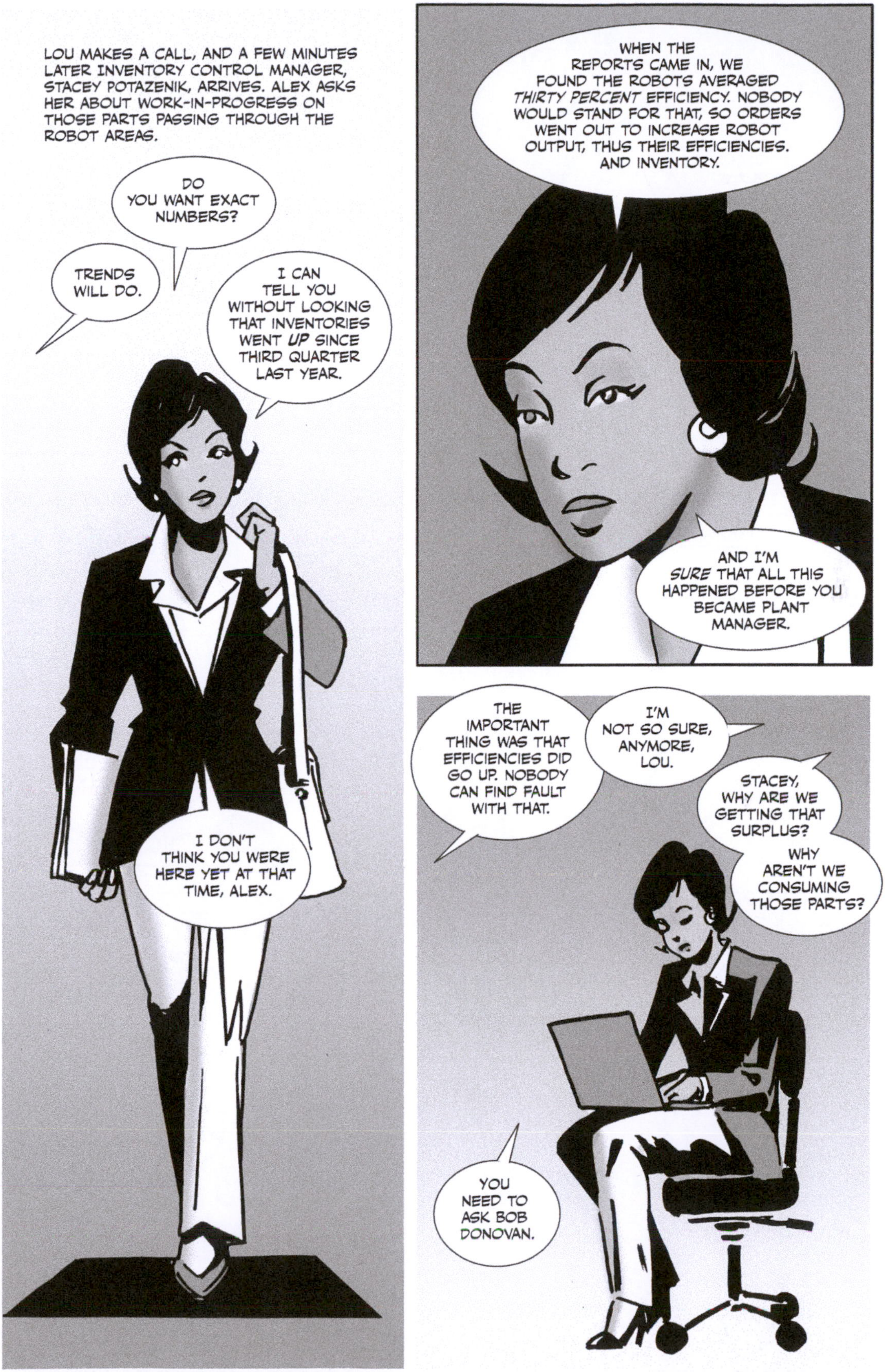
LOU MAKES A CALL, AND A FEW MINUTES LATER INVENTORY CONTROL MANAGER, STACEY POTAZENIK, ARRIVES. ALEX ASKS HER ABOUT WORK-IN-PROGRESS ON THOSE PARTS PASSING THROUGH THE ROBOT AREAS.
DO YOU WANT EXACT NUMBERS?
TRENDS WILL DO.
I CAN TELL YOU WITHOUT LOOKING THAT INVENTORIES WENT *UP* SINCE THIRD QUARTER LAST YEAR.
I DON'T THINK YOU WERE HERE YET AT THAT TIME, ALEX.
WHEN THE REPORTS CAME IN, WE FOUND THE ROBOTS AVERAGED *THIRTY PERCENT* EFFICIENCY. NOBODY WOULD STAND FOR THAT, SO ORDERS WENT OUT TO INCREASE ROBOT OUTPUT, THUS THEIR EFFICIENCIES. AND INVENTORY.
AND I'M *SURE* THAT ALL THIS HAPPENED BEFORE YOU BECAME PLANT MANAGER.
THE IMPORTANT THING WAS THAT EFFICIENCIES DID GO UP. NOBODY CAN FIND FAULT WITH THAT.
I'M NOT SO SURE, ANYMORE, LOU.
STACEY, WHY ARE WE GETTING THAT SURPLUS?
WHY AREN'T WE CONSUMING THOSE PARTS?
YOU NEED TO ASK BOB DONOVAN.

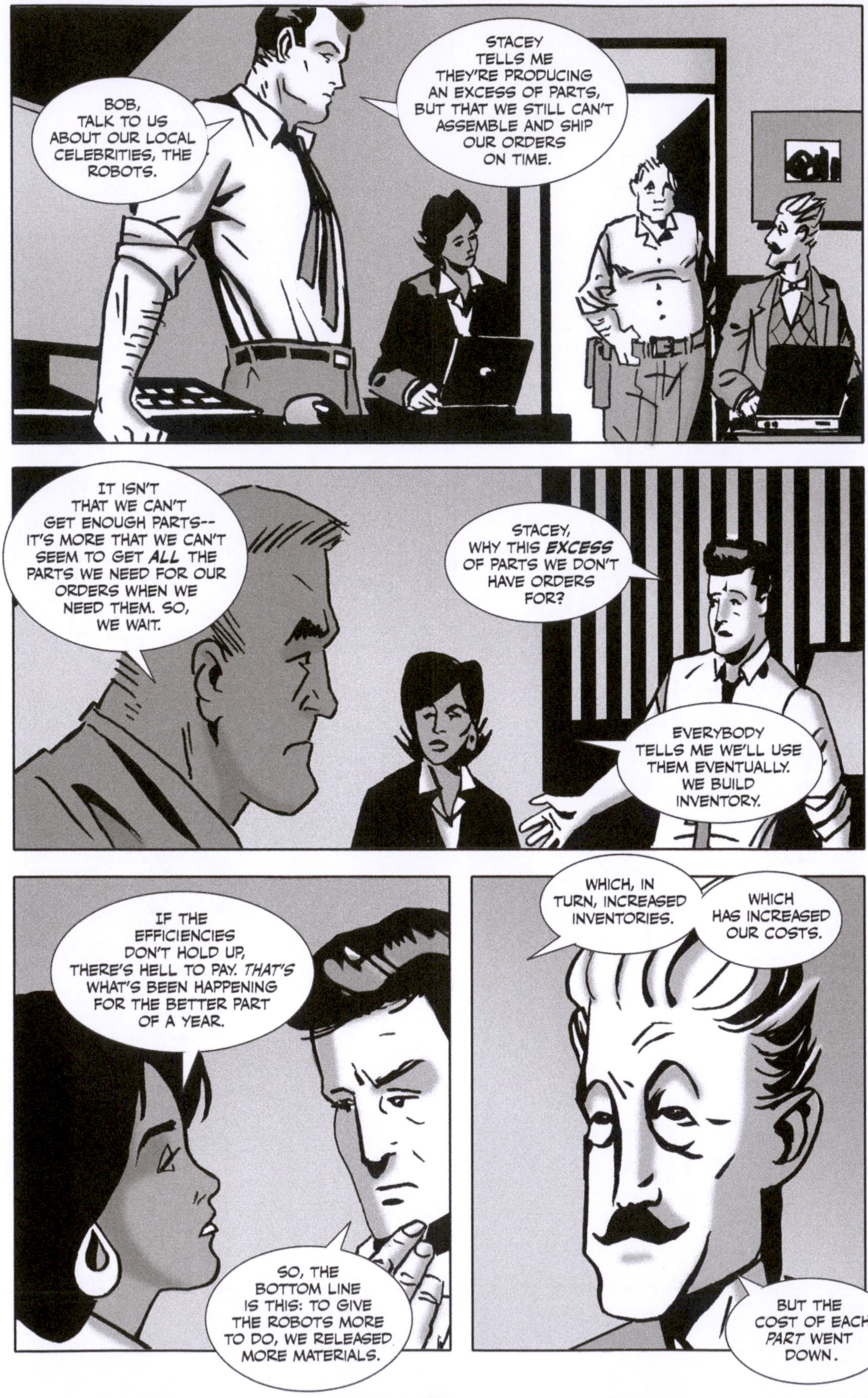
BOB, TALK TO US ABOUT OUR LOCAL CELEBRITIES, THE ROBOTS.
STACEY TELLS ME THEY'RE PRODUCING AN EXCESS OF PARTS, BUT THAT WE STILL CAN'T ASSEMBLE AND SHIP OUR ORDERS ON TIME.
IT ISN'T THAT WE CAN'T GET ENOUGH PARTS-- IT'S MORE THAT WE CAN'T SEEM TO GET *ALL* THE PARTS WE NEED FOR OUR ORDERS WHEN WE NEED THEM. SO, WE WAIT.
STACEY, WHY THIS *EXCESS* OF PARTS WE DON'T HAVE ORDERS FOR?
EVERYBODY TELLS ME WE'LL USE THEM EVENTUALLY. WE BUILD INVENTORY.
IF THE EFFICIENCIES DON'T HOLD UP, THERE'S HELL TO PAY. *THAT'S* WHAT'S BEEN HAPPENING FOR THE BETTER PART OF A YEAR.
SO, THE BOTTOM LINE IS THIS: TO GIVE THE ROBOTS MORE TO DO, WE RELEASED MORE MATERIALS.
WHICH, IN TURN, INCREASED INVENTORIES.
WHICH HAS INCREASED OUR COSTS.
BUT THE COST OF EACH *PART* WENT DOWN.

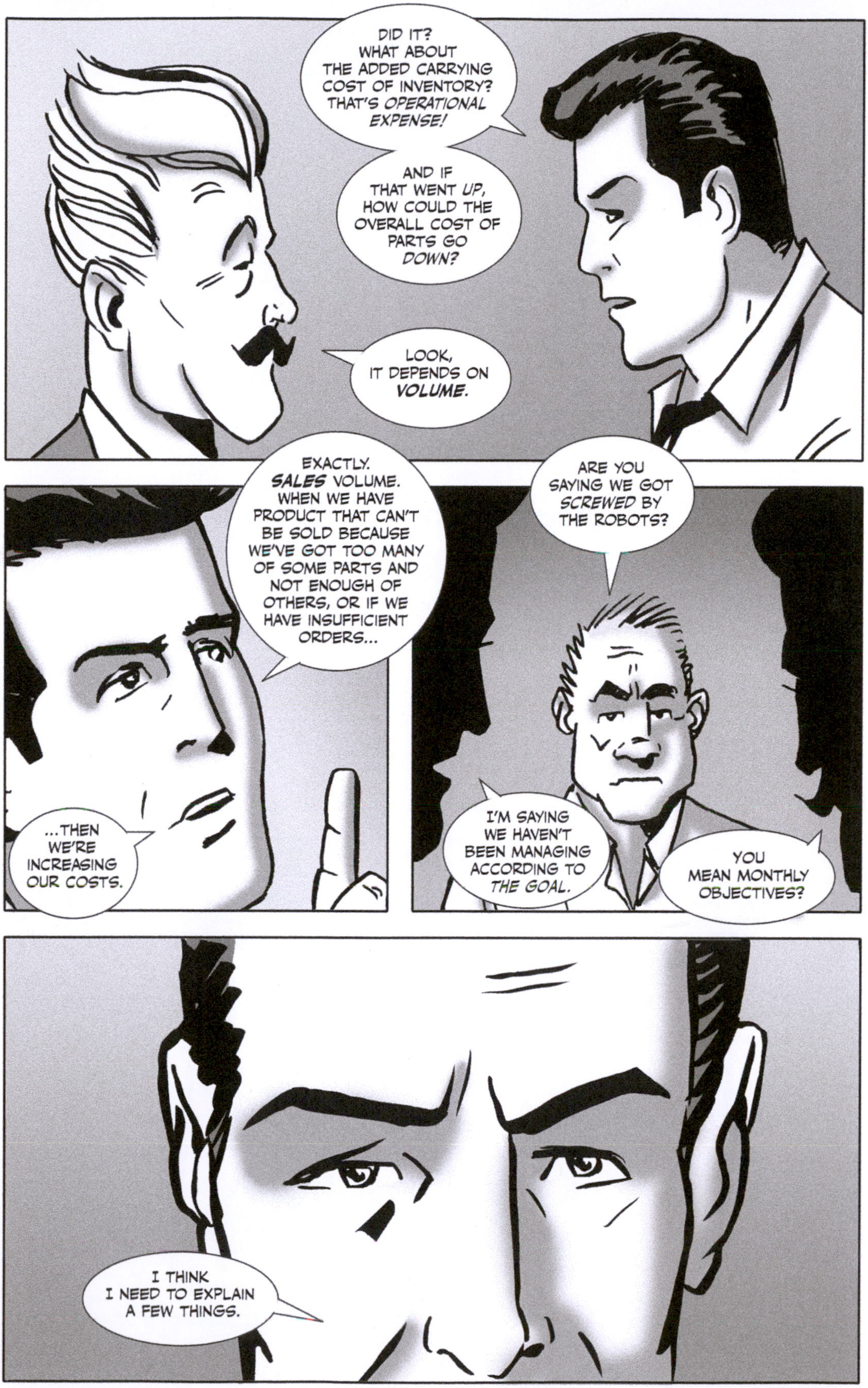
DID IT? WHAT ABOUT THE ADDED CARRYING COST OF INVENTORY? THAT'S *OPERATIONAL EXPENSE!*
AND IF THAT WENT *UP*, HOW COULD THE OVERALL COST OF PARTS GO *DOWN?*
LOOK, IT DEPENDS ON ***VOLUME***.
EXACTLY. ***SALES*** VOLUME. WHEN WE HAVE PRODUCT THAT CAN'T BE SOLD BECAUSE WE'VE GOT TOO MANY OF SOME PARTS AND NOT ENOUGH OF OTHERS, OR IF WE HAVE INSUFFICIENT ORDERS...
...THEN WE'RE INCREASING OUR COSTS.
ARE YOU SAYING WE GOT *SCREWED* BY THE ROBOTS?
I'M SAYING WE HAVEN'T BEEN MANAGING ACCORDING TO *THE GOAL*.
YOU MEAN MONTHLY OBJECTIVES?
I THINK I NEED TO EXPLAIN A FEW THINGS.

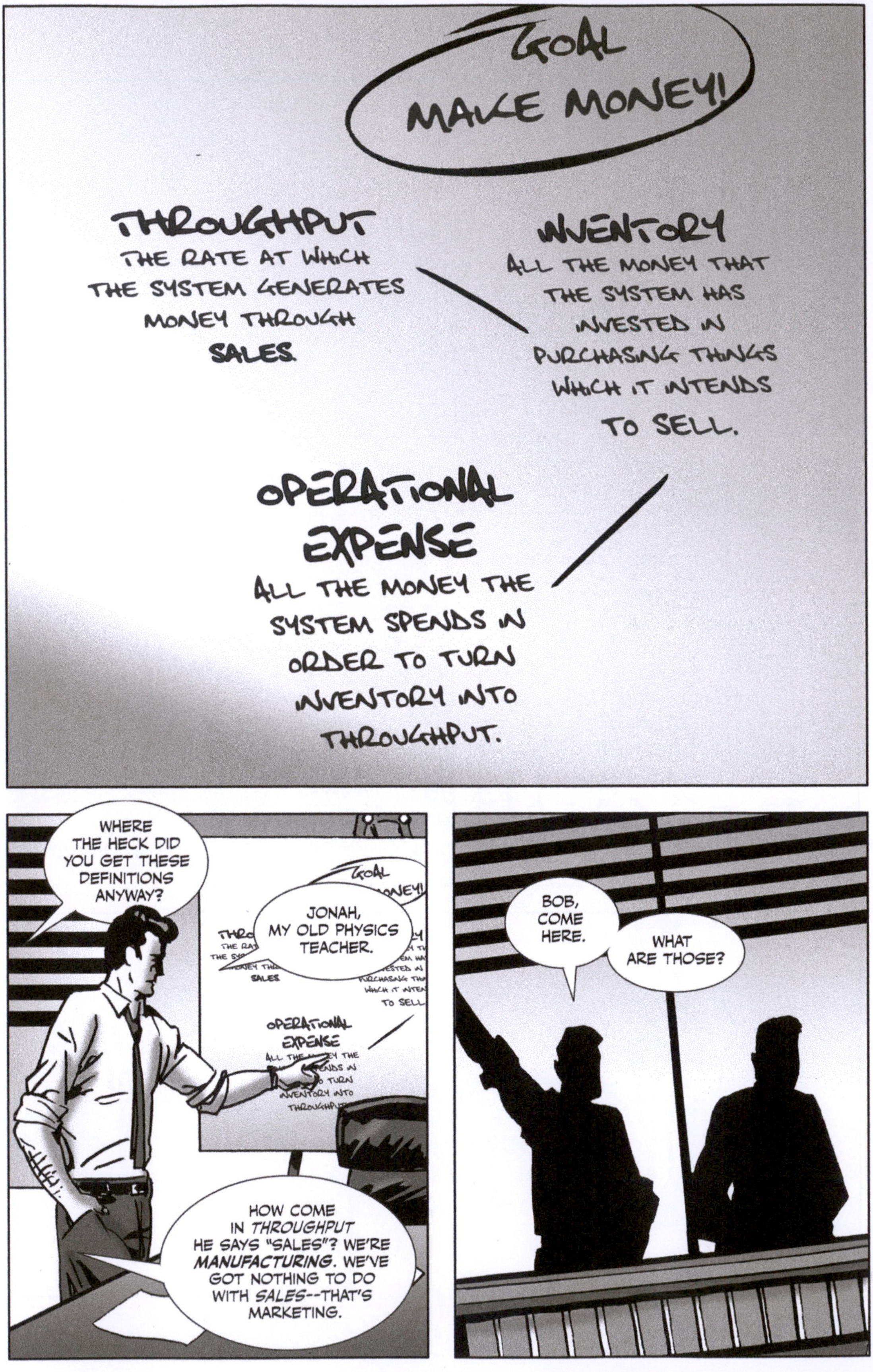
GOAL
MAKE MONEY!
THROUGHPUT
THE RATE AT WHICH THE SYSTEM GENERATES MONEY THROUGH SALES.
INVENTORY
ALL THE MONEY THAT THE SYSTEM HAS INVESTED IN PURCHASING THINGS WHICH IT INTENDS TO SELL.
OPERATIONAL EXPENSE
ALL THE MONEY THE SYSTEM SPENDS IN ORDER TO TURN INVENTORY INTO THROUGHPUT.
WHERE THE HECK DID YOU GET THESE DEFINITIONS ANYWAY?
JONAH, MY OLD PHYSICS TEACHER.
HOW COME IN *THROUGHPUT* HE SAYS "SALES"? WE'RE ***MANUFACTURING***. WE'VE GOT NOTHING TO DO WITH *SALES*--THAT'S MARKETING.
BOB, COME HERE.
WHAT ARE THOSE?

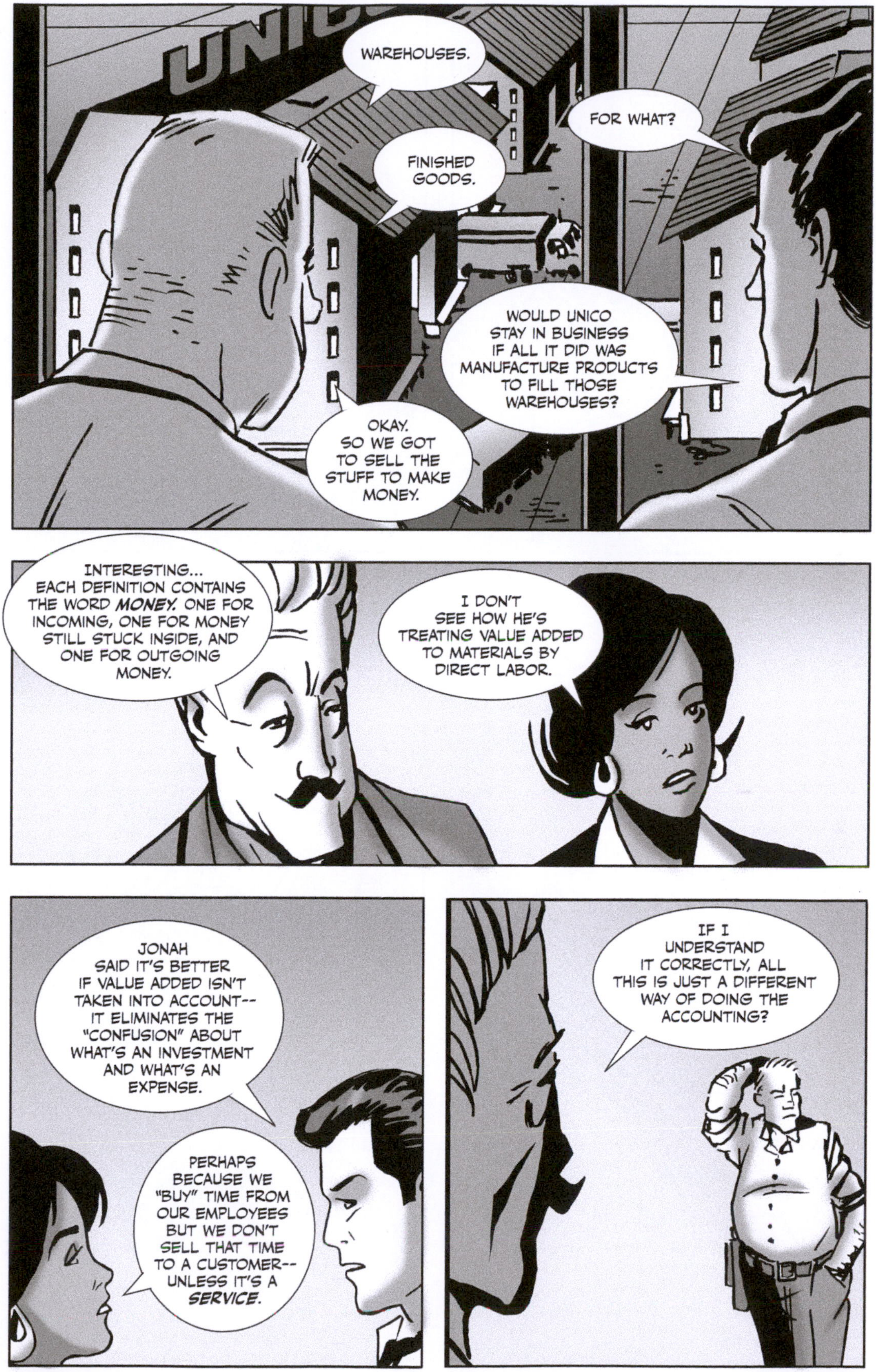
WAREHOUSES.
FOR WHAT?
FINISHED GOODS.
WOULD UNICO STAY IN BUSINESS IF ALL IT DID WAS MANUFACTURE PRODUCTS TO FILL THOSE WAREHOUSES?
OKAY. SO WE GOT TO SELL THE STUFF TO MAKE MONEY.
INTERESTING... EACH DEFINITION CONTAINS THE WORD **MONEY.** ONE FOR INCOMING, ONE FOR MONEY STILL STUCK INSIDE, AND ONE FOR OUTGOING MONEY.
I DON'T SEE HOW HE'S TREATING VALUE ADDED TO MATERIALS BY DIRECT LABOR.
JONAH SAID IT'S BETTER IF VALUE ADDED ISN'T TAKEN INTO ACCOUNT-- IT ELIMINATES THE "CONFUSION" ABOUT WHAT'S AN INVESTMENT AND WHAT'S AN EXPENSE.
PERHAPS BECAUSE WE "BUY" TIME FROM OUR EMPLOYEES BUT WE DON'T SELL THAT TIME TO A CUSTOMER-- UNLESS IT'S A ***SERVICE***.
IF I UNDERSTAND IT CORRECTLY, ALL THIS IS JUST A DIFFERENT WAY OF DOING THE ACCOUNTING?

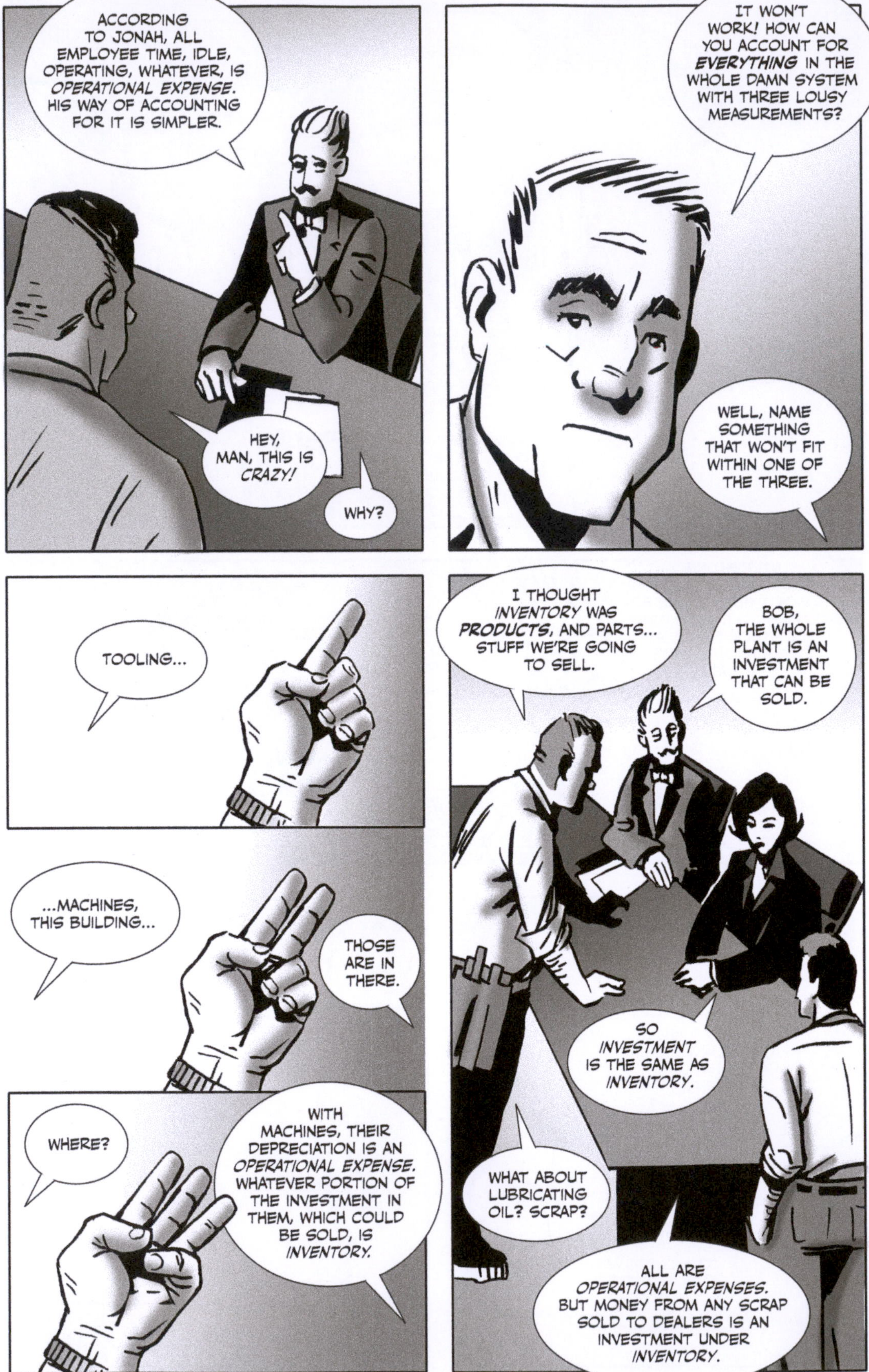

ACCORDING TO JONAH, ALL EMPLOYEE TIME, IDLE, OPERATING, WHATEVER, IS *OPERATIONAL EXPENSE*. HIS WAY OF ACCOUNTING FOR IT IS SIMPLER.
HEY, MAN, THIS IS *CRAZY!*
WHY?
IT WON'T WORK! HOW CAN YOU ACCOUNT FOR ***EVERYTHING*** IN THE WHOLE DAMN SYSTEM WITH THREE LOUSY MEASUREMENTS?
WELL, NAME SOMETHING THAT WON'T FIT WITHIN ONE OF THE THREE.
TOOLING...
...MACHINES, THIS BUILDING...
THOSE ARE IN THERE.
WHERE?
WITH MACHINES, THEIR DEPRECIATION IS AN *OPERATIONAL EXPENSE*. WHATEVER PORTION OF THE INVESTMENT IN THEM, WHICH COULD BE SOLD, IS *INVENTORY*.
I THOUGHT *INVENTORY* WAS ***PRODUCTS***, AND PARTS... STUFF WE'RE GOING TO SELL.
BOB, THE WHOLE PLANT IS AN INVESTMENT THAT CAN BE SOLD.
SO *INVESTMENT* IS THE SAME AS *INVENTORY*.
WHAT ABOUT LUBRICATING OIL? SCRAP?
ALL ARE *OPERATIONAL EXPENSES*. BUT MONEY FROM ANY SCRAP SOLD TO DEALERS IS AN INVESTMENT UNDER *INVENTORY*.

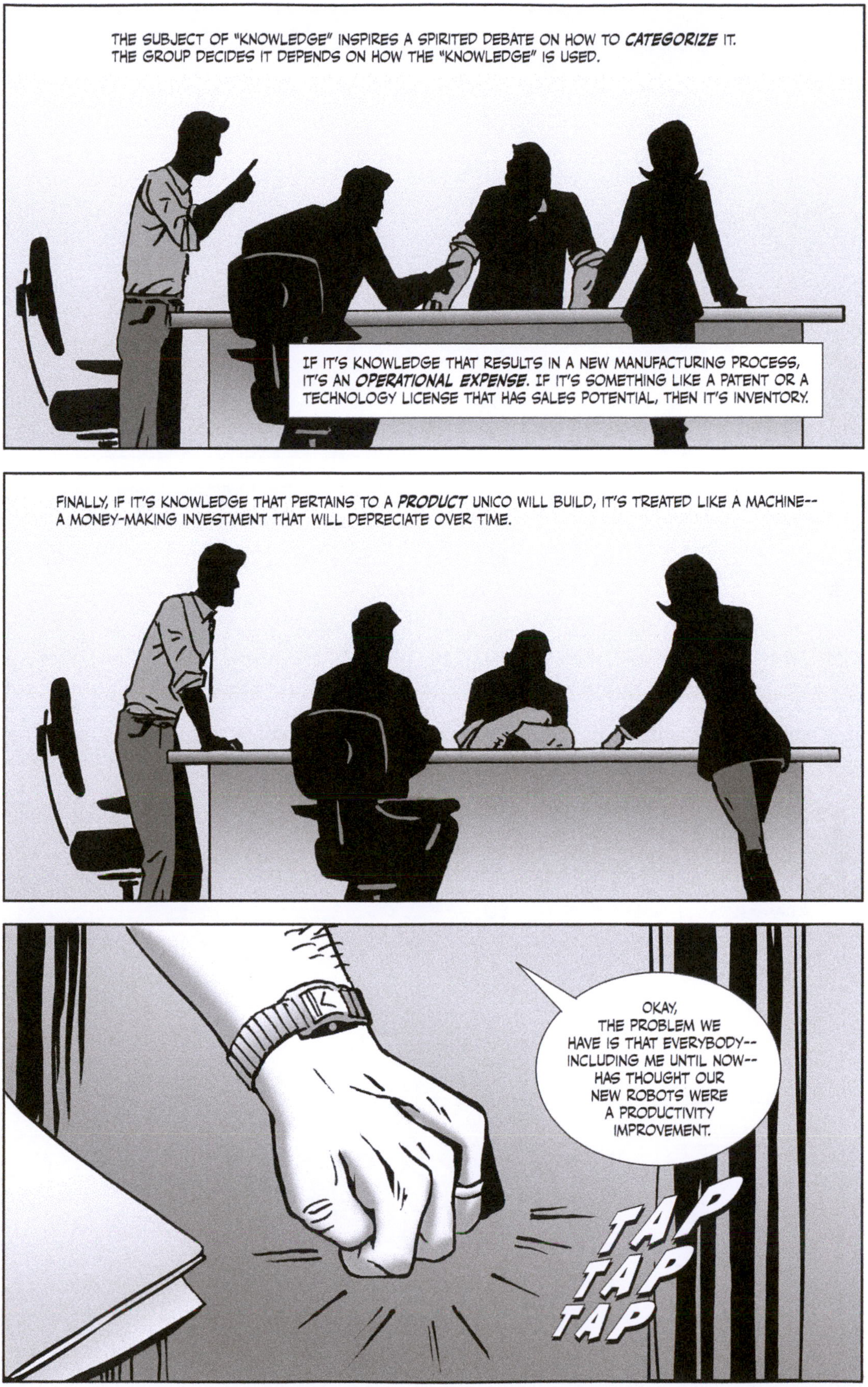
THE SUBJECT OF "KNOWLEDGE" INSPIRES A SPIRITED DEBATE ON HOW TO *CATEGORIZE* IT. THE GROUP DECIDES IT DEPENDS ON HOW THE "KNOWLEDGE" IS USED.
IF IT'S KNOWLEDGE THAT RESULTS IN A NEW MANUFACTURING PROCESS, IT'S AN *OPERATIONAL EXPENSE*. IF IT'S SOMETHING LIKE A PATENT OR A TECHNOLOGY LICENSE THAT HAS SALES POTENTIAL, THEN IT'S INVENTORY.
FINALLY, IF IT'S KNOWLEDGE THAT PERTAINS TO A *PRODUCT* UNICO WILL BUILD, IT'S TREATED LIKE A MACHINE-- A MONEY-MAKING INVESTMENT THAT WILL DEPRECIATE OVER TIME.
OKAY, THE PROBLEM WE HAVE IS THAT EVERYBODY-- INCLUDING ME UNTIL NOW-- HAS THOUGHT OUR NEW ROBOTS WERE A PRODUCTIVITY IMPROVEMENT.
TAP TAP TAP

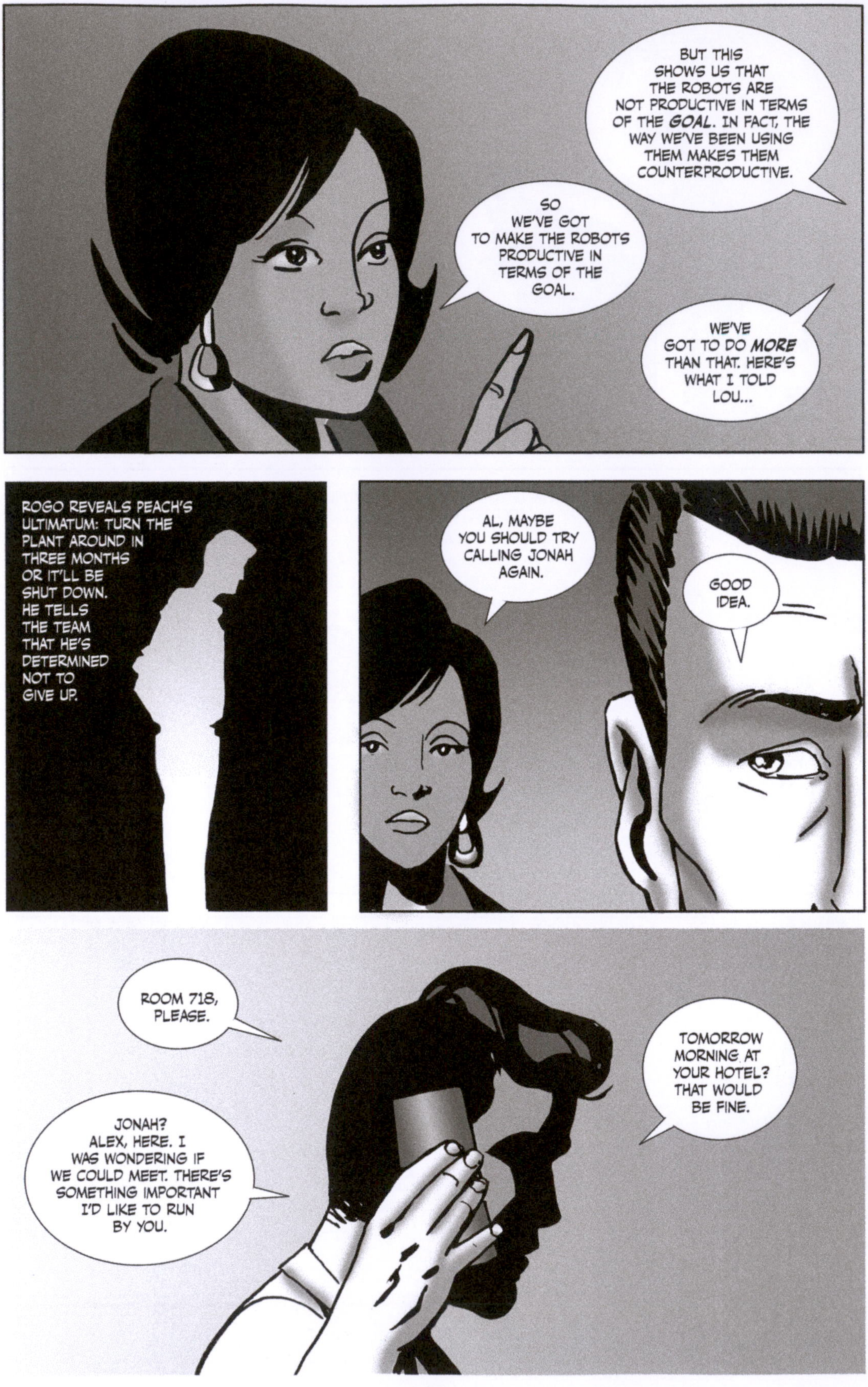
BUT THIS SHOWS US THAT THE ROBOTS ARE NOT PRODUCTIVE IN TERMS OF THE *GOAL*. IN FACT, THE WAY WE'VE BEEN USING THEM MAKES THEM COUNTERPRODUCTIVE.
SO WE'VE GOT TO MAKE THE ROBOTS PRODUCTIVE IN TERMS OF THE GOAL.
WE'VE GOT TO DO *MORE* THAN THAT. HERE'S WHAT I TOLD LOU...
ROGO REVEALS PEACH'S ULTIMATUM: TURN THE PLANT AROUND IN THREE MONTHS OR IT'LL BE SHUT DOWN. HE TELLS THE TEAM THAT HE'S DETERMINED NOT TO GIVE UP.
AL, MAYBE YOU SHOULD TRY CALLING JONAH AGAIN.
GOOD IDEA.
ROOM 718, PLEASE.
JONAH? ALEX, HERE. I WAS WONDERING IF WE COULD MEET. THERE'S SOMETHING IMPORTANT I'D LIKE TO RUN BY YOU.
TOMORROW MORNING AT YOUR HOTEL? THAT WOULD BE FINE.

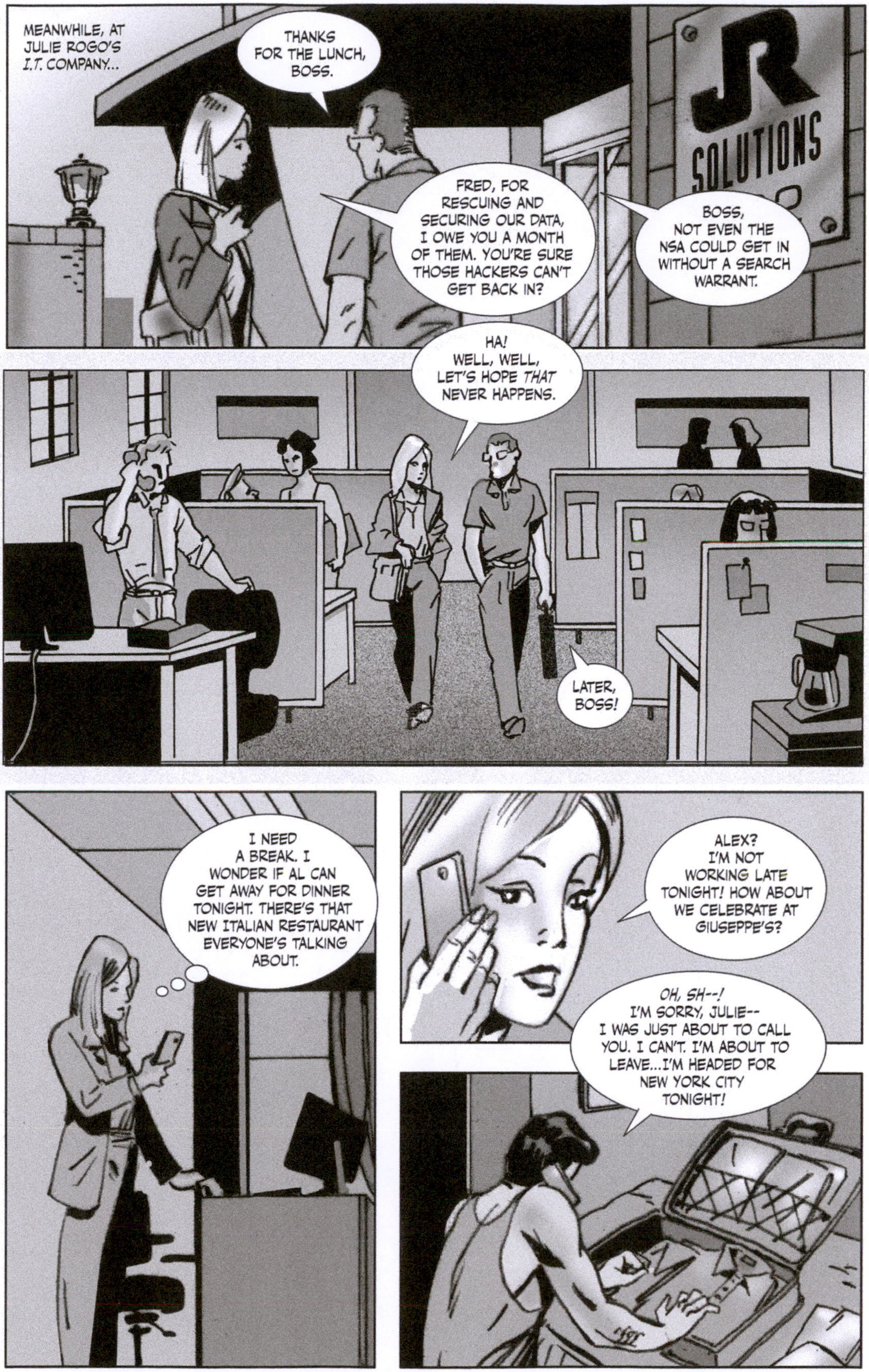
MEANWHILE, AT JULIE ROGO'S *I.T.* COMPANY...
THANKS FOR THE LUNCH, BOSS.
JR SOLUTIONS
FRED, FOR RESCUING AND SECURING OUR DATA, I OWE YOU A MONTH OF THEM. YOU'RE SURE THOSE HACKERS CAN'T GET BACK IN?
BOSS, NOT EVEN THE NSA COULD GET IN WITHOUT A SEARCH WARRANT.
HA! WELL, WELL, LET'S HOPE *THAT* NEVER HAPPENS.
LATER, BOSS!
I NEED A BREAK. I WONDER IF AL CAN GET AWAY FOR DINNER TONIGHT. THERE'S THAT NEW ITALIAN RESTAURANT EVERYONE'S TALKING ABOUT.
ALEX? I'M NOT WORKING LATE TONIGHT! HOW ABOUT WE CELEBRATE AT GIUSEPPE'S?
OH, SH--! I'M SORRY, JULIE-- I WAS JUST ABOUT TO CALL YOU. I CAN'T. I'M ABOUT TO LEAVE...I'M HEADED FOR NEW YORK CITY TONIGHT!

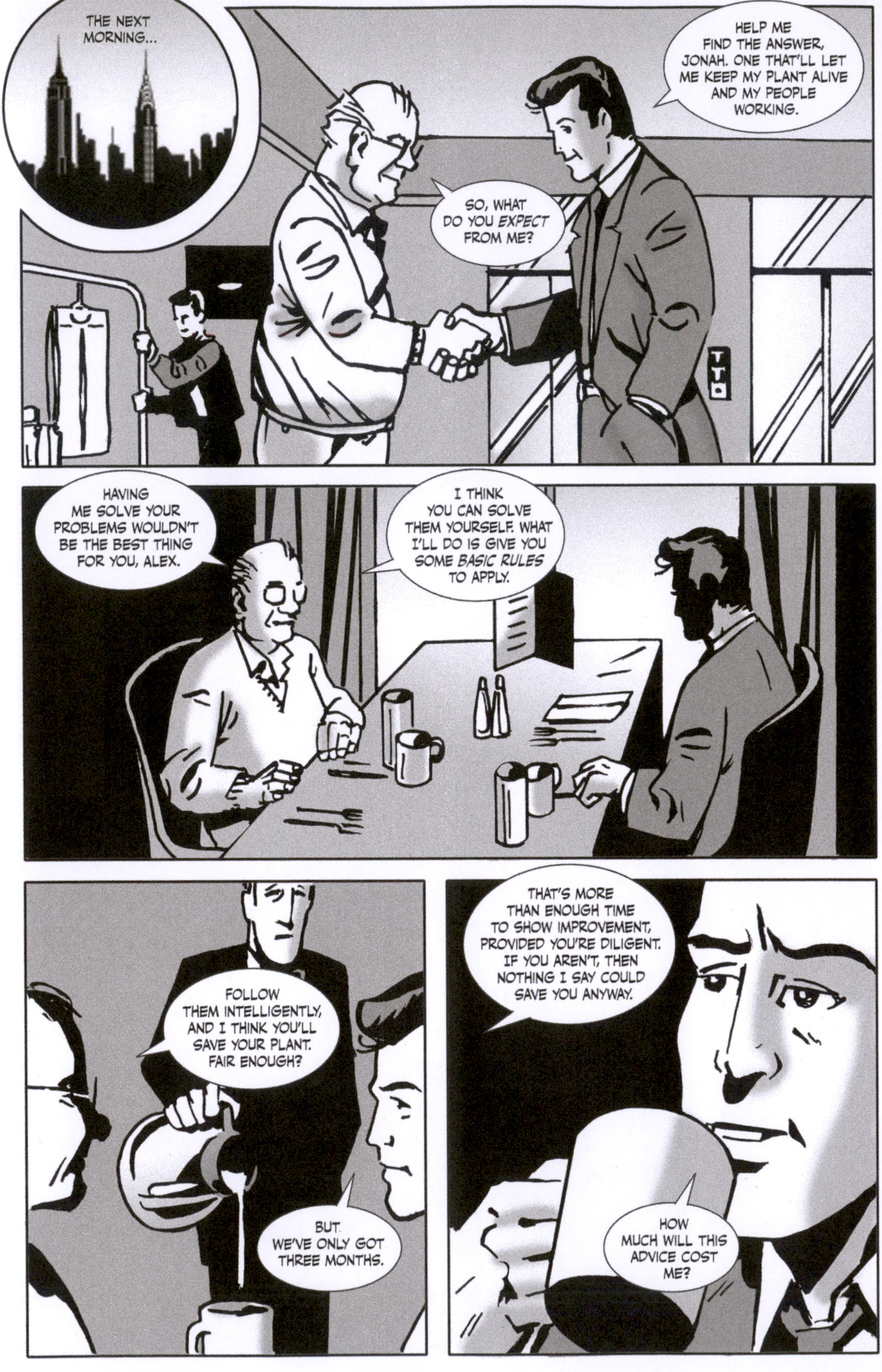
THE NEXT MORNING...
HELP ME FIND THE ANSWER, JONAH. ONE THAT'LL LET ME KEEP MY PLANT ALIVE AND MY PEOPLE WORKING.
SO, WHAT DO YOU *EXPECT* FROM ME?
HAVING ME SOLVE YOUR PROBLEMS WOULDN'T BE THE BEST THING FOR YOU, ALEX.
I THINK YOU CAN SOLVE THEM YOURSELF. WHAT I'LL DO IS GIVE YOU SOME *BASIC RULES* TO APPLY.
FOLLOW THEM INTELLIGENTLY, AND I THINK YOU'LL SAVE YOUR PLANT. FAIR ENOUGH?
BUT. WE'VE ONLY GOT THREE MONTHS.
THAT'S MORE THAN ENOUGH TIME TO SHOW IMPROVEMENT, PROVIDED YOU'RE DILIGENT. IF YOU AREN'T, THEN NOTHING I SAY COULD SAVE YOU ANYWAY.
HOW MUCH WILL THIS ADVICE COST ME?

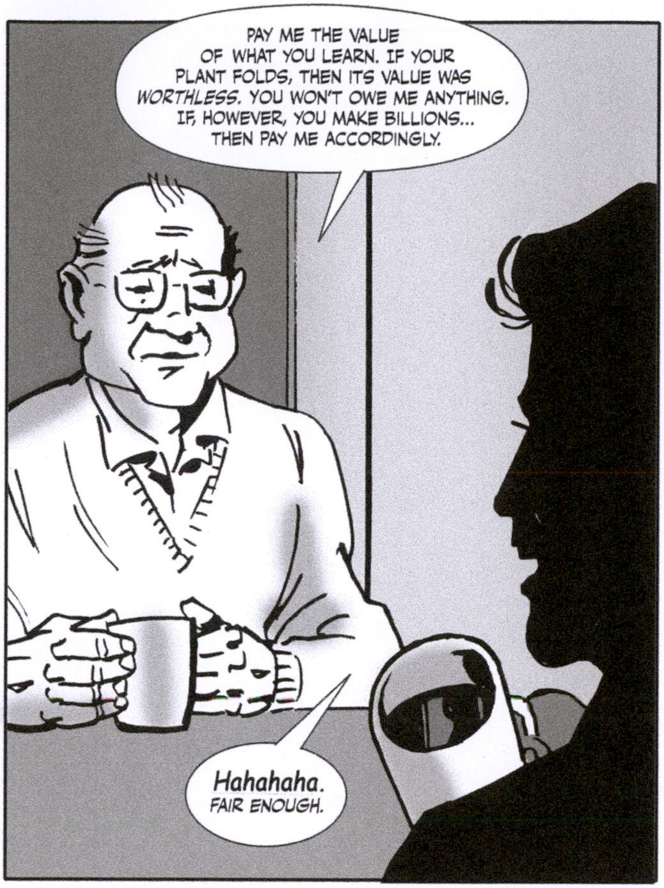
PAY ME THE VALUE OF WHAT YOU LEARN. IF YOUR PLANT FOLDS, THEN ITS VALUE WAS *WORTHLESS*. YOU WON'T OWE ME ANYTHING. IF, HOWEVER, YOU MAKE BILLIONS... THEN PAY ME ACCORDINGLY.
Hahahaha. FAIR ENOUGH.

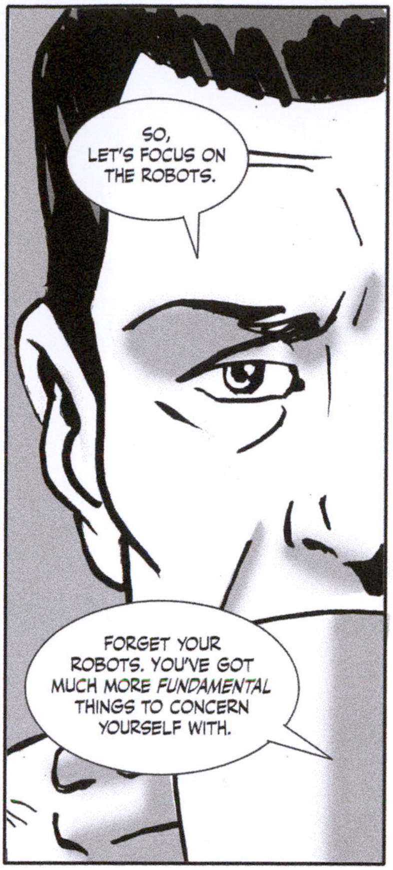
SO, LET'S FOCUS ON THE ROBOTS.
FORGET YOUR ROBOTS. YOU'VE GOT MUCH MORE *FUNDAMENTAL* THINGS TO CONCERN YOURSELF WITH.

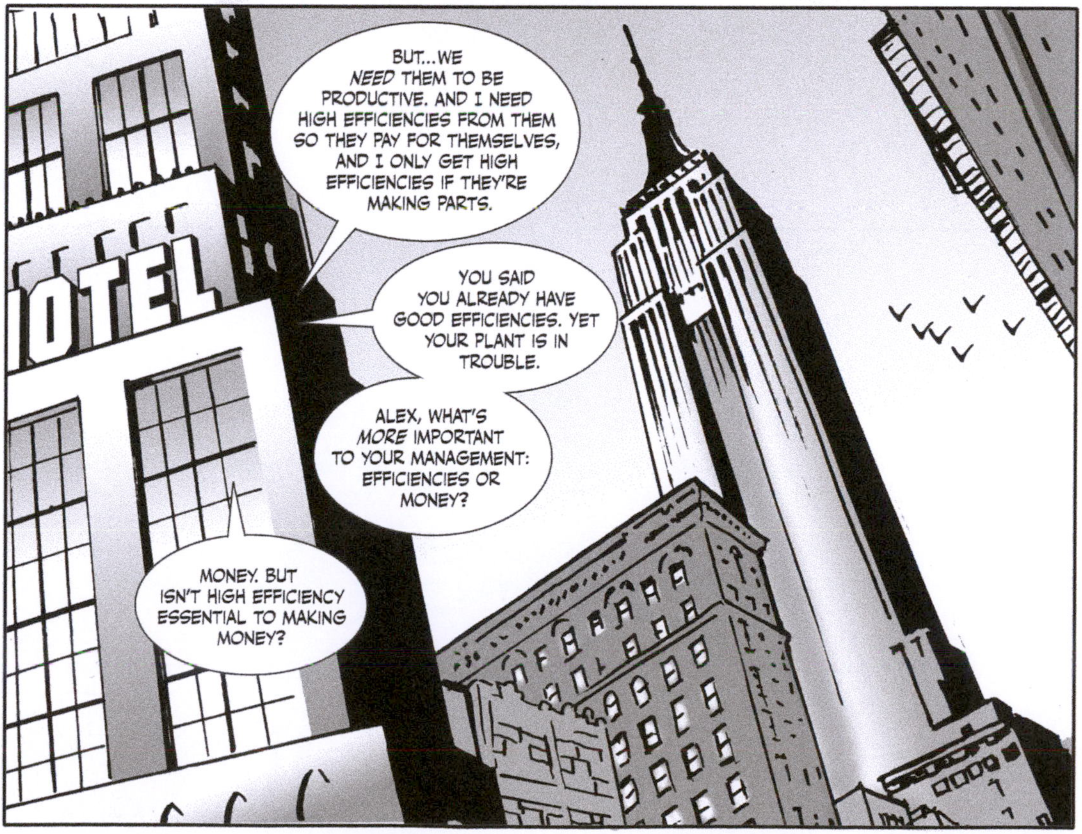
BUT...WE *NEED* THEM TO BE PRODUCTIVE. AND I NEED HIGH EFFICIENCIES FROM THEM SO THEY PAY FOR THEMSELVES, AND I ONLY GET HIGH EFFICIENCIES IF THEY'RE MAKING PARTS.
YOU SAID YOU ALREADY HAVE GOOD EFFICIENCIES. YET YOUR PLANT IS IN TROUBLE.
ALEX, WHAT'S *MORE* IMPORTANT TO YOUR MANAGEMENT: EFFICIENCIES OR MONEY?
MONEY. BUT ISN'T HIGH EFFICIENCY ESSENTIAL TO MAKING MONEY?
OTEL

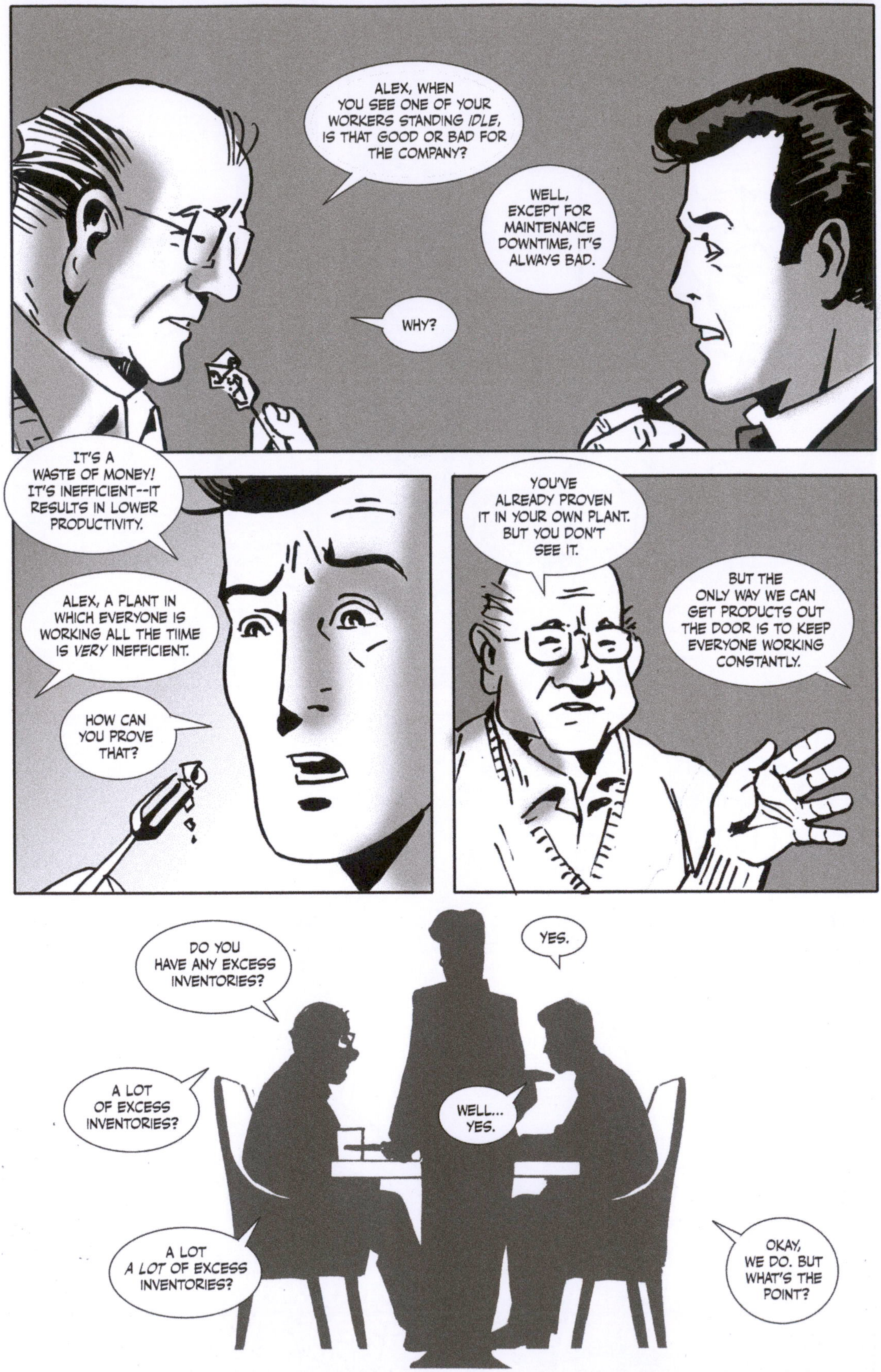
ALEX, WHEN YOU SEE ONE OF YOUR WORKERS STANDING *IDLE*, IS THAT GOOD OR BAD FOR THE COMPANY?
WELL, EXCEPT FOR MAINTENANCE DOWNTIME, IT'S ALWAYS BAD.
WHY?
IT'S A WASTE OF MONEY! IT'S INEFFICIENT--IT RESULTS IN LOWER PRODUCTIVITY.
ALEX, A PLANT IN WHICH EVERYONE IS WORKING ALL THE TIIME IS *VERY* INEFFICIENT.
HOW CAN YOU PROVE THAT?
YOU'VE ALREADY PROVEN IT IN YOUR OWN PLANT. BUT YOU DON'T SEE IT.
BUT THE ONLY WAY WE CAN GET PRODUCTS OUT THE DOOR IS TO KEEP EVERYONE WORKING CONSTANTLY.
DO YOU HAVE ANY EXCESS INVENTORIES?
YES.
A LOT OF EXCESS INVENTORIES?
WELL... YES.
A LOT *A LOT* OF EXCESS INVENTORIES?
OKAY, WE DO. BUT WHAT'S THE POINT?

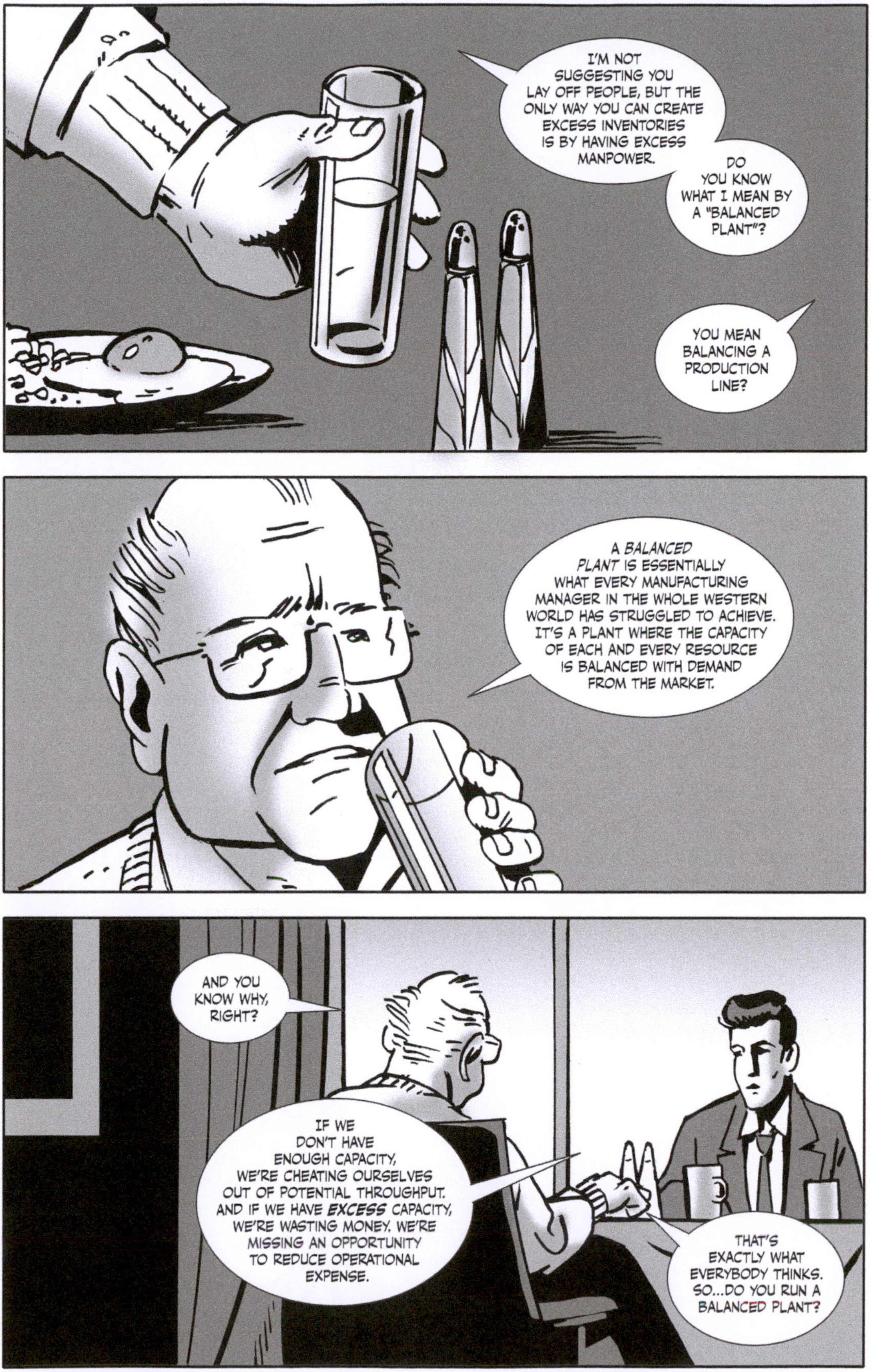
I'M NOT SUGGESTING YOU LAY OFF PEOPLE, BUT THE ONLY WAY YOU CAN CREATE EXCESS INVENTORIES IS BY HAVING EXCESS MANPOWER.
DO YOU KNOW WHAT I MEAN BY A "BALANCED PLANT"?
YOU MEAN BALANCING A PRODUCTION LINE?
A *BALANCED PLANT* IS ESSENTIALLY WHAT EVERY MANUFACTURING MANAGER IN THE WHOLE WESTERN WORLD HAS STRUGGLED TO ACHIEVE. IT'S A PLANT WHERE THE CAPACITY OF EACH AND EVERY RESOURCE IS BALANCED WITH DEMAND FROM THE MARKET.
AND YOU KNOW WHY, RIGHT?
IF WE DON'T HAVE ENOUGH CAPACITY, WE'RE CHEATING OURSELVES OUT OF POTENTIAL THROUGHPUT. AND IF WE HAVE ***EXCESS*** CAPACITY, WE'RE WASTING MONEY. WE'RE MISSING AN OPPORTUNITY TO REDUCE OPERATIONAL EXPENSE.
THAT'S EXACTLY WHAT EVERYBODY THINKS. SO...DO YOU RUN A BALANCED PLANT?

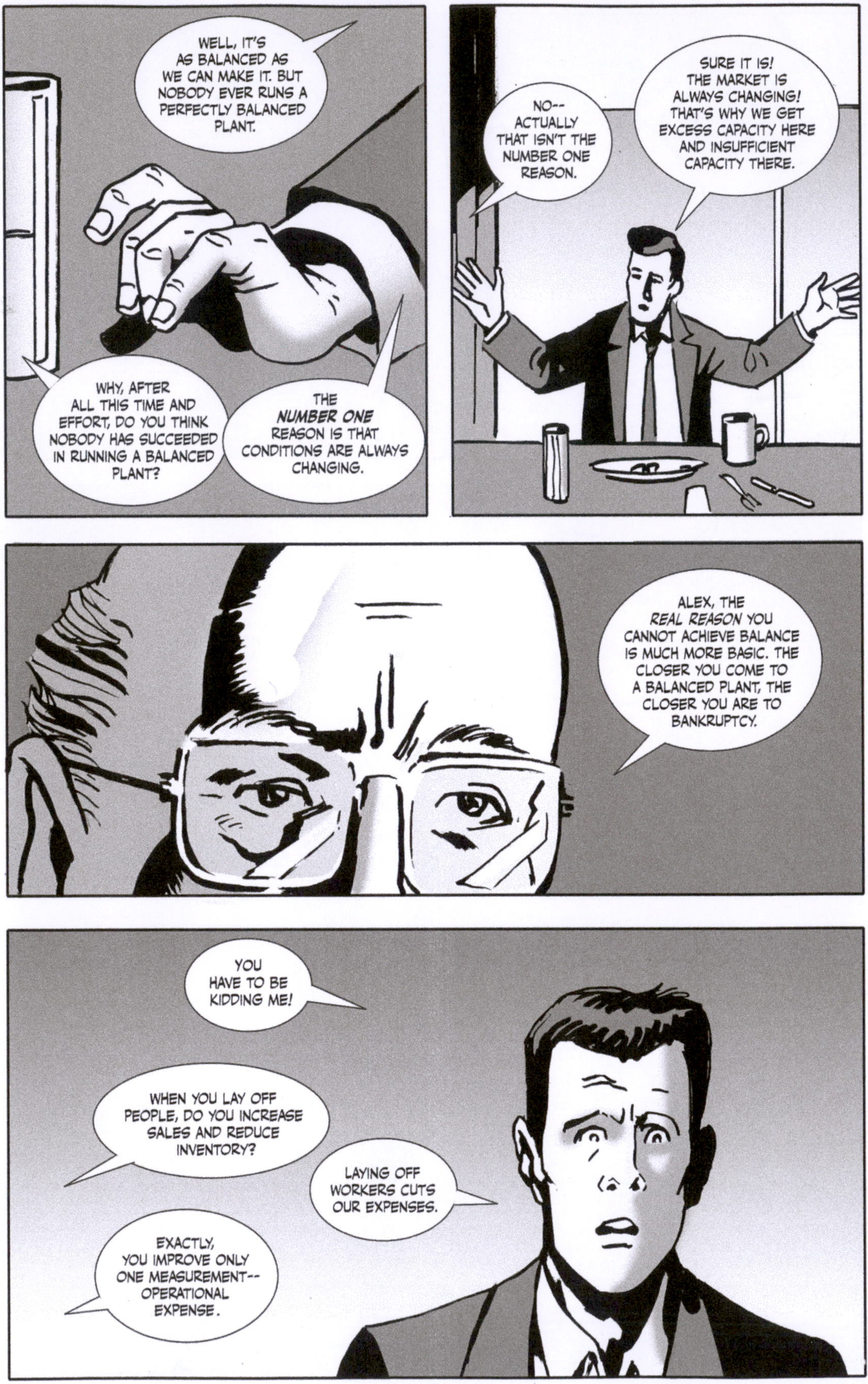
WELL, IT'S AS BALANCED AS WE CAN MAKE IT. BUT NOBODY EVER RUNS A PERFECTLY BALANCED PLANT.
WHY, AFTER ALL THIS TIME AND EFFORT, DO YOU THINK NOBODY HAS SUCCEEDED IN RUNNING A BALANCED PLANT?
THE *NUMBER ONE* REASON IS THAT CONDITIONS ARE ALWAYS CHANGING.
NO-- ACTUALLY THAT ISN'T THE NUMBER ONE REASON.
SURE IT IS! THE MARKET IS ALWAYS CHANGING! THAT'S WHY WE GET EXCESS CAPACITY HERE AND INSUFFICIENT CAPACITY THERE.
ALEX, THE *REAL REASON* YOU CANNOT ACHIEVE BALANCE IS MUCH MORE BASIC. THE CLOSER YOU COME TO A BALANCED PLANT, THE CLOSER YOU ARE TO BANKRUPTCY.
YOU HAVE TO BE KIDDING ME!
WHEN YOU LAY OFF PEOPLE, DO YOU INCREASE SALES AND REDUCE INVENTORY?
LAYING OFF WORKERS CUTS OUR EXPENSES.
EXACTLY, YOU IMPROVE ONLY ONE MEASUREMENT-- OPERATIONAL EXPENSE.

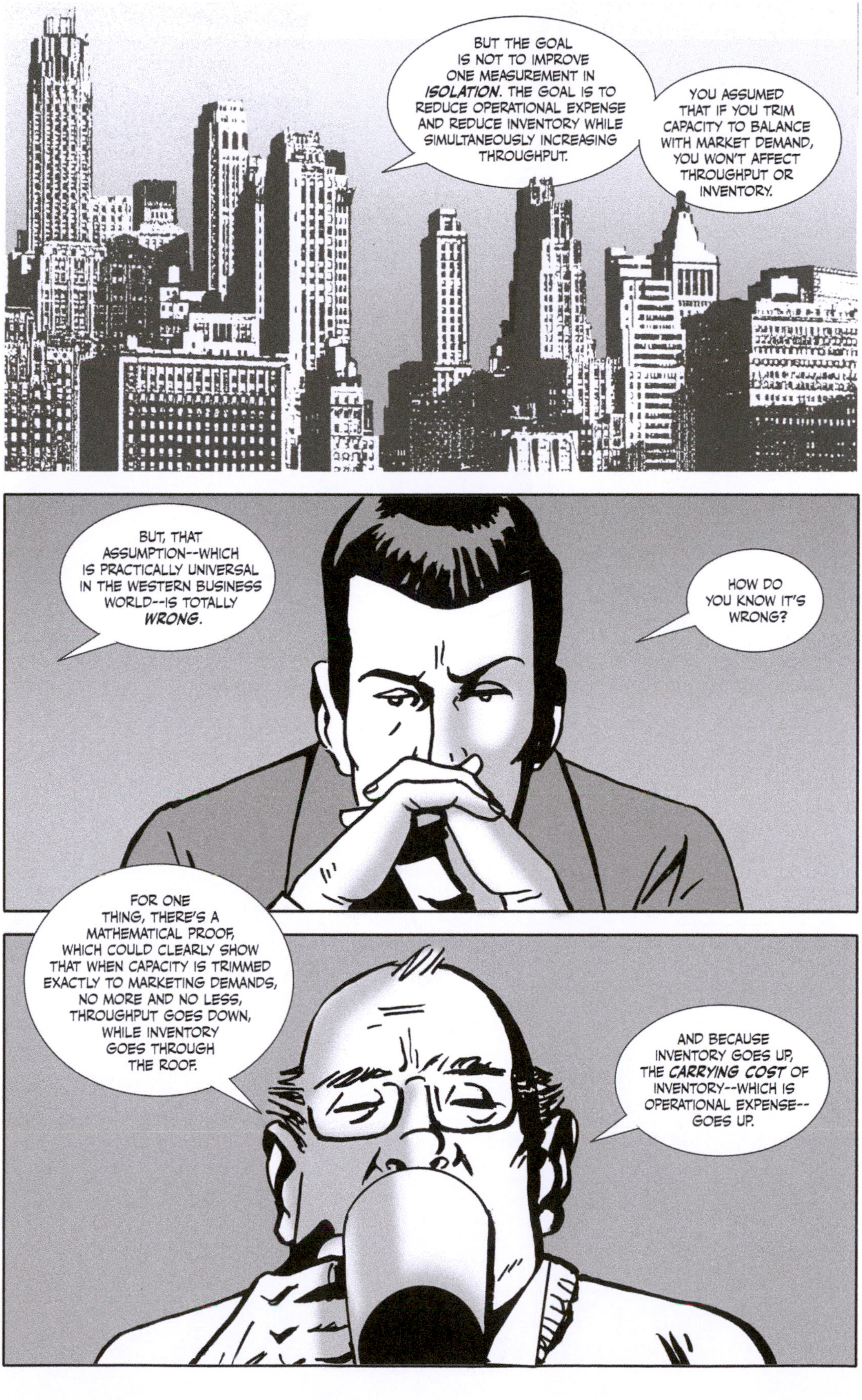

BUT THE GOAL IS NOT TO IMPROVE ONE MEASUREMENT IN *ISOLATION*. THE GOAL IS TO REDUCE OPERATIONAL EXPENSE AND REDUCE INVENTORY WHILE SIMULTANEOUSLY INCREASING THROUGHPUT.
YOU ASSUMED THAT IF YOU TRIM CAPACITY TO BALANCE WITH MARKET DEMAND, YOU WON'T AFFECT THROUGHPUT OR INVENTORY.
BUT, THAT ASSUMPTION--WHICH IS PRACTICALLY UNIVERSAL IN THE WESTERN BUSINESS WORLD--IS TOTALLY *WRONG*.
HOW DO YOU KNOW IT'S WRONG?
FOR ONE THING, THERE'S A MATHEMATICAL PROOF, WHICH COULD CLEARLY SHOW THAT WHEN CAPACITY IS TRIMMED EXACTLY TO MARKETING DEMANDS, NO MORE AND NO LESS, THROUGHPUT GOES DOWN, WHILE INVENTORY GOES THROUGH THE ROOF.
AND BECAUSE INVENTORY GOES UP, THE *CARRYING COST* OF INVENTORY--WHICH IS OPERATIONAL EXPENSE--GOES UP.

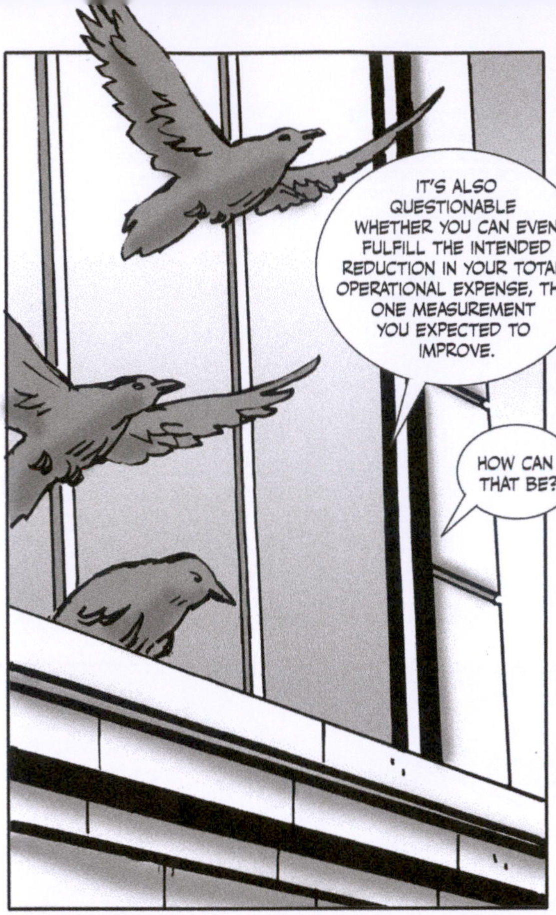
IT'S ALSO QUESTIONABLE WHETHER YOU CAN EVEN FULFILL THE INTENDED REDUCTION IN YOUR TOTAL OPERATIONAL EXPENSE, THE ONE MEASUREMENT YOU EXPECTED TO IMPROVE.
HOW CAN THAT BE?

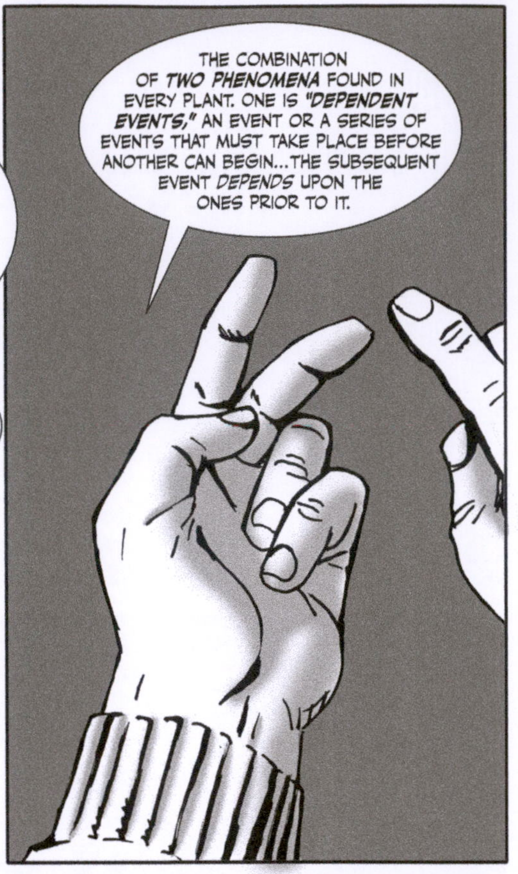
THE COMBINATION OF *TWO PHENOMENA* FOUND IN EVERY PLANT. ONE IS *"DEPENDENT EVENTS,"* AN EVENT OR A SERIES OF EVENTS THAT MUST TAKE PLACE BEFORE ANOTHER CAN BEGIN...THE SUBSEQUENT EVENT *DEPENDS* UPON THE ONES PRIOR TO IT.

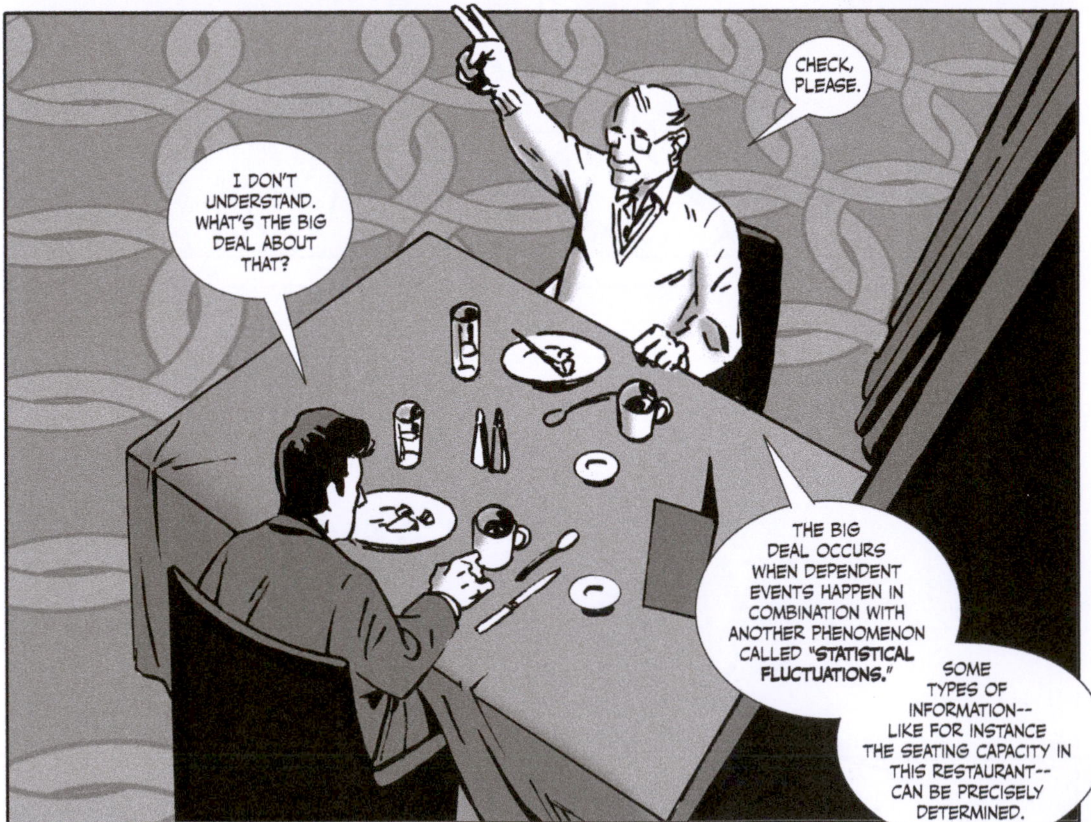
CHECK, PLEASE.
I DON'T UNDERSTAND. WHAT'S THE BIG DEAL ABOUT THAT?
THE BIG DEAL OCCURS WHEN DEPENDENT EVENTS HAPPEN IN COMBINATION WITH ANOTHER PHENOMENON CALLED **"STATISTICAL FLUCTUATIONS."**
SOME TYPES OF INFORMATION-- LIKE FOR INSTANCE THE SEATING CAPACITY IN THIS RESTAURANT-- CAN BE PRECISELY DETERMINED.

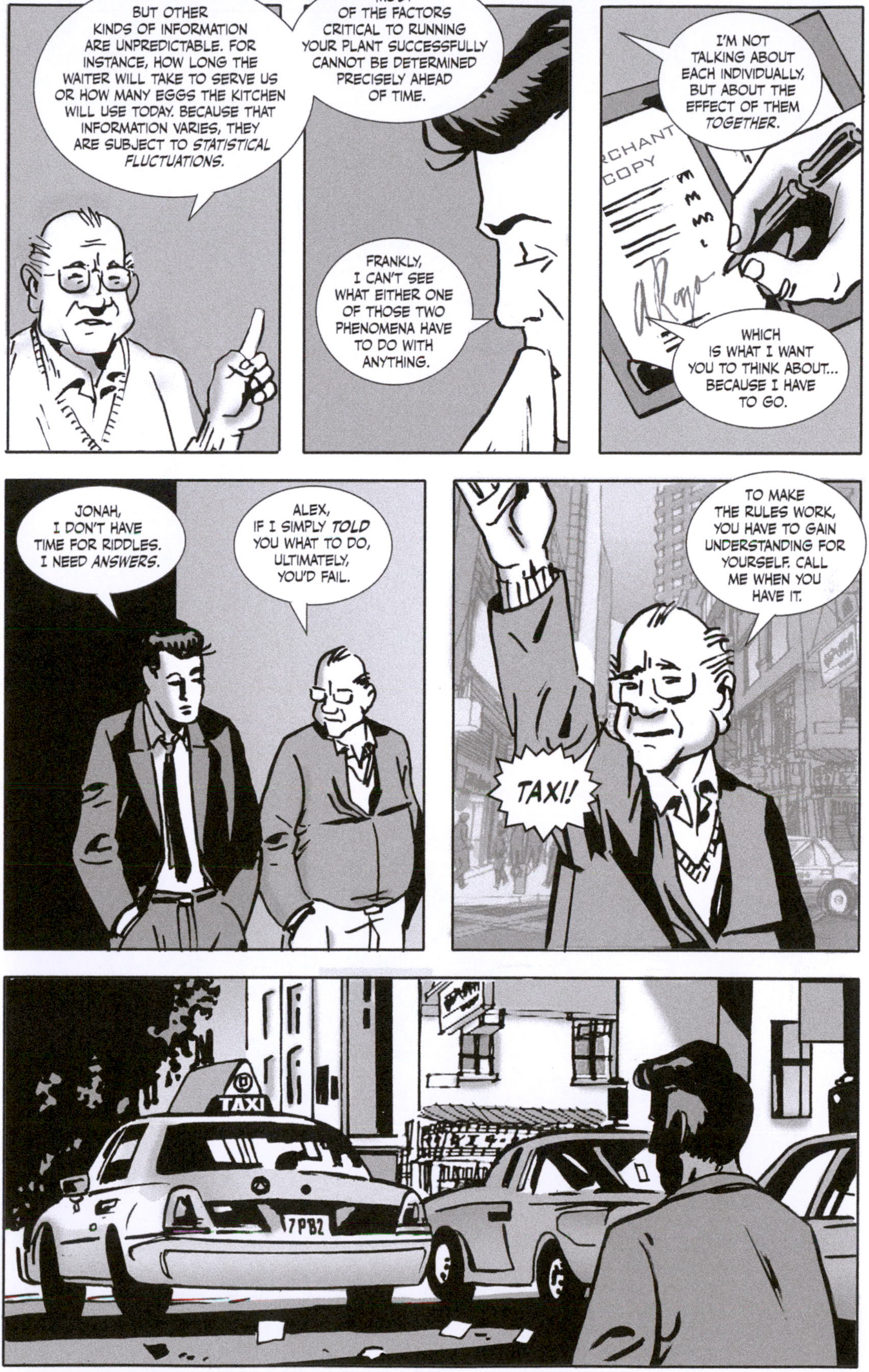
BUT OTHER KINDS OF INFORMATION ARE UNPREDICTABLE. FOR INSTANCE, HOW LONG THE WAITER WILL TAKE TO SERVE US OR HOW MANY EGGS THE KITCHEN WILL USE TODAY. BECAUSE THAT INFORMATION VARIES, THEY ARE SUBJECT TO *STATISTICAL FLUCTUATIONS*.
MOST OF THE FACTORS CRITICAL TO RUNNING YOUR PLANT SUCCESSFULLY CANNOT BE DETERMINED PRECISELY AHEAD OF TIME.
FRANKLY, I CAN'T SEE WHAT EITHER ONE OF THOSE TWO PHENOMENA HAVE TO DO WITH ANYTHING.
I'M NOT TALKING ABOUT EACH INDIVIDUALLY, BUT ABOUT THE EFFECT OF THEM *TOGETHER*.
WHICH IS WHAT I WANT YOU TO THINK ABOUT... BECAUSE I HAVE TO GO.
JONAH, I DON'T HAVE TIME FOR RIDDLES. I NEED *ANSWERS*.
ALEX, IF I SIMPLY *TOLD* YOU WHAT TO DO, ULTIMATELY, YOU'D FAIL.
TO MAKE THE RULES WORK, YOU HAVE TO GAIN UNDERSTANDING FOR YOURSELF. CALL ME WHEN YOU HAVE IT.
TAXI!
TAXI

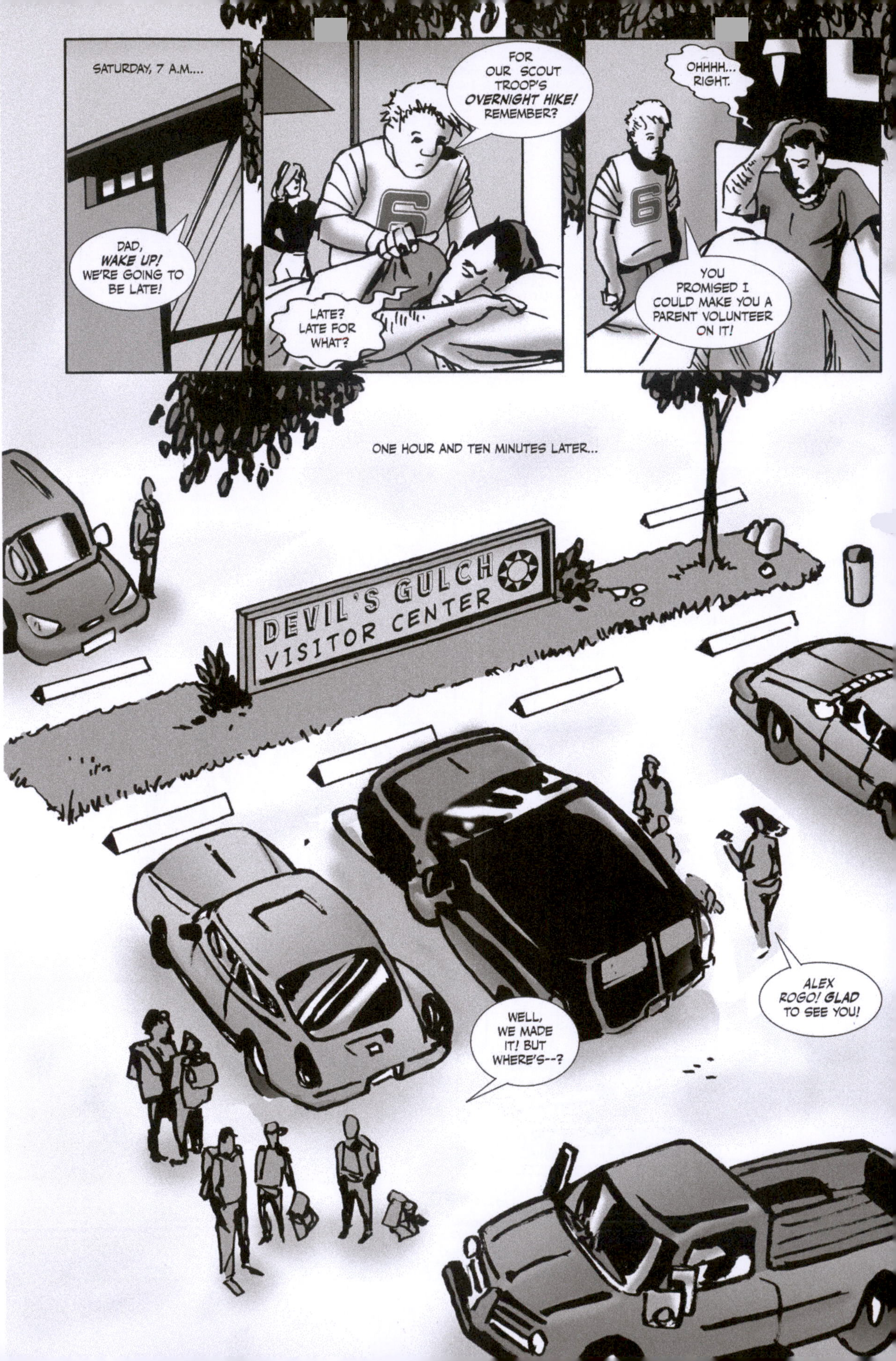
SATURDAY, 7 A.M....
DAD, WAKE UP! WE'RE GOING TO BE LATE!
LATE? LATE FOR WHAT?
FOR OUR SCOUT TROOP'S OVERNIGHT HIKE! REMEMBER?
OHHHH... RIGHT.
YOU PROMISED I COULD MAKE YOU A PARENT VOLUNTEER ON IT!
ONE HOUR AND TEN MINUTES LATER...
DEVIL'S GULCH VISITOR CENTER
WELL, WE MADE IT! BUT WHERE'S--?
ALEX ROGO! GLAD TO SEE YOU!

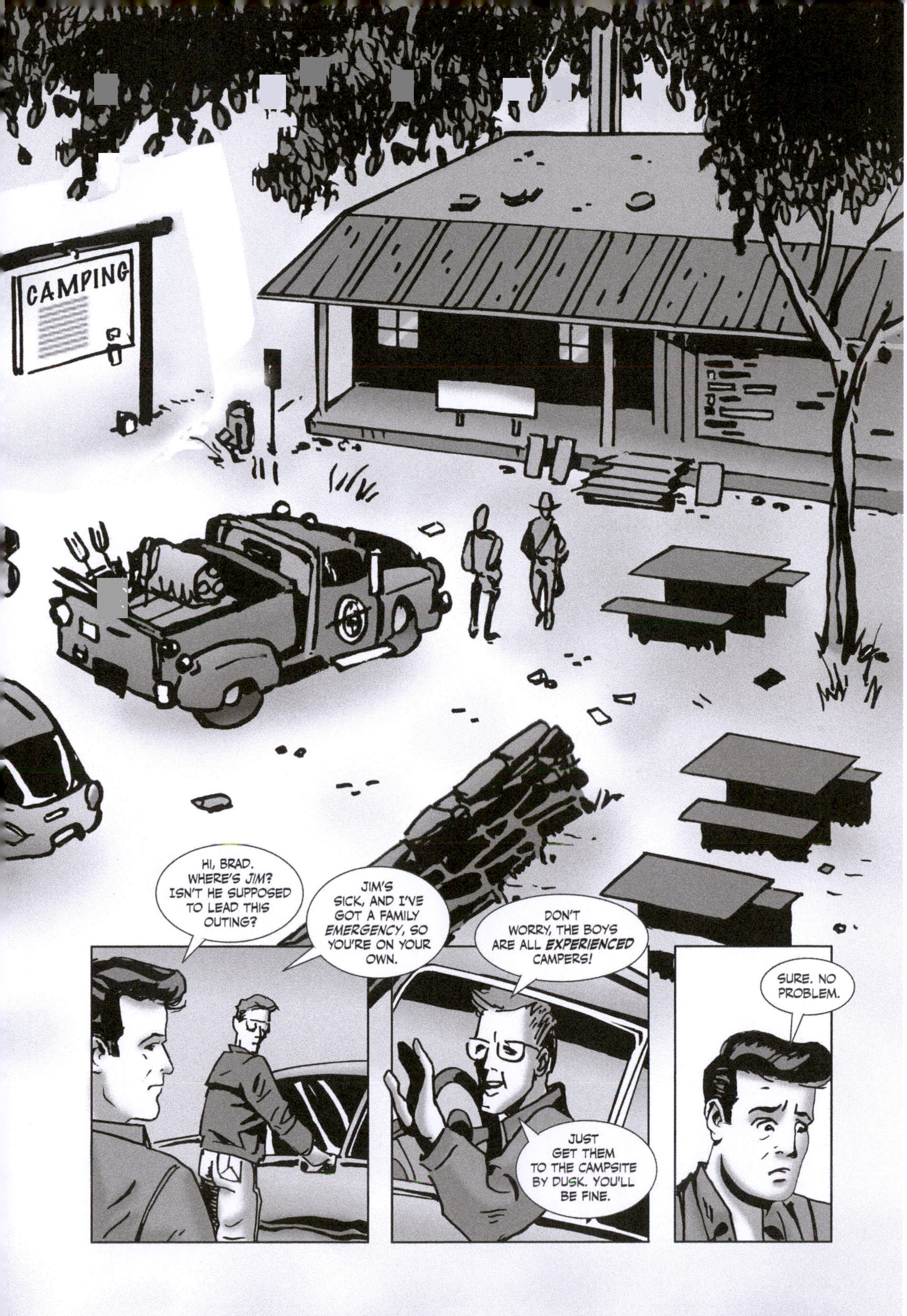
CAMPING
HI, BRAD. WHERE'S *JIM*? ISN'T HE SUPPOSED TO LEAD THIS OUTING?
JIM'S SICK, AND I'VE GOT A FAMILY *EMERGENCY*, SO YOU'RE ON YOUR OWN.
DON'T WORRY, THE BOYS ARE ALL *EXPERIENCED* CAMPERS!
JUST GET THEM TO THE CAMPSITE BY DUSK. YOU'LL BE FINE.
SURE. NO PROBLEM.

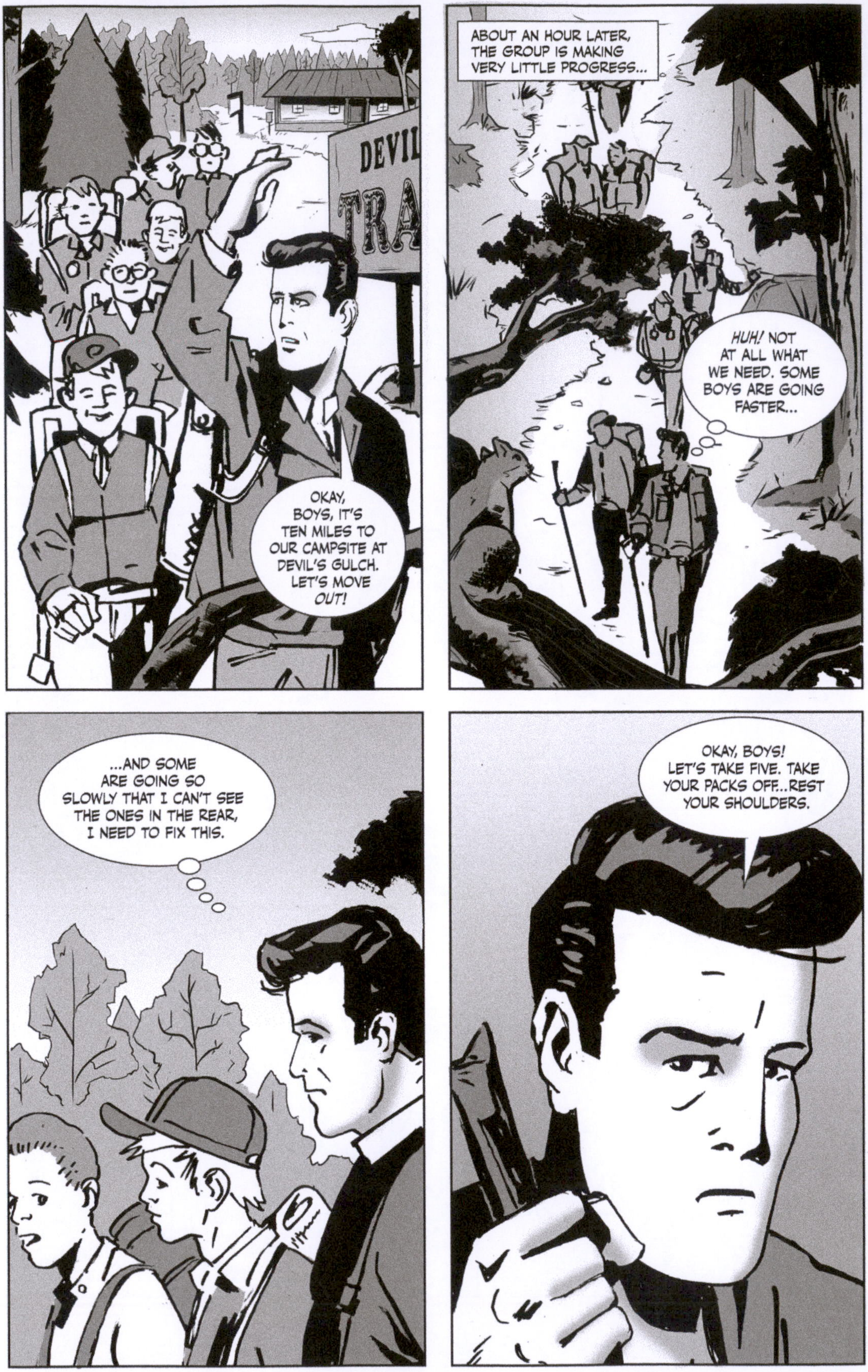

DEVIL
TRA
OKAY, BOYS, IT'S TEN MILES TO OUR CAMPSITE AT DEVIL'S GULCH. LET'S MOVE *OUT!*
ABOUT AN HOUR LATER, THE GROUP IS MAKING VERY LITTLE PROGRESS...
HUH! NOT AT ALL WHAT WE NEED. SOME BOYS ARE GOING FASTER...
...AND SOME ARE GOING SO SLOWLY THAT I CAN'T SEE THE ONES IN THE REAR, I NEED TO FIX THIS.
OKAY, BOYS! LET'S TAKE FIVE. TAKE YOUR PACKS OFF...REST YOUR SHOULDERS.

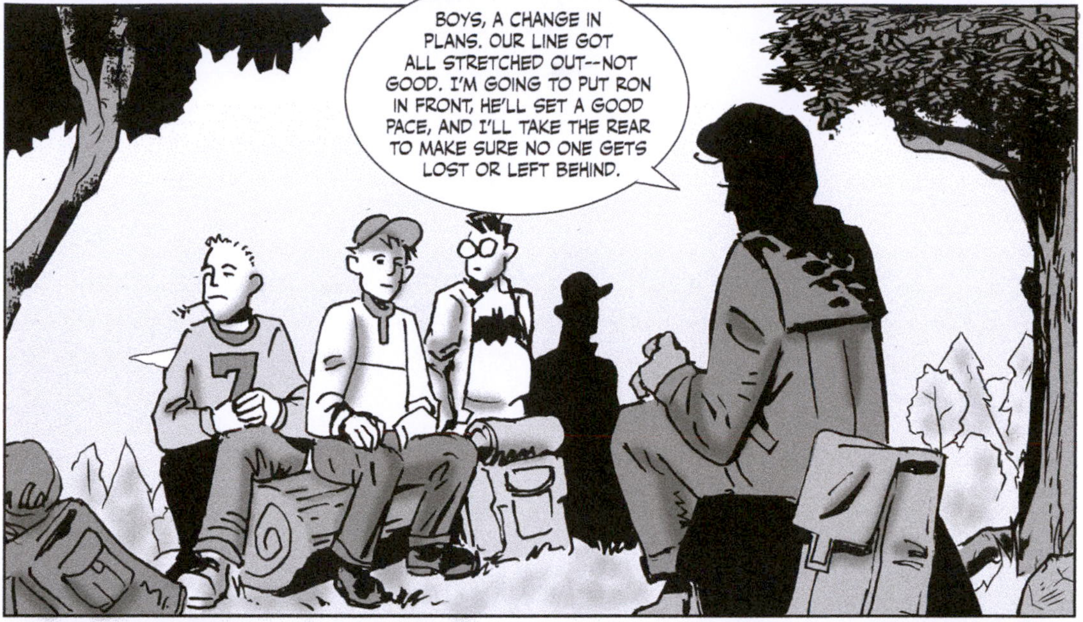
BOYS, A CHANGE IN PLANS. OUR LINE GOT ALL STRETCHED OUT--NOT GOOD. I'M GOING TO PUT RON IN FRONT, HE'LL SET A GOOD PACE, AND I'LL TAKE THE REAR TO MAKE SURE NO ONE GETS LOST OR LEFT BEHIND.

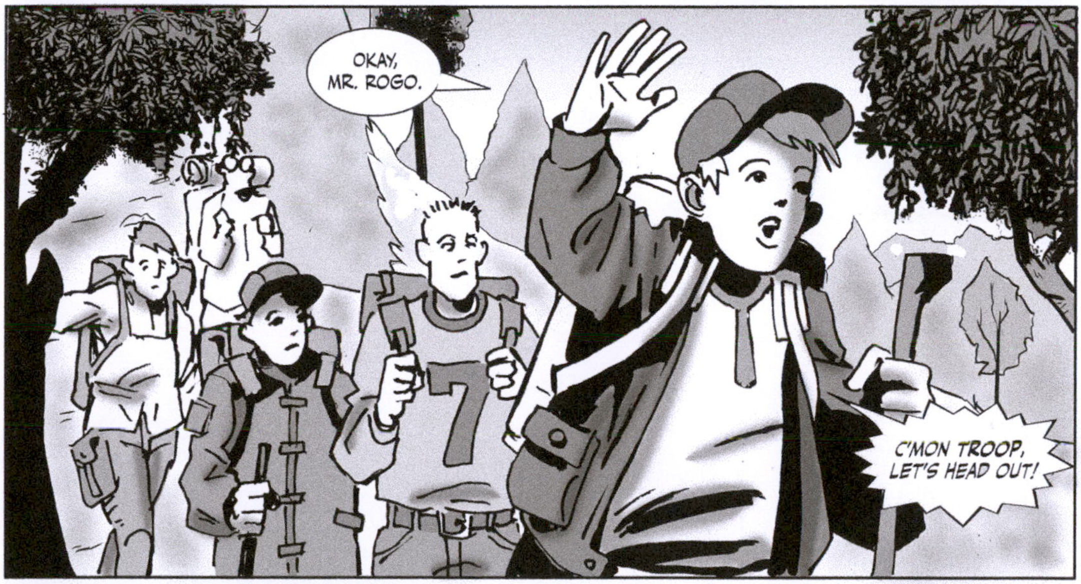
OKAY, MR. ROGO.
C'MON TROOP, LET'S HEAD OUT!

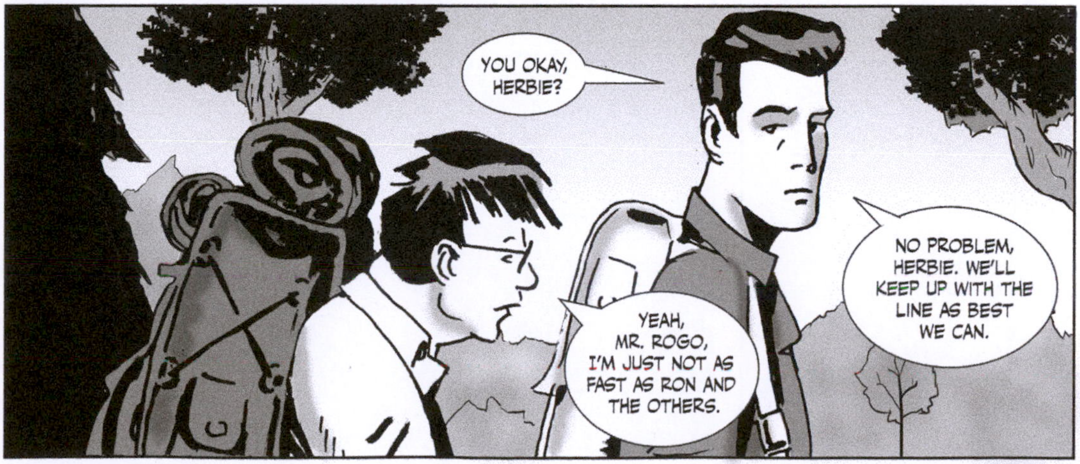
YOU OKAY, HERBIE?
YEAH, MR. ROGO, I'M JUST NOT AS FAST AS RON AND THE OTHERS.
NO PROBLEM, HERBIE. WE'LL KEEP UP WITH THE LINE AS BEST WE CAN.

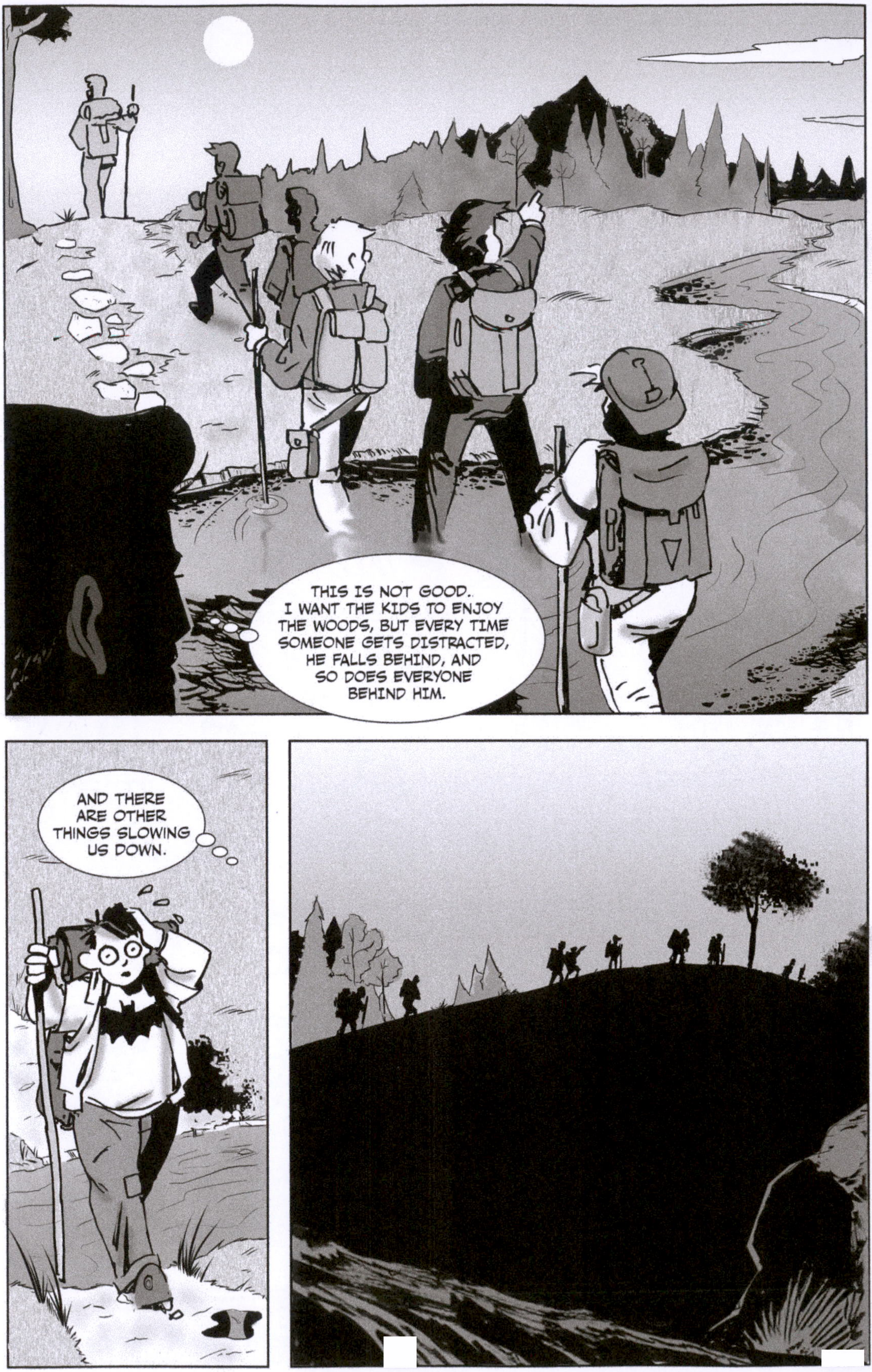
THIS IS NOT GOOD. I WANT THE KIDS TO ENJOY THE WOODS, BUT EVERY TIME SOMEONE GETS DISTRACTED, HE FALLS BEHIND, AND SO DOES EVERYONE BEHIND HIM.
AND THERE ARE OTHER THINGS SLOWING US DOWN.

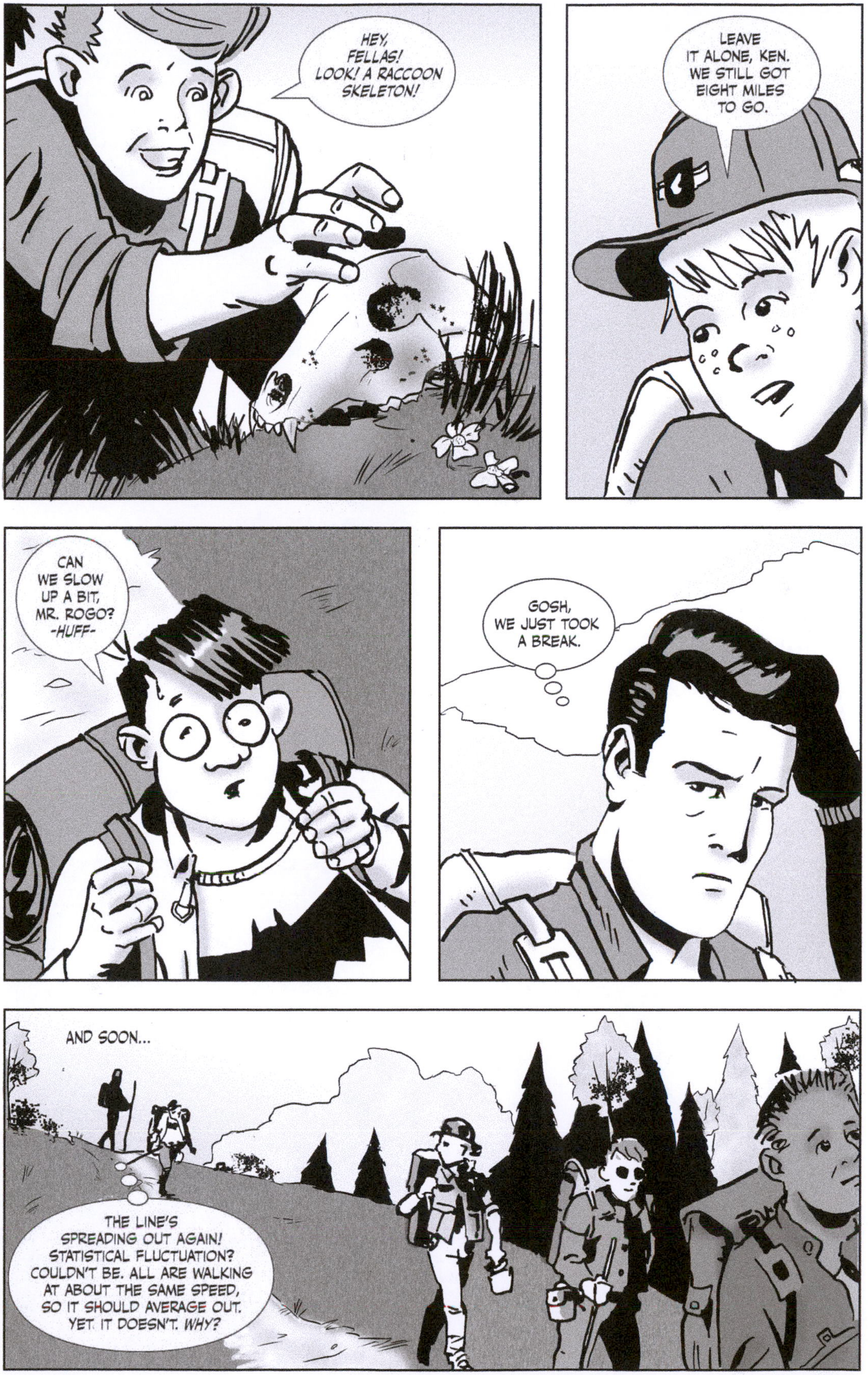
HEY, FELLAS! LOOK! A RACCOON SKELETON!
LEAVE IT ALONE, KEN. WE STILL GOT EIGHT MILES TO GO.
CAN WE SLOW UP A BIT, MR. ROGO? -HUFF-
GOSH, WE JUST TOOK A BREAK.
AND SOON...
THE LINE'S SPREADING OUT AGAIN! STATISTICAL FLUCTUATION? COULDN'T BE. ALL ARE WALKING AT ABOUT THE SAME SPEED, SO IT SHOULD AVERAGE OUT. YET. IT DOESN'T. WHY?

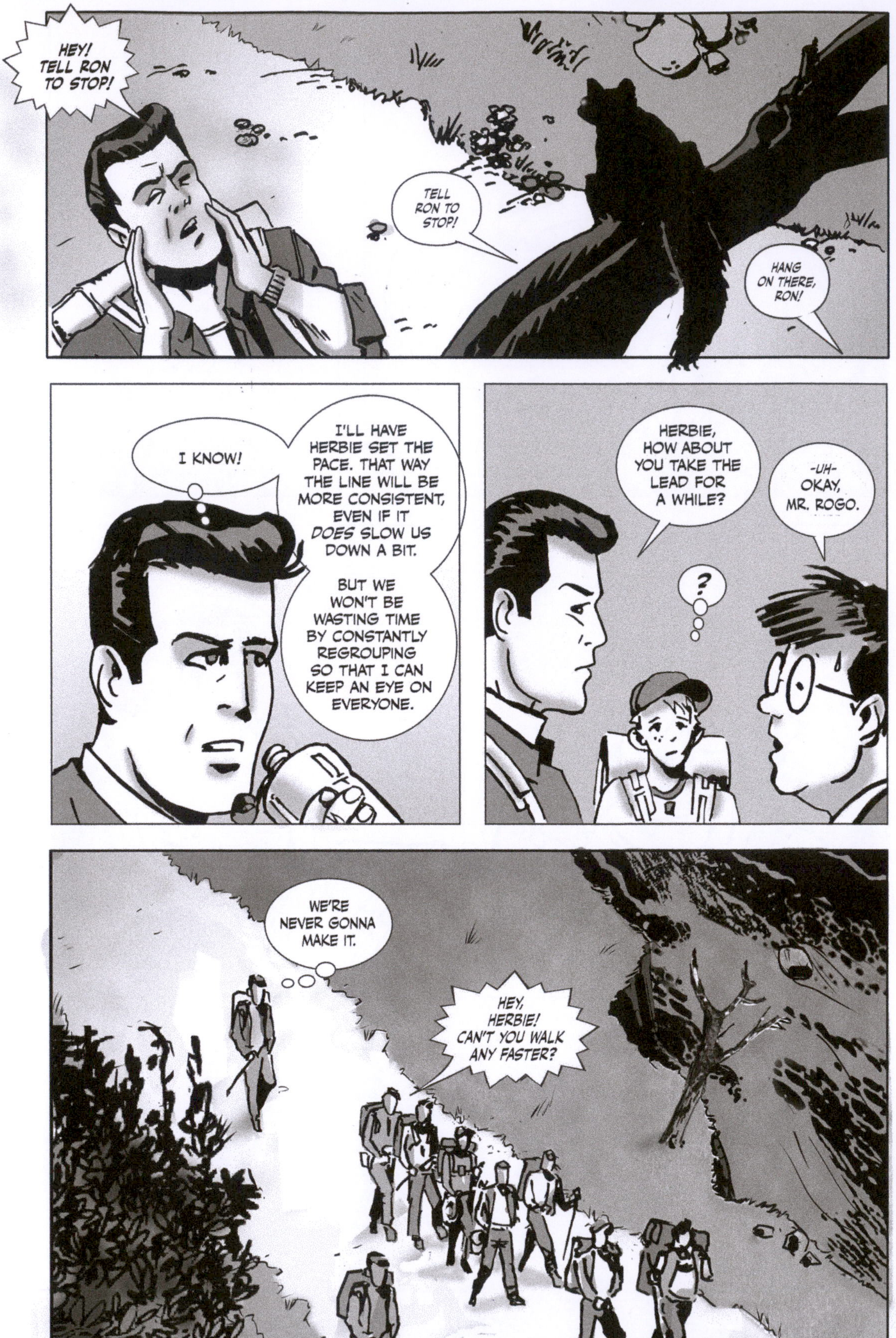
HEY! TELL RON TO STOP!
TELL RON TO STOP!
HANG ON THERE, RON!
I KNOW!
I'LL HAVE HERBIE SET THE PACE. THAT WAY THE LINE WILL BE MORE CONSISTENT, EVEN IF IT *DOES* SLOW US DOWN A BIT.
BUT WE WON'T BE WASTING TIME BY CONSTANTLY REGROUPING SO THAT I CAN KEEP AN EYE ON EVERYONE.
HERBIE, HOW ABOUT YOU TAKE THE LEAD FOR A WHILE?
?
-UH- OKAY, MR. ROGO.
WE'RE NEVER GONNA MAKE IT.
HEY, HERBIE! CAN'T YOU WALK ANY FASTER?

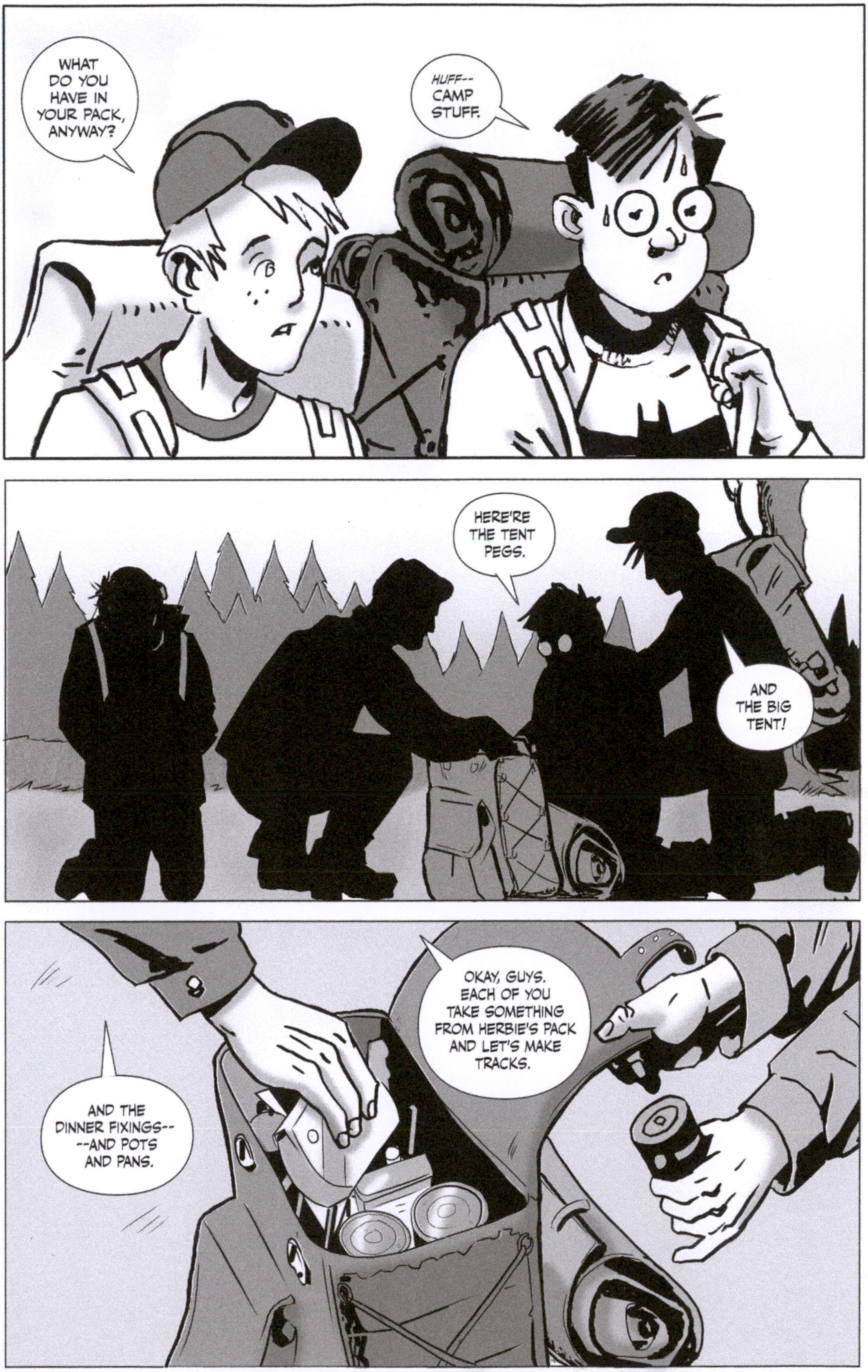
WHAT DO YOU HAVE IN YOUR PACK, ANYWAY?
HUFF-- CAMP STUFF.
HERE'RE THE TENT PEGS.
AND THE BIG TENT!
OKAY, GUYS. EACH OF YOU TAKE SOMETHING FROM HERBIE'S PACK AND LET'S MAKE TRACKS.
AND THE DINNER FIXINGS-- --AND POTS AND PANS.

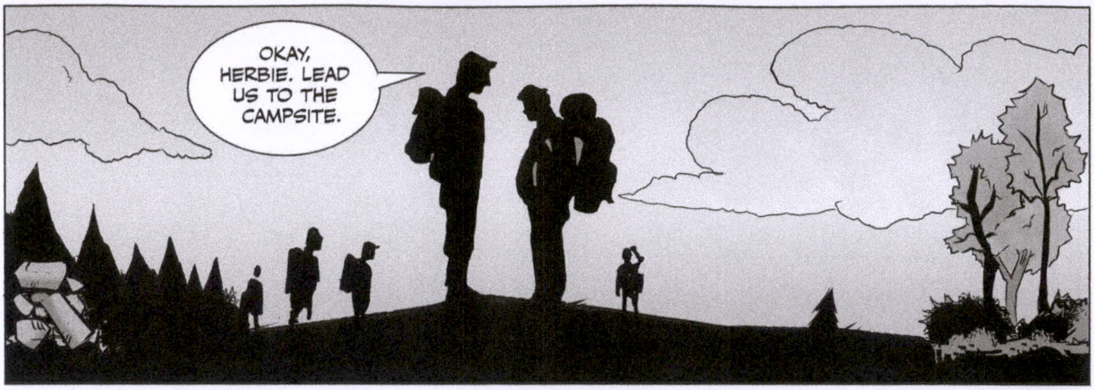
OKAY, HERBIE. LEAD US TO THE CAMPSITE.

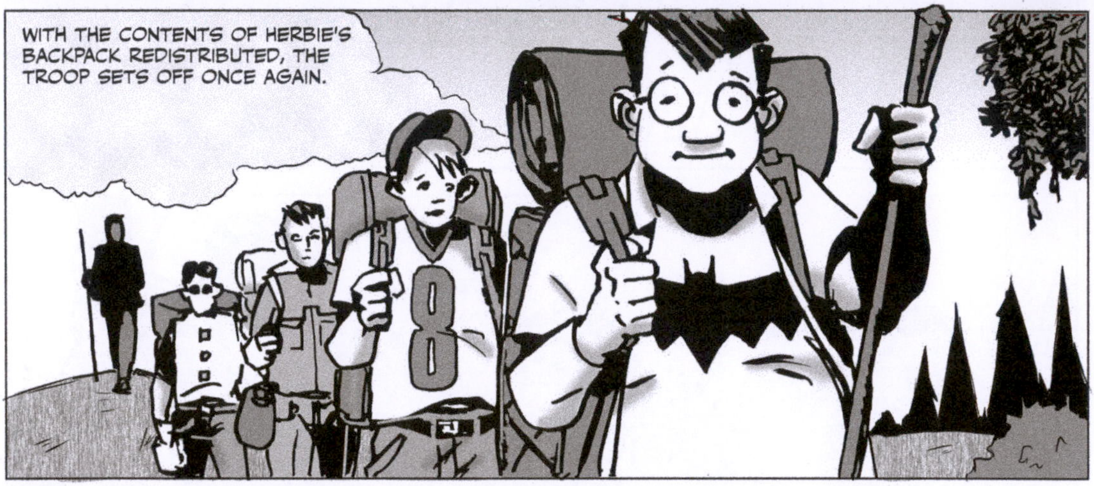
WITH THE CONTENTS OF HERBIE'S BACKPACK REDISTRIBUTED, THE TROOP SETS OFF ONCE AGAIN.

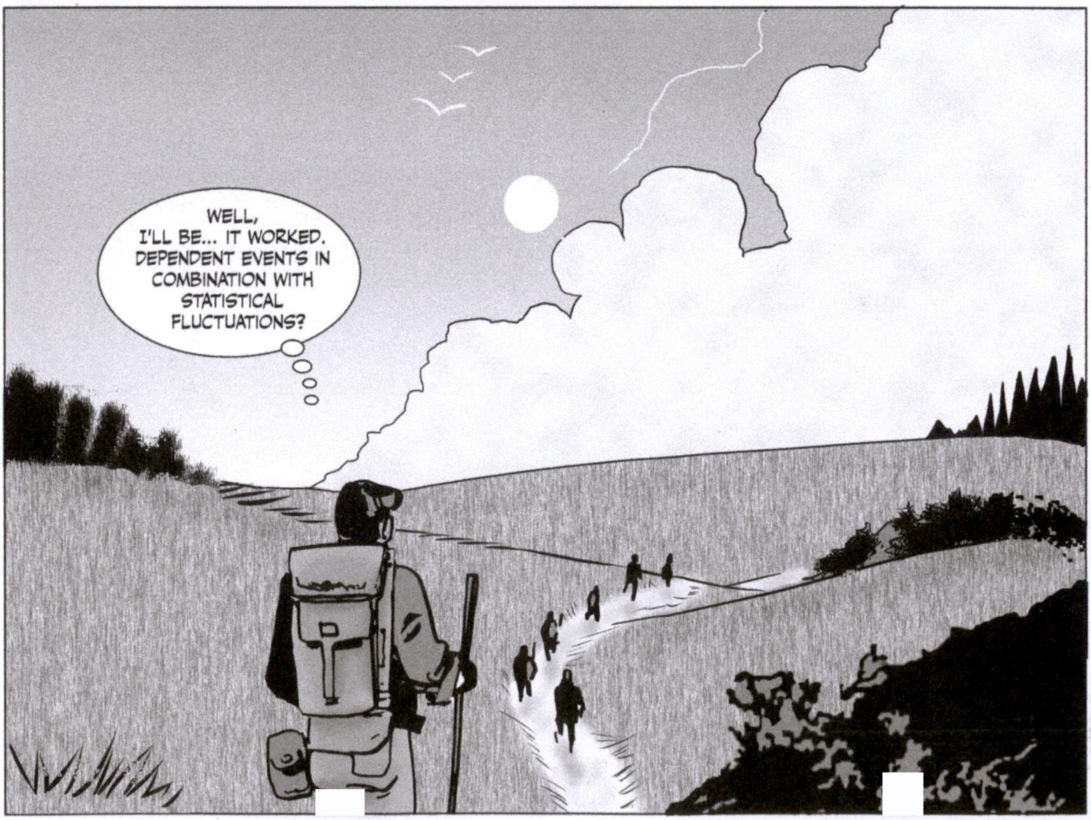
WELL, I'LL BE... IT WORKED. DEPENDENT EVENTS IN COMBINATION WITH STATISTICAL FLUCTUATIONS?

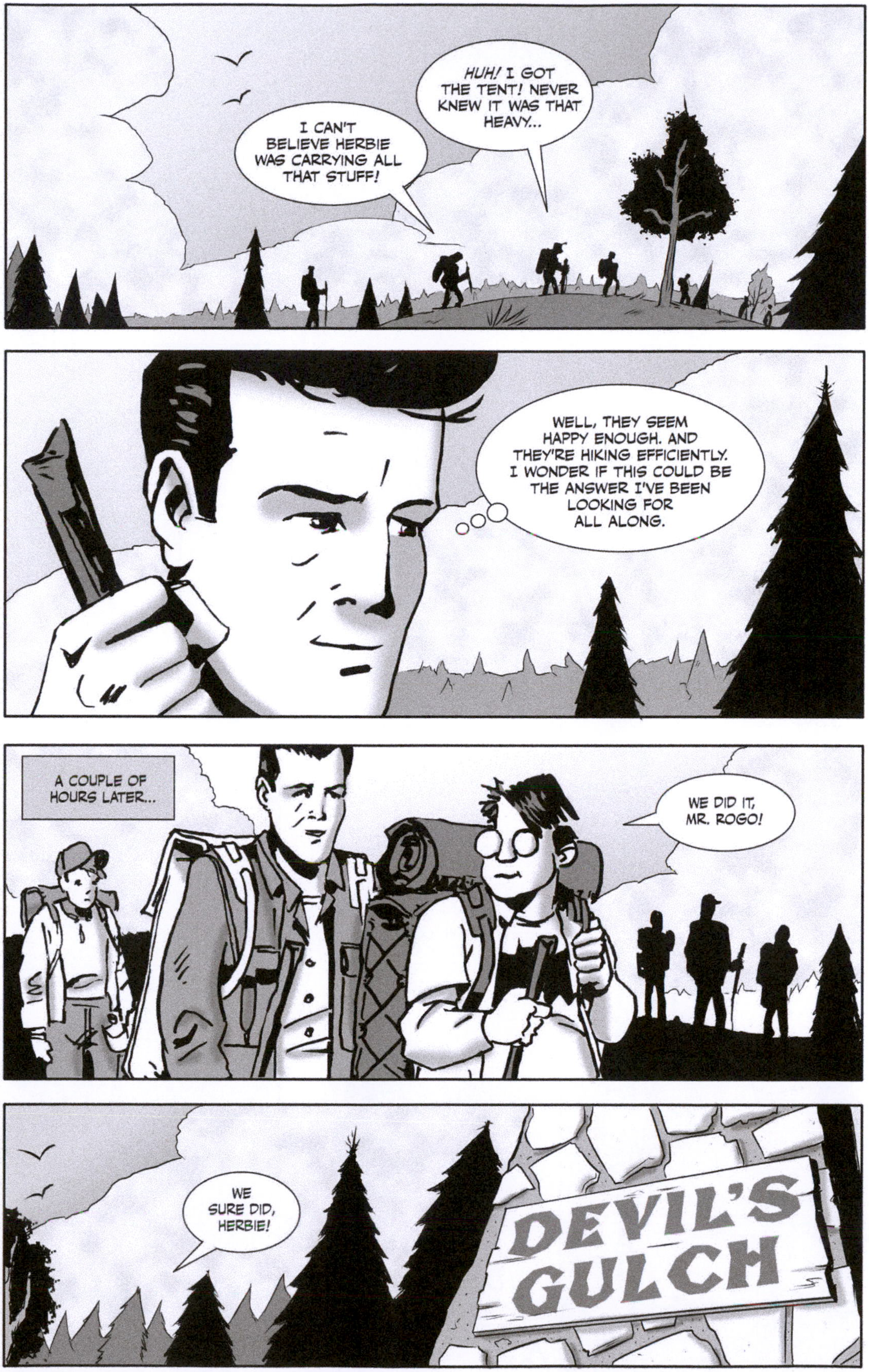
I CAN'T BELIEVE HERBIE WAS CARRYING ALL THAT STUFF!
HUH! I GOT THE TENT! NEVER KNEW IT WAS THAT HEAVY...
WELL, THEY SEEM HAPPY ENOUGH. AND THEY'RE HIKING EFFICIENTLY. I WONDER IF THIS COULD BE THE ANSWER I'VE BEEN LOOKING FOR ALL ALONG.
A COUPLE OF HOURS LATER...
WE DID IT, MR. ROGO!
WE SURE DID, HERBIE!
DEVIL'S GULCH

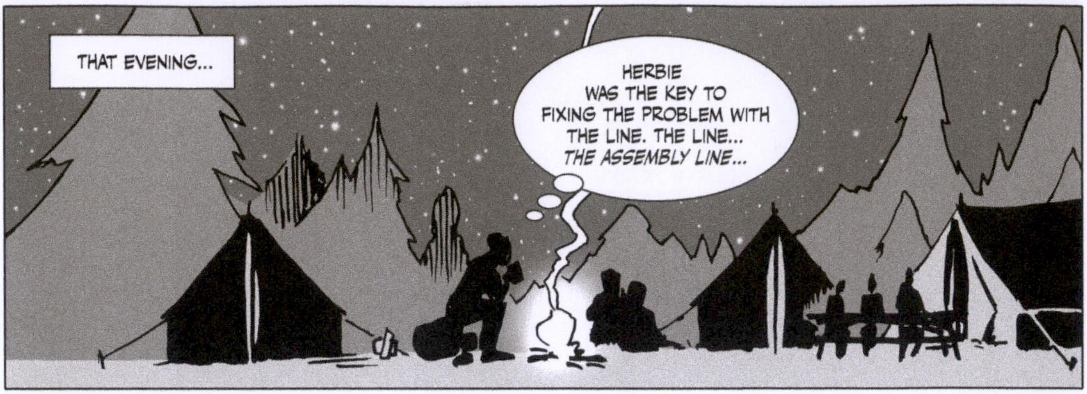
THAT EVENING...
HERBIE WAS THE KEY TO FIXING THE PROBLEM WITH THE LINE. THE LINE... *THE ASSEMBLY LINE*...

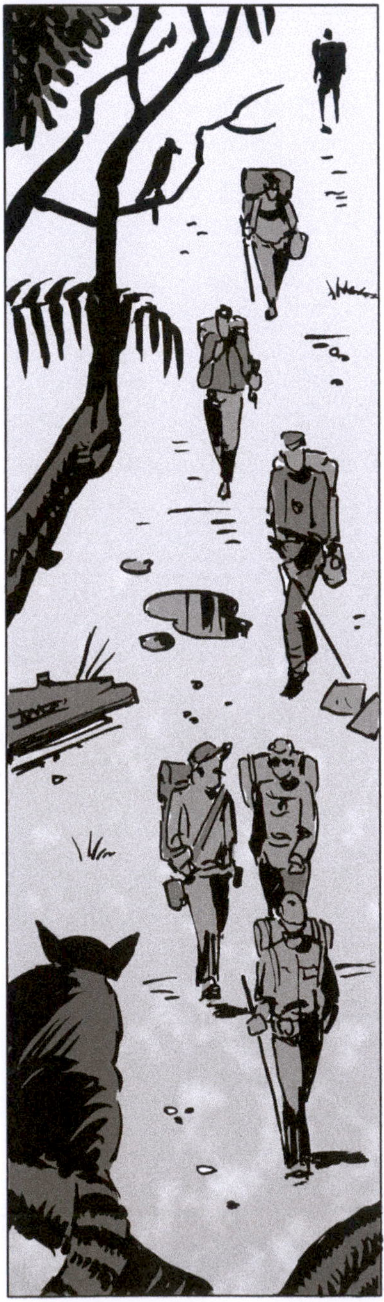

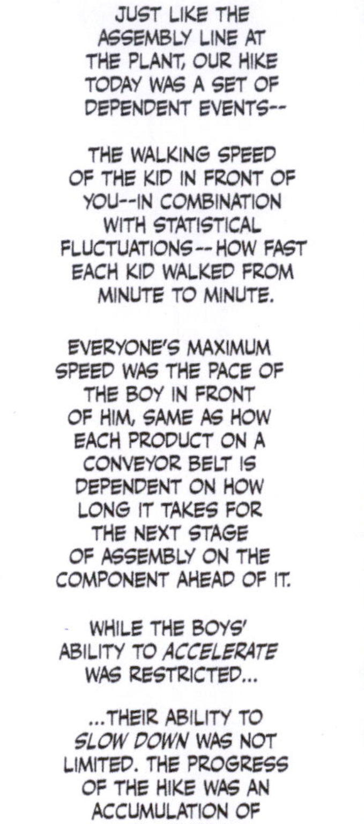
JUST LIKE THE ASSEMBLY LINE AT THE PLANT, OUR HIKE TODAY WAS A SET OF DEPENDENT EVENTS--
THE WALKING SPEED OF THE KID IN FRONT OF YOU--IN COMBINATION WITH STATISTICAL FLUCTUATIONS--HOW FAST EACH KID WALKED FROM MINUTE TO MINUTE.
EVERYONE'S MAXIMUM SPEED WAS THE PACE OF THE BOY IN FRONT OF HIM, SAME AS HOW EACH PRODUCT ON A CONVEYOR BELT IS DEPENDENT ON HOW LONG IT TAKES FOR THE NEXT STAGE OF ASSEMBLY ON THE COMPONENT AHEAD OF IT.
WHILE THE BOYS' ABILITY TO *ACCELERATE* WAS RESTRICTED...
...THEIR ABILITY TO *SLOW DOWN* WAS NOT LIMITED. THE PROGRESS OF THE HIKE WAS AN ACCUMULATION OF SLOWNESS FLUCTUATIONS...

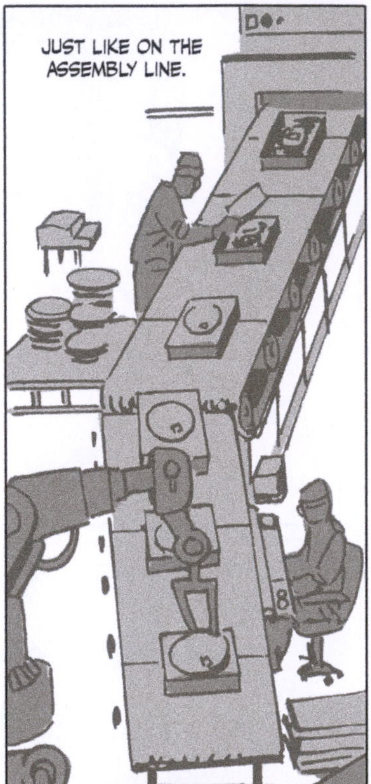
JUST LIKE ON THE ASSEMBLY LINE.

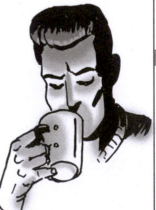

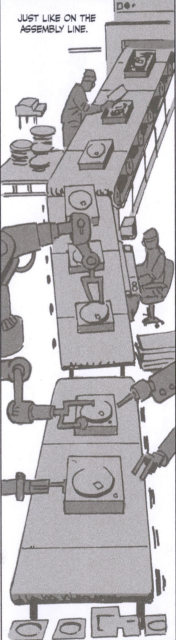

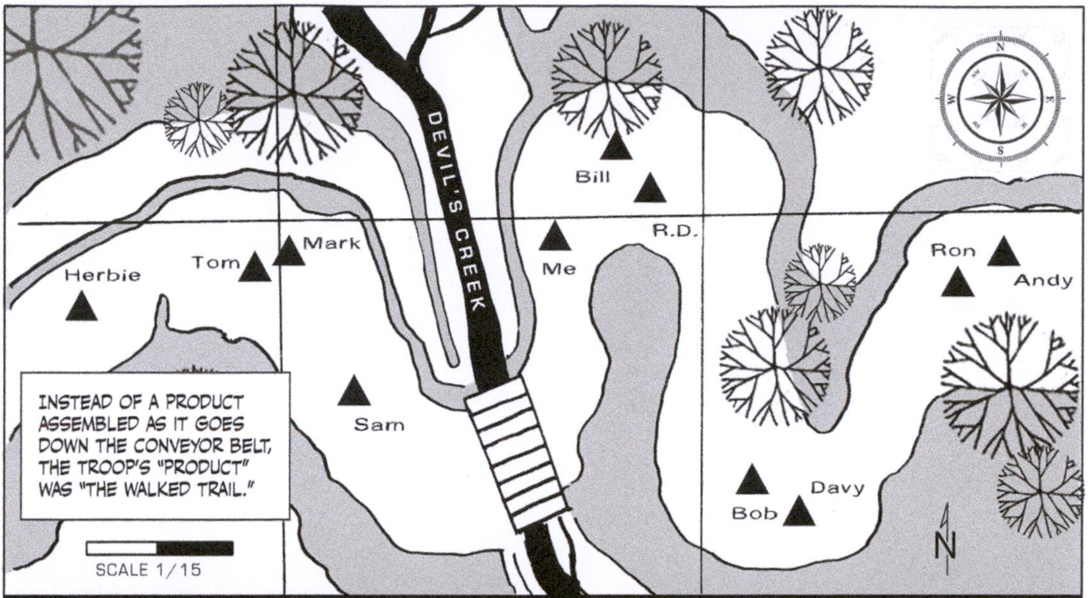
INSTEAD OF A PRODUCT ASSEMBLED AS IT GOES DOWN THE CONVEYOR BELT, THE TROOP'S "PRODUCT" WAS "THE WALKED TRAIL."
DEVIL'S CREEK
Herbie
Tom
Mark
Sam
Me
R.D.
Bill
Ron
Andy
Davy
Bob
SCALE 1/15
N

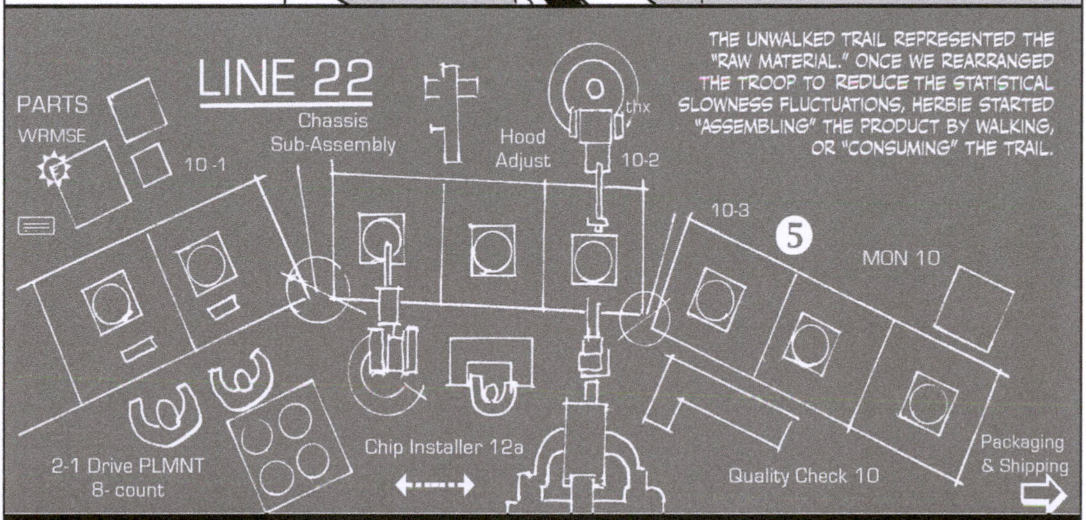
THE UNWALKED TRAIL REPRESENTED THE "RAW MATERIAL." ONCE WE REARRANGED THE TROOP TO REDUCE THE STATISTICAL SLOWNESS FLUCTUATIONS, HERBIE STARTED "ASSEMBLING" THE PRODUCT BY WALKING, OR "CONSUMING" THE TRAIL.
LINE 22
PARTS
WRMSE
Chassis Sub-Assembly
Hood Adjust
thx
10-1
10-2
10-3
5
MON 10
2-1 Drive PLMNT 8- count
Chip Installer 12a
Quality Check 10
Packaging & Shipping

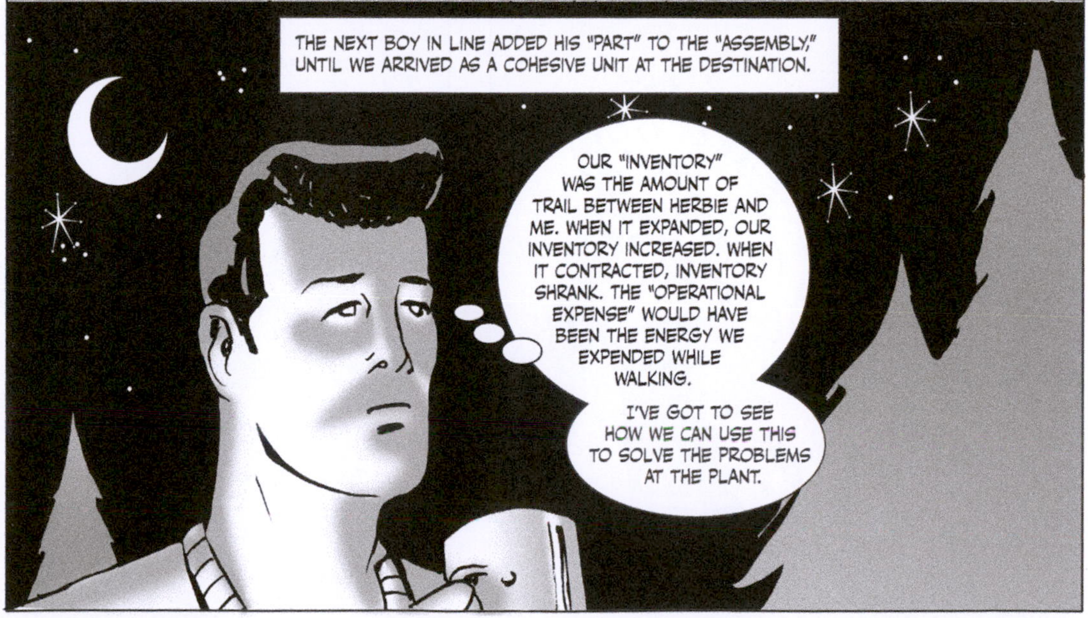
THE NEXT BOY IN LINE ADDED HIS "PART" TO THE "ASSEMBLY," UNTIL WE ARRIVED AS A COHESIVE UNIT AT THE DESTINATION.
OUR "INVENTORY" WAS THE AMOUNT OF TRAIL BETWEEN HERBIE AND ME. WHEN IT EXPANDED, OUR INVENTORY INCREASED. WHEN IT CONTRACTED, INVENTORY SHRANK. THE "OPERATIONAL EXPENSE" WOULD HAVE BEEN THE ENERGY WE EXPENDED WHILE WALKING.
I'VE GOT TO SEE HOW WE CAN USE THIS TO SOLVE THE PROBLEMS AT THE PLANT.

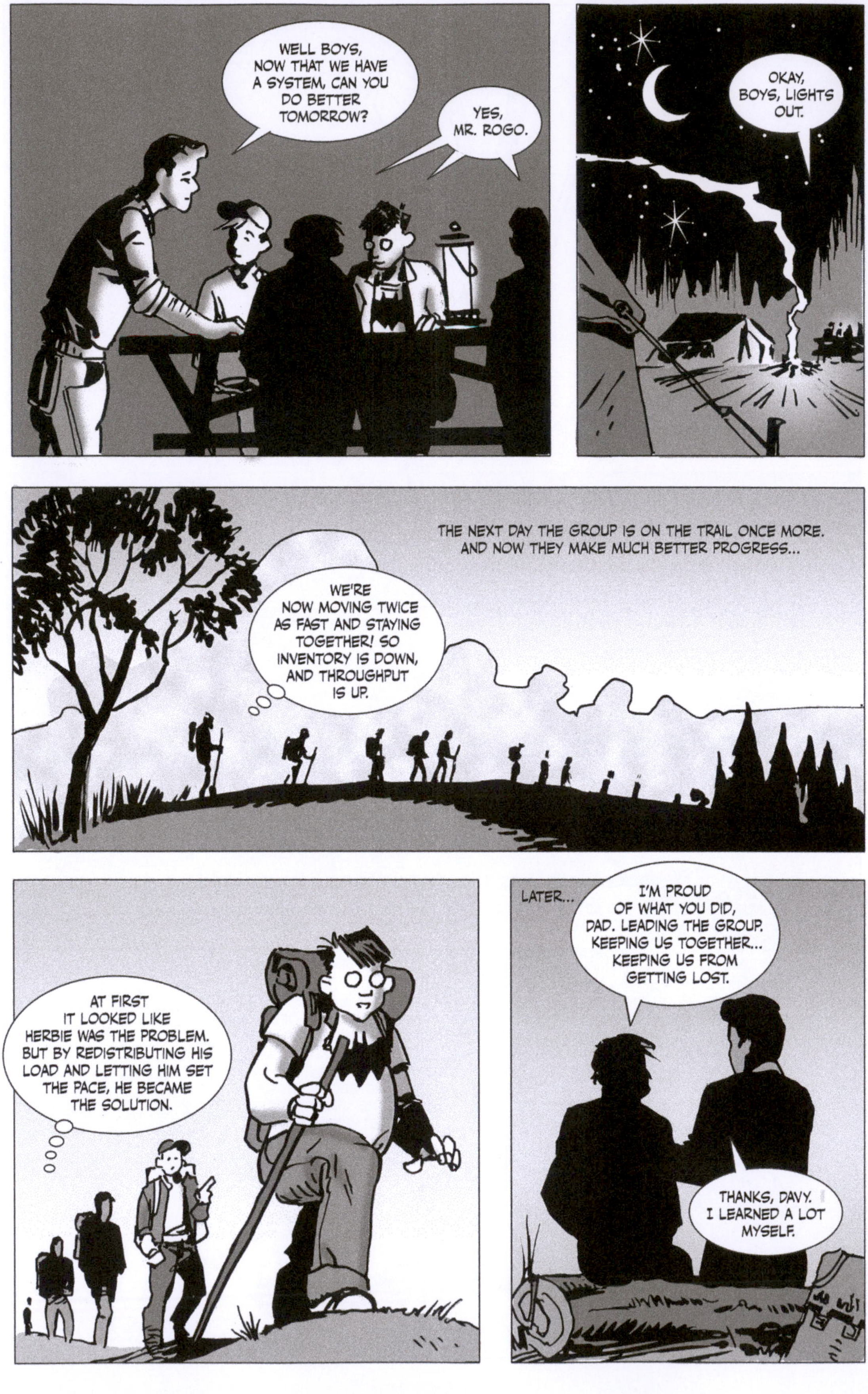
WELL BOYS, NOW THAT WE HAVE A SYSTEM, CAN YOU DO BETTER TOMORROW?
YES, MR. ROGO.
OKAY, BOYS, LIGHTS OUT.
THE NEXT DAY THE GROUP IS ON THE TRAIL ONCE MORE. AND NOW THEY MAKE MUCH BETTER PROGRESS...
WE'RE NOW MOVING TWICE AS FAST AND STAYING TOGETHER! SO INVENTORY IS DOWN, AND THROUGHPUT IS UP.
AT FIRST IT LOOKED LIKE HERBIE WAS THE PROBLEM. BUT BY REDISTRIBUTING HIS LOAD AND LETTING HIM SET THE PACE, HE BECAME THE SOLUTION.
LATER...
I'M PROUD OF WHAT YOU DID, DAD. LEADING THE GROUP. KEEPING US TOGETHER... KEEPING US FROM GETTING LOST.
THANKS, DAVY. I LEARNED A LOT MYSELF.

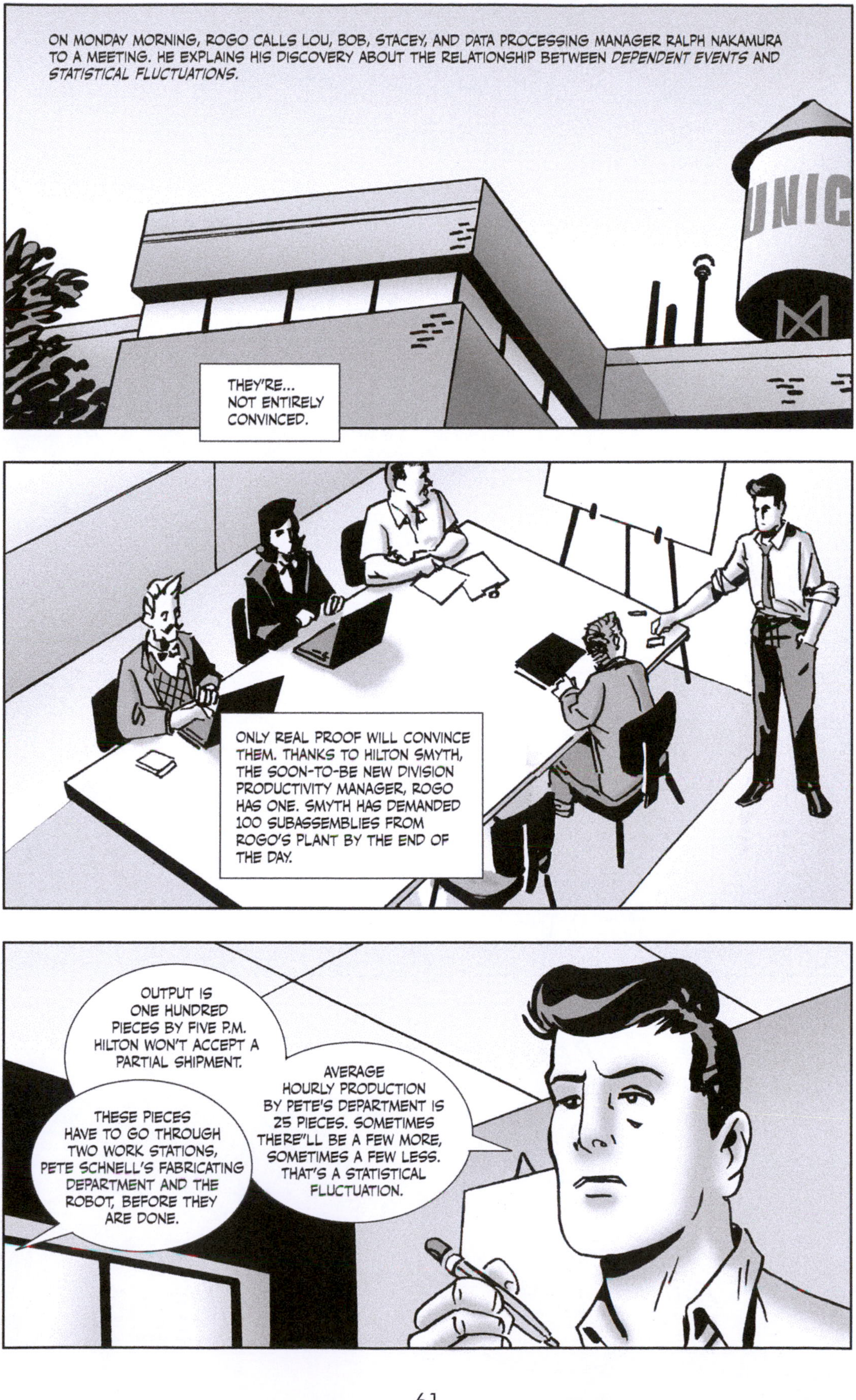
ON MONDAY MORNING, ROGO CALLS LOU, BOB, STACEY, AND DATA PROCESSING MANAGER RALPH NAKAMURA TO A MEETING. HE EXPLAINS HIS DISCOVERY ABOUT THE RELATIONSHIP BETWEEN *DEPENDENT EVENTS* AND *STATISTICAL FLUCTUATIONS*.
UNIC
THEY'RE... NOT ENTIRELY CONVINCED.
ONLY REAL PROOF WILL CONVINCE THEM. THANKS TO HILTON SMYTH, THE SOON-TO-BE NEW DIVISION PRODUCTIVITY MANAGER, ROGO HAS ONE. SMYTH HAS DEMANDED 100 SUBASSEMBLIES FROM ROGO'S PLANT BY THE END OF THE DAY.
OUTPUT IS ONE HUNDRED PIECES BY FIVE P.M. HILTON WON'T ACCEPT A PARTIAL SHIPMENT.
THESE PIECES HAVE TO GO THROUGH TWO WORK STATIONS, PETE SCHNELL'S FABRICATING DEPARTMENT AND THE ROBOT, BEFORE THEY ARE DONE.
AVERAGE HOURLY PRODUCTION BY PETE'S DEPARTMENT IS 25 PIECES. SOMETIMES THERE'LL BE A FEW MORE, SOMETIMES A FEW LESS. THAT'S A STATISTICAL FLUCTUATION.

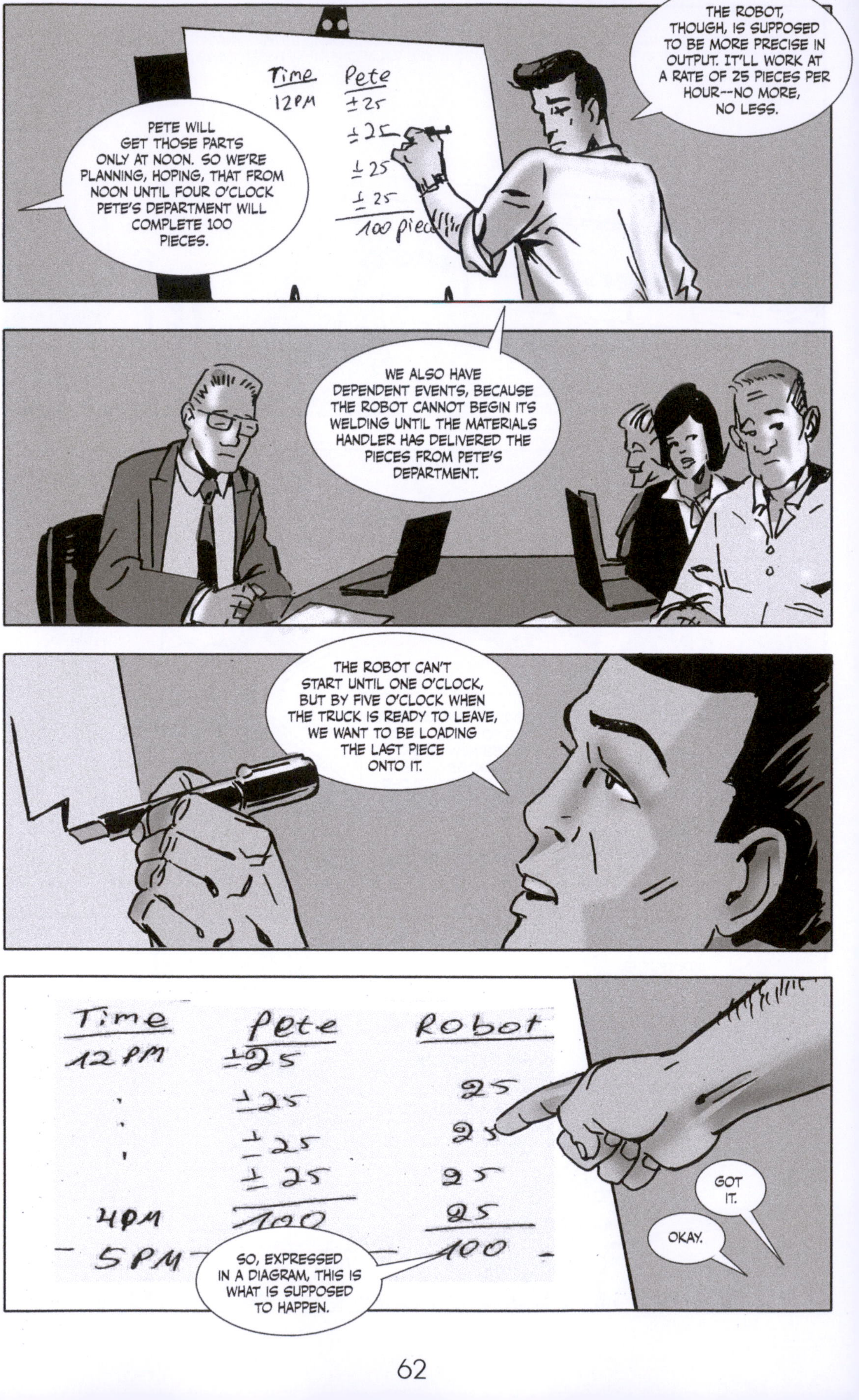
Time Pete
12PM ±25
±25
±25
±25
100 piec
PETE WILL GET THOSE PARTS ONLY AT NOON. SO WE'RE PLANNING, HOPING, THAT FROM NOON UNTIL FOUR O'CLOCK PETE'S DEPARTMENT WILL COMPLETE 100 PIECES.
THE ROBOT, THOUGH, IS SUPPOSED TO BE MORE PRECISE IN OUTPUT. IT'LL WORK AT A RATE OF 25 PIECES PER HOUR--NO MORE, NO LESS.
WE ALSO HAVE DEPENDENT EVENTS, BECAUSE THE ROBOT CANNOT BEGIN ITS WELDING UNTIL THE MATERIALS HANDLER HAS DELIVERED THE PIECES FROM PETE'S DEPARTMENT.
THE ROBOT CAN'T START UNTIL ONE O'CLOCK, BUT BY FIVE O'CLOCK WHEN THE TRUCK IS READY TO LEAVE, WE WANT TO BE LOADING THE LAST PIECE ONTO IT.
Time Pete Robot
12PM ±25
±25 25
±25 25
±25 25
4PM 100 25
5PM 100
SO, EXPRESSED IN A DIAGRAM, THIS IS WHAT IS SUPPOSED TO HAPPEN.
GOT IT.
OKAY.

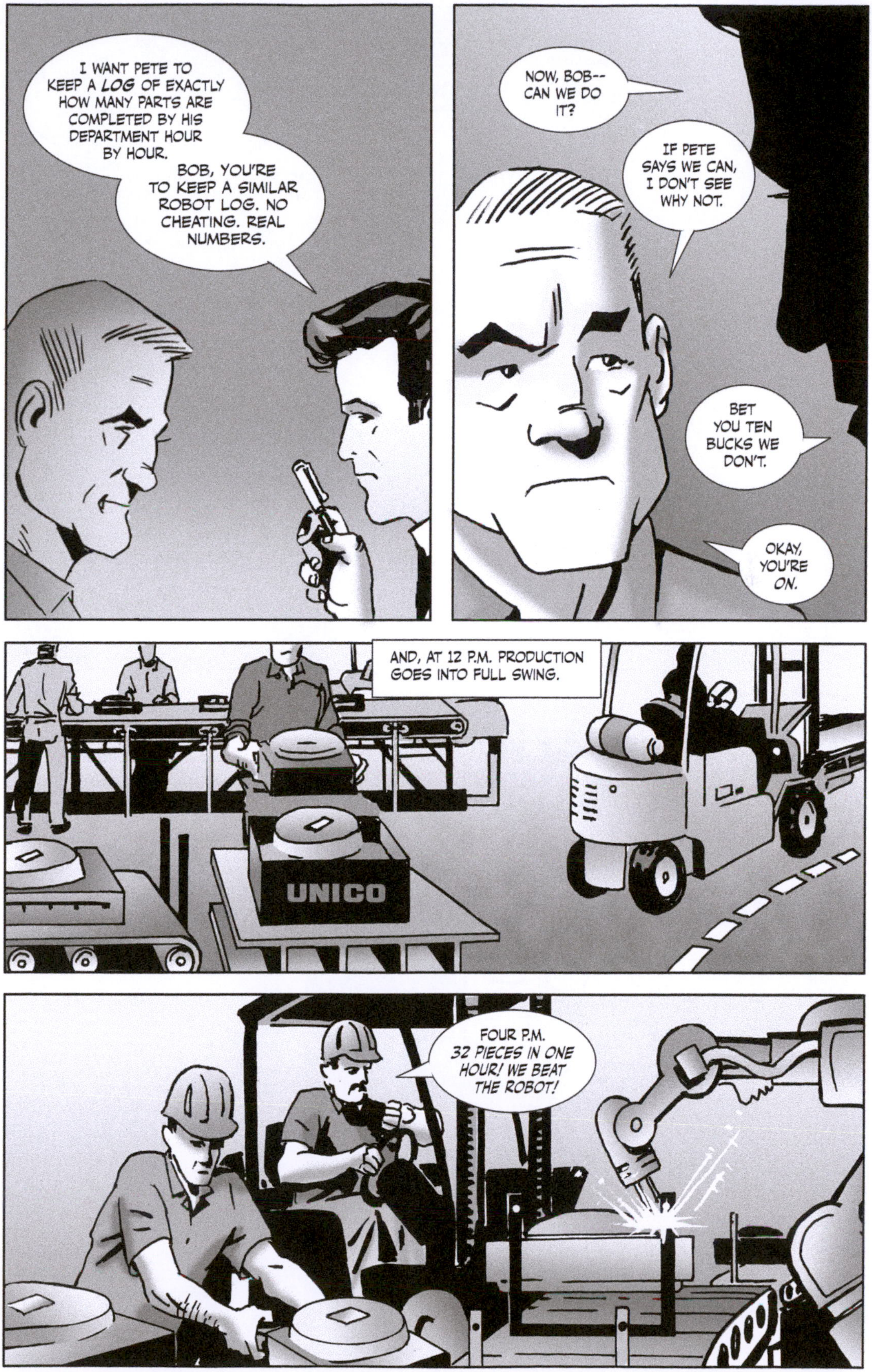
I WANT PETE TO KEEP A LOG OF EXACTLY HOW MANY PARTS ARE COMPLETED BY HIS DEPARTMENT HOUR BY HOUR.
BOB, YOU'RE TO KEEP A SIMILAR ROBOT LOG. NO CHEATING. REAL NUMBERS.
NOW, BOB-- CAN WE DO IT?
IF PETE SAYS WE CAN, I DON'T SEE WHY NOT.
BET YOU TEN BUCKS WE DON'T.
OKAY, YOU'RE ON.
AND, AT 12 P.M. PRODUCTION GOES INTO FULL SWING.
UNICO
FOUR P.M. 32 PIECES IN ONE HOUR! WE BEAT THE ROBOT!

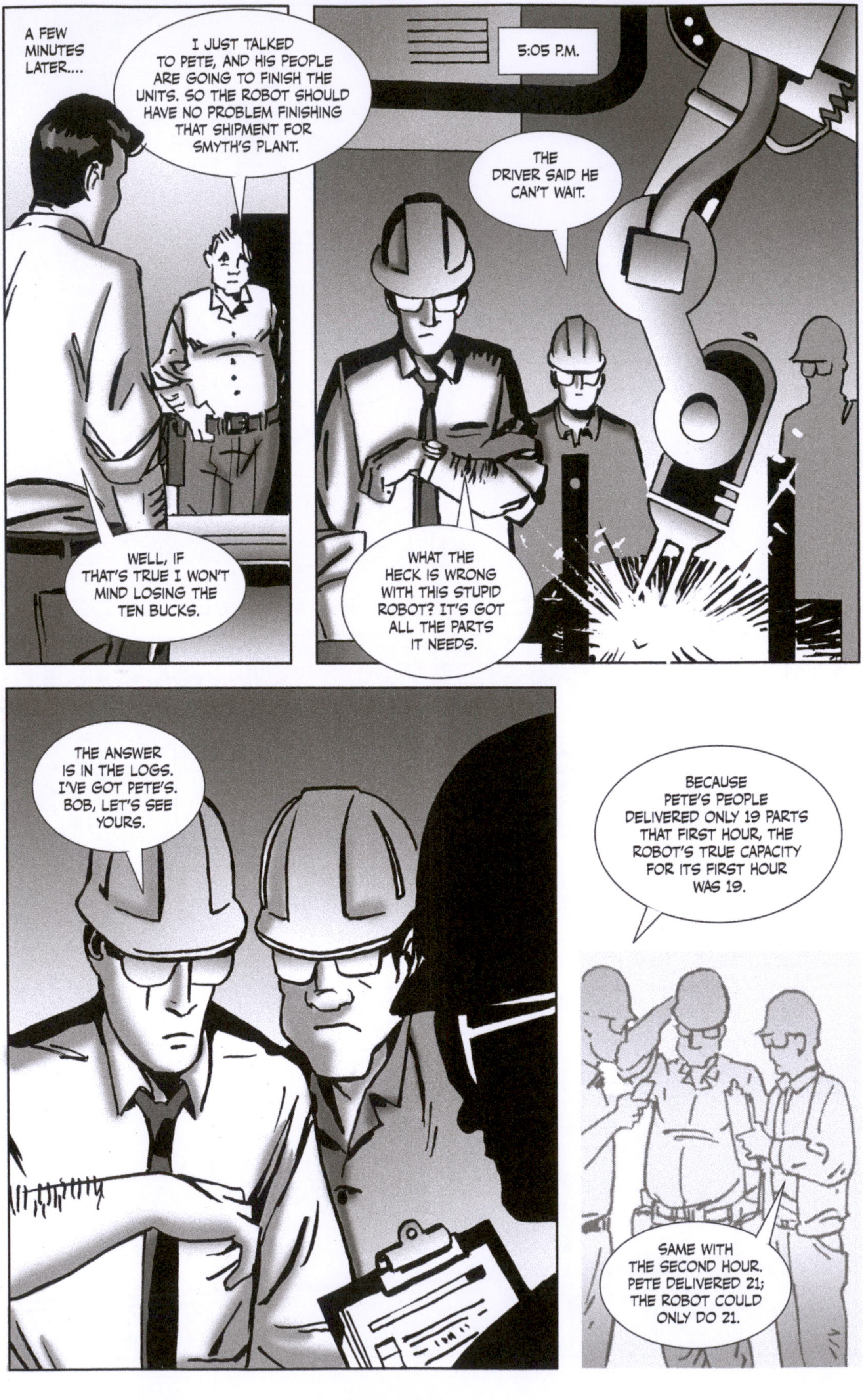

A FEW MINUTES LATER....
I JUST TALKED TO PETE, AND HIS PEOPLE ARE GOING TO FINISH THE UNITS. SO THE ROBOT SHOULD HAVE NO PROBLEM FINISHING THAT SHIPMENT FOR SMYTH'S PLANT.
WELL, IF THAT'S TRUE I WON'T MIND LOSING THE TEN BUCKS.
5:05 P.M.
THE DRIVER SAID HE CAN'T WAIT.
WHAT THE HECK IS WRONG WITH THIS STUPID ROBOT? IT'S GOT ALL THE PARTS IT NEEDS.
THE ANSWER IS IN THE LOGS. I'VE GOT PETE'S. BOB, LET'S SEE YOURS.
BECAUSE PETE'S PEOPLE DELIVERED ONLY 19 PARTS THAT FIRST HOUR, THE ROBOT'S TRUE CAPACITY FOR ITS FIRST HOUR WAS 19.
SAME WITH THE SECOND HOUR. PETE DELIVERED 21; THE ROBOT COULD ONLY DO 21.

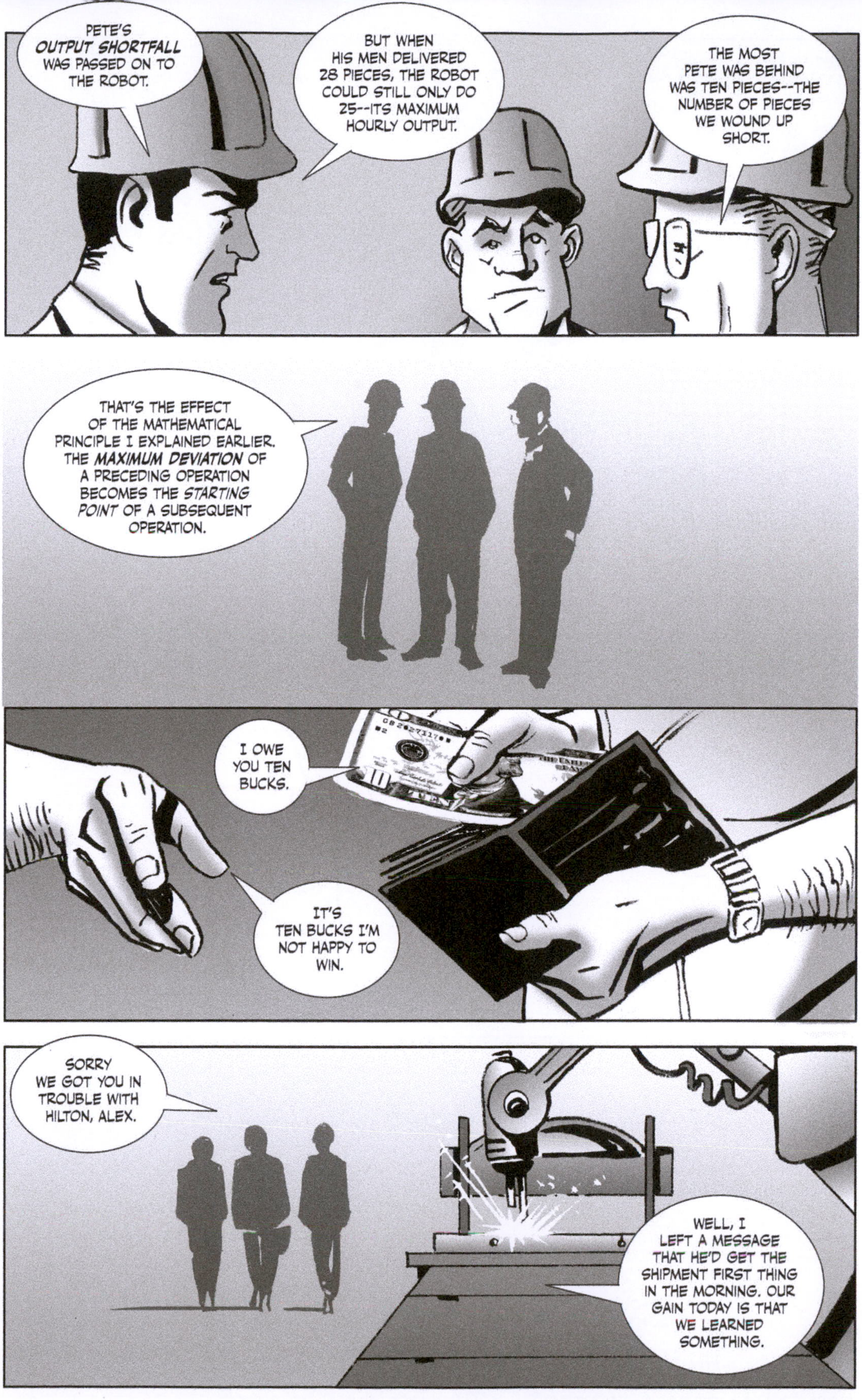
PETE'S OUTPUT SHORTFALL WAS PASSED ON TO THE ROBOT.
BUT WHEN HIS MEN DELIVERED 28 PIECES, THE ROBOT COULD STILL ONLY DO 25--ITS MAXIMUM HOURLY OUTPUT.
THE MOST PETE WAS BEHIND WAS TEN PIECES--THE NUMBER OF PIECES WE WOUND UP SHORT.
THAT'S THE EFFECT OF THE MATHEMATICAL PRINCIPLE I EXPLAINED EARLIER. THE MAXIMUM DEVIATION OF A PRECEDING OPERATION BECOMES THE STARTING POINT OF A SUBSEQUENT OPERATION.
I OWE YOU TEN BUCKS.
IT'S TEN BUCKS I'M NOT HAPPY TO WIN.
SORRY WE GOT YOU IN TROUBLE WITH HILTON, ALEX.
WELL, I LEFT A MESSAGE THAT HE'D GET THE SHIPMENT FIRST THING IN THE MORNING. OUR GAIN TODAY IS THAT WE LEARNED SOMETHING.

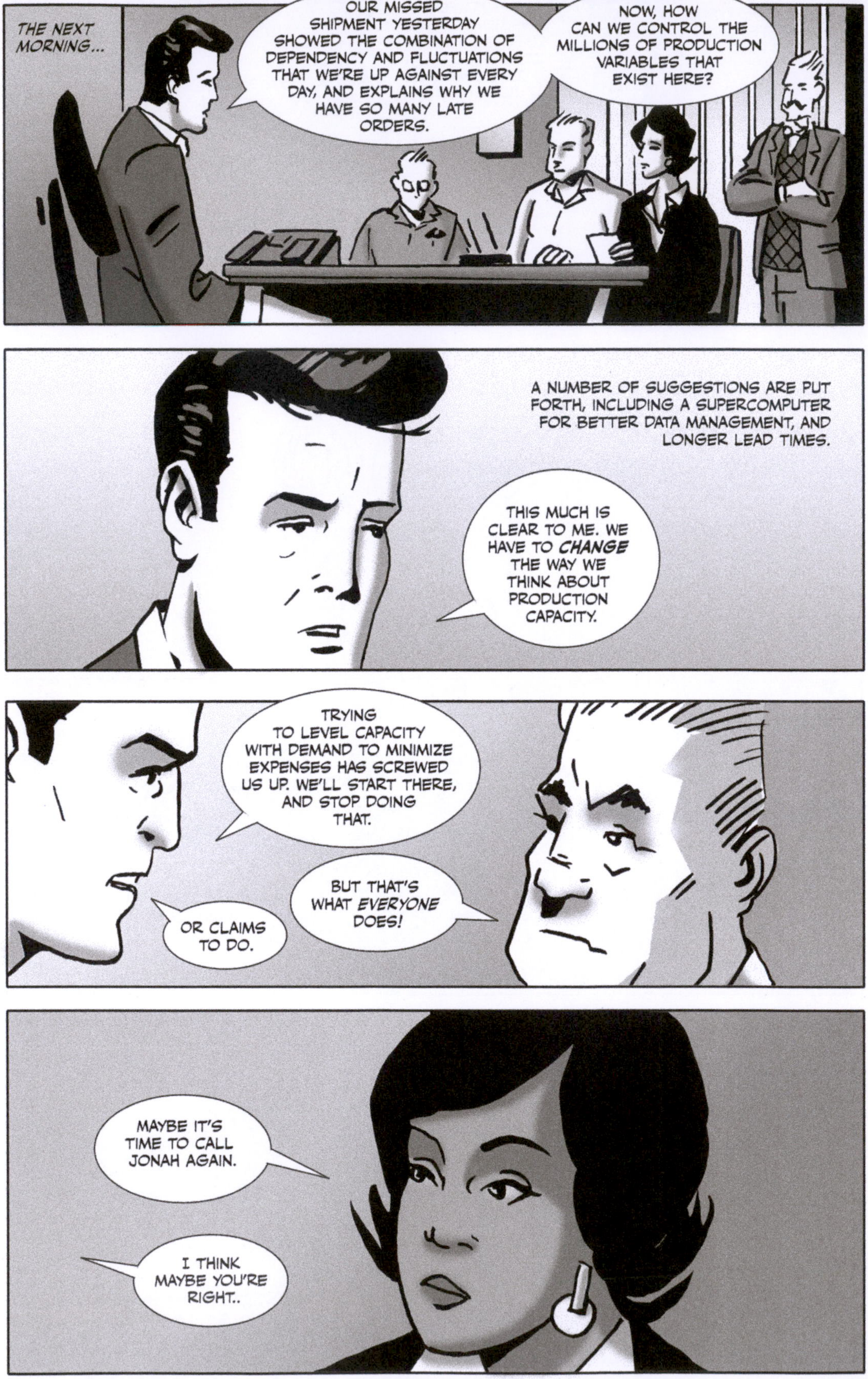
THE NEXT MORNING...
OUR MISSED SHIPMENT YESTERDAY SHOWED THE COMBINATION OF DEPENDENCY AND FLUCTUATIONS THAT WE'RE UP AGAINST EVERY DAY, AND EXPLAINS WHY WE HAVE SO MANY LATE ORDERS.
NOW, HOW CAN WE CONTROL THE MILLIONS OF PRODUCTION VARIABLES THAT EXIST HERE?
A NUMBER OF SUGGESTIONS ARE PUT FORTH, INCLUDING A SUPERCOMPUTER FOR BETTER DATA MANAGEMENT, AND LONGER LEAD TIMES.
THIS MUCH IS CLEAR TO ME. WE HAVE TO *CHANGE* THE WAY WE THINK ABOUT PRODUCTION CAPACITY.
TRYING TO LEVEL CAPACITY WITH DEMAND TO MINIMIZE EXPENSES HAS SCREWED US UP. WE'LL START THERE, AND STOP DOING THAT.
BUT THAT'S WHAT *EVERYONE* DOES!
OR CLAIMS TO DO.
MAYBE IT'S TIME TO CALL JONAH AGAIN.
I THINK MAYBE YOU'RE RIGHT..

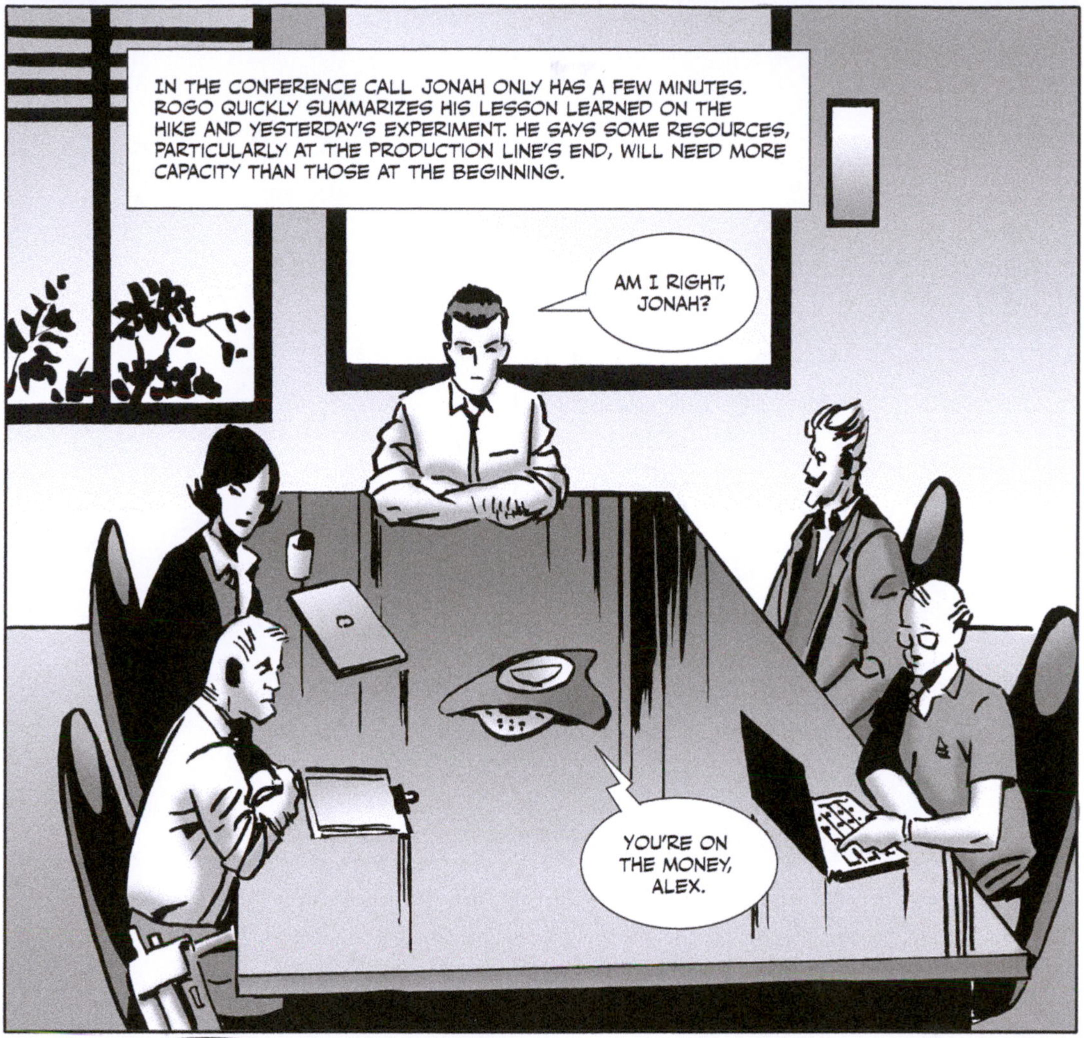
IN THE CONFERENCE CALL JONAH ONLY HAS A FEW MINUTES. ROGO QUICKLY SUMMARIZES HIS LESSON LEARNED ON THE HIKE AND YESTERDAY'S EXPERIMENT. HE SAYS SOME RESOURCES, PARTICULARLY AT THE PRODUCTION LINE'S END, WILL NEED MORE CAPACITY THAN THOSE AT THE BEGINNING.
AM I RIGHT, JONAH?
YOU'RE ON THE MONEY, ALEX.

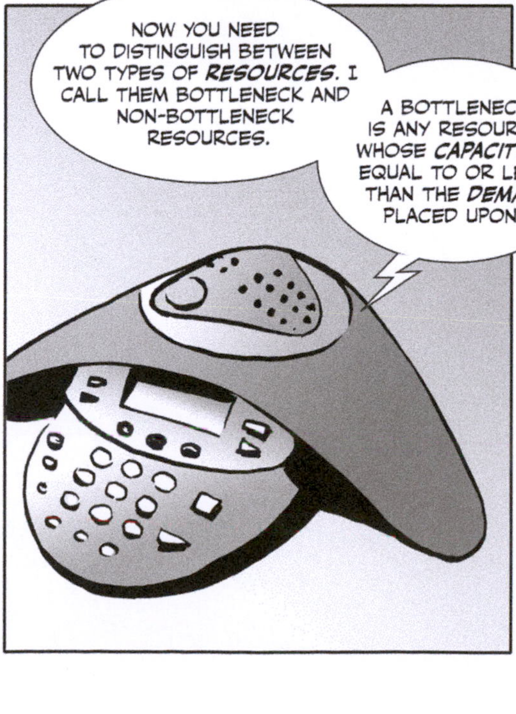
NOW YOU NEED TO DISTINGUISH BETWEEN TWO TYPES OF ***RESOURCES***. I CALL THEM BOTTLENECK AND NON-BOTTLENECK RESOURCES.
A BOTTLENECK IS ANY RESOURCE WHOSE ***CAPACITY*** IS EQUAL TO OR LESS THAN THE ***DEMAND*** PLACED UPON IT.

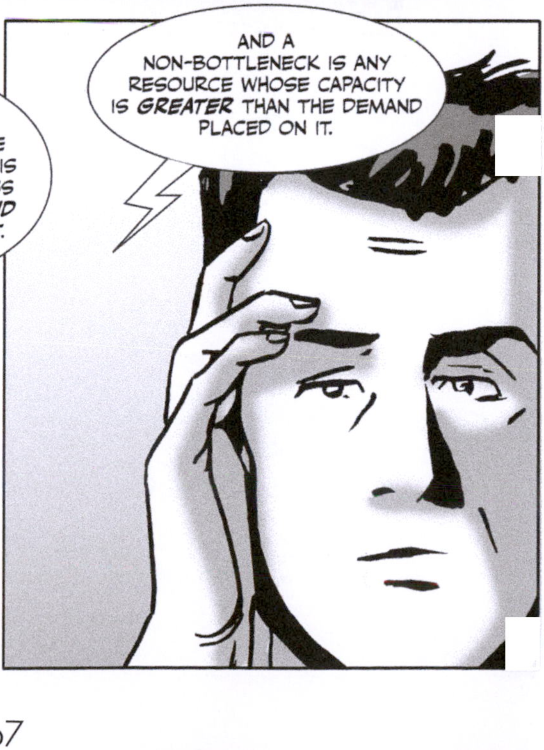
AND A NON-BOTTLENECK IS ANY RESOURCE WHOSE CAPACITY IS ***GREATER*** THAN THE DEMAND PLACED ON IT.

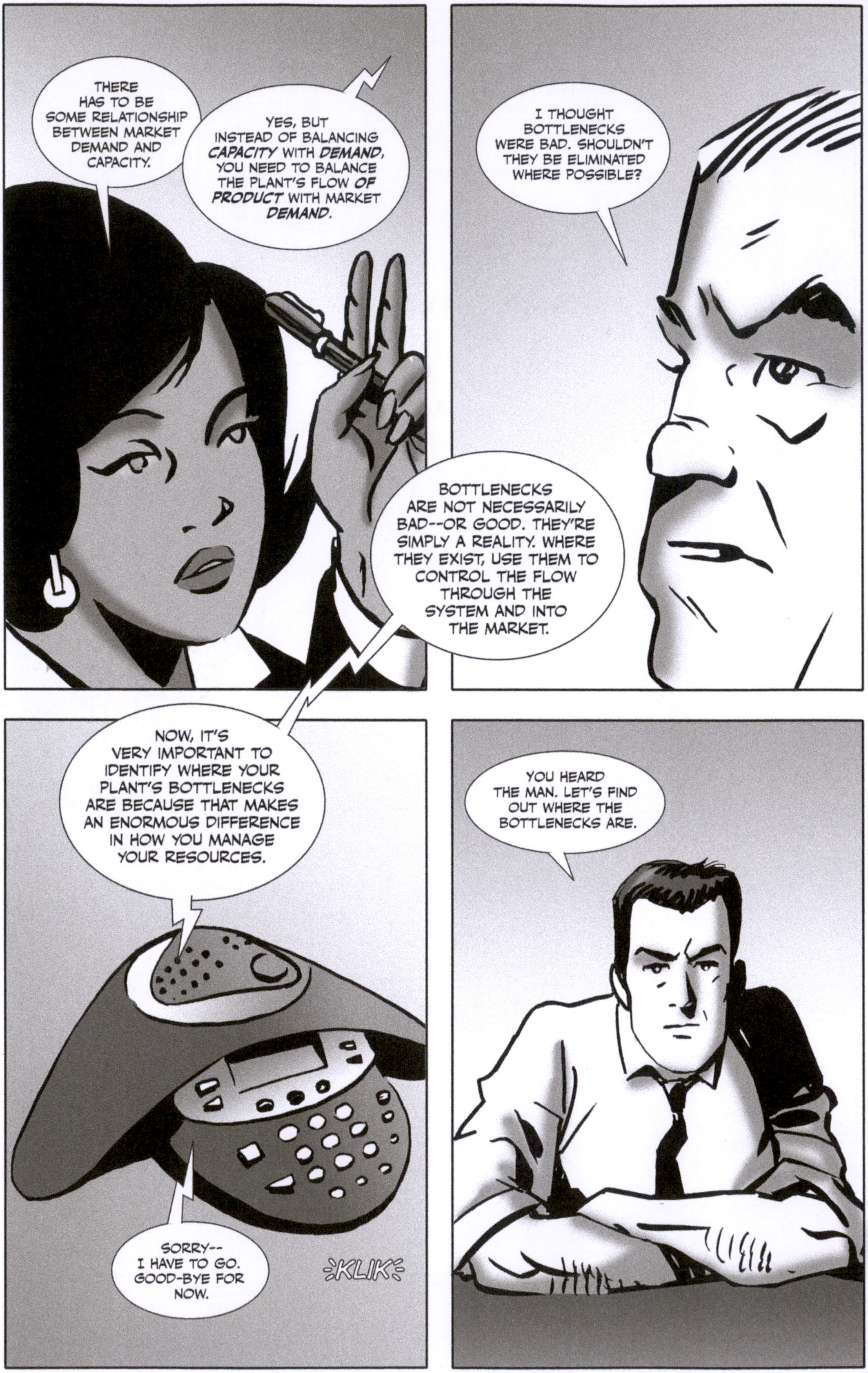
THERE HAS TO BE SOME RELATIONSHIP BETWEEN MARKET DEMAND AND CAPACITY.
YES, BUT INSTEAD OF BALANCING *CAPACITY* WITH *DEMAND*, YOU NEED TO BALANCE THE PLANT'S FLOW *OF PRODUCT* WITH MARKET *DEMAND*.
I THOUGHT BOTTLENECKS WERE BAD. SHOULDN'T THEY BE ELIMINATED WHERE POSSIBLE?
BOTTLENECKS ARE NOT NECESSARILY BAD--OR GOOD. THEY'RE SIMPLY A REALITY. WHERE THEY EXIST, USE THEM TO CONTROL THE FLOW THROUGH THE SYSTEM AND INTO THE MARKET.
NOW, IT'S VERY IMPORTANT TO IDENTIFY WHERE YOUR PLANT'S BOTTLENECKS ARE BECAUSE THAT MAKES AN ENORMOUS DIFFERENCE IN HOW YOU MANAGE YOUR RESOURCES.
SORRY-- I HAVE TO GO. GOOD-BYE FOR NOW.
KLIK
YOU HEARD THE MAN. LET'S FIND OUT WHERE THE BOTTLENECKS ARE.

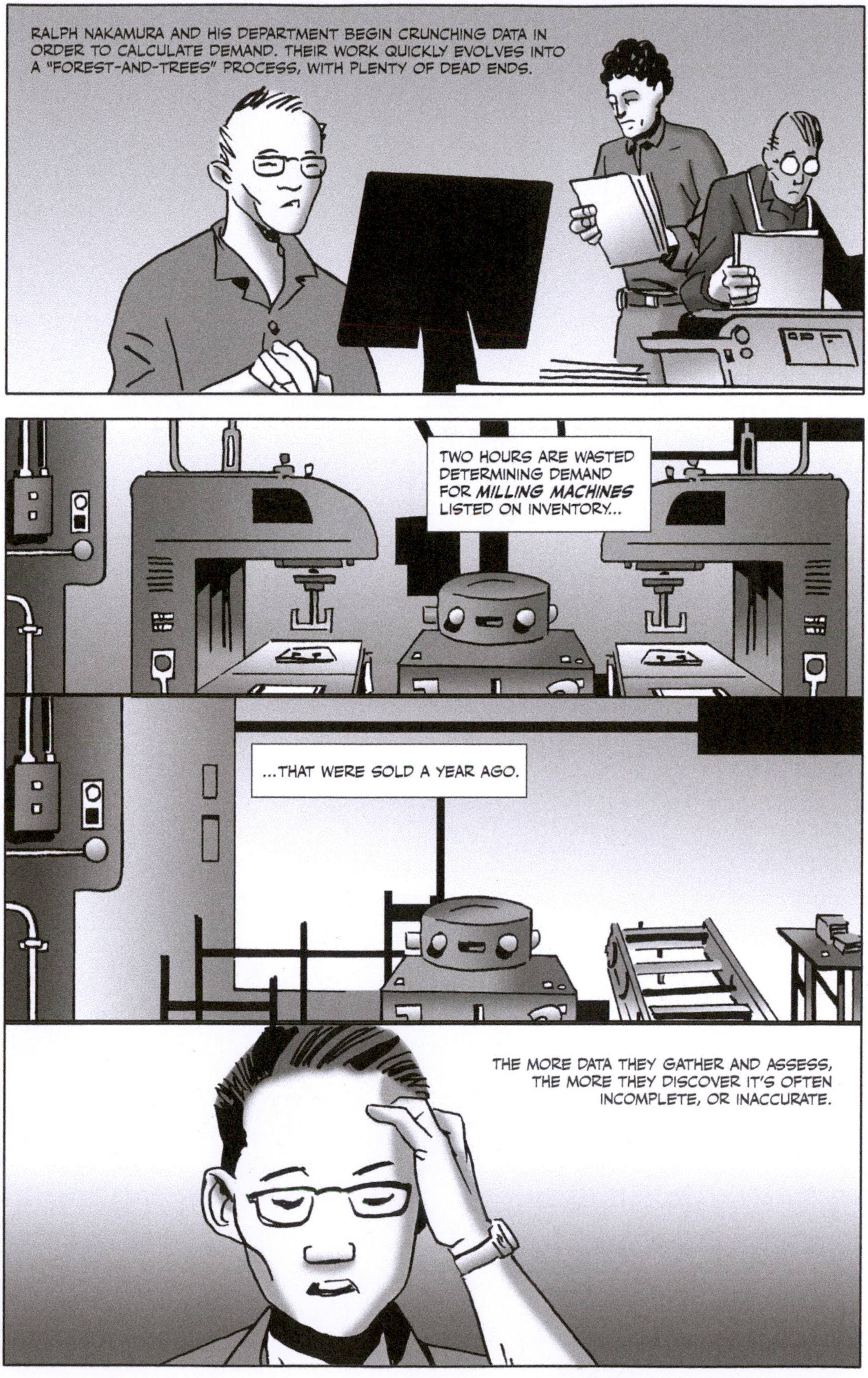
RALPH NAKAMURA AND HIS DEPARTMENT BEGIN CRUNCHING DATA IN ORDER TO CALCULATE DEMAND. THEIR WORK QUICKLY EVOLVES INTO A "FOREST-AND-TREES" PROCESS, WITH PLENTY OF DEAD ENDS.
TWO HOURS ARE WASTED DETERMINING DEMAND FOR *MILLING MACHINES* LISTED ON INVENTORY...
...THAT WERE SOLD A YEAR AGO.
THE MORE DATA THEY GATHER AND ASSESS, THE MORE THEY DISCOVER IT'S OFTEN INCOMPLETE, OR INACCURATE.

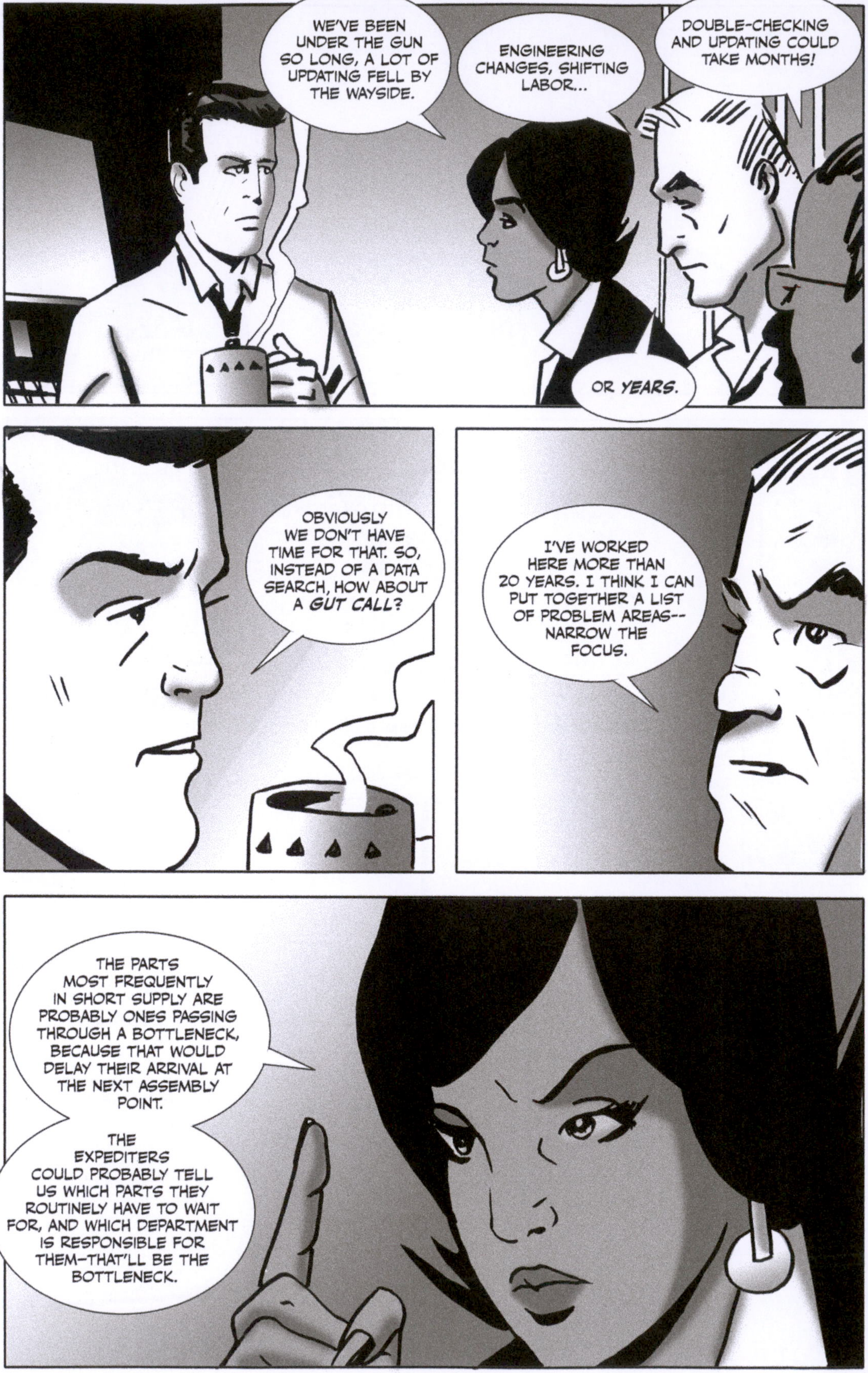
WE'VE BEEN UNDER THE GUN SO LONG, A LOT OF UPDATING FELL BY THE WAYSIDE.
ENGINEERING CHANGES, SHIFTING LABOR...
DOUBLE-CHECKING AND UPDATING COULD TAKE MONTHS!
OR *YEARS*.
OBVIOUSLY WE DON'T HAVE TIME FOR THAT. SO, INSTEAD OF A DATA SEARCH, HOW ABOUT A *GUT CALL*?
I'VE WORKED HERE MORE THAN 20 YEARS. I THINK I CAN PUT TOGETHER A LIST OF PROBLEM AREAS--NARROW THE FOCUS.
THE PARTS MOST FREQUENTLY IN SHORT SUPPLY ARE PROBABLY ONES PASSING THROUGH A BOTTLENECK, BECAUSE THAT WOULD DELAY THEIR ARRIVAL AT THE NEXT ASSEMBLY POINT.
THE EXPEDITERS COULD PROBABLY TELL US WHICH PARTS THEY ROUTINELY HAVE TO WAIT FOR, AND WHICH DEPARTMENT IS RESPONSIBLE FOR THEM–THAT'LL BE THE BOTTLENECK.

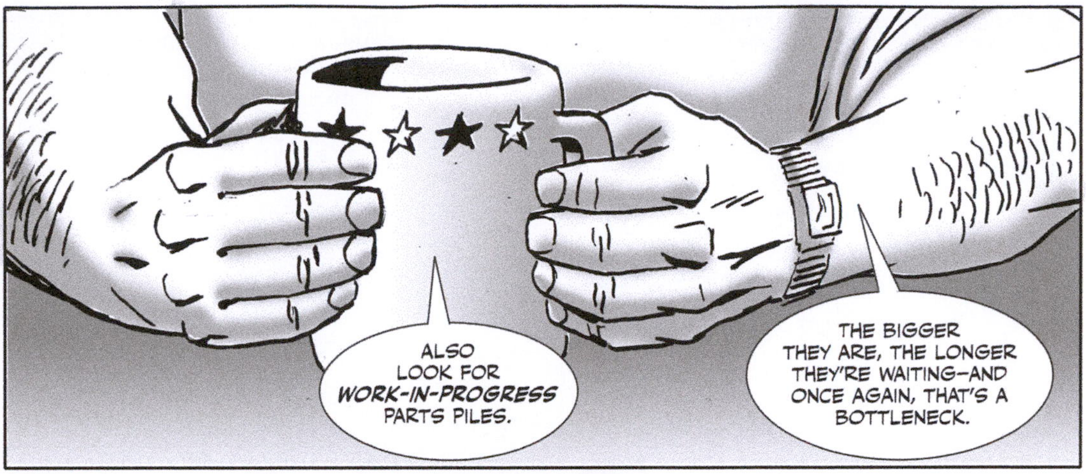
ALSO LOOK FOR *WORK-IN-PROGRESS* PARTS PILES.
THE BIGGER THEY ARE, THE LONGER THEY'RE WAITING–AND ONCE AGAIN, THAT'S A BOTTLENECK.

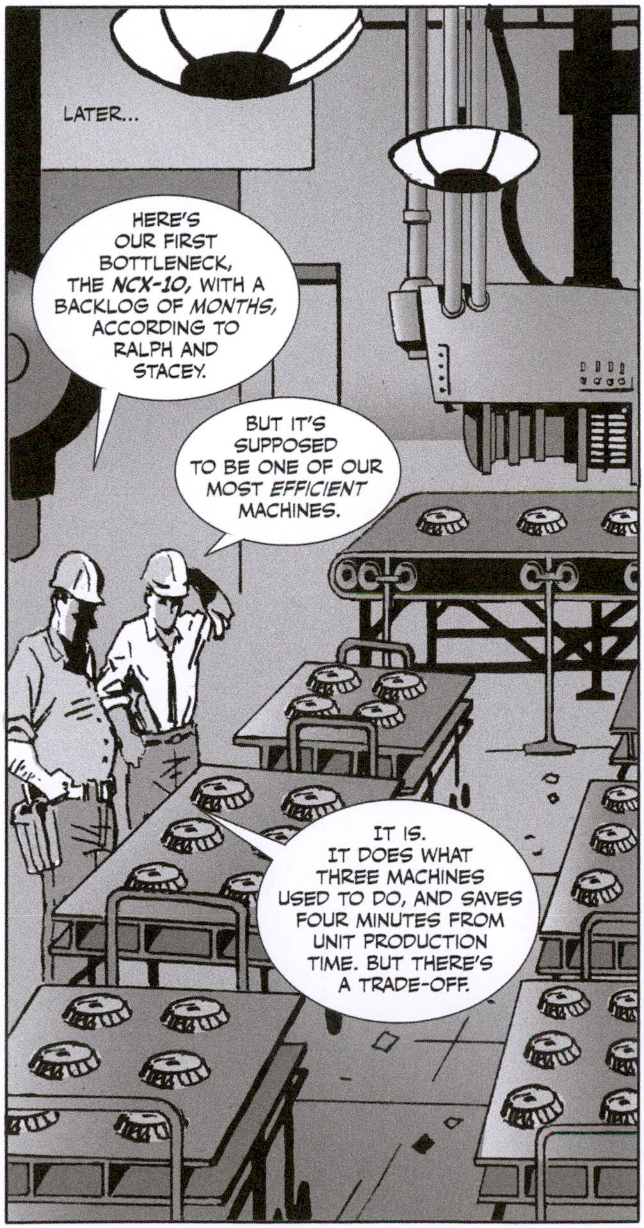
LATER...
HERE'S OUR FIRST BOTTLENECK, THE *NCX-10,* WITH A BACKLOG OF *MONTHS,* ACCORDING TO RALPH AND STACEY.
BUT IT'S SUPPOSED TO BE ONE OF OUR MOST *EFFICIENT* MACHINES.
IT IS. IT DOES WHAT THREE MACHINES USED TO DO, AND SAVES FOUR MINUTES FROM UNIT PRODUCTION TIME. BUT THERE'S A TRADE-OFF.

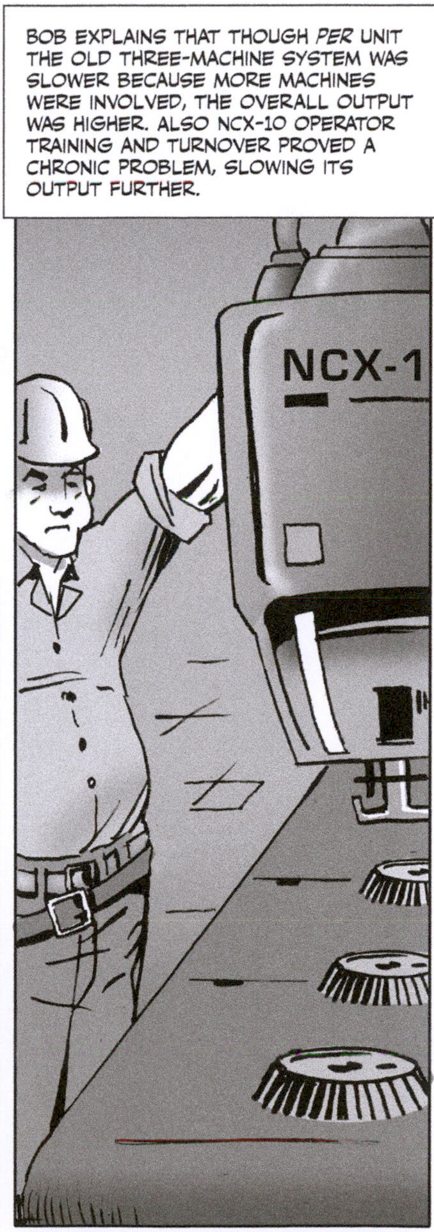
BOB EXPLAINS THAT THOUGH *PER* UNIT THE OLD THREE-MACHINE SYSTEM WAS SLOWER BECAUSE MORE MACHINES WERE INVOLVED, THE OVERALL OUTPUT WAS HIGHER. ALSO NCX-10 OPERATOR TRAINING AND TURNOVER PROVED A CHRONIC PROBLEM, SLOWING ITS OUTPUT FURTHER.
NCX-1

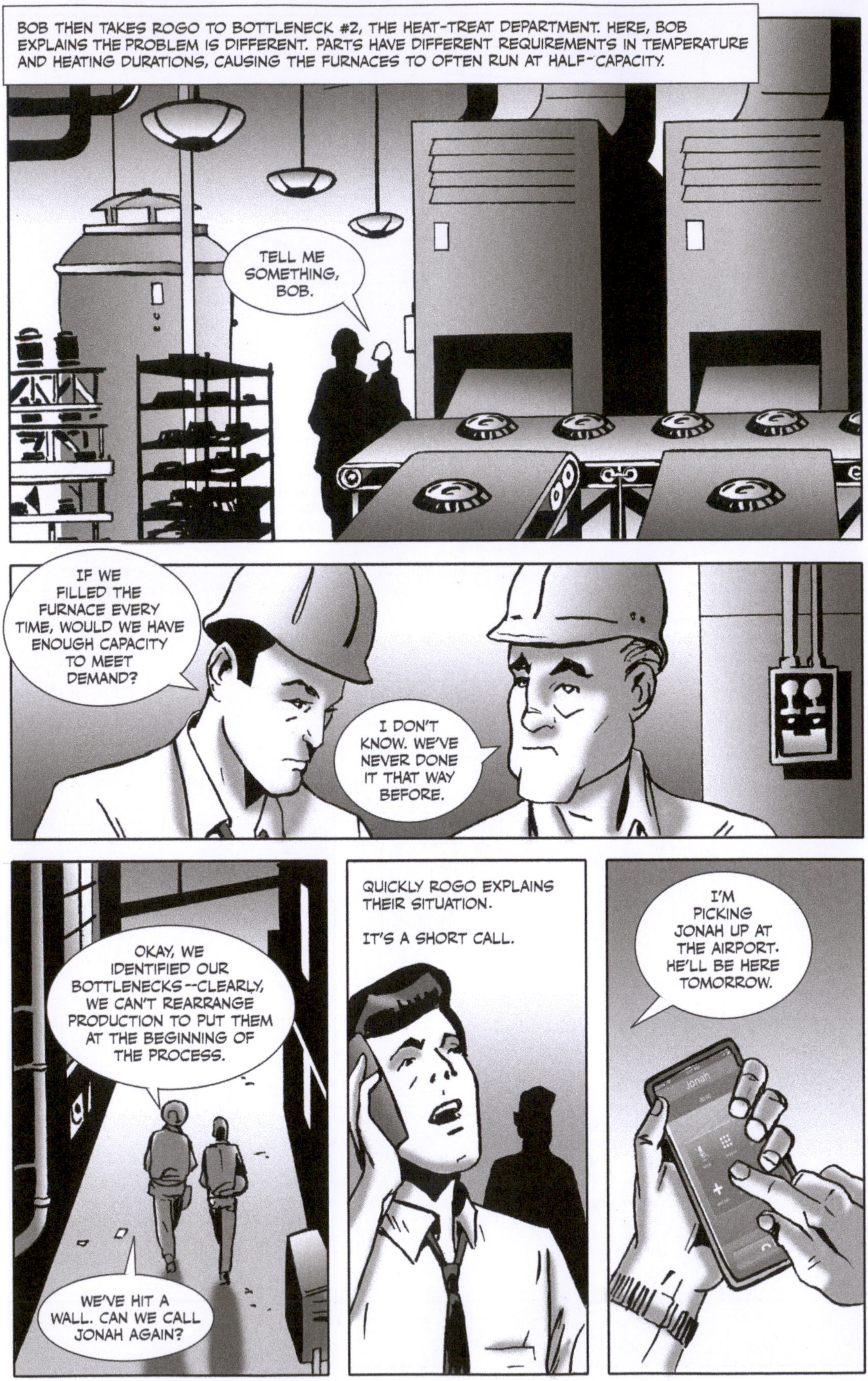
BOB THEN TAKES ROGO TO BOTTLENECK #2, THE HEAT-TREAT DEPARTMENT. HERE, BOB EXPLAINS THE PROBLEM IS DIFFERENT. PARTS HAVE DIFFERENT REQUIREMENTS IN TEMPERATURE AND HEATING DURATIONS, CAUSING THE FURNACES TO OFTEN RUN AT HALF-CAPACITY.
TELL ME SOMETHING, BOB.
IF WE FILLED THE FURNACE EVERY TIME, WOULD WE HAVE ENOUGH CAPACITY TO MEET DEMAND?
I DON'T KNOW. WE'VE NEVER DONE IT THAT WAY BEFORE.
OKAY, WE IDENTIFIED OUR BOTTLENECKS--CLEARLY, WE CAN'T REARRANGE PRODUCTION TO PUT THEM AT THE BEGINNING OF THE PROCESS.
WE'VE HIT A WALL. CAN WE CALL JONAH AGAIN?
QUICKLY ROGO EXPLAINS THEIR SITUATION.
IT'S A SHORT CALL.
I'M PICKING JONAH UP AT THE AIRPORT. HE'LL BE HERE TOMORROW.

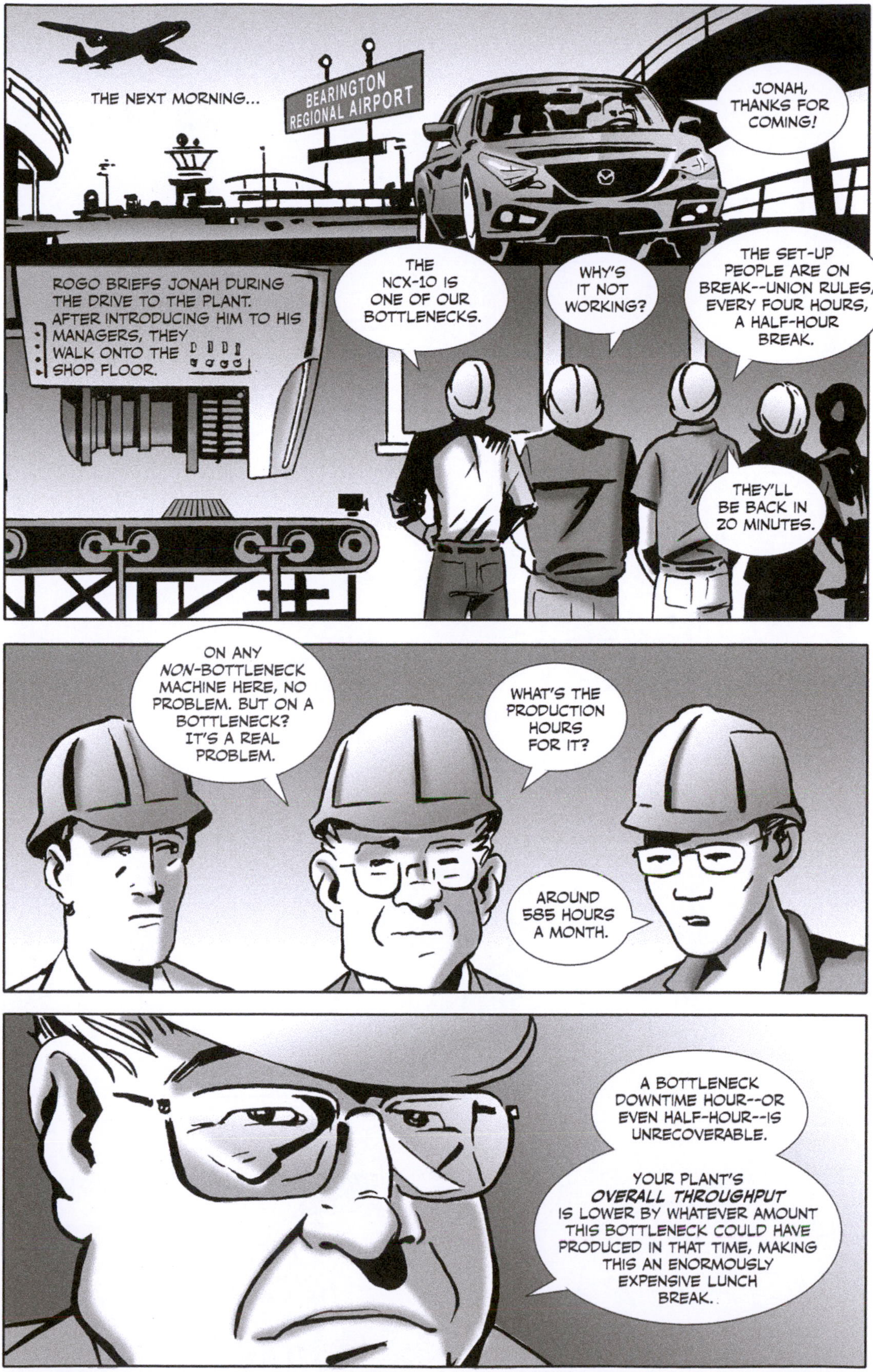
THE NEXT MORNING...
BEARINGTON REGIONAL AIRPORT
JONAH, THANKS FOR COMING!
ROGO BRIEFS JONAH DURING THE DRIVE TO THE PLANT. AFTER INTRODUCING HIM TO HIS MANAGERS, THEY WALK ONTO THE SHOP FLOOR.
THE NCX-10 IS ONE OF OUR BOTTLENECKS.
WHY'S IT NOT WORKING?
THE SET-UP PEOPLE ARE ON BREAK--UNION RULES, EVERY FOUR HOURS, A HALF-HOUR BREAK.
THEY'LL BE BACK IN 20 MINUTES.
ON ANY *NON*-BOTTLENECK MACHINE HERE, NO PROBLEM. BUT ON A BOTTLENECK? IT'S A REAL PROBLEM.
WHAT'S THE PRODUCTION HOURS FOR IT?
AROUND 585 HOURS A MONTH.
A BOTTLENECK DOWNTIME HOUR--OR EVEN HALF-HOUR--IS UNRECOVERABLE.
YOUR PLANT'S ***OVERALL THROUGHPUT*** IS LOWER BY WHATEVER AMOUNT THIS BOTTLENECK COULD HAVE PRODUCED IN THAT TIME, MAKING THIS AN ENORMOUSLY EXPENSIVE LUNCH BREAK.

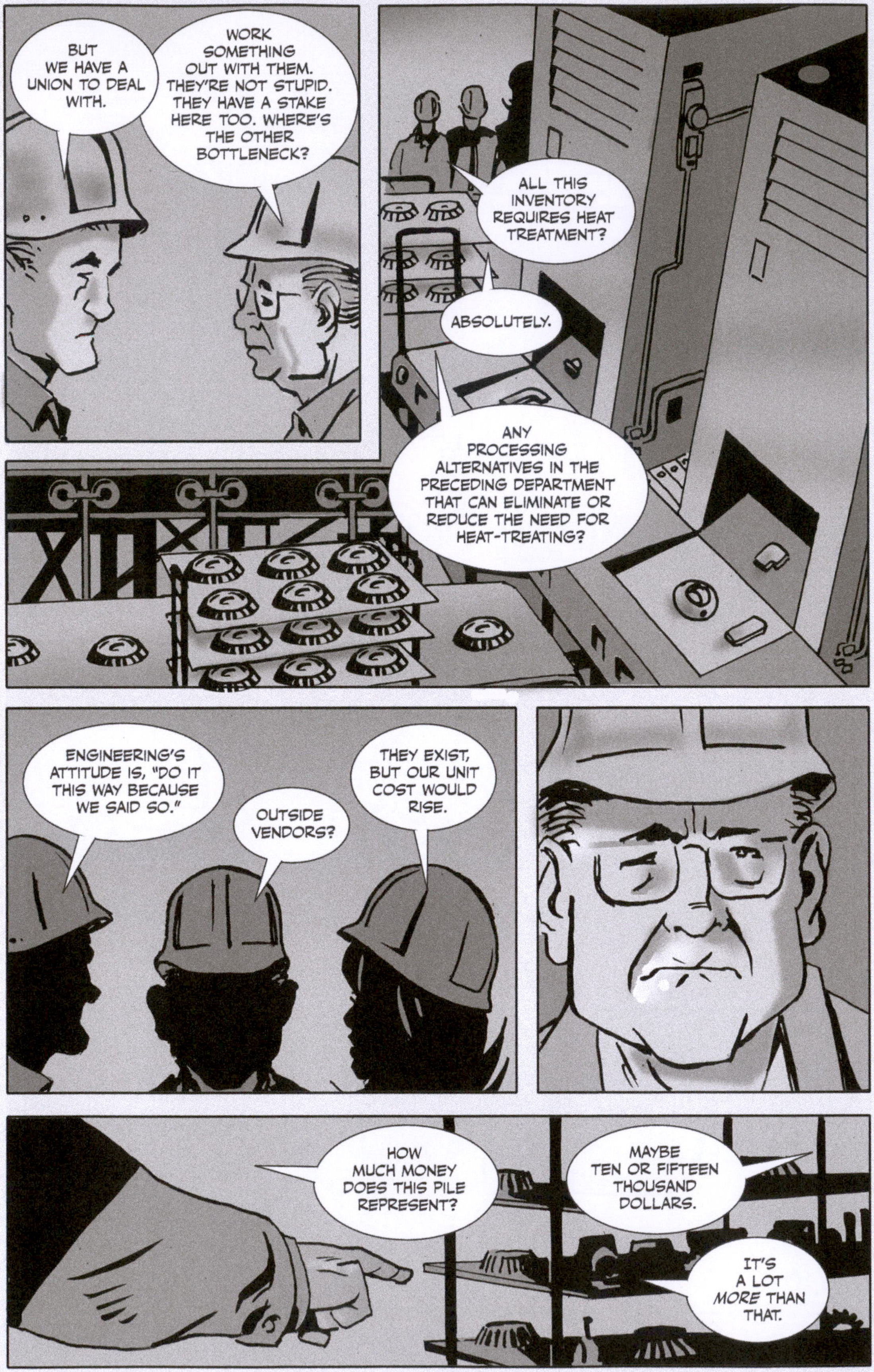
BUT WE HAVE A UNION TO DEAL WITH.
WORK SOMETHING OUT WITH THEM. THEY'RE NOT STUPID. THEY HAVE A STAKE HERE TOO. WHERE'S THE OTHER BOTTLENECK?
ALL THIS INVENTORY REQUIRES HEAT TREATMENT?
ABSOLUTELY.
ANY PROCESSING ALTERNATIVES IN THE PRECEDING DEPARTMENT THAT CAN ELIMINATE OR REDUCE THE NEED FOR HEAT-TREATING?
ENGINEERING'S ATTITUDE IS, "DO IT THIS WAY BECAUSE WE SAID SO."
OUTSIDE VENDORS?
THEY EXIST, BUT OUR UNIT COST WOULD RISE.
HOW MUCH MONEY DOES THIS PILE REPRESENT?
MAYBE TEN OR FIFTEEN THOUSAND DOLLARS.
IT'S A LOT *MORE* THAN THAT.

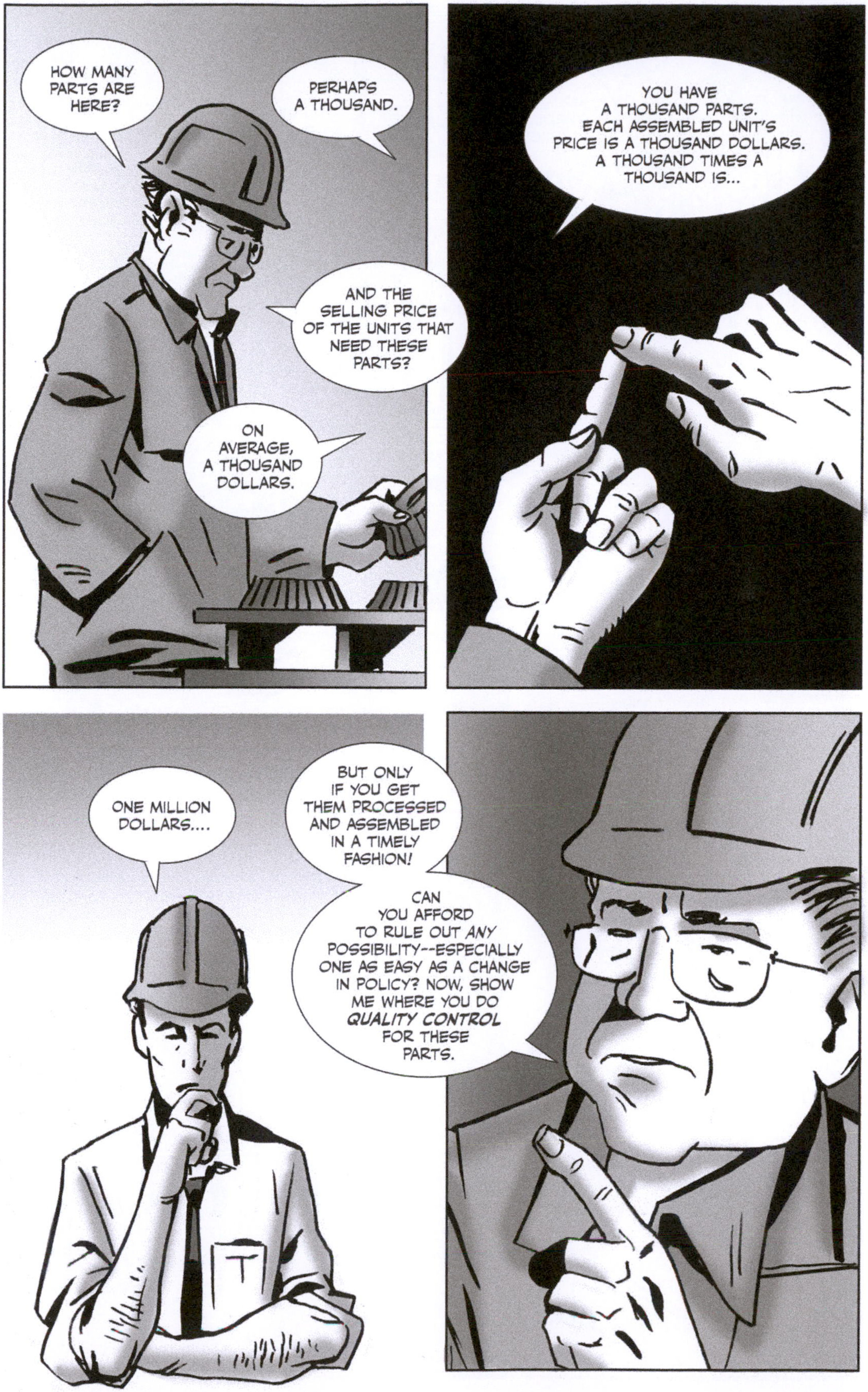
HOW MANY PARTS ARE HERE?
PERHAPS A THOUSAND.
AND THE SELLING PRICE OF THE UNITS THAT NEED THESE PARTS?
ON AVERAGE, A THOUSAND DOLLARS.
YOU HAVE A THOUSAND PARTS. EACH ASSEMBLED UNIT'S PRICE IS A THOUSAND DOLLARS. A THOUSAND TIMES A THOUSAND IS...
ONE MILLION DOLLARS....
BUT ONLY IF YOU GET THEM PROCESSED AND ASSEMBLED IN A TIMELY FASHION!
CAN YOU AFFORD TO RULE OUT *ANY* POSSIBILITY--ESPECIALLY ONE AS EASY AS A CHANGE IN POLICY? NOW, SHOW ME WHERE YOU DO ***QUALITY CONTROL*** FOR THESE PARTS.

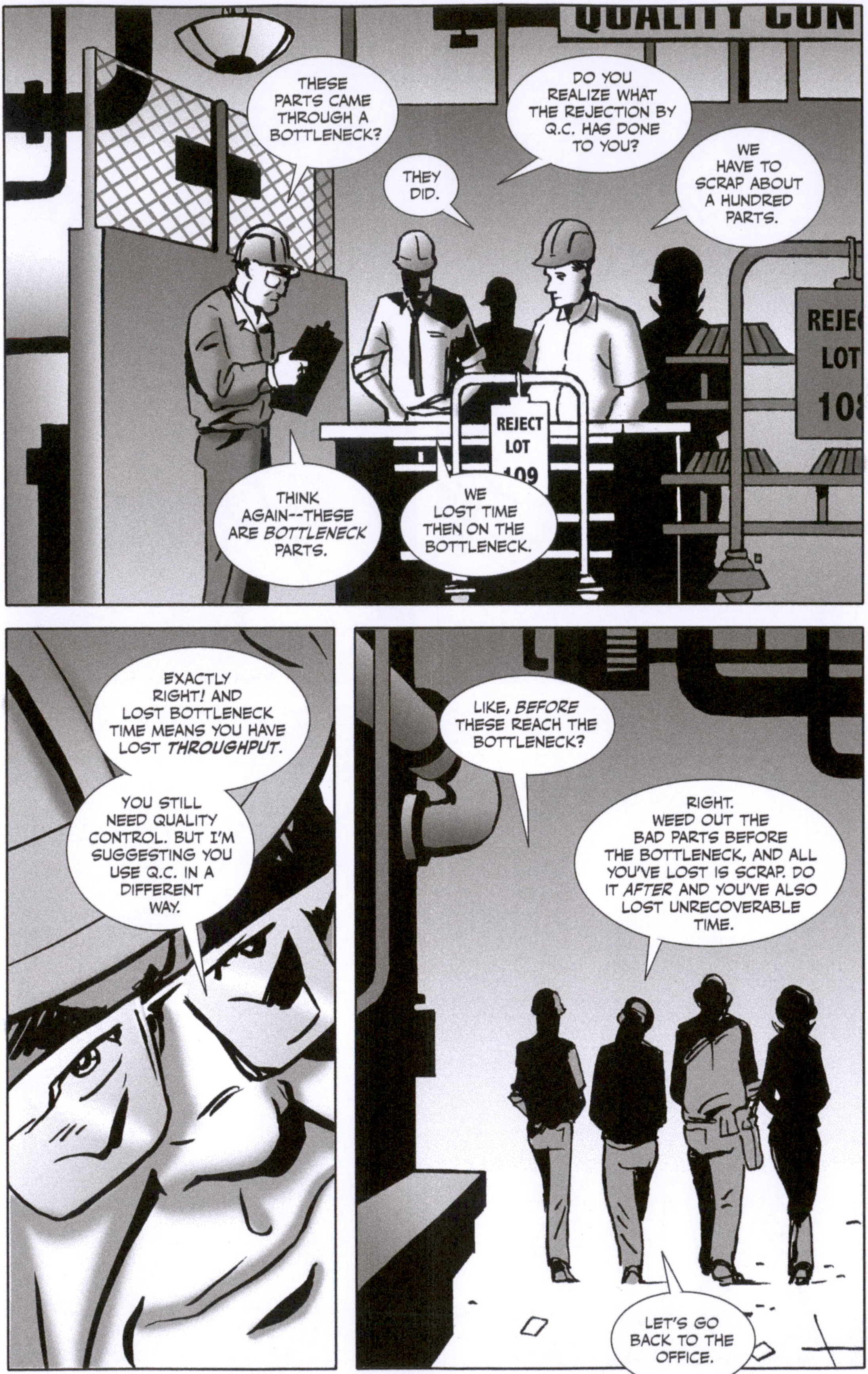
THESE PARTS CAME THROUGH A BOTTLENECK?
THEY DID.
DO YOU REALIZE WHAT THE REJECTION BY Q.C. HAS DONE TO YOU?
WE HAVE TO SCRAP ABOUT A HUNDRED PARTS.
REJECT LOT 109
THINK AGAIN--THESE ARE *BOTTLENECK* PARTS.
WE LOST TIME THEN ON THE BOTTLENECK.
EXACTLY RIGHT! AND LOST BOTTLENECK TIME MEANS YOU HAVE LOST ***THROUGHPUT***.
YOU STILL NEED QUALITY CONTROL. BUT I'M SUGGESTING YOU USE Q.C. IN A DIFFERENT WAY.
LIKE, *BEFORE* THESE REACH THE BOTTLENECK?
RIGHT. WEED OUT THE BAD PARTS BEFORE THE BOTTLENECK, AND ALL YOU'VE LOST IS SCRAP. DO IT *AFTER* AND YOU'VE ALSO LOST UNRECOVERABLE TIME.
LET'S GO BACK TO THE OFFICE.

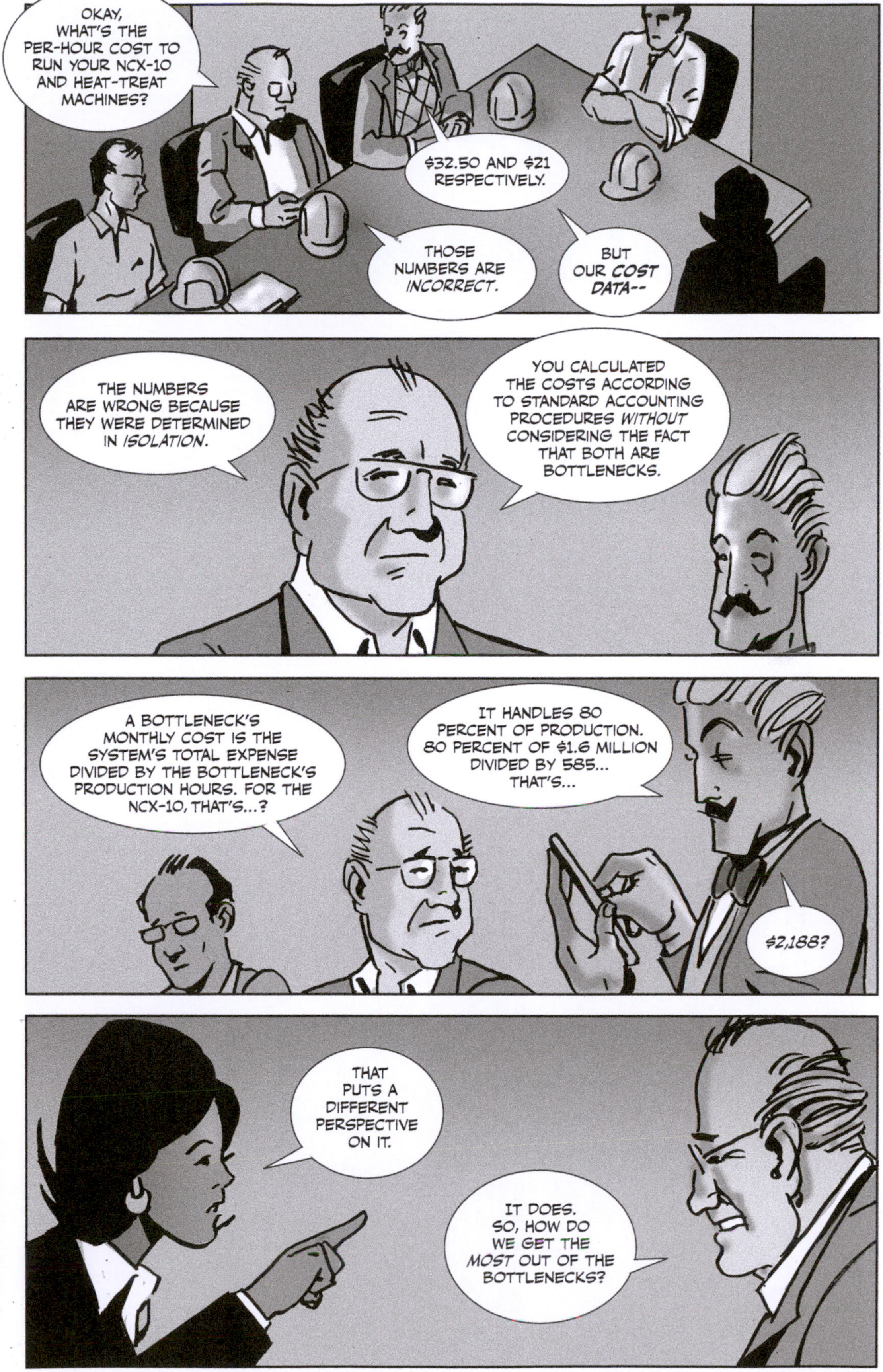
OKAY, WHAT'S THE PER-HOUR COST TO RUN YOUR NCX-10 AND HEAT-TREAT MACHINES?
$32.50 AND $21 RESPECTIVELY.
THOSE NUMBERS ARE *INCORRECT*.
BUT OUR *COST DATA*--
THE NUMBERS ARE WRONG BECAUSE THEY WERE DETERMINED IN *ISOLATION*.
YOU CALCULATED THE COSTS ACCORDING TO STANDARD ACCOUNTING PROCEDURES *WITHOUT* CONSIDERING THE FACT THAT BOTH ARE BOTTLENECKS.
A BOTTLENECK'S MONTHLY COST IS THE SYSTEM'S TOTAL EXPENSE DIVIDED BY THE BOTTLENECK'S PRODUCTION HOURS. FOR THE NCX-10, THAT'S...?
IT HANDLES 80 PERCENT OF PRODUCTION. 80 PERCENT OF $1.6 MILLION DIVIDED BY 585... THAT'S...
$2,188?
THAT PUTS A DIFFERENT PERSPECTIVE ON IT.
IT DOES. SO, HOW DO WE GET THE *MOST* OUT OF THE BOTTLENECKS?

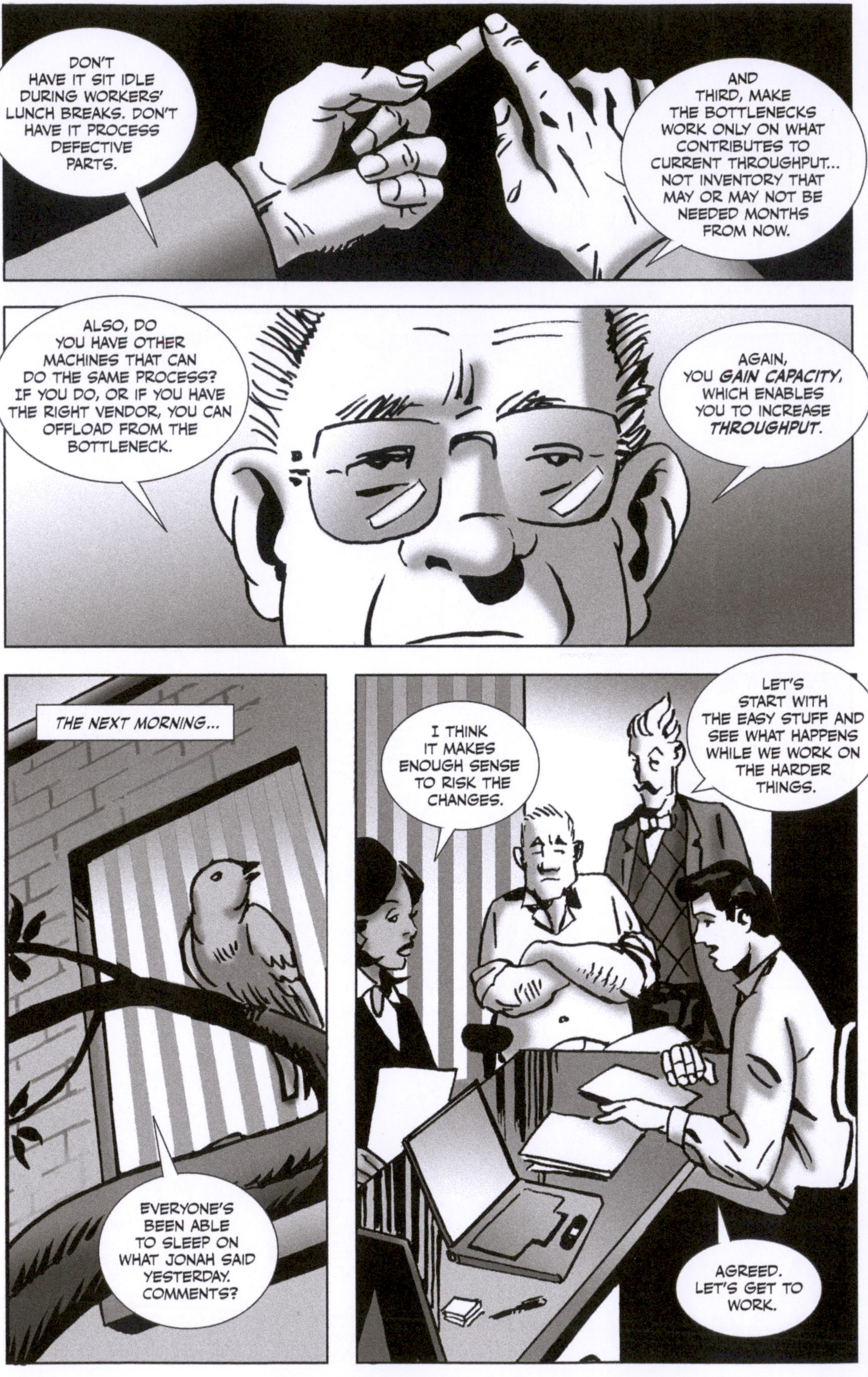

DON'T HAVE IT SIT IDLE DURING WORKERS' LUNCH BREAKS. DON'T HAVE IT PROCESS DEFECTIVE PARTS.
AND THIRD, MAKE THE BOTTLENECKS WORK ONLY ON WHAT CONTRIBUTES TO CURRENT THROUGHPUT... NOT INVENTORY THAT MAY OR MAY NOT BE NEEDED MONTHS FROM NOW.
ALSO, DO YOU HAVE OTHER MACHINES THAT CAN DO THE SAME PROCESS? IF YOU DO, OR IF YOU HAVE THE RIGHT VENDOR, YOU CAN OFFLOAD FROM THE BOTTLENECK.
AGAIN, YOU *GAIN CAPACITY*, WHICH ENABLES YOU TO INCREASE *THROUGHPUT*.
THE NEXT MORNING...
EVERYONE'S BEEN ABLE TO SLEEP ON WHAT JONAH SAID YESTERDAY. COMMENTS?
I THINK IT MAKES ENOUGH SENSE TO RISK THE CHANGES.
LET'S START WITH THE EASY STUFF AND SEE WHAT HAPPENS WHILE WE WORK ON THE HARDER THINGS.
AGREED. LET'S GET TO WORK.

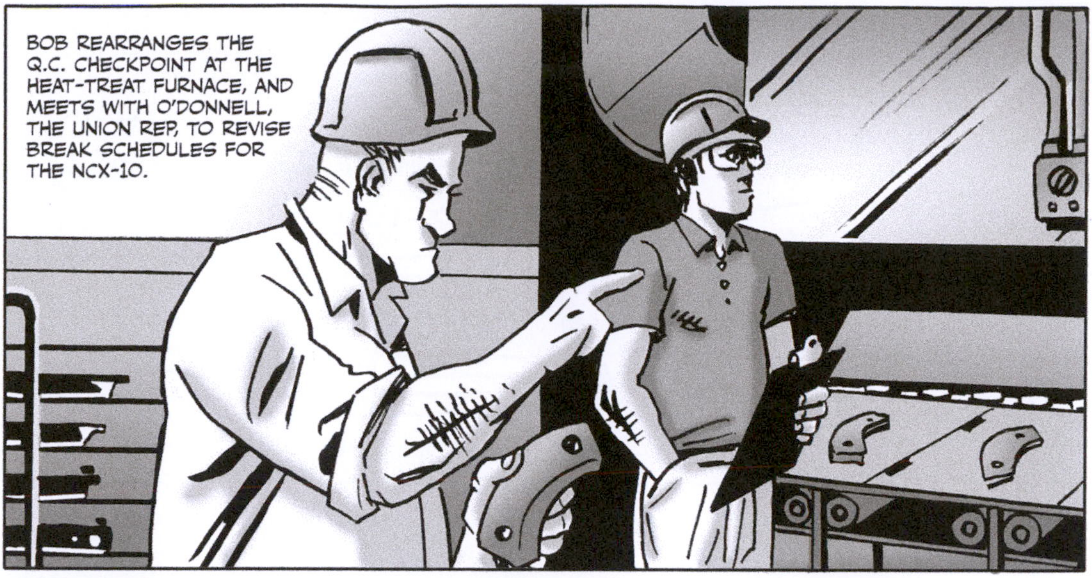
BOB REARRANGES THE Q.C. CHECKPOINT AT THE HEAT-TREAT FURNACE, AND MEETS WITH O'DONNELL, THE UNION REP, TO REVISE BREAK SCHEDULES FOR THE NCX-10.

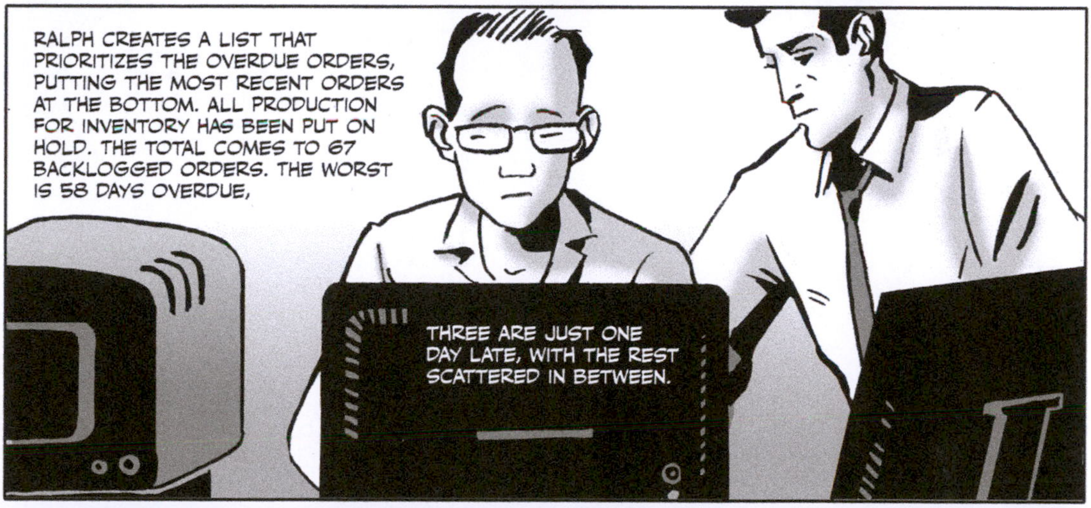
RALPH CREATES A LIST THAT PRIORITIZES THE OVERDUE ORDERS, PUTTING THE MOST RECENT ORDERS AT THE BOTTOM. ALL PRODUCTION FOR INVENTORY HAS BEEN PUT ON HOLD. THE TOTAL COMES TO 67 BACKLOGGED ORDERS. THE WORST IS 58 DAYS OVERDUE,
THREE ARE JUST ONE DAY LATE, WITH THE REST SCATTERED IN BETWEEN.

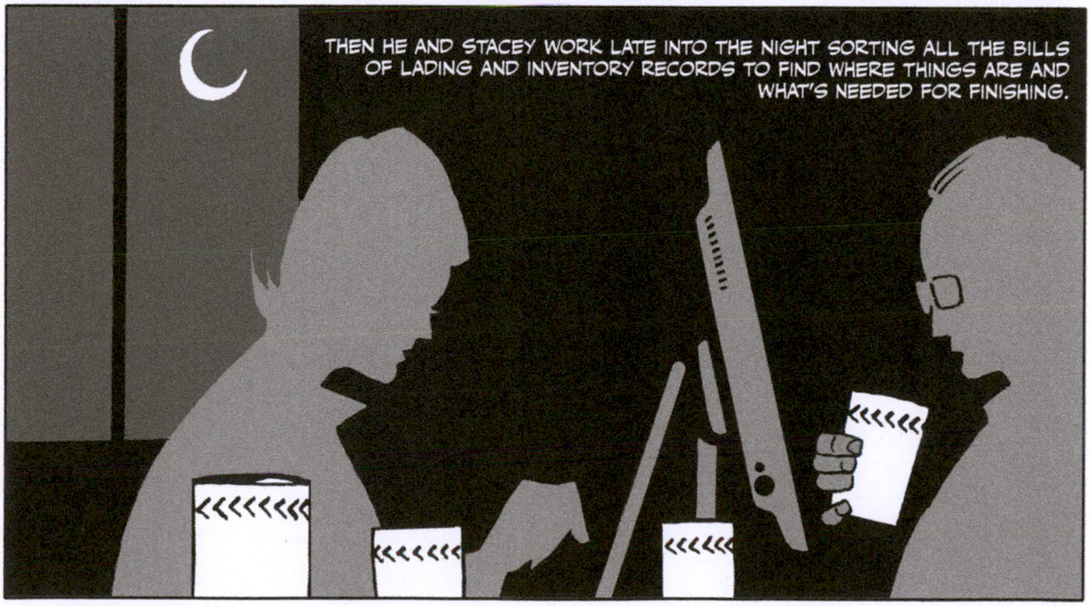
THEN HE AND STACEY WORK LATE INTO THE NIGHT SORTING ALL THE BILLS OF LADING AND INVENTORY RECORDS TO FIND WHERE THINGS ARE AND WHAT'S NEEDED FOR FINISHING.

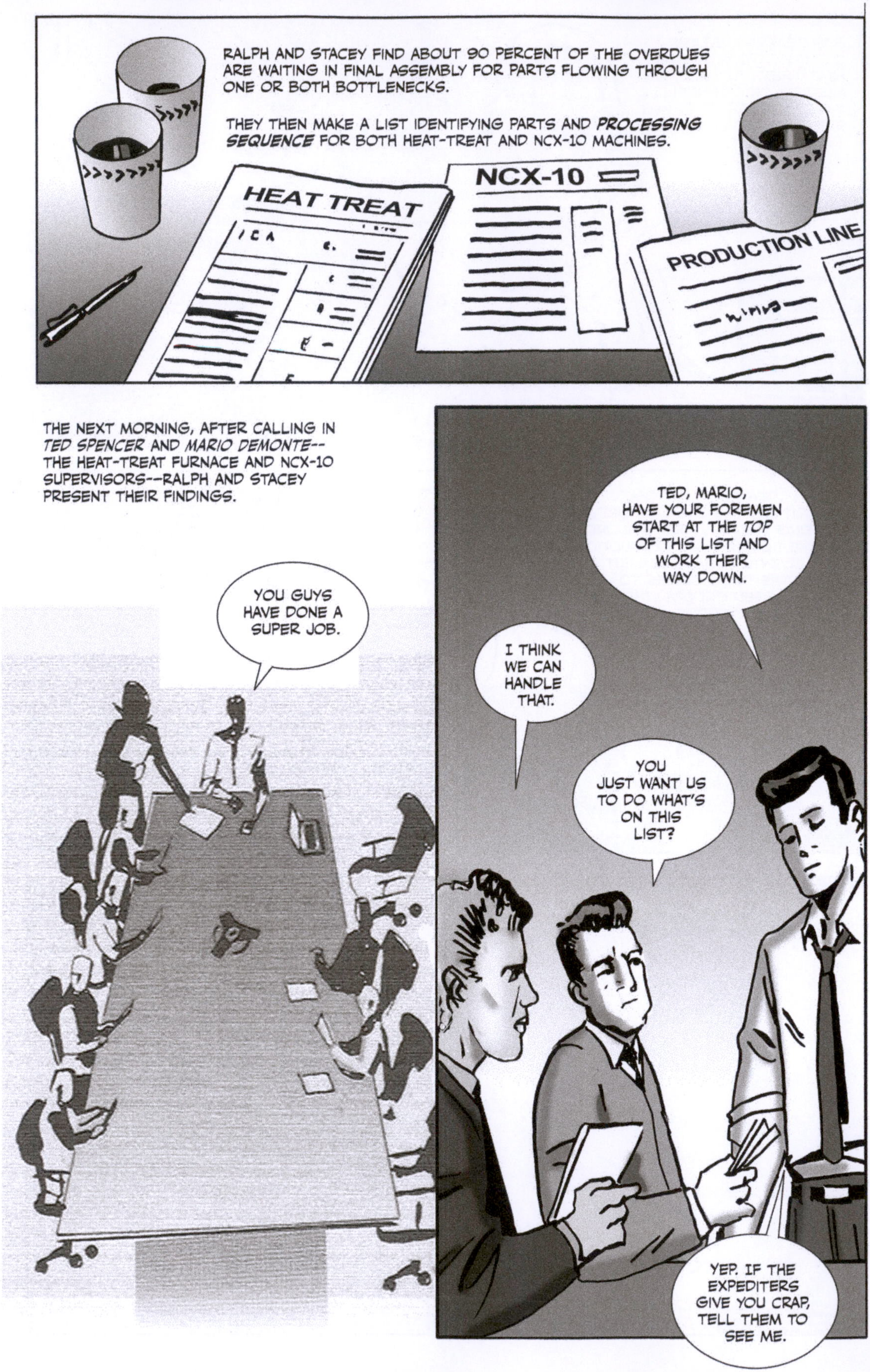
RALPH AND STACEY FIND ABOUT 90 PERCENT OF THE OVERDUES ARE WAITING IN FINAL ASSEMBLY FOR PARTS FLOWING THROUGH ONE OR BOTH BOTTLENECKS.
THEY THEN MAKE A LIST IDENTIFYING PARTS AND *PROCESSING SEQUENCE* FOR BOTH HEAT-TREAT AND NCX-10 MACHINES.
HEAT TREAT
NCX-10
PRODUCTION LINE
THE NEXT MORNING, AFTER CALLING IN *TED SPENCER* AND *MARIO DEMONTE*--THE HEAT-TREAT FURNACE AND NCX-10 SUPERVISORS--RALPH AND STACEY PRESENT THEIR FINDINGS.
YOU GUYS HAVE DONE A SUPER JOB.
TED, MARIO, HAVE YOUR FOREMEN START AT THE *TOP* OF THIS LIST AND WORK THEIR WAY DOWN.
I THINK WE CAN HANDLE THAT.
YOU JUST WANT US TO DO WHAT'S ON THIS LIST?
YEP. IF THE EXPEDITERS GIVE YOU CRAP, TELL THEM TO SEE ME.

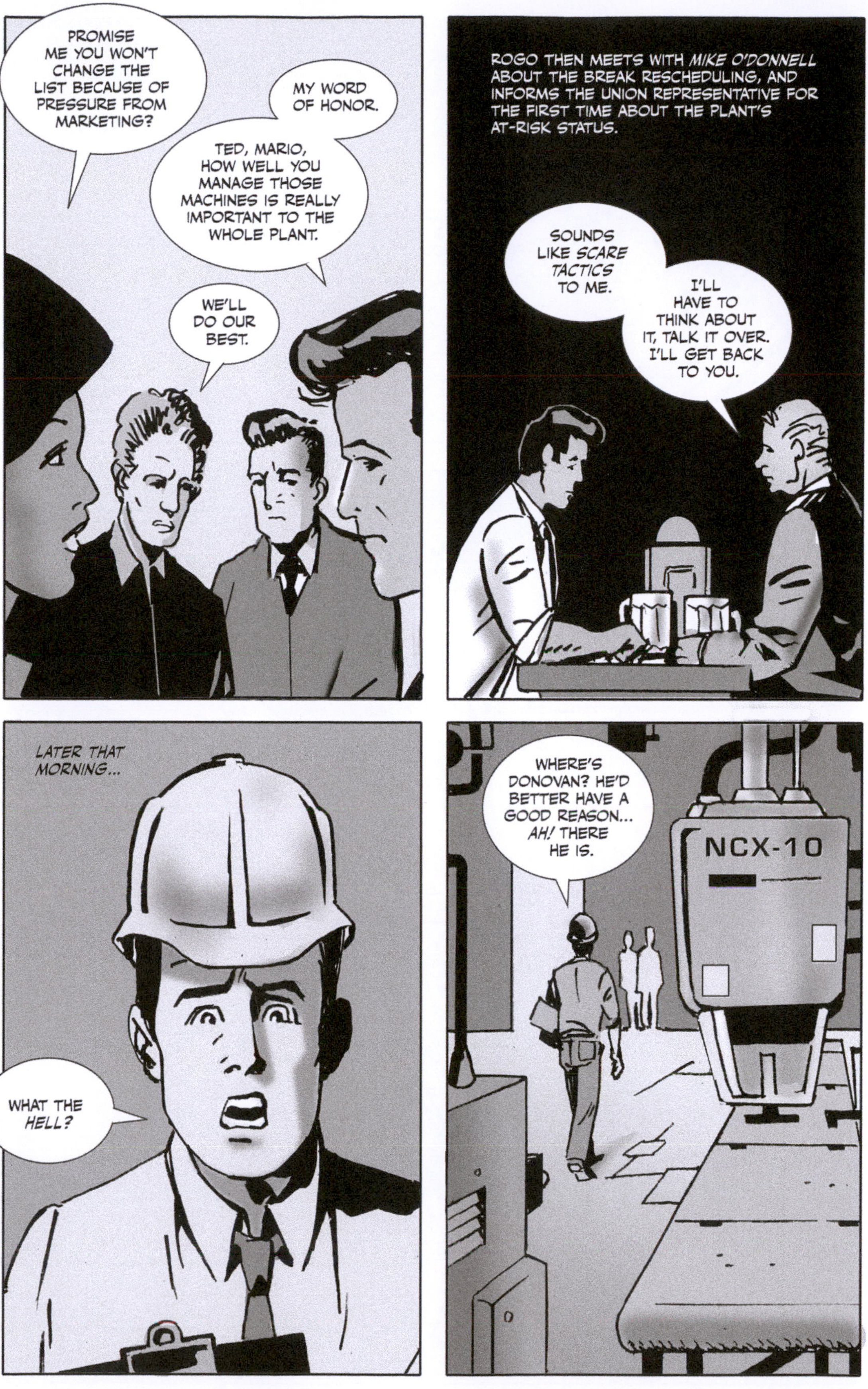
PROMISE ME YOU WON'T CHANGE THE LIST BECAUSE OF PRESSURE FROM MARKETING?
MY WORD OF HONOR.
TED, MARIO, HOW WELL YOU MANAGE THOSE MACHINES IS REALLY IMPORTANT TO THE WHOLE PLANT.
WE'LL DO OUR BEST.
ROGO THEN MEETS WITH *MIKE O'DONNELL* ABOUT THE BREAK RESCHEDULING, AND INFORMS THE UNION REPRESENTATIVE FOR THE FIRST TIME ABOUT THE PLANT'S AT-RISK STATUS.
SOUNDS LIKE *SCARE TACTICS* TO ME.
I'LL HAVE TO THINK ABOUT IT, TALK IT OVER. I'LL GET BACK TO YOU.
LATER THAT MORNING...
WHAT THE *HELL?*
WHERE'S DONOVAN? HE'D BETTER HAVE A GOOD REASON... *AH!* THERE HE IS.
NCX-10

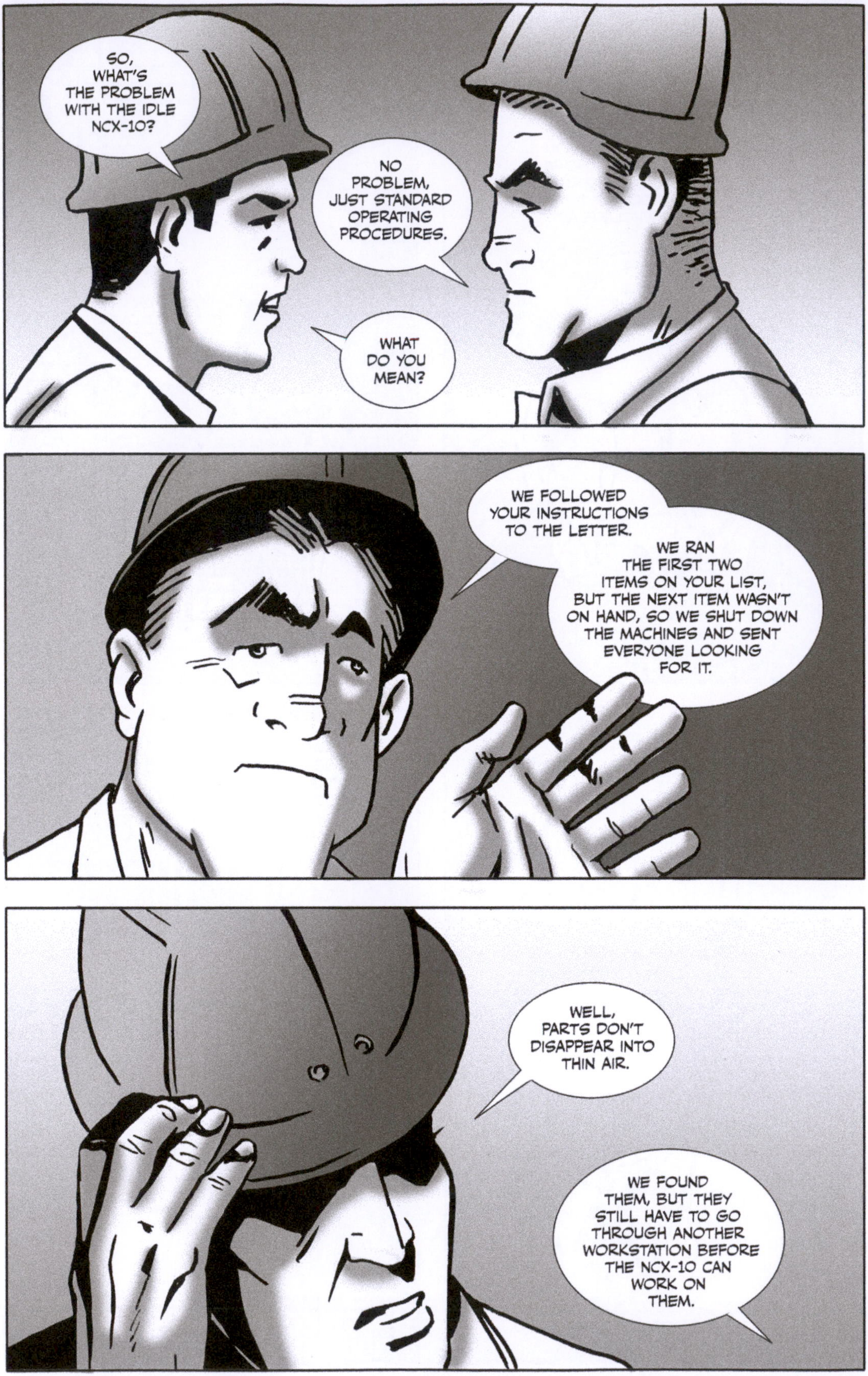
SO, WHAT'S THE PROBLEM WITH THE IDLE NCX-10?
NO PROBLEM, JUST STANDARD OPERATING PROCEDURES.
WHAT DO YOU MEAN?
WE FOLLOWED YOUR INSTRUCTIONS TO THE LETTER.
WE RAN THE FIRST TWO ITEMS ON YOUR LIST, BUT THE NEXT ITEM WASN'T ON HAND, SO WE SHUT DOWN THE MACHINES AND SENT EVERYONE LOOKING FOR IT.
WELL, PARTS DON'T DISAPPEAR INTO THIN AIR.
WE FOUND THEM, BUT THEY STILL HAVE TO GO THROUGH ANOTHER WORKSTATION BEFORE THE NCX-10 CAN WORK ON THEM.

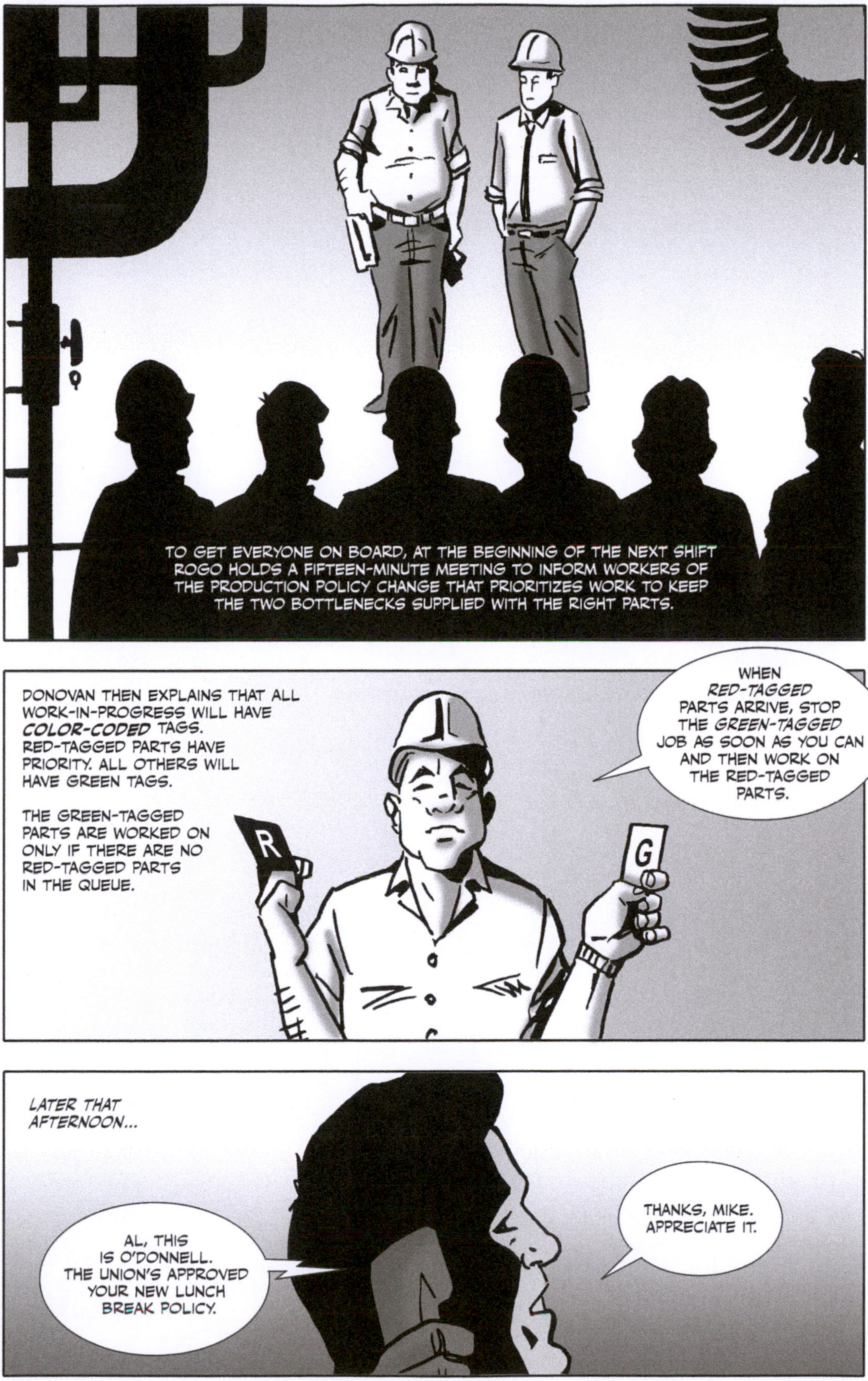
TO GET EVERYONE ON BOARD, AT THE BEGINNING OF THE NEXT SHIFT ROGO HOLDS A FIFTEEN-MINUTE MEETING TO INFORM WORKERS OF THE PRODUCTION POLICY CHANGE THAT PRIORITIZES WORK TO KEEP THE TWO BOTTLENECKS SUPPLIED WITH THE RIGHT PARTS.
DONOVAN THEN EXPLAINS THAT ALL WORK-IN-PROGRESS WILL HAVE *COLOR-CODED* TAGS. RED-TAGGED PARTS HAVE PRIORITY. ALL OTHERS WILL HAVE GREEN TAGS.
THE GREEN-TAGGED PARTS ARE WORKED ON ONLY IF THERE ARE NO RED-TAGGED PARTS IN THE QUEUE.
R
G
WHEN *RED-TAGGED* PARTS ARRIVE, STOP THE *GREEN-TAGGED* JOB AS SOON AS YOU CAN AND THEN WORK ON THE RED-TAGGED PARTS.
LATER THAT AFTERNOON...
AL, THIS IS O'DONNELL. THE UNION'S APPROVED YOUR NEW LUNCH BREAK POLICY.
THANKS, MIKE. APPRECIATE IT.

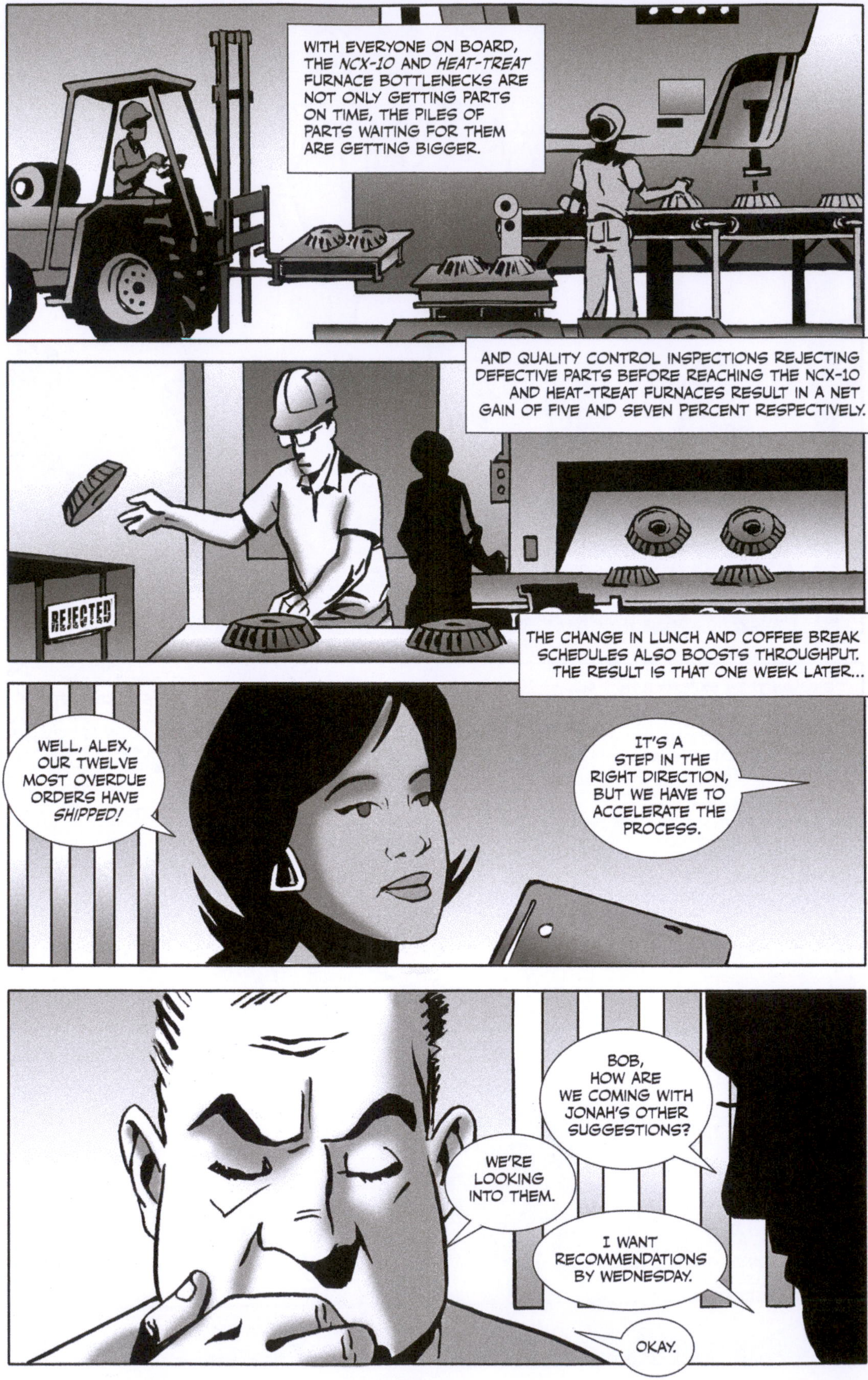
WITH EVERYONE ON BOARD, THE *NCX-10* AND *HEAT-TREAT* FURNACE BOTTLENECKS ARE NOT ONLY GETTING PARTS ON TIME, THE PILES OF PARTS WAITING FOR THEM ARE GETTING BIGGER.
AND QUALITY CONTROL INSPECTIONS REJECTING DEFECTIVE PARTS BEFORE REACHING THE NCX-10 AND HEAT-TREAT FURNACES RESULT IN A NET GAIN OF FIVE AND SEVEN PERCENT RESPECTIVELY.
REJECTED
THE CHANGE IN LUNCH AND COFFEE BREAK SCHEDULES ALSO BOOSTS THROUGHPUT. THE RESULT IS THAT ONE WEEK LATER...
WELL, ALEX, OUR TWELVE MOST OVERDUE ORDERS HAVE *SHIPPED!*
IT'S A STEP IN THE RIGHT DIRECTION, BUT WE HAVE TO ACCELERATE THE PROCESS.
BOB, HOW ARE WE COMING WITH JONAH'S OTHER SUGGESTIONS?
WE'RE LOOKING INTO THEM.
I WANT RECOMMENDATIONS BY WEDNESDAY.
OKAY.

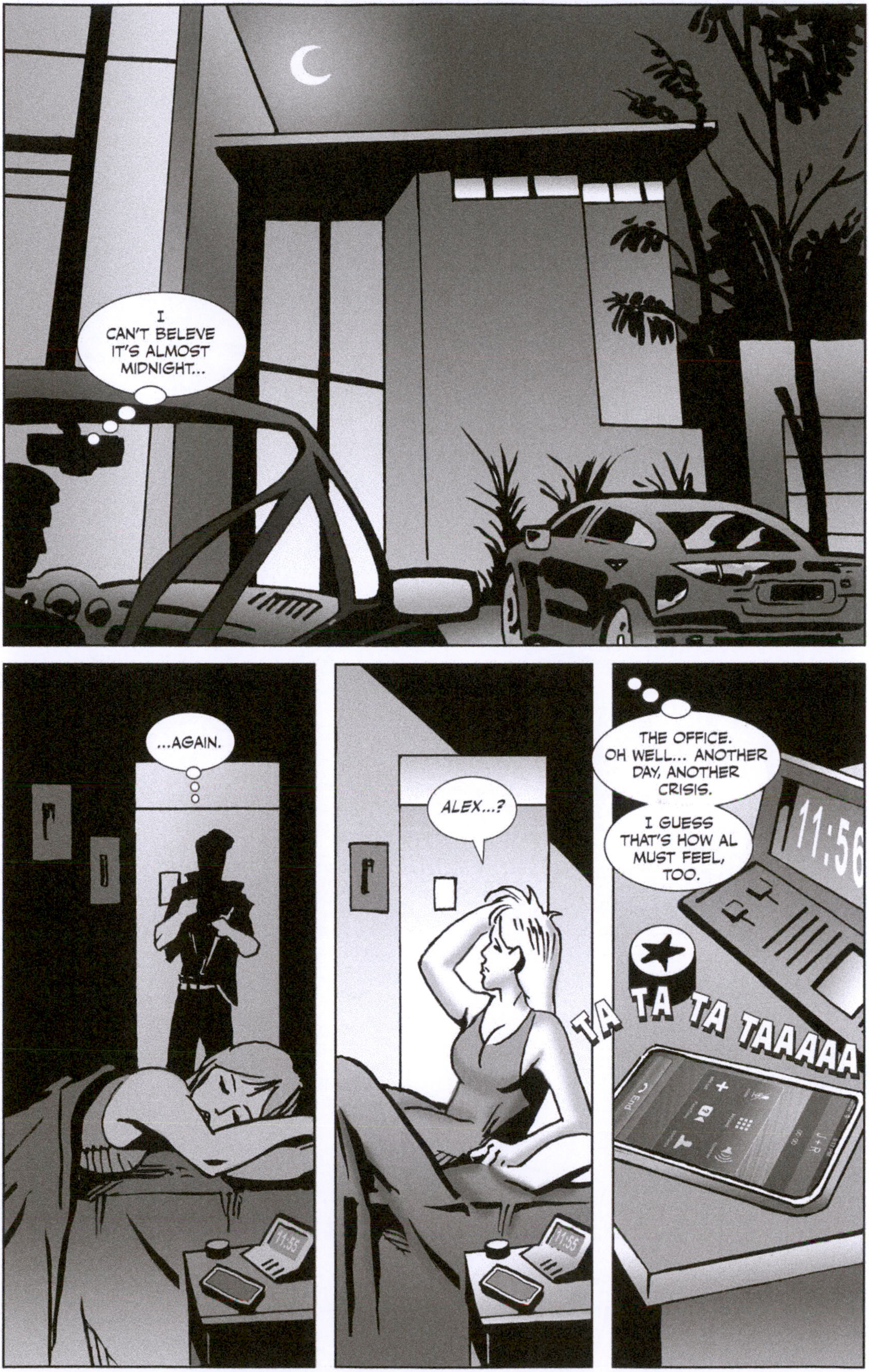
I CAN'T BELEVE IT'S ALMOST MIDNIGHT...
...AGAIN.
ALEX...?
THE OFFICE. OH WELL... ANOTHER DAY, ANOTHER CRISIS.
I GUESS THAT'S HOW AL MUST FEEL, TOO.
11:56
TA TA TA TAAAAA

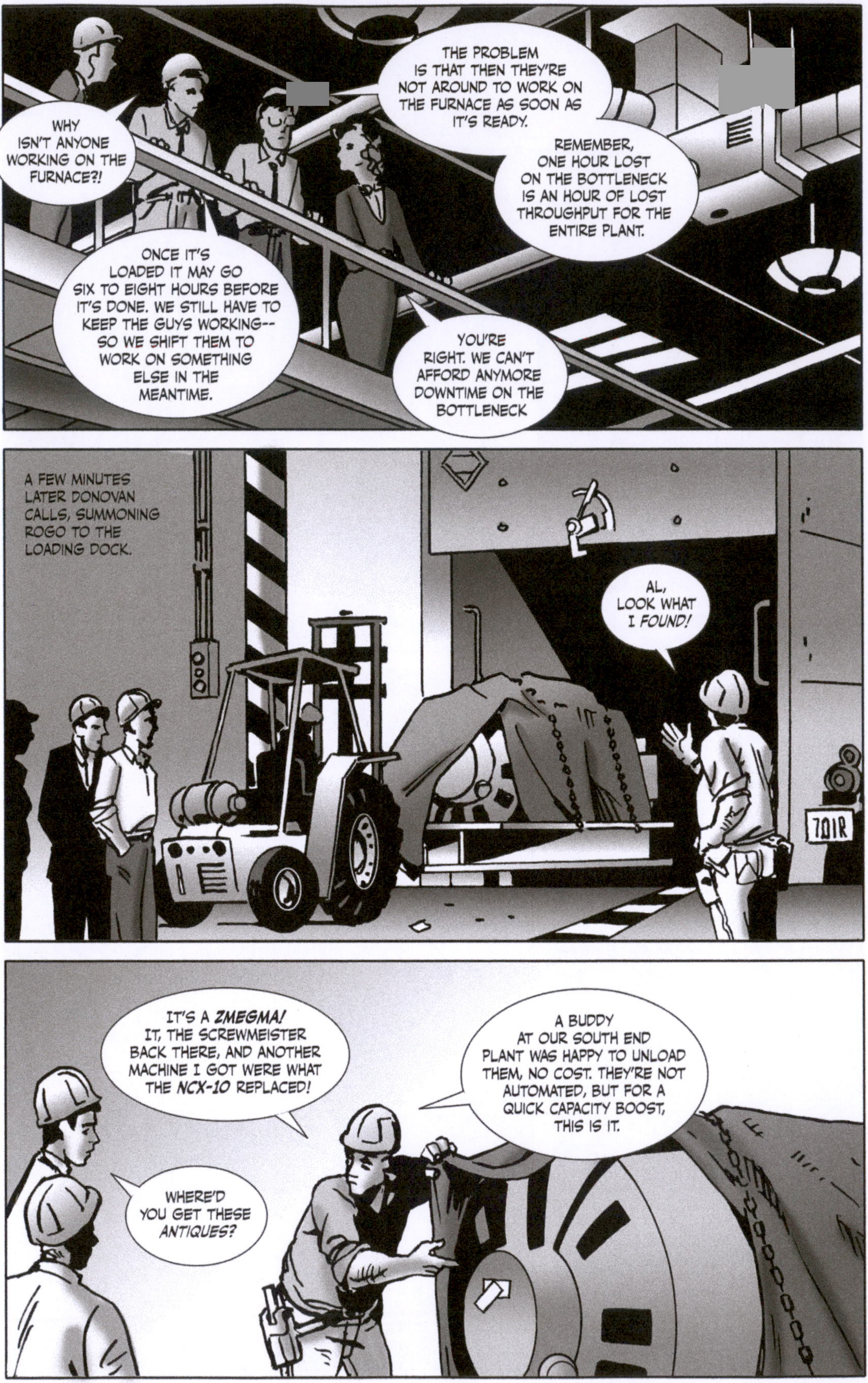
WHY ISN'T ANYONE WORKING ON THE FURNACE?!
THE PROBLEM IS THAT THEN THEY'RE NOT AROUND TO WORK ON THE FURNACE AS SOON AS IT'S READY.
REMEMBER, ONE HOUR LOST ON THE BOTTLENECK IS AN HOUR OF LOST THROUGHPUT FOR THE ENTIRE PLANT.
ONCE IT'S LOADED IT MAY GO SIX TO EIGHT HOURS BEFORE IT'S DONE. WE STILL HAVE TO KEEP THE GUYS WORKING-- SO WE SHIFT THEM TO WORK ON SOMETHING ELSE IN THE MEANTIME.
YOU'RE RIGHT. WE CAN'T AFFORD ANYMORE DOWNTIME ON THE BOTTLENECK
A FEW MINUTES LATER DONOVAN CALLS, SUMMONING ROGO TO THE LOADING DOCK.
AL, LOOK WHAT I *FOUND!*
701R
IT'S A ***ZMEGMA!*** IT, THE SCREWMEISTER BACK THERE, AND ANOTHER MACHINE I GOT WERE WHAT THE ***NCX-10*** REPLACED!
A BUDDY AT OUR SOUTH END PLANT WAS HAPPY TO UNLOAD THEM, NO COST. THEY'RE NOT AUTOMATED, BUT FOR A QUICK CAPACITY BOOST, THIS IS IT.
WHERE'D YOU GET THESE *ANTIQUES?*

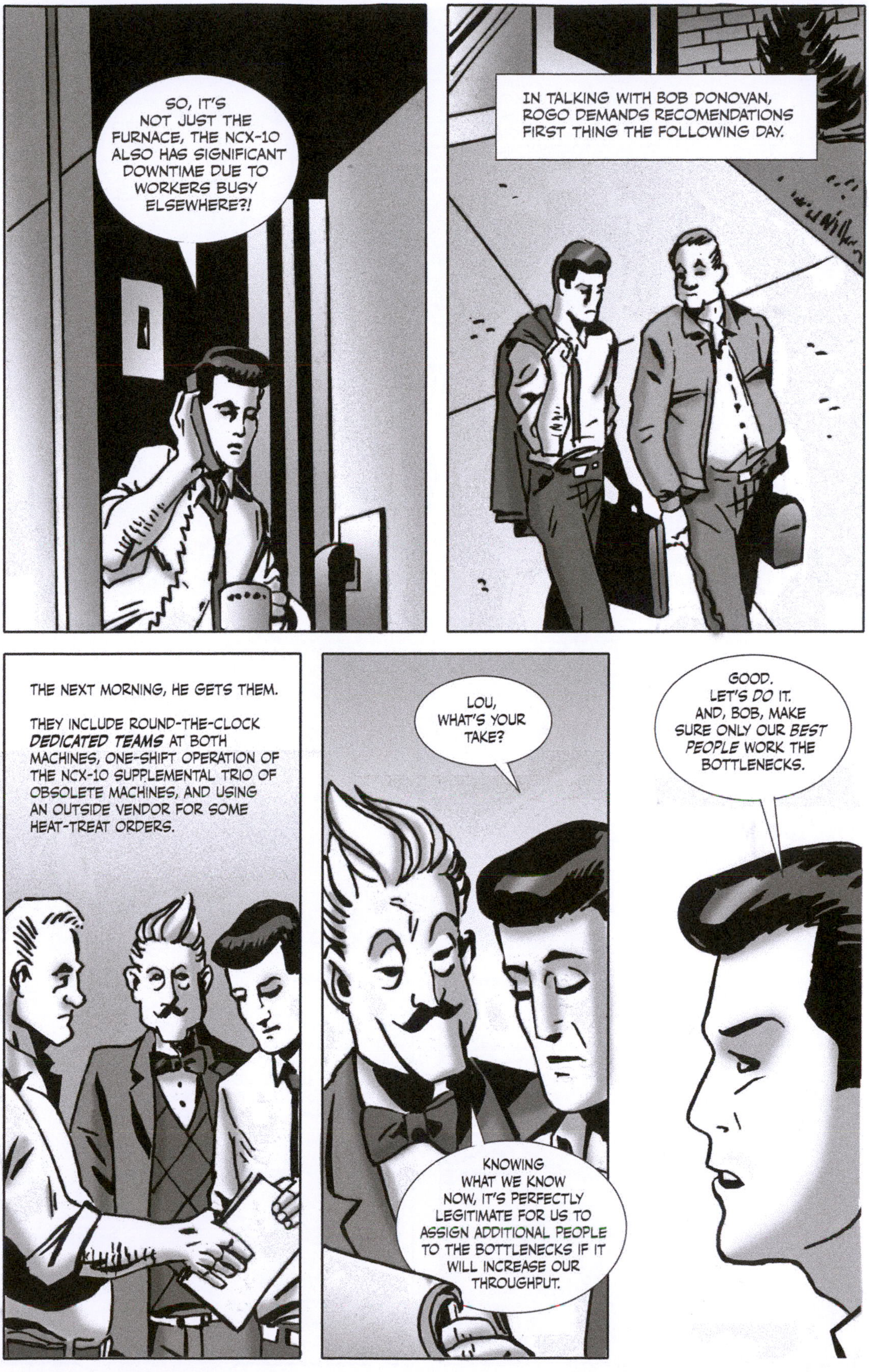
SO, IT'S NOT JUST THE FURNACE, THE NCX-10 ALSO HAS SIGNIFICANT DOWNTIME DUE TO WORKERS BUSY ELSEWHERE?!
IN TALKING WITH BOB DONOVAN, ROGO DEMANDS RECOMENDATIONS FIRST THING THE FOLLOWING DAY.
THE NEXT MORNING, HE GETS THEM.
THEY INCLUDE ROUND-THE-CLOCK ***DEDICATED TEAMS*** AT BOTH MACHINES, ONE-SHIFT OPERATION OF THE NCX-10 SUPPLEMENTAL TRIO OF OBSOLETE MACHINES, AND USING AN OUTSIDE VENDOR FOR SOME HEAT-TREAT ORDERS.
LOU, WHAT'S YOUR TAKE?
KNOWING WHAT WE KNOW NOW, IT'S PERFECTLY LEGITIMATE FOR US TO ASSIGN ADDITIONAL PEOPLE TO THE BOTTLENECKS IF IT WILL INCREASE OUR THROUGHPUT.
GOOD. LET'S *DO* IT. AND, BOB, MAKE SURE ONLY OUR *BEST PEOPLE* WORK THE BOTTLENECKS.

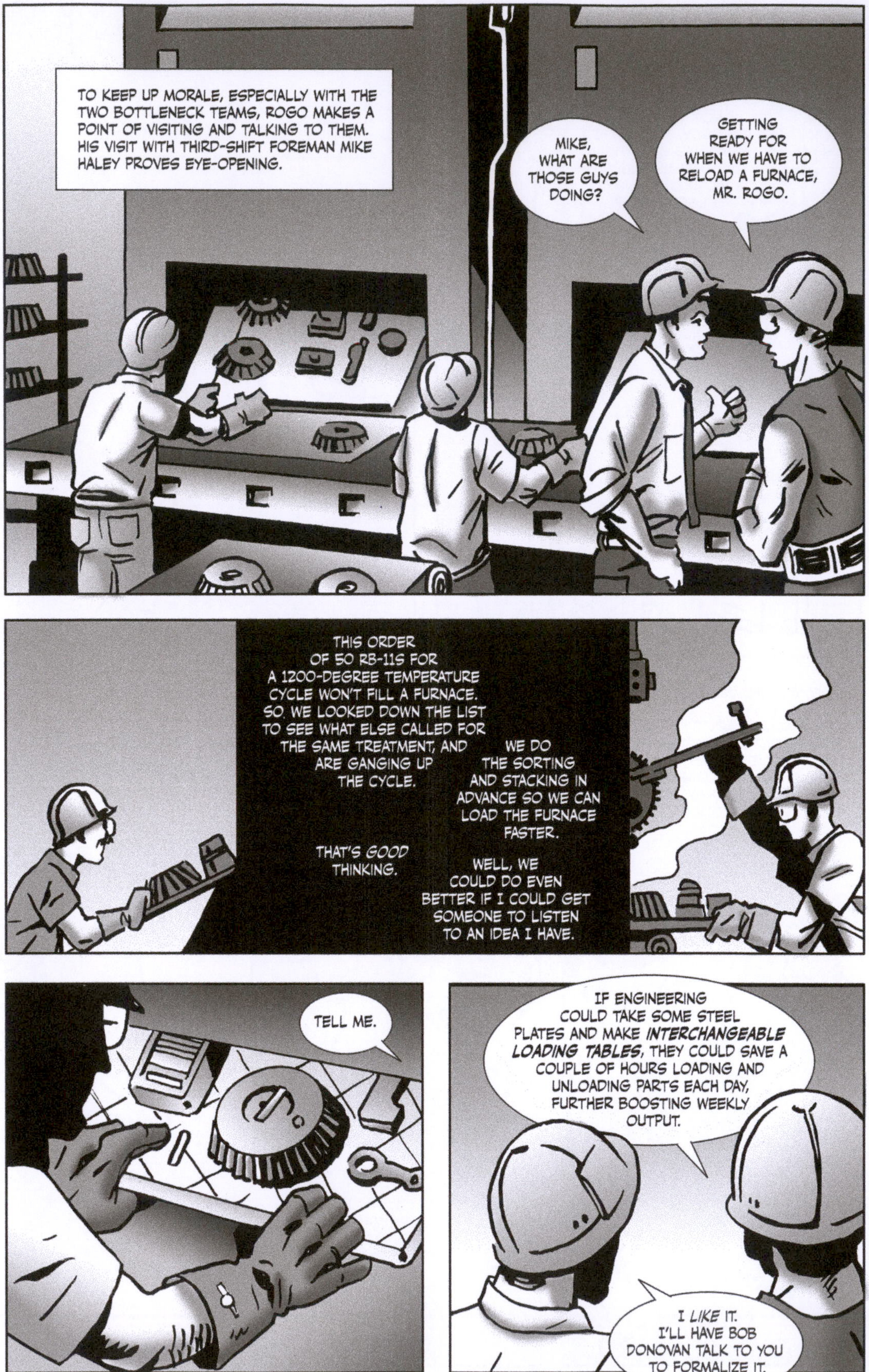
TO KEEP UP MORALE, ESPECIALLY WITH THE TWO BOTTLENECK TEAMS, ROGO MAKES A POINT OF VISITING AND TALKING TO THEM. HIS VISIT WITH THIRD-SHIFT FOREMAN MIKE HALEY PROVES EYE-OPENING.
MIKE, WHAT ARE THOSE GUYS DOING?
GETTING READY FOR WHEN WE HAVE TO RELOAD A FURNACE, MR. ROGO.
THIS ORDER OF 50 RB-11S FOR A 1200-DEGREE TEMPERATURE CYCLE WON'T FILL A FURNACE. SO, WE LOOKED DOWN THE LIST TO SEE WHAT ELSE CALLED FOR THE SAME TREATMENT, AND ARE GANGING UP THE CYCLE.
WE DO THE SORTING AND STACKING IN ADVANCE SO WE CAN LOAD THE FURNACE FASTER.
THAT'S *GOOD* THINKING.
WELL, WE COULD DO EVEN BETTER IF I COULD GET SOMEONE TO LISTEN TO AN IDEA I HAVE.
TELL ME.
IF ENGINEERING COULD TAKE SOME STEEL PLATES AND MAKE ***INTERCHANGEABLE LOADING TABLES***, THEY COULD SAVE A COUPLE OF HOURS LOADING AND UNLOADING PARTS EACH DAY, FURTHER BOOSTING WEEKLY OUTPUT.
I *LIKE* IT. I'LL HAVE BOB DONOVAN TALK TO YOU TO FORMALIZE IT.

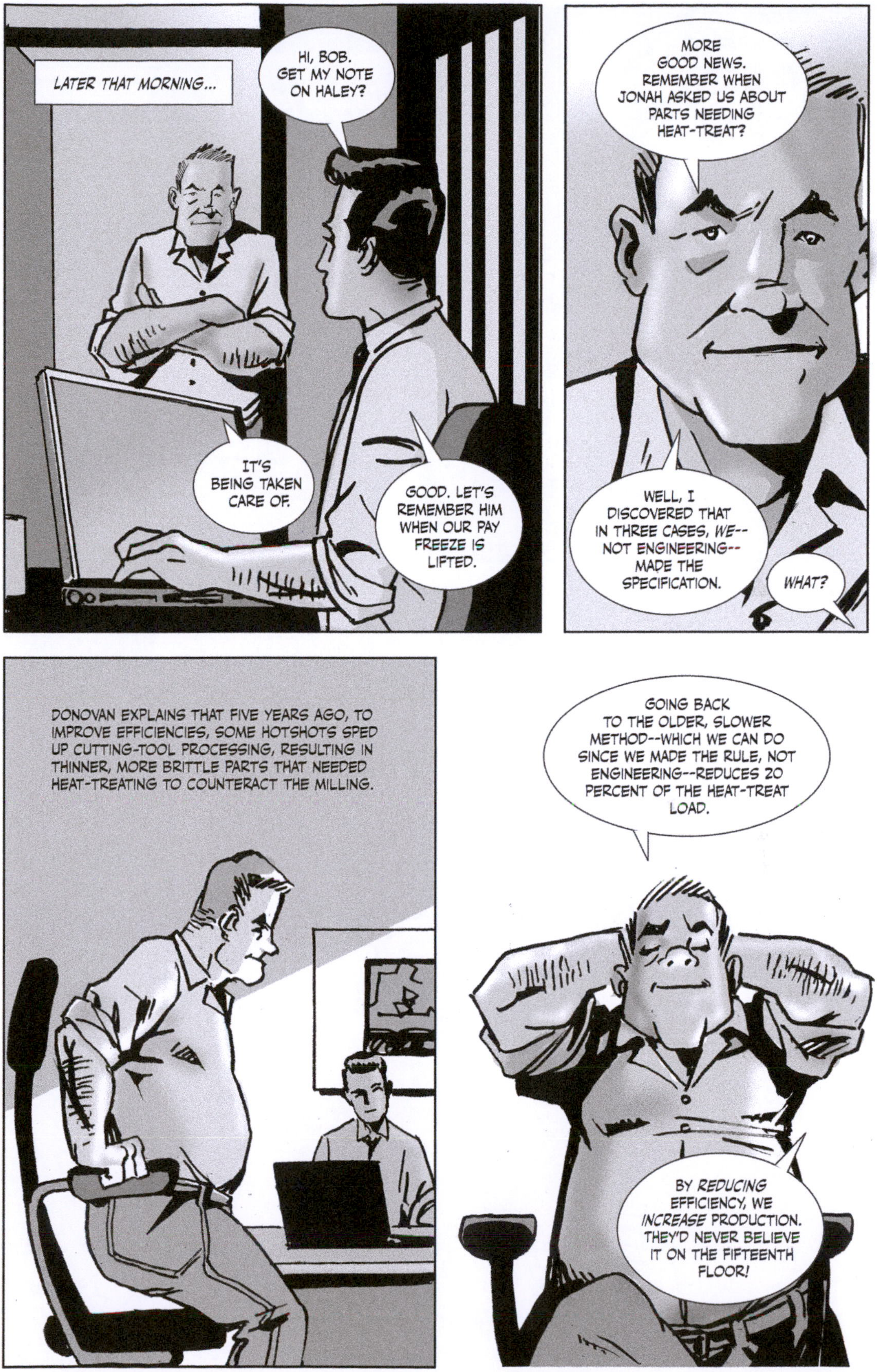
LATER THAT MORNING...
HI, BOB. GET MY NOTE ON HALEY?
IT'S BEING TAKEN CARE OF.
GOOD. LET'S REMEMBER HIM WHEN OUR PAY FREEZE IS LIFTED.
MORE GOOD NEWS. REMEMBER WHEN JONAH ASKED US ABOUT PARTS NEEDING HEAT-TREAT?
WELL, I DISCOVERED THAT IN THREE CASES, *WE*--NOT ENGINEERING--MADE THE SPECIFICATION.
WHAT?
DONOVAN EXPLAINS THAT FIVE YEARS AGO, TO IMPROVE EFFICIENCIES, SOME HOTSHOTS SPED UP CUTTING-TOOL PROCESSING, RESULTING IN THINNER, MORE BRITTLE PARTS THAT NEEDED HEAT-TREATING TO COUNTERACT THE MILLING.
GOING BACK TO THE OLDER, SLOWER METHOD--WHICH WE CAN DO SINCE WE MADE THE RULE, NOT ENGINEERING--REDUCES 20 PERCENT OF THE HEAT-TREAT LOAD.
BY *REDUCING* EFFICIENCY, WE *INCREASE* PRODUCTION. THEY'D NEVER BELIEVE IT ON THE FIFTEENTH FLOOR!

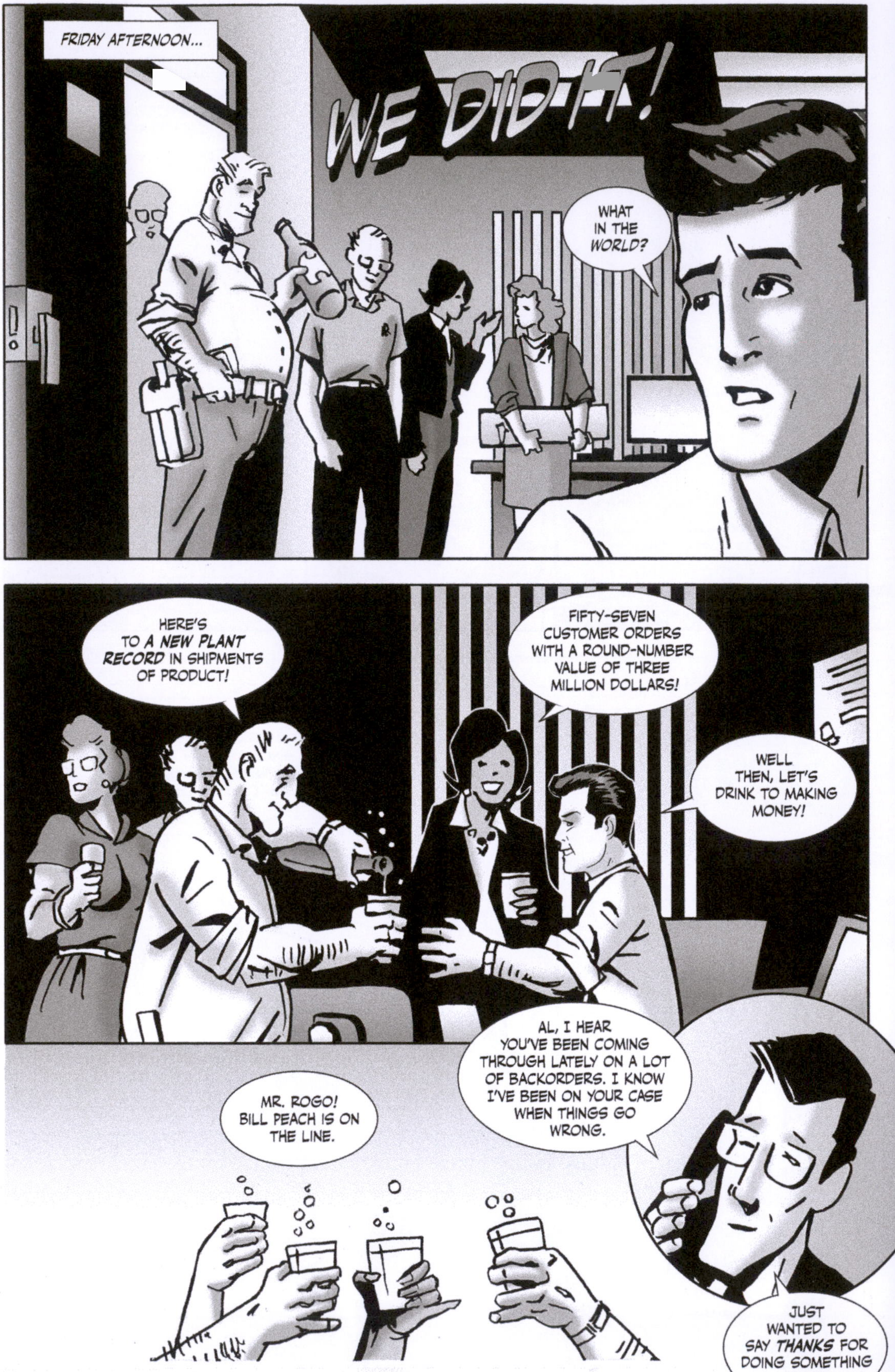
FRIDAY AFTERNOON...
WE DID IT!
WHAT IN THE WORLD?
HERE'S TO A NEW PLANT RECORD IN SHIPMENTS OF PRODUCT!
FIFTY-SEVEN CUSTOMER ORDERS WITH A ROUND-NUMBER VALUE OF THREE MILLION DOLLARS!
WELL THEN, LET'S DRINK TO MAKING MONEY!
MR. ROGO! BILL PEACH IS ON THE LINE.
AL, I HEAR YOU'VE BEEN COMING THROUGH LATELY ON A LOT OF BACKORDERS. I KNOW I'VE BEEN ON YOUR CASE WHEN THINGS GO WRONG.
JUST WANTED TO SAY THANKS FOR DOING SOMETHING RIGHT.

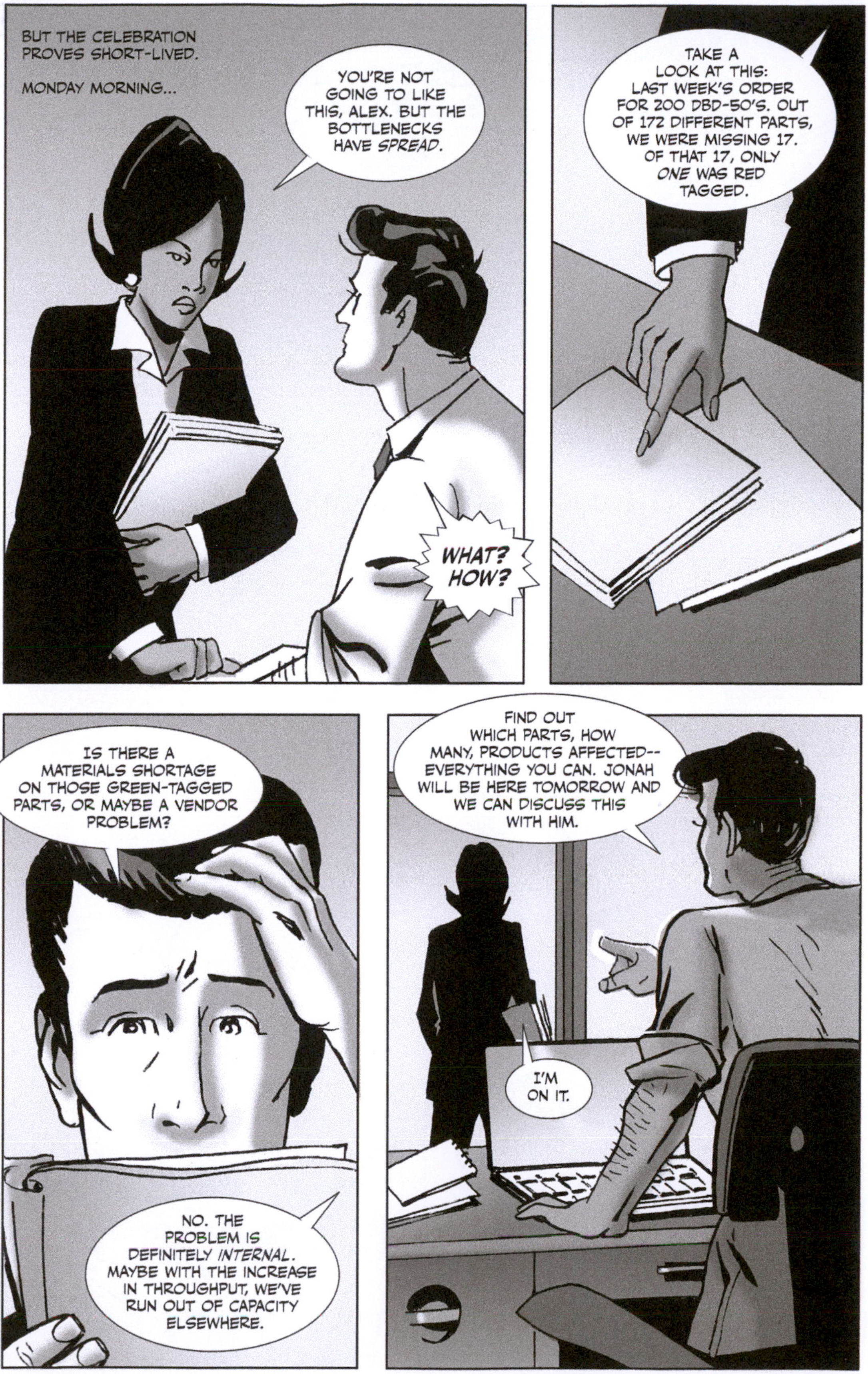
BUT THE CELEBRATION PROVES SHORT-LIVED.
MONDAY MORNING...
YOU'RE NOT GOING TO LIKE THIS, ALEX. BUT THE BOTTLENECKS HAVE *SPREAD*.
WHAT? HOW?
TAKE A LOOK AT THIS: LAST WEEK'S ORDER FOR 200 DBD-50'S. OUT OF 172 DIFFERENT PARTS, WE WERE MISSING 17. OF THAT 17, ONLY *ONE* WAS RED TAGGED.
IS THERE A MATERIALS SHORTAGE ON THOSE GREEN-TAGGED PARTS, OR MAYBE A VENDOR PROBLEM?
NO. THE PROBLEM IS DEFINITELY *INTERNAL*. MAYBE WITH THE INCREASE IN THROUGHPUT, WE'VE RUN OUT OF CAPACITY ELSEWHERE.
FIND OUT WHICH PARTS, HOW MANY, PRODUCTS AFFECTED-- EVERYTHING YOU CAN. JONAH WILL BE HERE TOMORROW AND WE CAN DISCUSS THIS WITH HIM.
I'M ON IT.

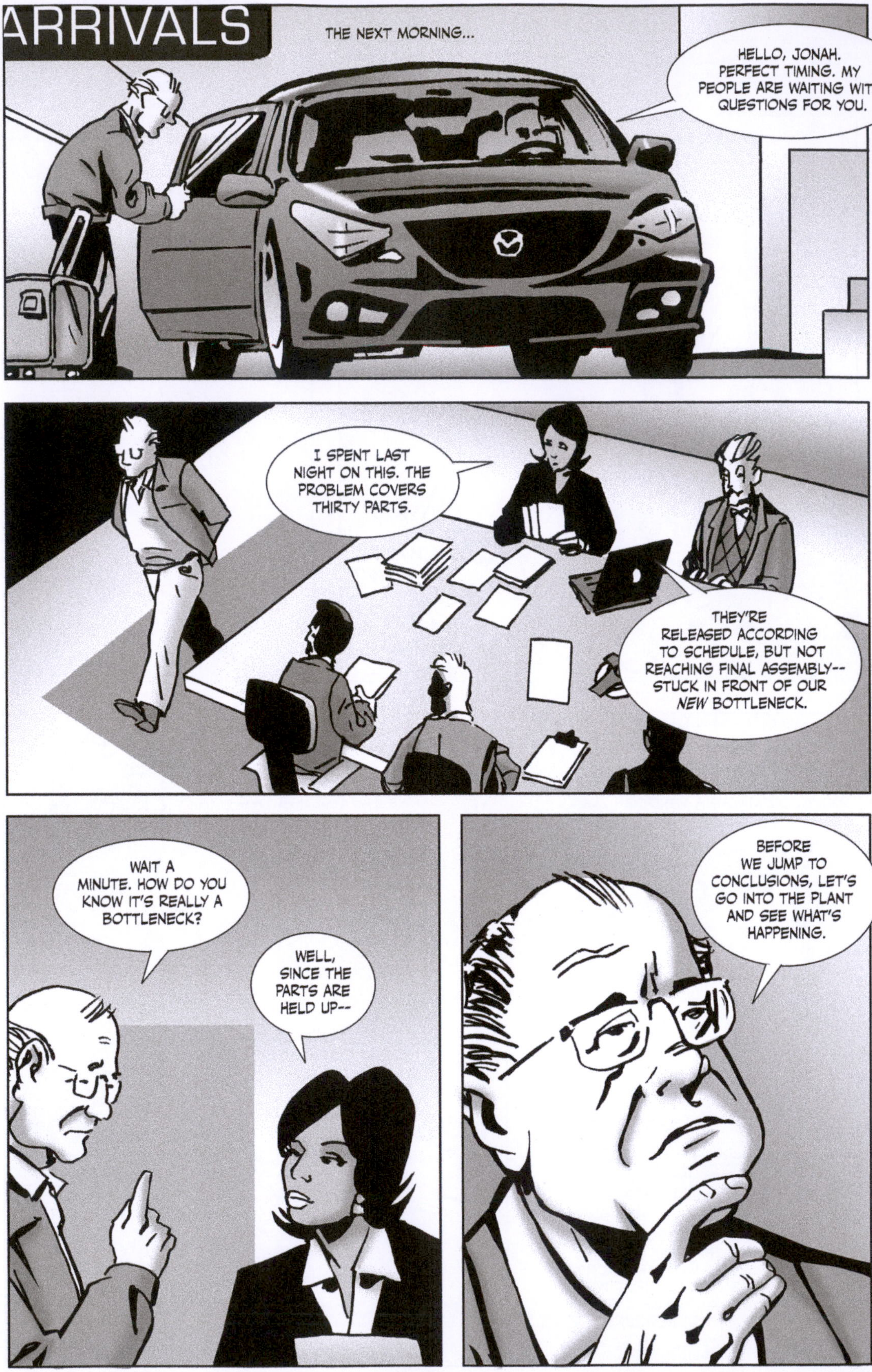
ARRIVALS
THE NEXT MORNING...
HELLO, JONAH. PERFECT TIMING. MY PEOPLE ARE WAITING WITH QUESTIONS FOR YOU.
I SPENT LAST NIGHT ON THIS. THE PROBLEM COVERS THIRTY PARTS.
THEY'RE RELEASED ACCORDING TO SCHEDULE, BUT NOT REACHING FINAL ASSEMBLY-- STUCK IN FRONT OF OUR *NEW* BOTTLENECK.
WAIT A MINUTE. HOW DO YOU KNOW IT'S REALLY A BOTTLENECK?
WELL, SINCE THE PARTS ARE HELD UP--
BEFORE WE JUMP TO CONCLUSIONS, LET'S GO INTO THE PLANT AND SEE WHAT'S HAPPENING.

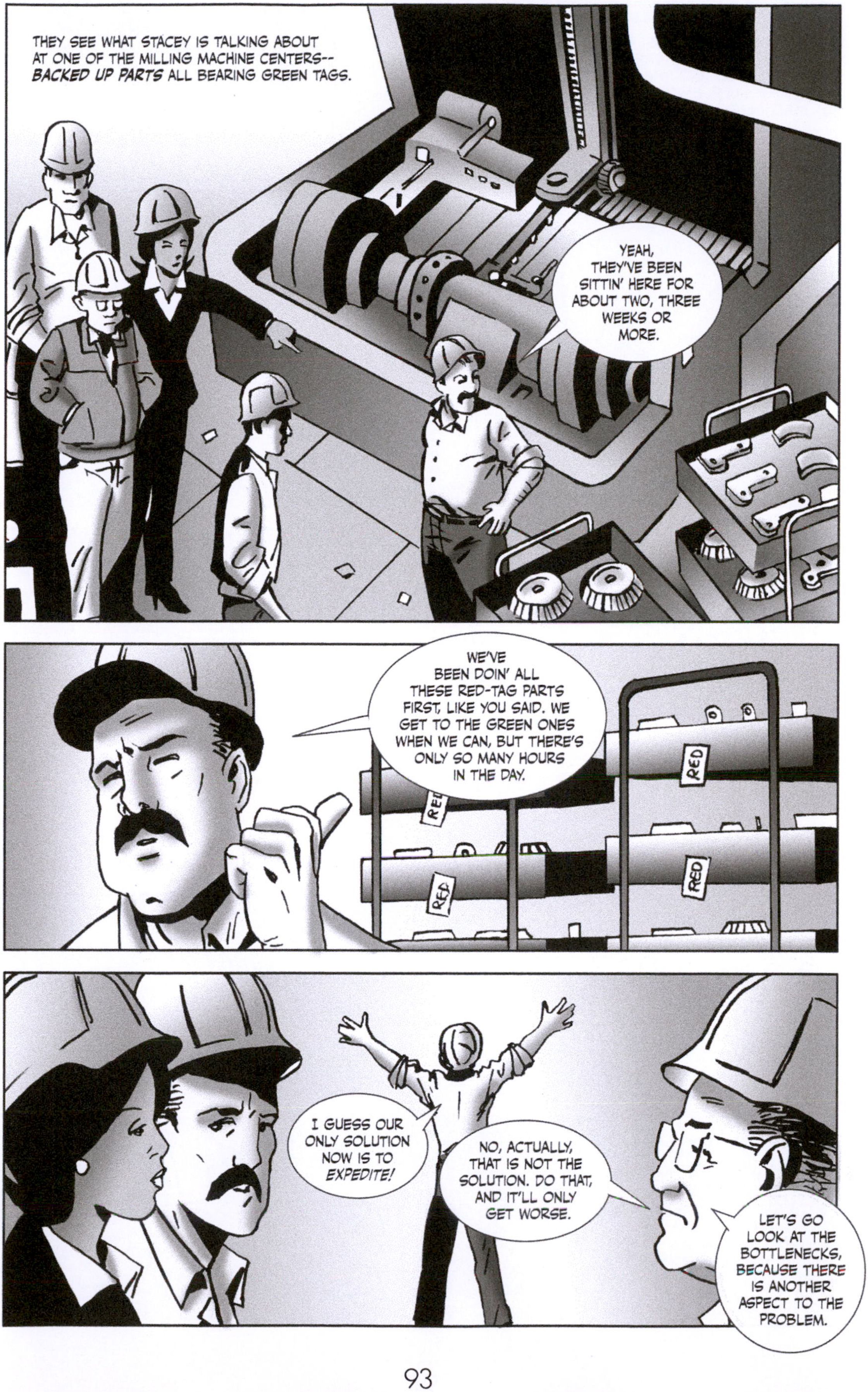
THEY SEE WHAT STACEY IS TALKING ABOUT AT ONE OF THE MILLING MACHINE CENTERS-- *BACKED UP PARTS* ALL BEARING GREEN TAGS.
YEAH, THEY'VE BEEN SITTIN' HERE FOR ABOUT TWO, THREE WEEKS OR MORE.
WE'VE BEEN DOIN' ALL THESE RED-TAG PARTS FIRST, LIKE YOU SAID. WE GET TO THE GREEN ONES WHEN WE CAN, BUT THERE'S ONLY SO MANY HOURS IN THE DAY.
RED
RED
RED
RED
I GUESS OUR ONLY SOLUTION NOW IS TO *EXPEDITE!*
NO, ACTUALLY, THAT IS NOT THE SOLUTION. DO THAT, AND IT'LL ONLY GET WORSE.
LET'S GO LOOK AT THE BOTTLENECKS, BECAUSE THERE IS ANOTHER ASPECT TO THE PROBLEM.

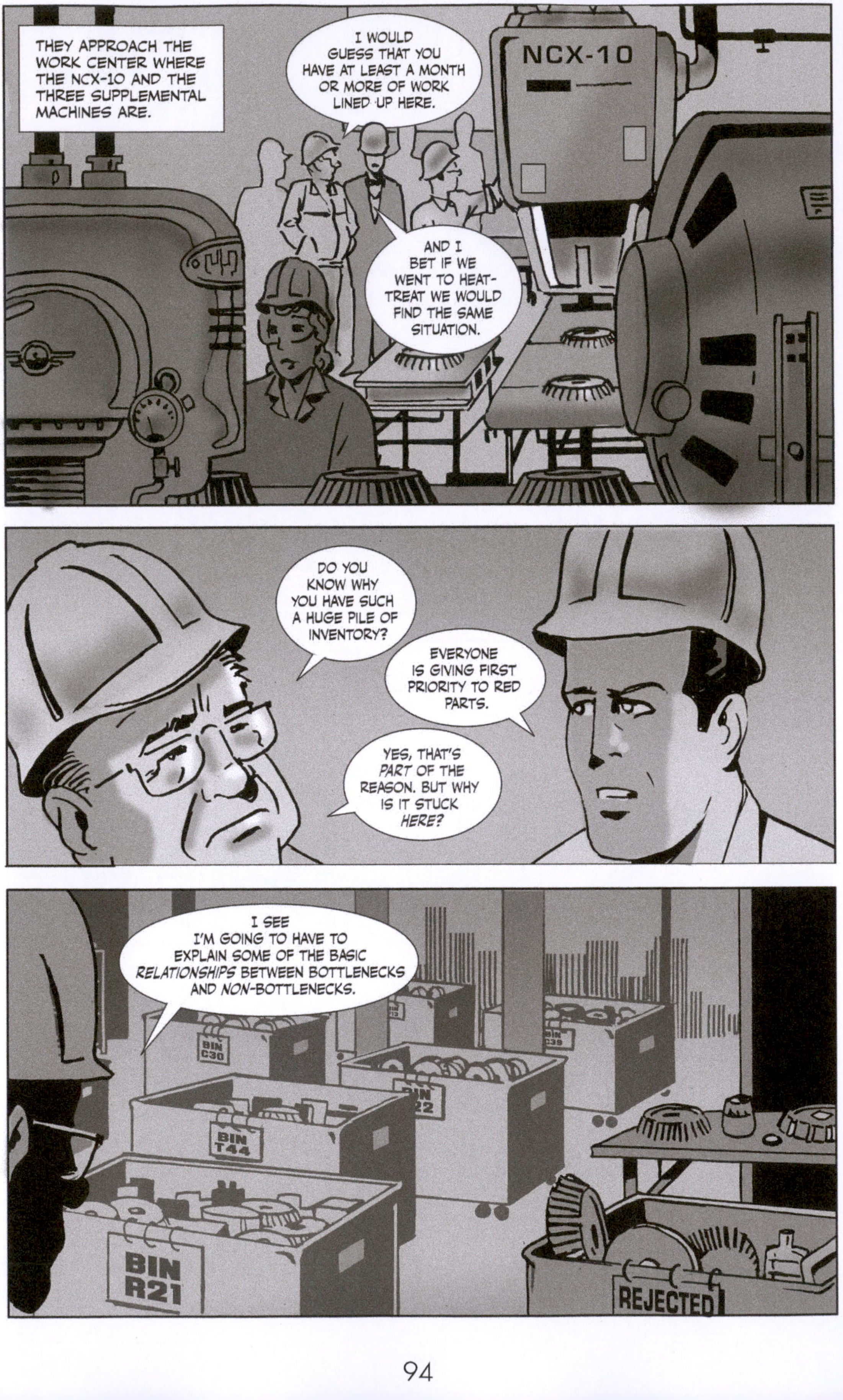
THEY APPROACH THE WORK CENTER WHERE THE NCX-10 AND THE THREE SUPPLEMENTAL MACHINES ARE.
I WOULD GUESS THAT YOU HAVE AT LEAST A MONTH OR MORE OF WORK LINED UP HERE.
NCX-10
AND I BET IF WE WENT TO HEAT-TREAT WE WOULD FIND THE SAME SITUATION.
DO YOU KNOW WHY YOU HAVE SUCH A HUGE PILE OF INVENTORY?
EVERYONE IS GIVING FIRST PRIORITY TO RED PARTS.
YES, THAT'S *PART* OF THE REASON. BUT WHY IS IT STUCK *HERE*?
I SEE I'M GOING TO HAVE TO EXPLAIN SOME OF THE BASIC *RELATIONSHIPS* BETWEEN BOTTLENECKS AND *NON*-BOTTLENECKS.
BIN C30
BIN C39
BIN T44
BIN R21
REJECTED

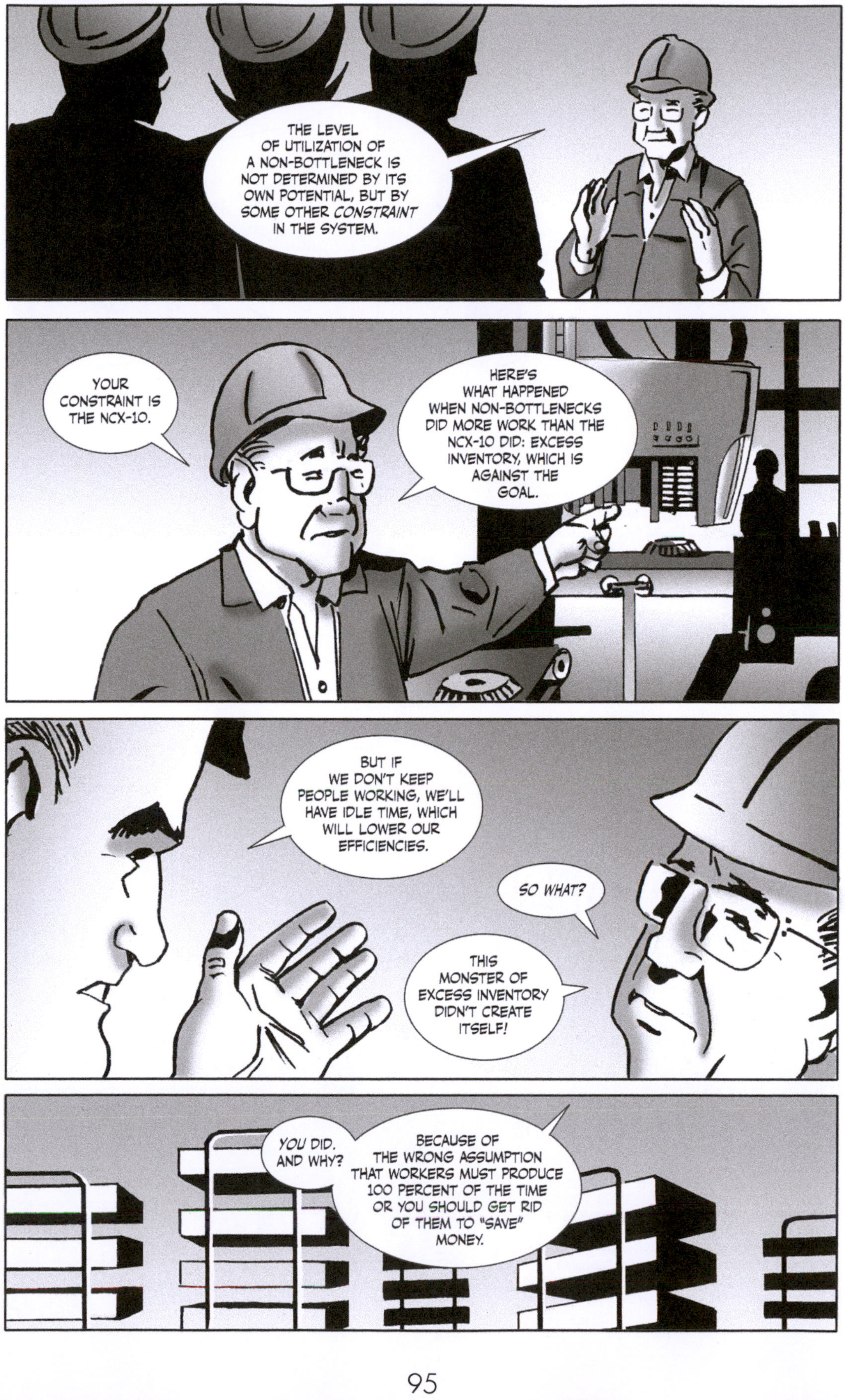
THE LEVEL OF UTILIZATION OF A NON-BOTTLENECK IS NOT DETERMINED BY ITS OWN POTENTIAL, BUT BY SOME OTHER *CONSTRAINT* IN THE SYSTEM.
YOUR CONSTRAINT IS THE NCX-10.
HERE'S WHAT HAPPENED WHEN NON-BOTTLENECKS DID MORE WORK THAN THE NCX-10 DID: EXCESS INVENTORY, WHICH IS AGAINST THE GOAL.
BUT IF WE DON'T KEEP PEOPLE WORKING, WE'LL HAVE IDLE TIME, WHICH WILL LOWER OUR EFFICIENCIES.
SO WHAT?
THIS MONSTER OF EXCESS INVENTORY DIDN'T CREATE ITSELF!
YOU DID. AND WHY?
BECAUSE OF THE WRONG ASSUMPTION THAT WORKERS MUST PRODUCE 100 PERCENT OF THE TIME OR YOU SHOULD GET RID OF THEM TO "SAVE" MONEY.

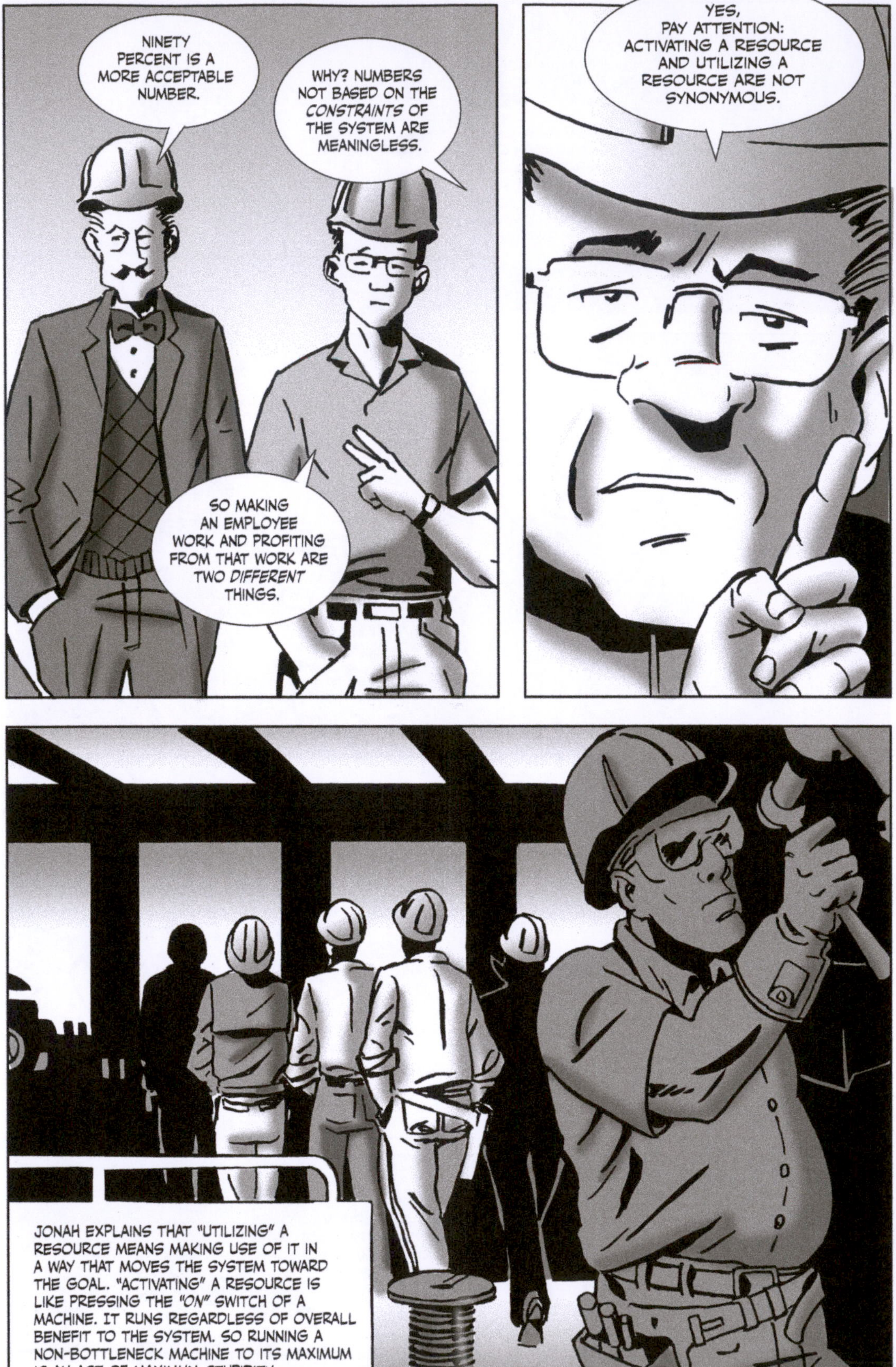
NINETY PERCENT IS A MORE ACCEPTABLE NUMBER.
WHY? NUMBERS NOT BASED ON THE *CONSTRAINTS* OF THE SYSTEM ARE MEANINGLESS.
SO MAKING AN EMPLOYEE WORK AND PROFITING FROM THAT WORK ARE TWO *DIFFERENT* THINGS.
YES, PAY ATTENTION: ACTIVATING A RESOURCE AND UTILIZING A RESOURCE ARE NOT SYNONYMOUS.
JONAH EXPLAINS THAT "UTILIZING" A RESOURCE MEANS MAKING USE OF IT IN A WAY THAT MOVES THE SYSTEM TOWARD THE GOAL. "ACTIVATING" A RESOURCE IS LIKE PRESSING THE *"ON"* SWITCH OF A MACHINE. IT RUNS REGARDLESS OF OVERALL BENEFIT TO THE SYSTEM. SO RUNNING A NON-BOTTLENECK MACHINE TO ITS MAXIMUM IS AN ACT OF MAXIMUM STUPIDITY.

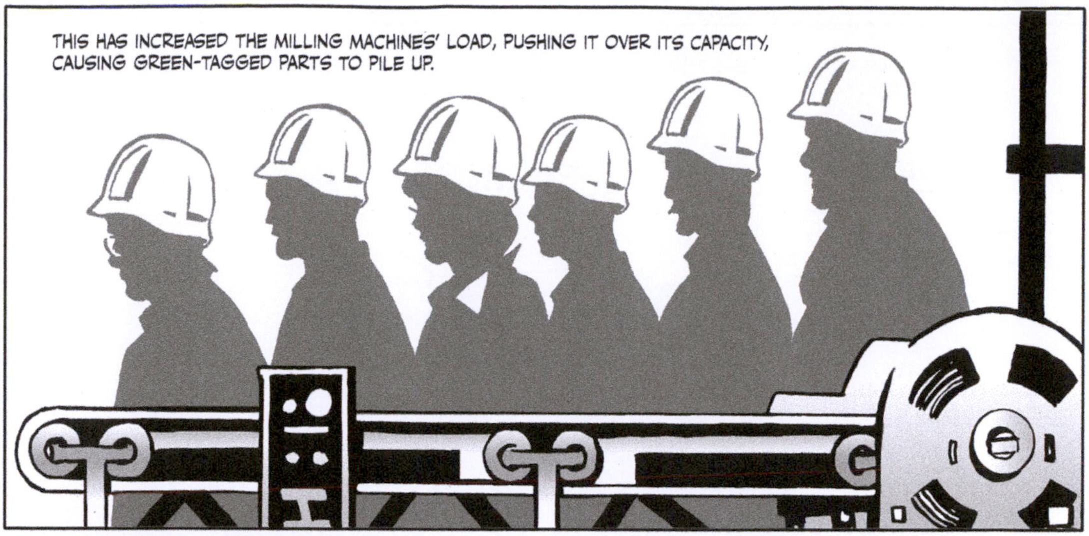
THIS HAS INCREASED THE MILLING MACHINES' LOAD, PUSHING IT OVER ITS CAPACITY, CAUSING GREEN-TAGGED PARTS TO PILE UP.

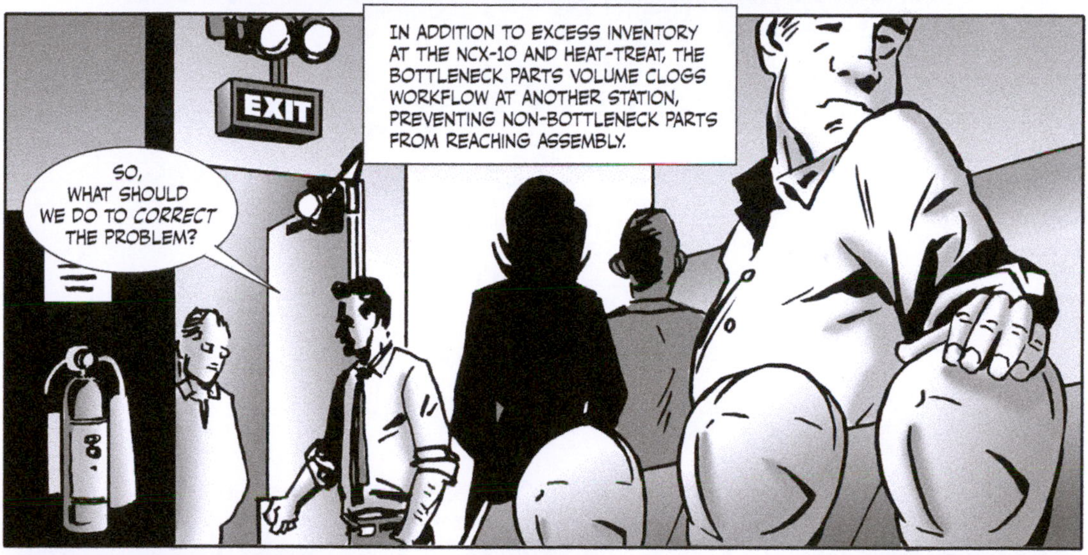
EXIT
IN ADDITION TO EXCESS INVENTORY AT THE NCX-10 AND HEAT-TREAT, THE BOTTLENECK PARTS VOLUME CLOGS WORKFLOW AT ANOTHER STATION, PREVENTING NON-BOTTLENECK PARTS FROM REACHING ASSEMBLY.
SO, WHAT SHOULD WE DO TO *CORRECT* THE PROBLEM?

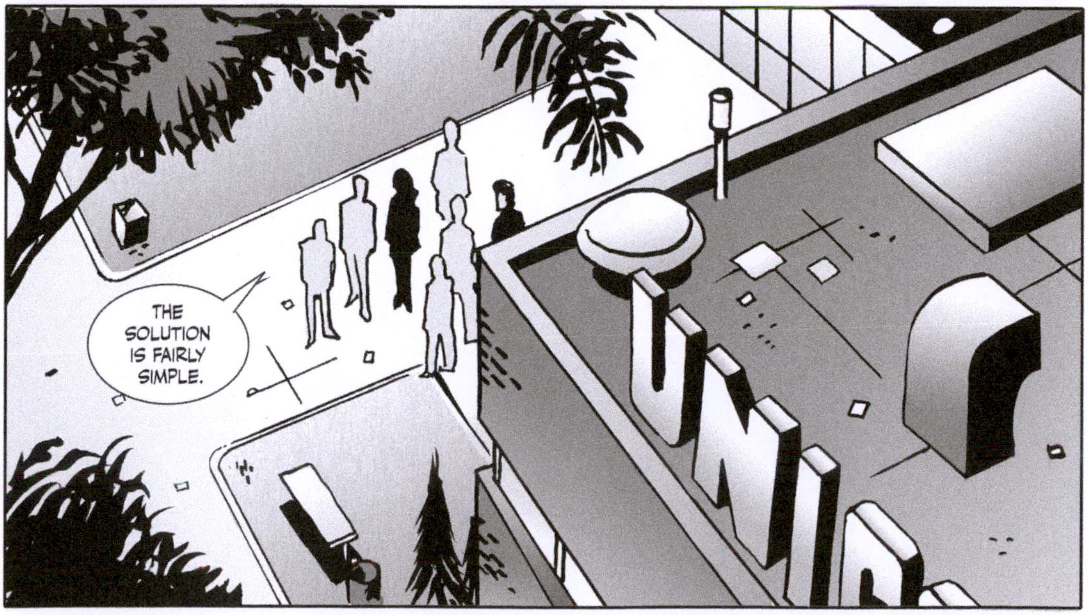
THE SOLUTION IS FAIRLY SIMPLE.

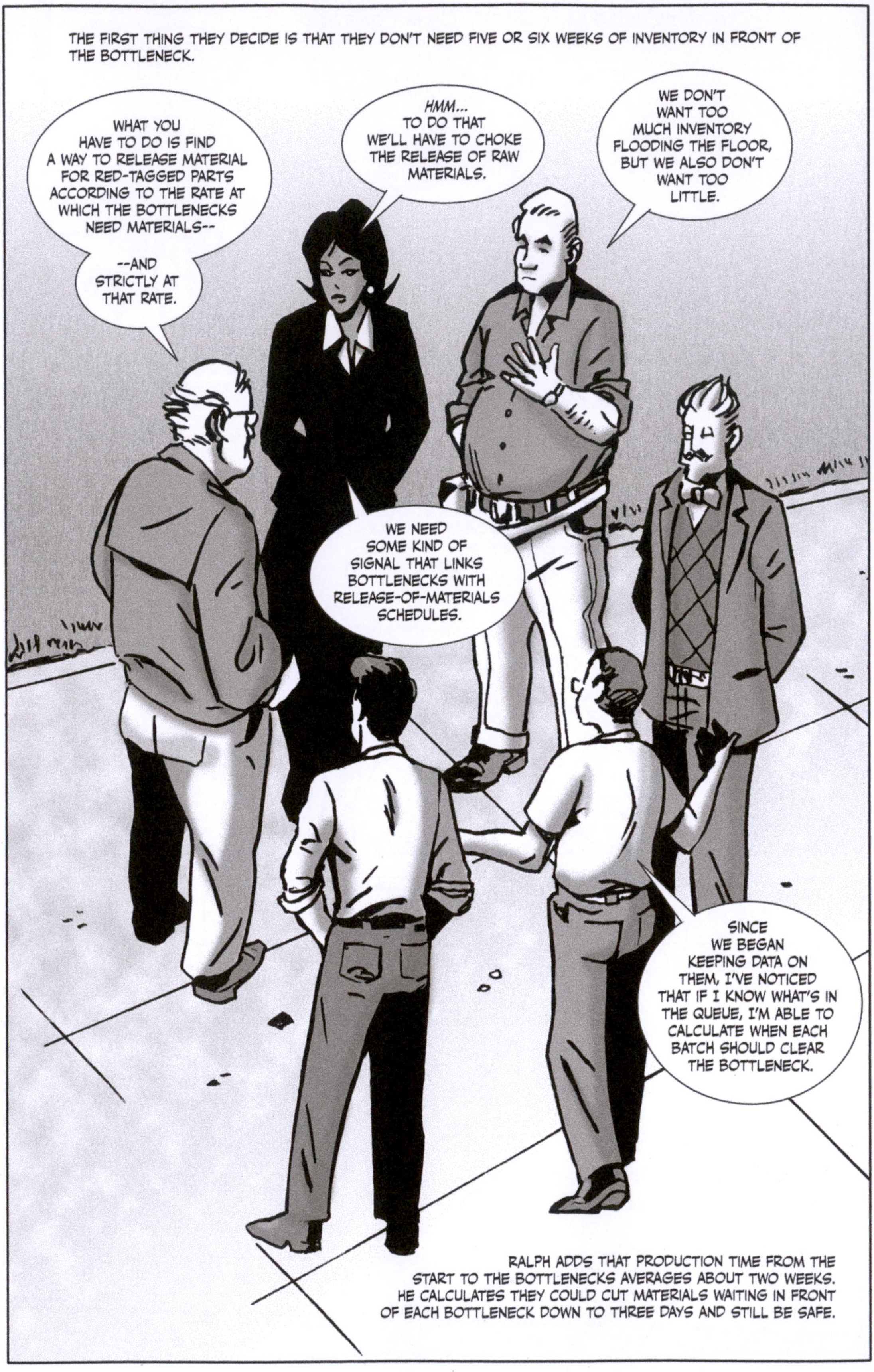
THE FIRST THING THEY DECIDE IS THAT THEY DON'T NEED FIVE OR SIX WEEKS OF INVENTORY IN FRONT OF THE BOTTLENECK.
WHAT YOU HAVE TO DO IS FIND A WAY TO RELEASE MATERIAL FOR RED-TAGGED PARTS ACCORDING TO THE RATE AT WHICH THE BOTTLENECKS NEED MATERIALS--
--AND STRICTLY AT THAT RATE.
HMM... TO DO THAT WE'LL HAVE TO CHOKE THE RELEASE OF RAW MATERIALS.
WE DON'T WANT TOO MUCH INVENTORY FLOODING THE FLOOR, BUT WE ALSO DON'T WANT TOO LITTLE.
WE NEED SOME KIND OF SIGNAL THAT LINKS BOTTLENECKS WITH RELEASE-OF-MATERIALS SCHEDULES.
SINCE WE BEGAN KEEPING DATA ON THEM, I'VE NOTICED THAT IF I KNOW WHAT'S IN THE QUEUE, I'M ABLE TO CALCULATE WHEN EACH BATCH SHOULD CLEAR THE BOTTLENECK.
RALPH ADDS THAT PRODUCTION TIME FROM THE START TO THE BOTTLENECKS AVERAGES ABOUT TWO WEEKS. HE CALCULATES THEY COULD CUT MATERIALS WAITING IN FRONT OF EACH BOTTLENECK DOWN TO THREE DAYS AND STILL BE SAFE.

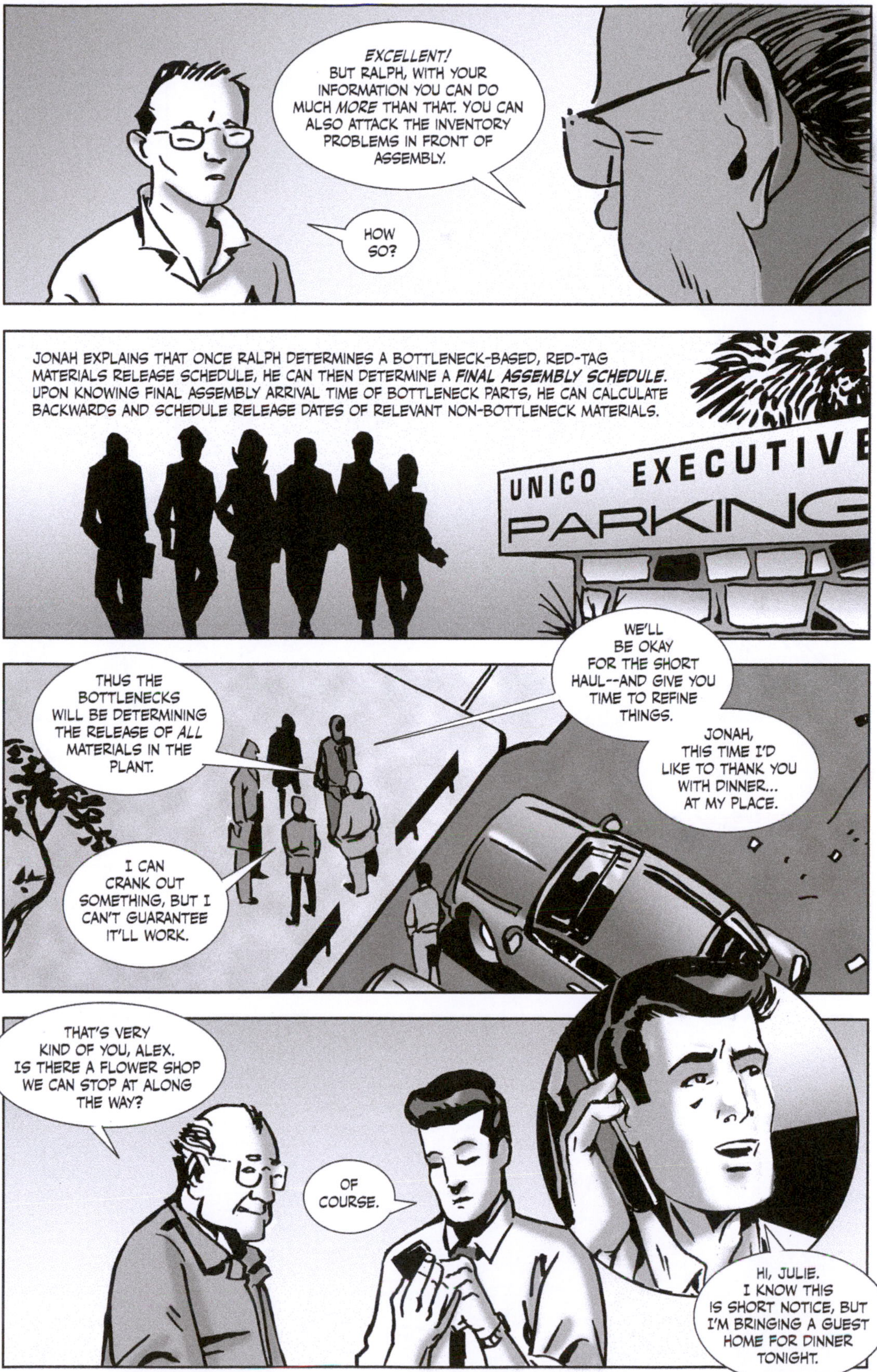
EXCELLENT! BUT RALPH, WITH YOUR INFORMATION YOU CAN DO MUCH MORE THAN THAT. YOU CAN ALSO ATTACK THE INVENTORY PROBLEMS IN FRONT OF ASSEMBLY.
HOW SO?
JONAH EXPLAINS THAT ONCE RALPH DETERMINES A BOTTLENECK-BASED, RED-TAG MATERIALS RELEASE SCHEDULE, HE CAN THEN DETERMINE A FINAL ASSEMBLY SCHEDULE. UPON KNOWING FINAL ASSEMBLY ARRIVAL TIME OF BOTTLENECK PARTS, HE CAN CALCULATE BACKWARDS AND SCHEDULE RELEASE DATES OF RELEVANT NON-BOTTLENECK MATERIALS.
UNICO EXECUTIVE
PARKING
THUS THE BOTTLENECKS WILL BE DETERMINING THE RELEASE OF ALL MATERIALS IN THE PLANT.
I CAN CRANK OUT SOMETHING, BUT I CAN'T GUARANTEE IT'LL WORK.
WE'LL BE OKAY FOR THE SHORT HAUL--AND GIVE YOU TIME TO REFINE THINGS.
JONAH, THIS TIME I'D LIKE TO THANK YOU WITH DINNER... AT MY PLACE.
THAT'S VERY KIND OF YOU, ALEX. IS THERE A FLOWER SHOP WE CAN STOP AT ALONG THE WAY?
OF COURSE.
HI, JULIE. I KNOW THIS IS SHORT NOTICE, BUT I'M BRINGING A GUEST HOME FOR DINNER TONIGHT.

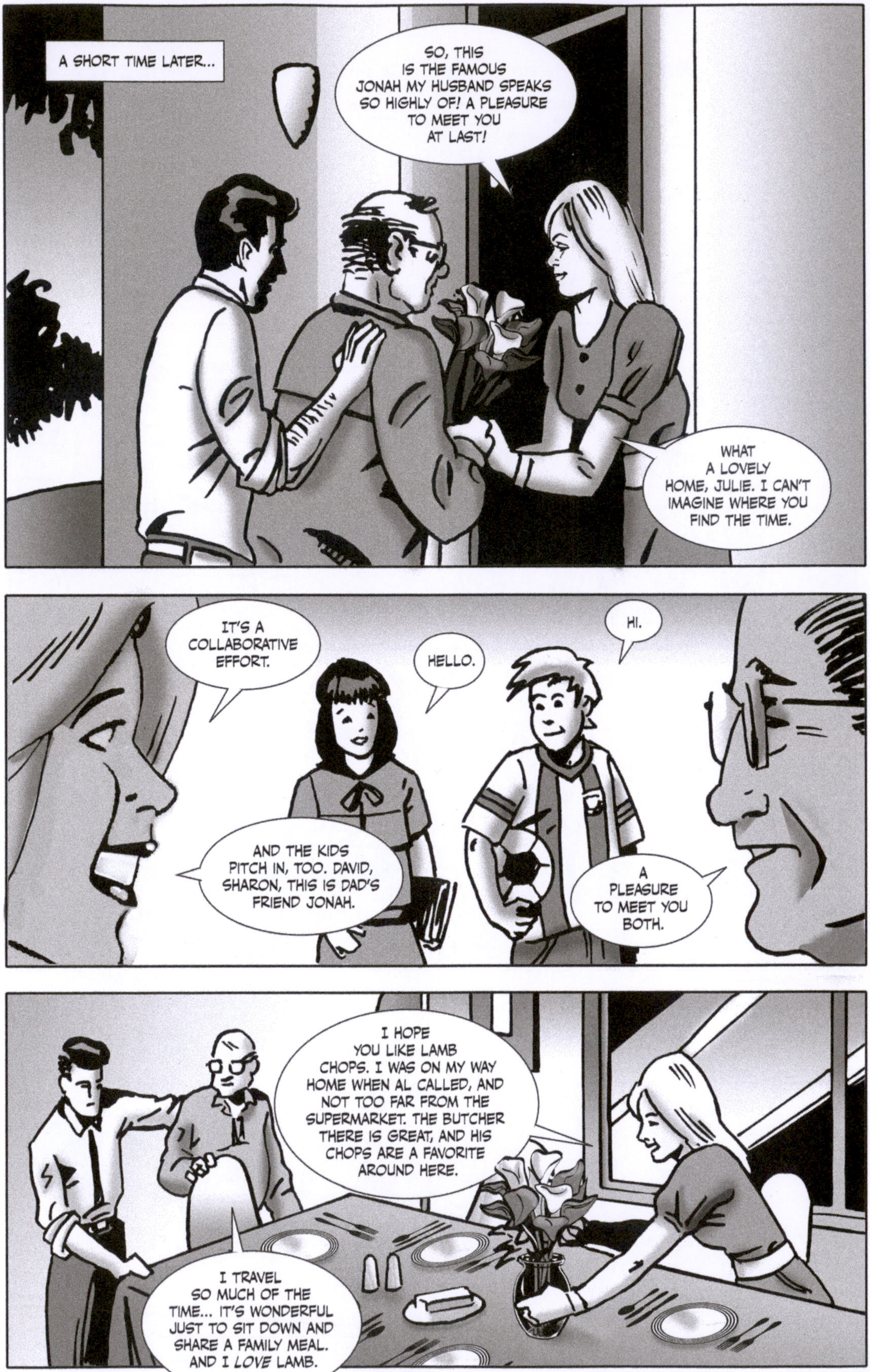
A SHORT TIME LATER...
SO, THIS IS THE FAMOUS JONAH MY HUSBAND SPEAKS SO HIGHLY OF! A PLEASURE TO MEET YOU AT LAST!
WHAT A LOVELY HOME, JULIE. I CAN'T IMAGINE WHERE YOU FIND THE TIME.
IT'S A COLLABORATIVE EFFORT.
HELLO.
HI.
AND THE KIDS PITCH IN, TOO. DAVID, SHARON, THIS IS DAD'S FRIEND JONAH.
A PLEASURE TO MEET YOU BOTH.
I HOPE YOU LIKE LAMB CHOPS. I WAS ON MY WAY HOME WHEN AL CALLED, AND NOT TOO FAR FROM THE SUPERMARKET. THE BUTCHER THERE IS GREAT, AND HIS CHOPS ARE A FAVORITE AROUND HERE.
I TRAVEL SO MUCH OF THE TIME... IT'S WONDERFUL JUST TO SIT DOWN AND SHARE A FAMILY MEAL. AND I *LOVE* LAMB.

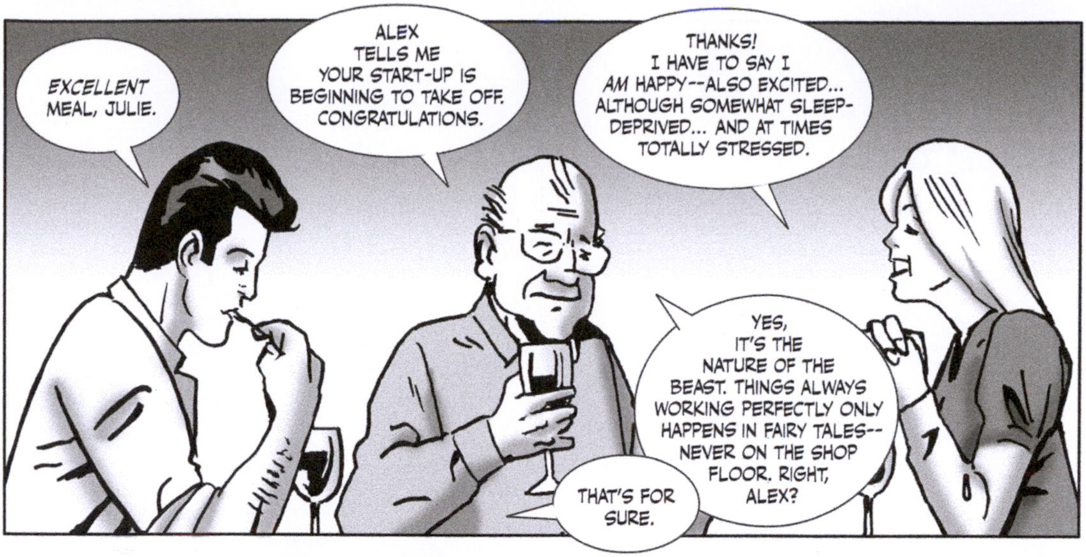
EXCELLENT MEAL, JULIE.
ALEX TELLS ME YOUR START-UP IS BEGINNING TO TAKE OFF. CONGRATULATIONS.
THANKS! I HAVE TO SAY I AM HAPPY--ALSO EXCITED... ALTHOUGH SOMEWHAT SLEEP-DEPRIVED... AND AT TIMES TOTALLY STRESSED.
YES, IT'S THE NATURE OF THE BEAST. THINGS ALWAYS WORKING PERFECTLY ONLY HAPPENS IN FAIRY TALES-- NEVER ON THE SHOP FLOOR. RIGHT, ALEX?
THAT'S FOR SURE.

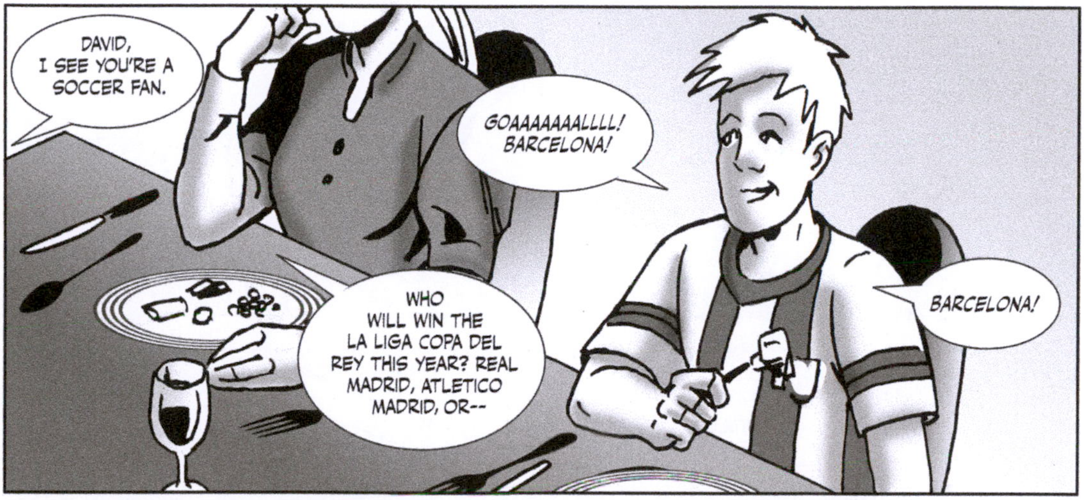
DAVID, I SEE YOU'RE A SOCCER FAN.
GOAAAAAAALLLL! BARCELONA!
WHO WILL WIN THE LA LIGA COPA DEL REY THIS YEAR? REAL MADRID, ATLETICO MADRID, OR--
BARCELONA!

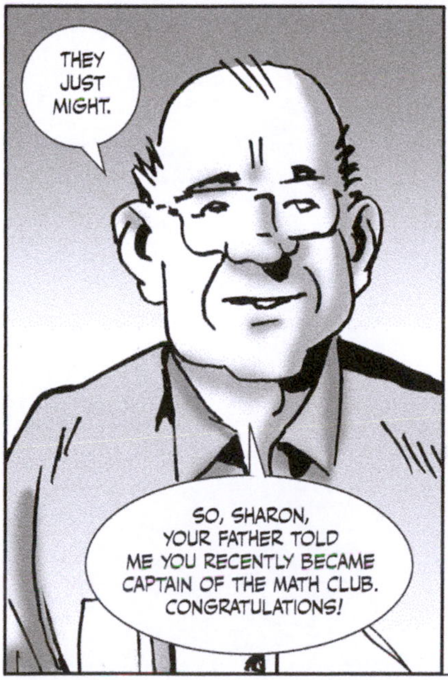
THEY JUST MIGHT.
SO, SHARON, YOUR FATHER TOLD ME YOU RECENTLY BECAME CAPTAIN OF THE MATH CLUB. CONGRATULATIONS!

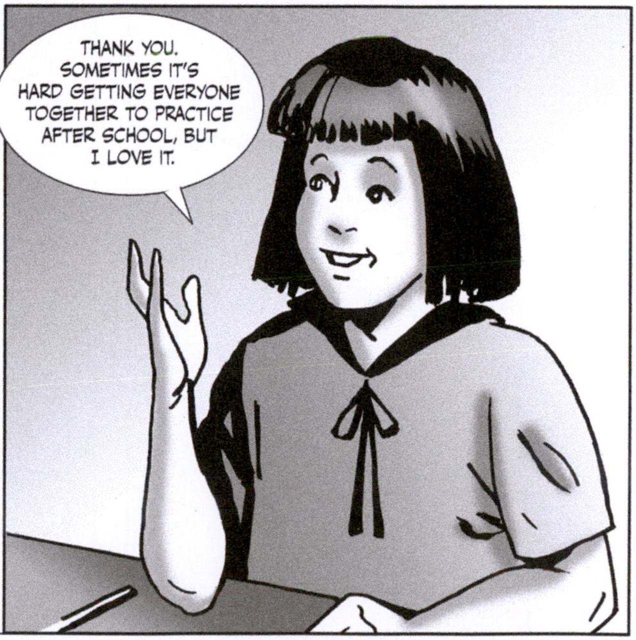
THANK YOU. SOMETIMES IT'S HARD GETTING EVERYONE TOGETHER TO PRACTICE AFTER SCHOOL, BUT I LOVE IT.

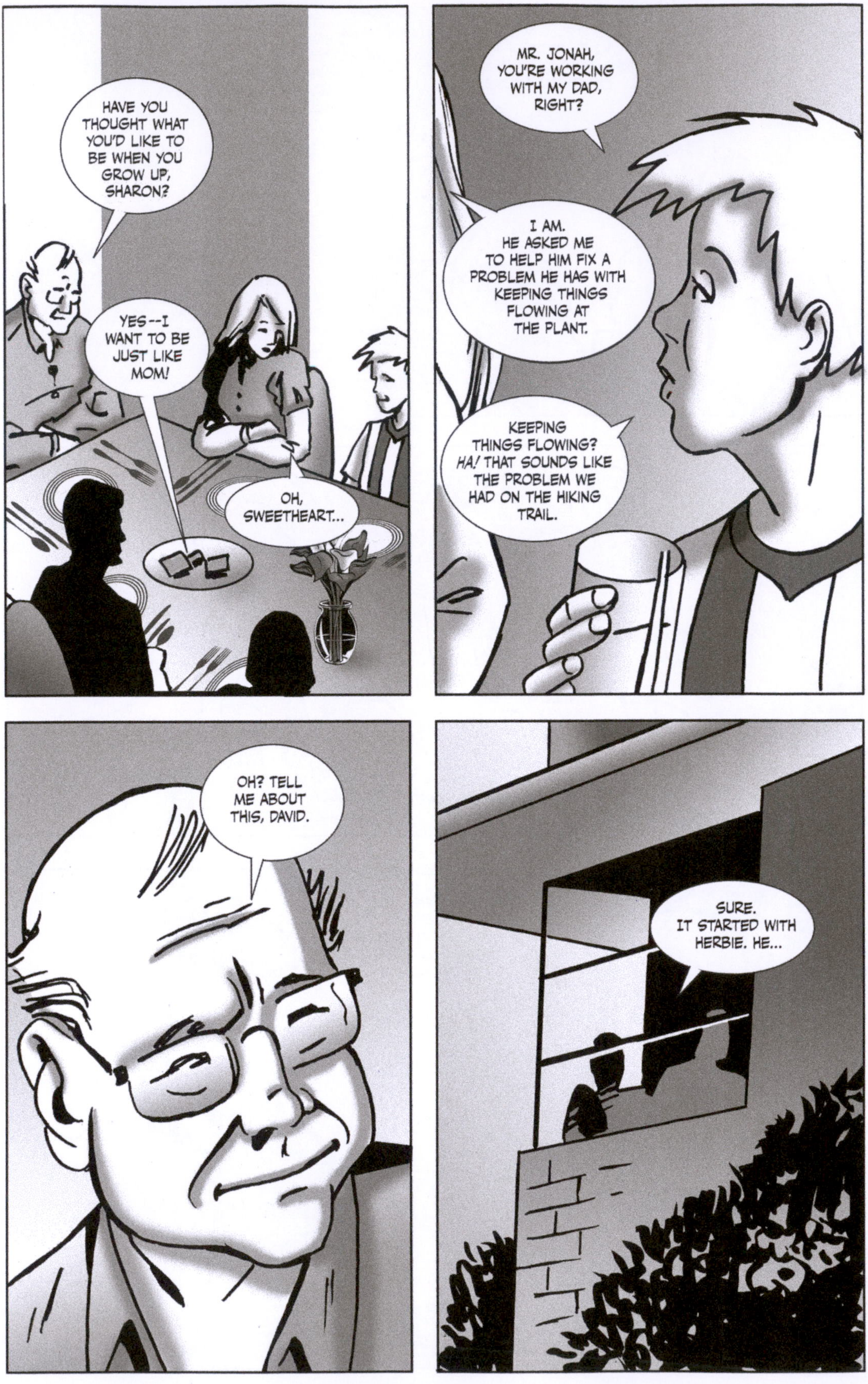
HAVE YOU THOUGHT WHAT YOU'D LIKE TO BE WHEN YOU GROW UP, SHARON?
YES--I WANT TO BE JUST LIKE MOM!
OH, SWEETHEART...
MR. JONAH, YOU'RE WORKING WITH MY DAD, RIGHT?
I AM. HE ASKED ME TO HELP HIM FIX A PROBLEM HE HAS WITH KEEPING THINGS FLOWING AT THE PLANT.
KEEPING THINGS FLOWING? HA! THAT SOUNDS LIKE THE PROBLEM WE HAD ON THE HIKING TRAIL.
OH? TELL ME ABOUT THIS, DAVID.
SURE. IT STARTED WITH HERBIE. HE...

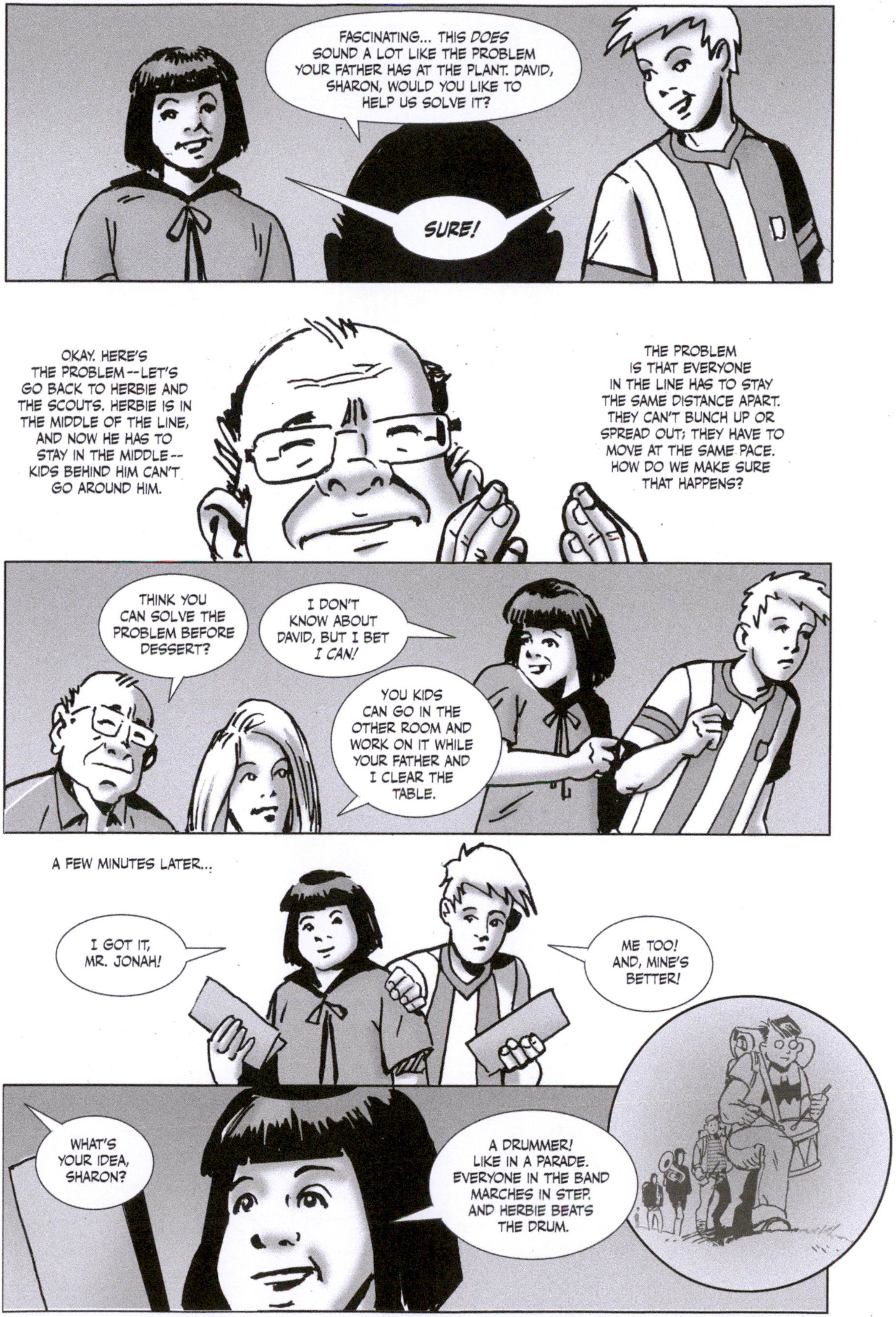

FASCINATING... THIS DOES SOUND A LOT LIKE THE PROBLEM YOUR FATHER HAS AT THE PLANT. DAVID, SHARON, WOULD YOU LIKE TO HELP US SOLVE IT?
SURE!
OKAY. HERE'S THE PROBLEM--LET'S GO BACK TO HERBIE AND THE SCOUTS. HERBIE IS IN THE MIDDLE OF THE LINE, AND NOW HE HAS TO STAY IN THE MIDDLE--KIDS BEHIND HIM CAN'T GO AROUND HIM.
THE PROBLEM IS THAT EVERYONE IN THE LINE HAS TO STAY THE SAME DISTANCE APART. THEY CAN'T BUNCH UP OR SPREAD OUT; THEY HAVE TO MOVE AT THE SAME PACE. HOW DO WE MAKE SURE THAT HAPPENS?
THINK YOU CAN SOLVE THE PROBLEM BEFORE DESSERT?
I DON'T KNOW ABOUT DAVID, BUT I BET I CAN!
YOU KIDS CAN GO IN THE OTHER ROOM AND WORK ON IT WHILE YOUR FATHER AND I CLEAR THE TABLE.
A FEW MINUTES LATER...
I GOT IT, MR. JONAH!
ME TOO! AND, MINE'S BETTER!
WHAT'S YOUR IDEA, SHARON?
A DRUMMER! LIKE IN A PARADE. EVERYONE IN THE BAND MARCHES IN STEP. AND HERBIE BEATS THE DRUM.

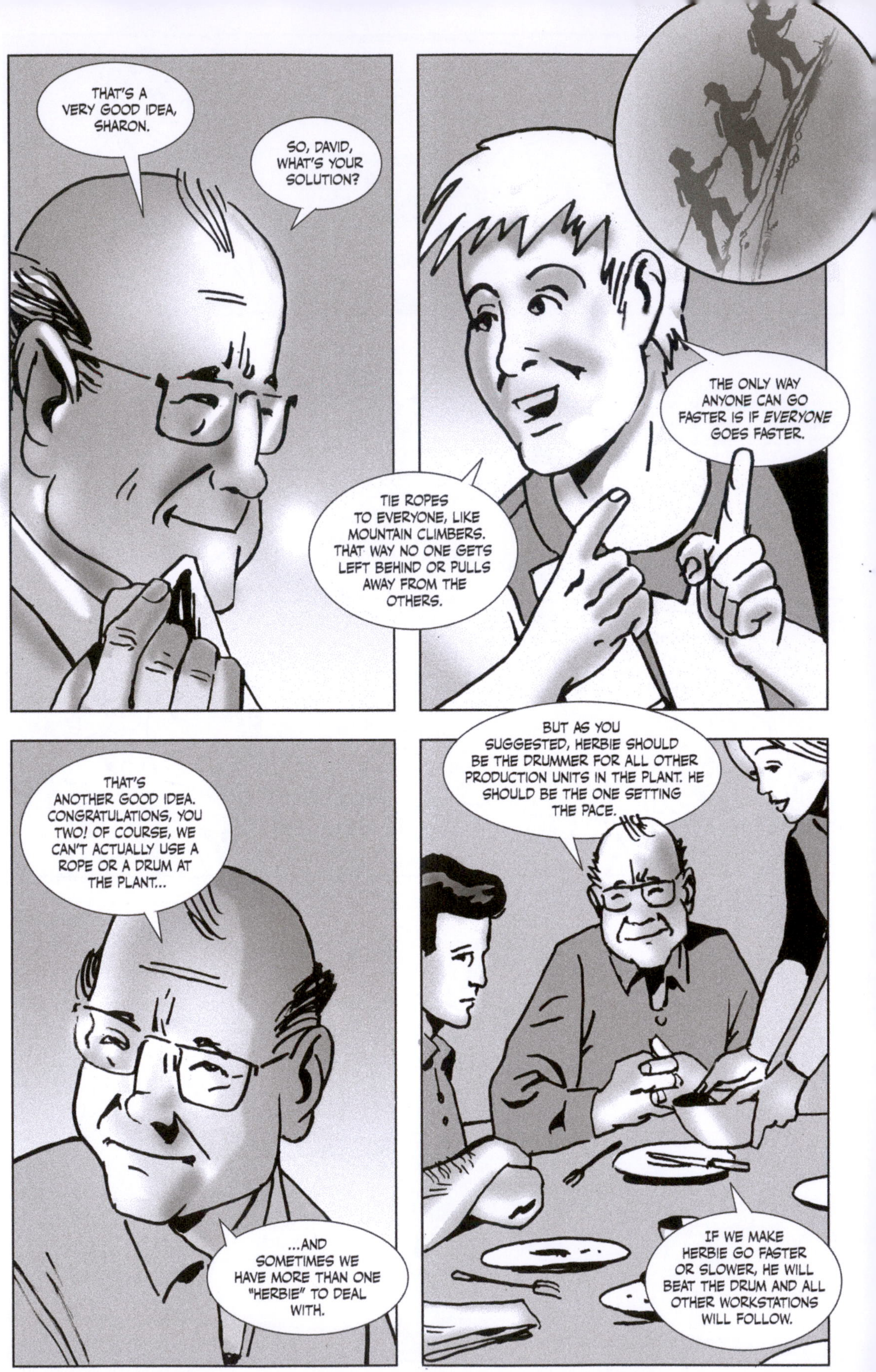
THAT'S A VERY GOOD IDEA, SHARON.
SO, DAVID, WHAT'S YOUR SOLUTION?
TIE ROPES TO EVERYONE, LIKE MOUNTAIN CLIMBERS. THAT WAY NO ONE GETS LEFT BEHIND OR PULLS AWAY FROM THE OTHERS.
THE ONLY WAY ANYONE CAN GO FASTER IS IF *EVERYONE* GOES FASTER.
THAT'S ANOTHER GOOD IDEA. CONGRATULATIONS, YOU TWO! OF COURSE, WE CAN'T ACTUALLY USE A ROPE OR A DRUM AT THE PLANT...
...AND SOMETIMES WE HAVE MORE THAN ONE "HERBIE" TO DEAL WITH.
BUT AS YOU SUGGESTED, HERBIE SHOULD BE THE DRUMMER FOR ALL OTHER PRODUCTION UNITS IN THE PLANT. HE SHOULD BE THE ONE SETTING THE PACE.
IF WE MAKE HERBIE GO FASTER OR SLOWER, HE WILL BEAT THE DRUM AND ALL OTHER WORKSTATIONS WILL FOLLOW.

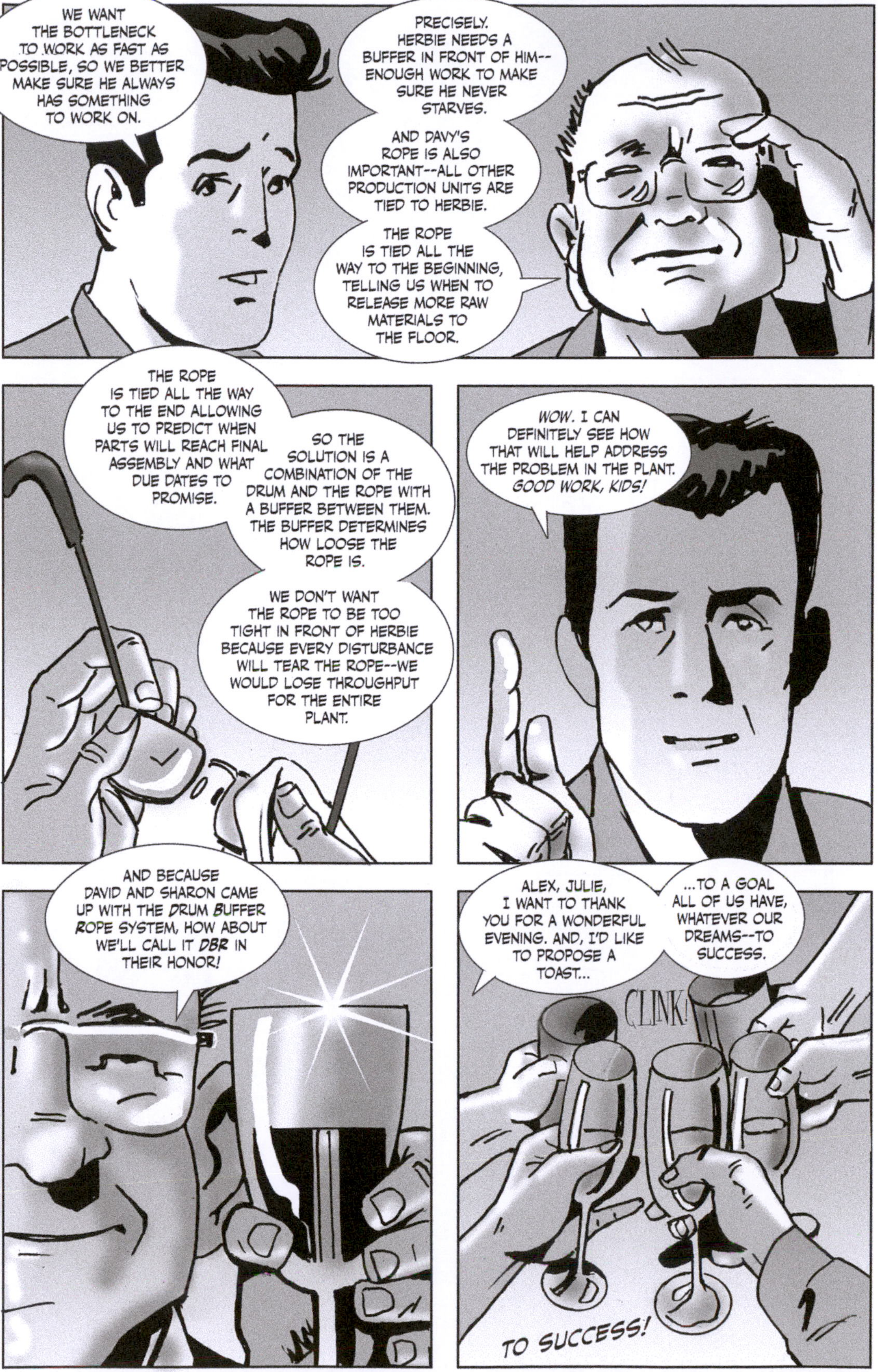
WE WANT THE BOTTLENECK TO WORK AS FAST AS POSSIBLE, SO WE BETTER MAKE SURE HE ALWAYS HAS SOMETHING TO WORK ON.
PRECISELY. HERBIE NEEDS A BUFFER IN FRONT OF HIM--ENOUGH WORK TO MAKE SURE HE NEVER STARVES.
AND DAVY'S ROPE IS ALSO IMPORTANT--ALL OTHER PRODUCTION UNITS ARE TIED TO HERBIE.
THE ROPE IS TIED ALL THE WAY TO THE BEGINNING, TELLING US WHEN TO RELEASE MORE RAW MATERIALS TO THE FLOOR.
THE ROPE IS TIED ALL THE WAY TO THE END ALLOWING US TO PREDICT WHEN PARTS WILL REACH FINAL ASSEMBLY AND WHAT DUE DATES TO PROMISE.
SO THE SOLUTION IS A COMBINATION OF THE DRUM AND THE ROPE WITH A BUFFER BETWEEN THEM. THE BUFFER DETERMINES HOW LOOSE THE ROPE IS.
WE DON'T WANT THE ROPE TO BE TOO TIGHT IN FRONT OF HERBIE BECAUSE EVERY DISTURBANCE WILL TEAR THE ROPE--WE WOULD LOSE THROUGHPUT FOR THE ENTIRE PLANT.
WOW. I CAN DEFINITELY SEE HOW THAT WILL HELP ADDRESS THE PROBLEM IN THE PLANT. *GOOD WORK, KIDS!*
AND BECAUSE DAVID AND SHARON CAME UP WITH THE *DRUM BUFFER ROPE* SYSTEM, HOW ABOUT WE'LL CALL IT *DBR* IN THEIR HONOR!
ALEX, JULIE, I WANT TO THANK YOU FOR A WONDERFUL EVENING. AND, I'D LIKE TO PROPOSE A TOAST...
...TO A GOAL ALL OF US HAVE, WHATEVER OUR DREAMS--TO SUCCESS.
CLINK!
TO SUCCESS!

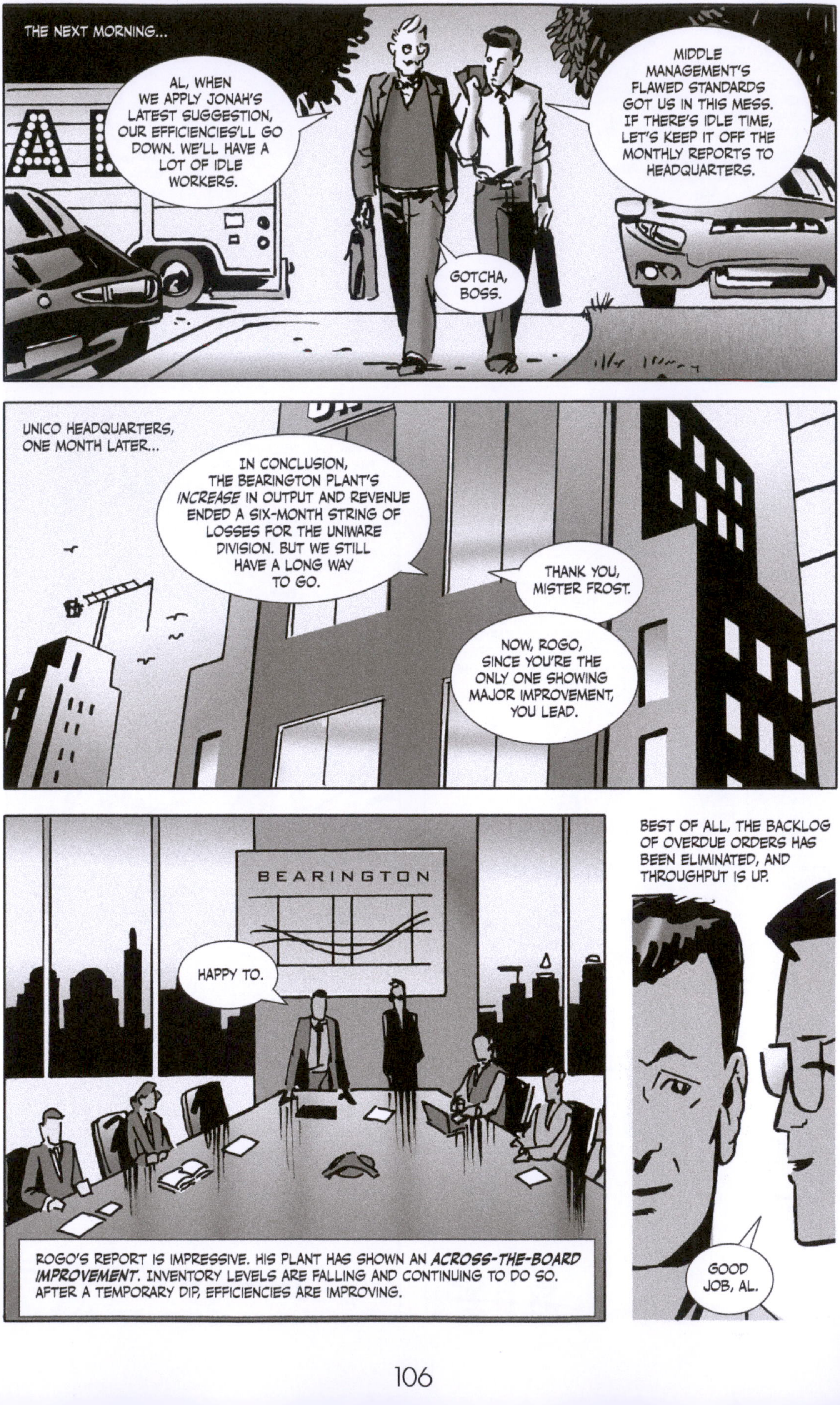
THE NEXT MORNING...
AL, WHEN WE APPLY JONAH'S LATEST SUGGESTION, OUR EFFICIENCIES'LL GO DOWN. WE'LL HAVE A LOT OF IDLE WORKERS.
MIDDLE MANAGEMENT'S FLAWED STANDARDS GOT US IN THIS MESS. IF THERE'S IDLE TIME, LET'S KEEP IT OFF THE MONTHLY REPORTS TO HEADQUARTERS.
GOTCHA, BOSS.
UNICO HEADQUARTERS, ONE MONTH LATER...
IN CONCLUSION, THE BEARINGTON PLANT'S *INCREASE* IN OUTPUT AND REVENUE ENDED A SIX-MONTH STRING OF LOSSES FOR THE UNIWARE DIVISION. BUT WE STILL HAVE A LONG WAY TO GO.
THANK YOU, MISTER FROST.
NOW, ROGO, SINCE YOU'RE THE ONLY ONE SHOWING MAJOR IMPROVEMENT, YOU LEAD.
BEARINGTON
HAPPY TO.
ROGO'S REPORT IS IMPRESSIVE. HIS PLANT HAS SHOWN AN ***ACROSS-THE-BOARD IMPROVEMENT***. INVENTORY LEVELS ARE FALLING AND CONTINUING TO DO SO. AFTER A TEMPORARY DIP, EFFICIENCIES ARE IMPROVING.
BEST OF ALL, THE BACKLOG OF OVERDUE ORDERS HAS BEEN ELIMINATED, AND THROUGHPUT IS UP.
GOOD JOB, AL.

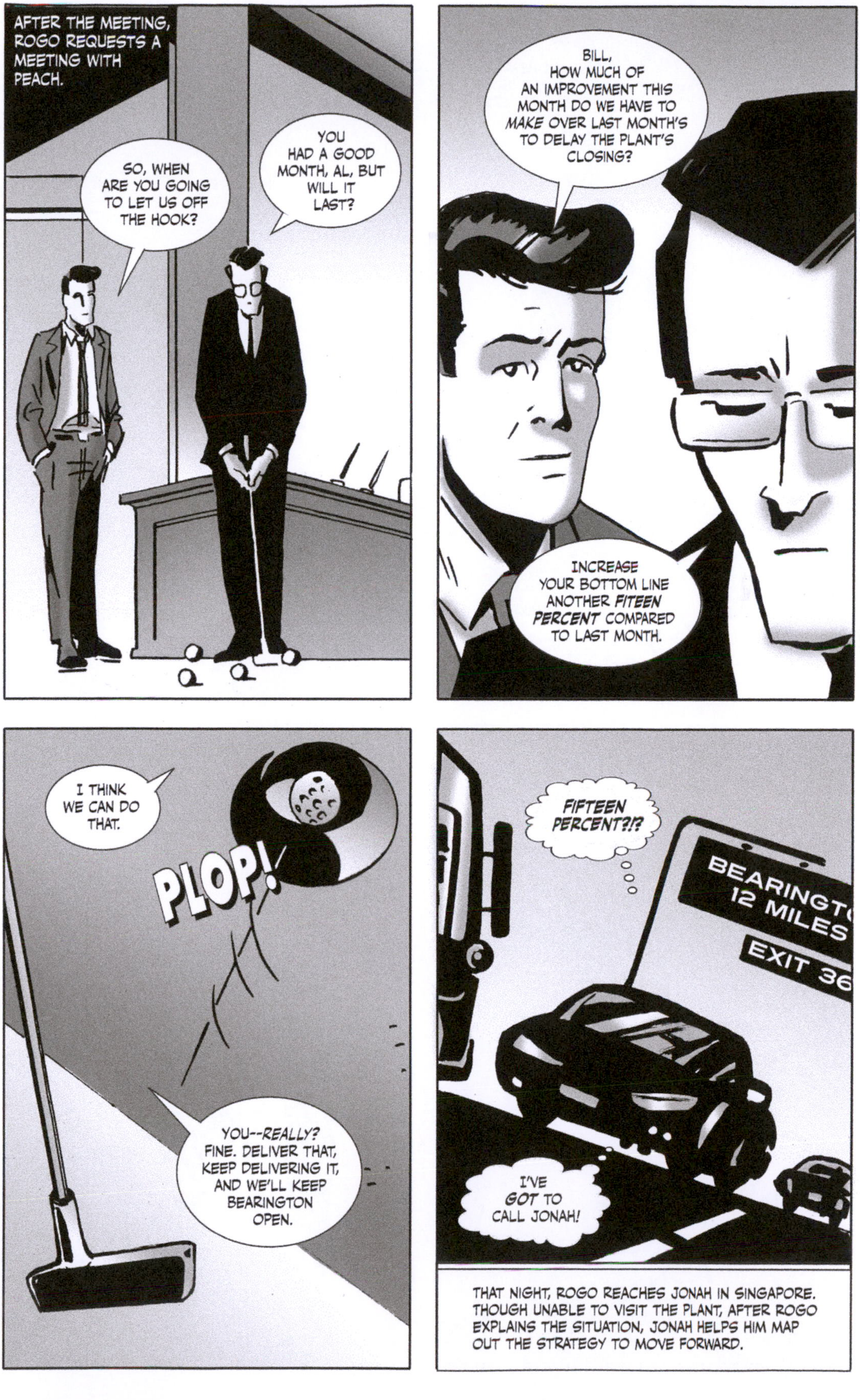
AFTER THE MEETING, ROGO REQUESTS A MEETING WITH PEACH.
SO, WHEN ARE YOU GOING TO LET US OFF THE HOOK?
YOU HAD A GOOD MONTH, AL, BUT WILL IT LAST?
BILL, HOW MUCH OF AN IMPROVEMENT THIS MONTH DO WE HAVE TO *MAKE* OVER LAST MONTH'S TO DELAY THE PLANT'S CLOSING?
INCREASE YOUR BOTTOM LINE ANOTHER *FITEEN PERCENT* COMPARED TO LAST MONTH.
I THINK WE CAN DO THAT.
PLOP!
YOU--*REALLY?* FINE. DELIVER THAT, KEEP DELIVERING IT, AND WE'LL KEEP BEARINGTON OPEN.
FIFTEEN PERCENT?!?
BEARINGTO
12 MILES
EXIT 36
I'VE *GOT* TO CALL JONAH!
THAT NIGHT, ROGO REACHES JONAH IN SINGAPORE. THOUGH UNABLE TO VISIT THE PLANT, AFTER ROGO EXPLAINS THE SITUATION, JONAH HELPS HIM MAP OUT THE STRATEGY TO MOVE FORWARD.

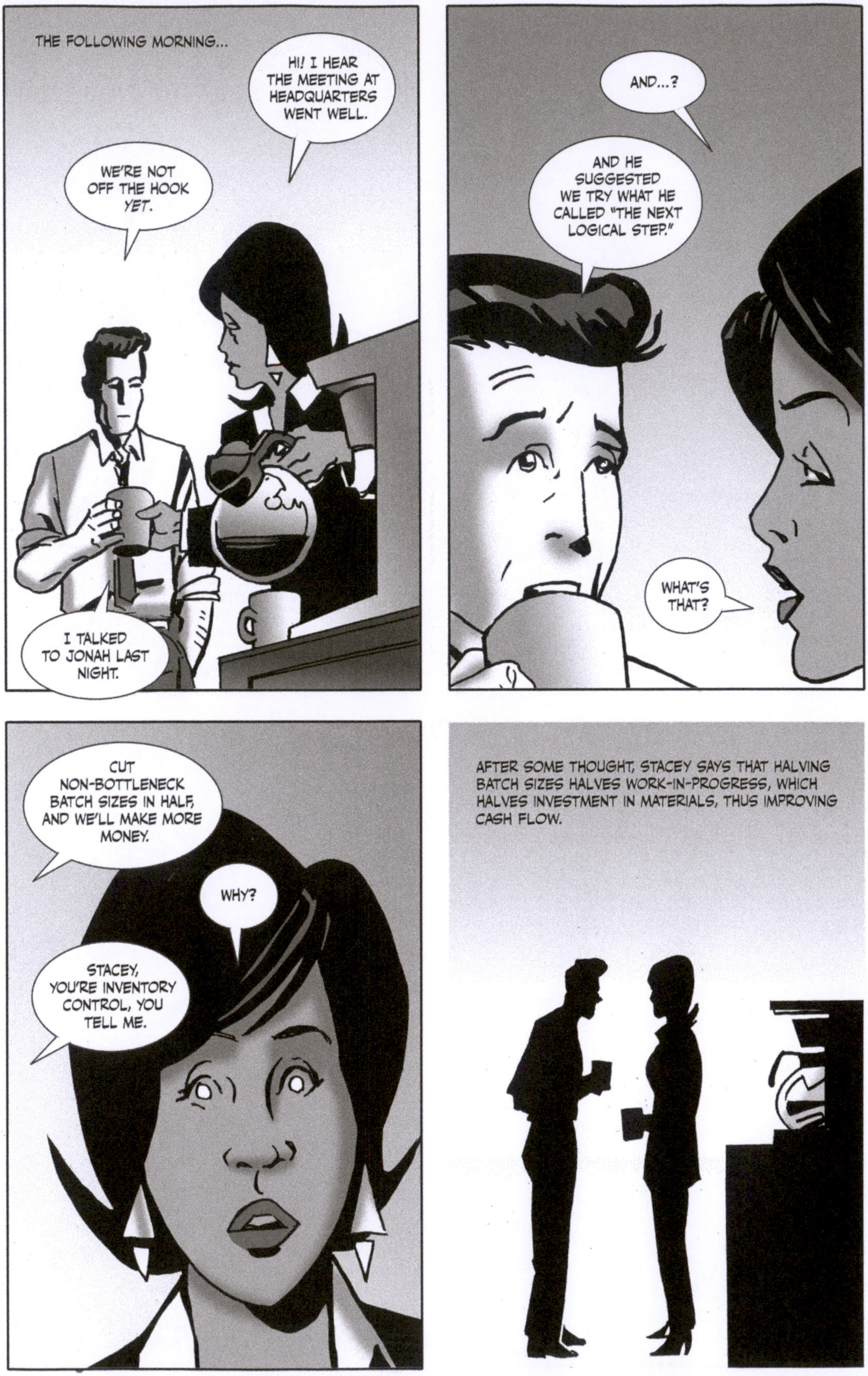
THE FOLLOWING MORNING...
HI! I HEAR THE MEETING AT HEADQUARTERS WENT WELL.
WE'RE NOT OFF THE HOOK YET.
I TALKED TO JONAH LAST NIGHT.
AND...?
AND HE SUGGESTED WE TRY WHAT HE CALLED "THE NEXT LOGICAL STEP."
WHAT'S THAT?
CUT NON-BOTTLENECK BATCH SIZES IN HALF, AND WE'LL MAKE MORE MONEY.
WHY?
STACEY, YOU'RE INVENTORY CONTROL, YOU TELL ME.
AFTER SOME THOUGHT, STACEY SAYS THAT HALVING BATCH SIZES HALVES WORK-IN-PROGRESS, WHICH HALVES INVESTMENT IN MATERIALS, THUS IMPROVING CASH FLOW.

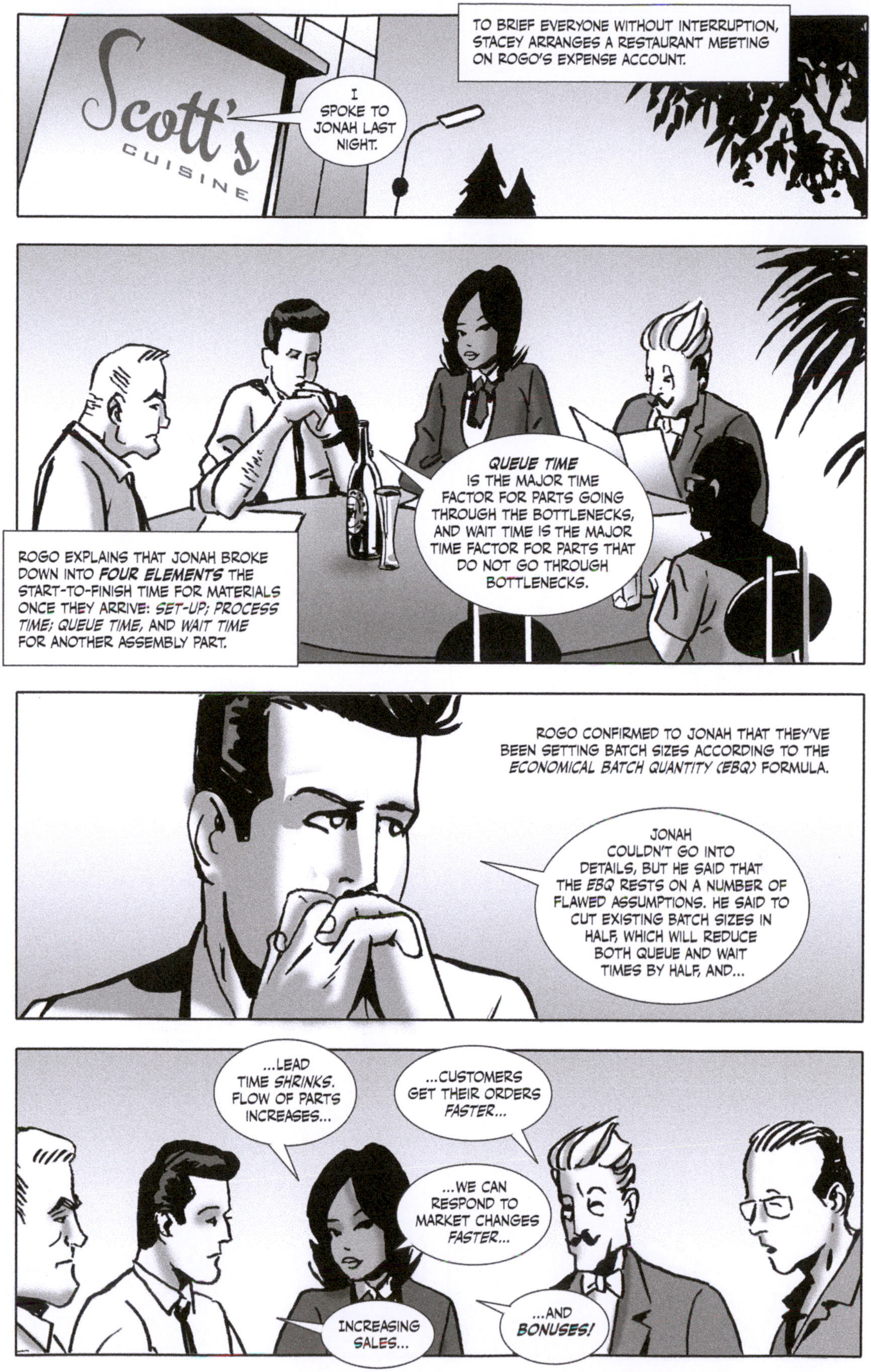

TO BRIEF EVERYONE WITHOUT INTERRUPTION, STACEY ARRANGES A RESTAURANT MEETING ON ROGO'S EXPENSE ACCOUNT.
Scott's CUISINE
I SPOKE TO JONAH LAST NIGHT.
ROGO EXPLAINS THAT JONAH BROKE DOWN INTO *FOUR ELEMENTS* THE START-TO-FINISH TIME FOR MATERIALS ONCE THEY ARRIVE: *SET-UP; PROCESS TIME; QUEUE TIME,* AND *WAIT TIME* FOR ANOTHER ASSEMBLY PART.
QUEUE TIME IS THE MAJOR TIME FACTOR FOR PARTS GOING THROUGH THE BOTTLENECKS, AND WAIT TIME IS THE MAJOR TIME FACTOR FOR PARTS THAT DO NOT GO THROUGH BOTTLENECKS.
ROGO CONFIRMED TO JONAH THAT THEY'VE BEEN SETTING BATCH SIZES ACCORDING TO THE *ECONOMICAL BATCH QUANTITY (EBQ)* FORMULA.
JONAH COULDN'T GO INTO DETAILS, BUT HE SAID THAT THE *EBQ* RESTS ON A NUMBER OF FLAWED ASSUMPTIONS. HE SAID TO CUT EXISTING BATCH SIZES IN HALF, WHICH WILL REDUCE BOTH QUEUE AND WAIT TIMES BY HALF, AND...
...LEAD TIME *SHRINKS*. FLOW OF PARTS INCREASES...
...CUSTOMERS GET THEIR ORDERS *FASTER*...
...WE CAN RESPOND TO MARKET CHANGES *FASTER*...
INCREASING SALES...
...AND *BONUSES!*

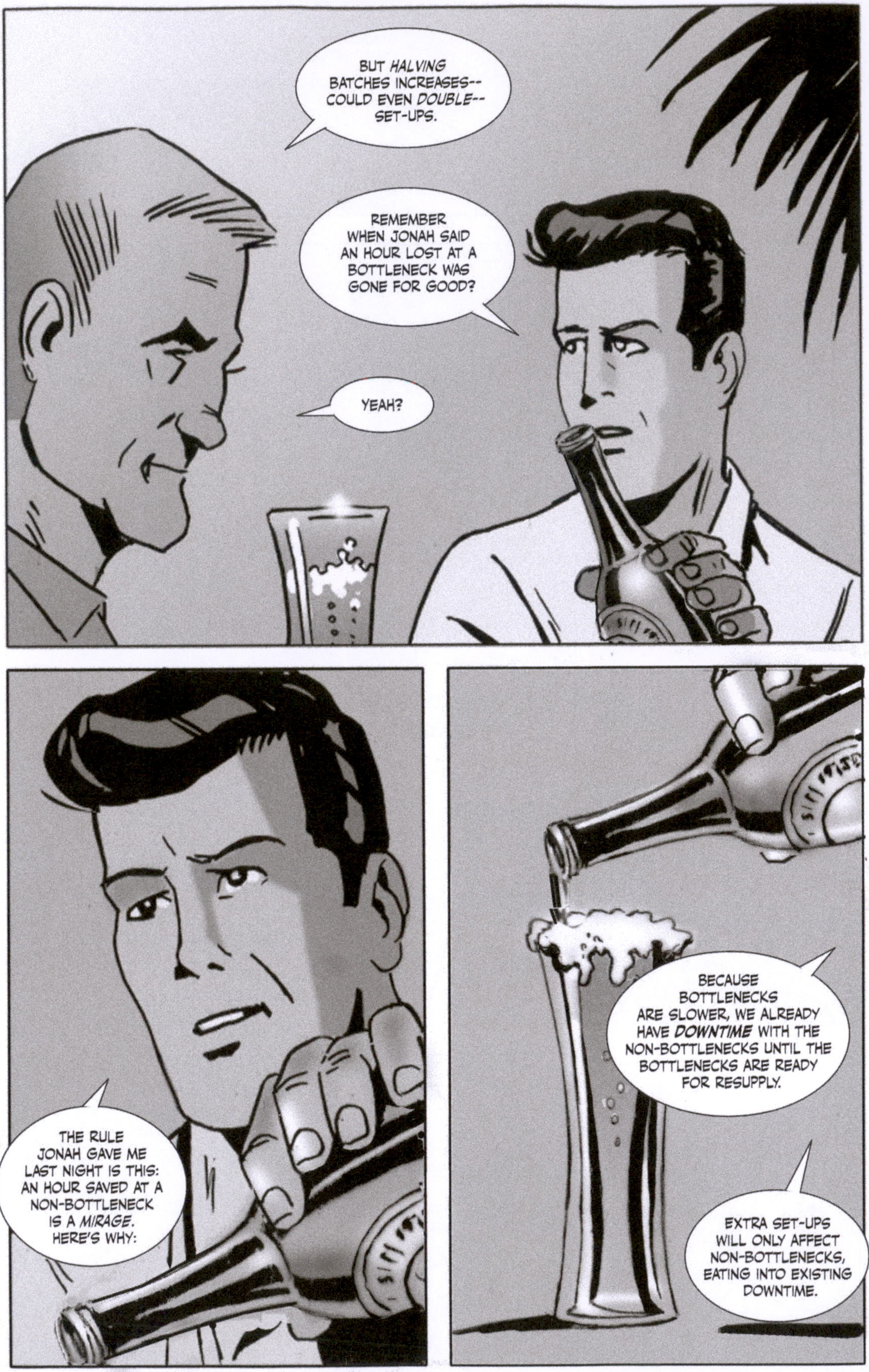
BUT *HALVING* BATCHES INCREASES-- COULD EVEN *DOUBLE*-- SET-UPS.
REMEMBER WHEN JONAH SAID AN HOUR LOST AT A BOTTLENECK WAS GONE FOR GOOD?
YEAH?
THE RULE JONAH GAVE ME LAST NIGHT IS THIS: AN HOUR SAVED AT A NON-BOTTLENECK IS A *MIRAGE*. HERE'S WHY:
BECAUSE BOTTLENECKS ARE SLOWER, WE ALREADY HAVE ***DOWNTIME*** WITH THE NON-BOTTLENECKS UNTIL THE BOTTLENECKS ARE READY FOR RESUPPLY.
EXTRA SET-UPS WILL ONLY AFFECT NON-BOTTLENECKS, EATING INTO EXISTING DOWNTIME.

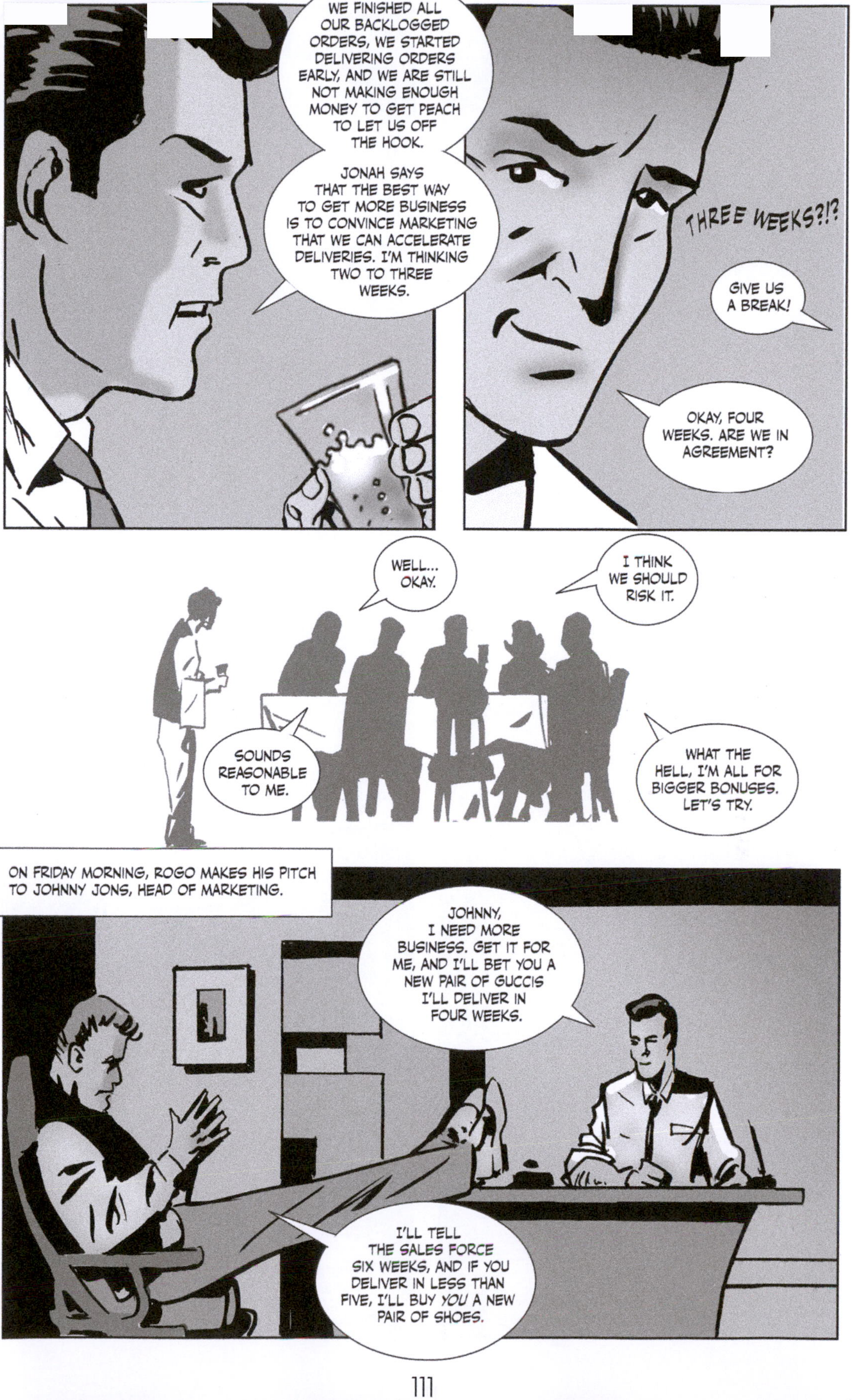
WE FINISHED ALL OUR BACKLOGGED ORDERS, WE STARTED DELIVERING ORDERS EARLY, AND WE ARE STILL NOT MAKING ENOUGH MONEY TO GET PEACH TO LET US OFF THE HOOK.
JONAH SAYS THAT THE BEST WAY TO GET MORE BUSINESS IS TO CONVINCE MARKETING THAT WE CAN ACCELERATE DELIVERIES. I'M THINKING TWO TO THREE WEEKS.
THREE WEEKS?!?
GIVE US A BREAK!
OKAY, FOUR WEEKS. ARE WE IN AGREEMENT?
WELL... OKAY.
I THINK WE SHOULD RISK IT.
SOUNDS REASONABLE TO ME.
WHAT THE HELL, I'M ALL FOR BIGGER BONUSES. LET'S TRY.
ON FRIDAY MORNING, ROGO MAKES HIS PITCH TO JOHNNY JONS, HEAD OF MARKETING.
JOHNNY, I NEED MORE BUSINESS. GET IT FOR ME, AND I'LL BET YOU A NEW PAIR OF GUCCIS I'LL DELIVER IN FOUR WEEKS.
I'LL TELL THE SALES FORCE SIX WEEKS, AND IF YOU DELIVER IN LESS THAN FIVE, I'LL BUY *YOU* A NEW PAIR OF SHOES.

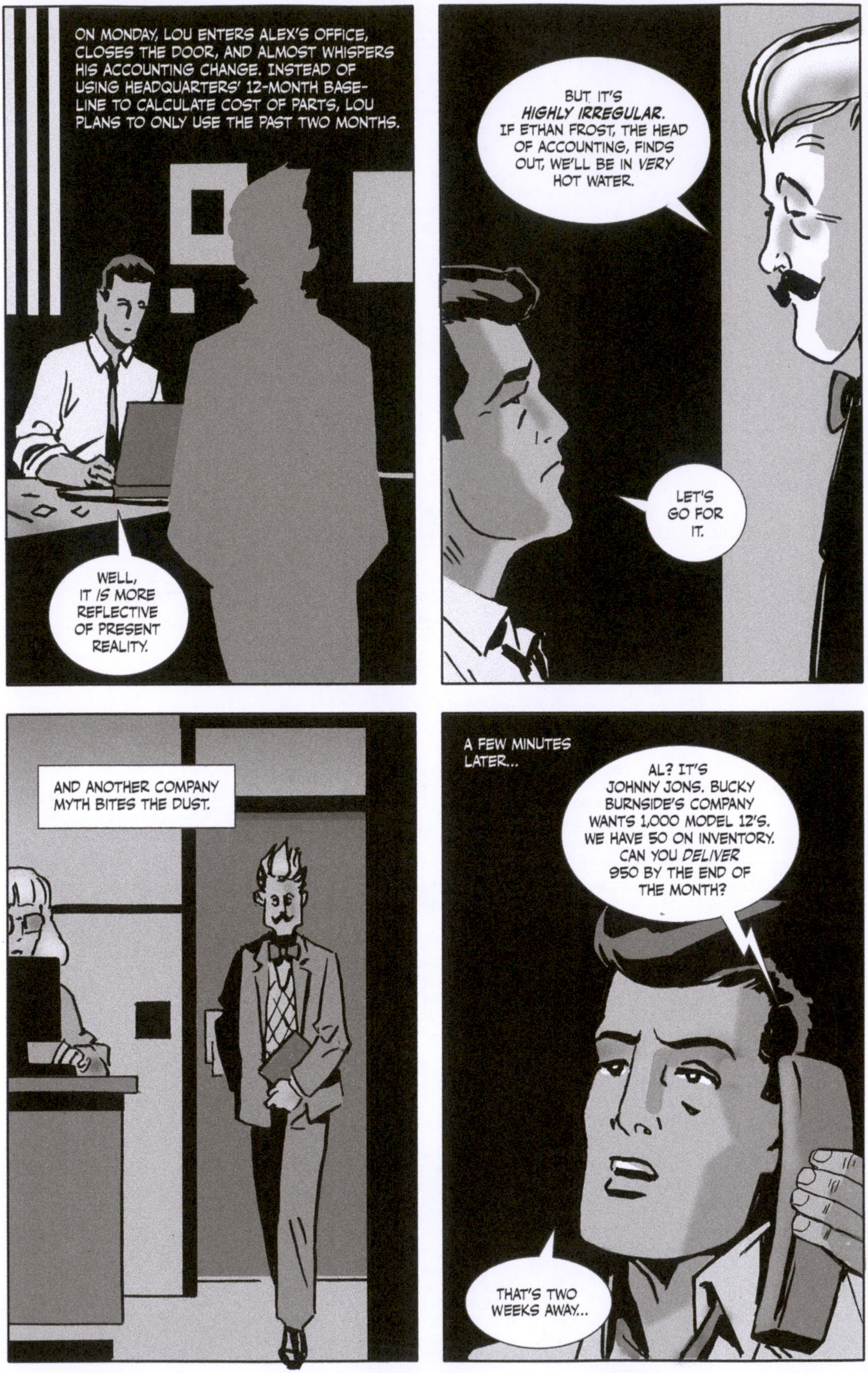
ON MONDAY, LOU ENTERS ALEX'S OFFICE, CLOSES THE DOOR, AND ALMOST WHISPERS HIS ACCOUNTING CHANGE. INSTEAD OF USING HEADQUARTERS' 12-MONTH BASE-LINE TO CALCULATE COST OF PARTS, LOU PLANS TO ONLY USE THE PAST TWO MONTHS.
WELL, IT *IS* MORE REFLECTIVE OF PRESENT REALITY.
BUT IT'S ***HIGHLY IRREGULAR.*** IF ETHAN FROST, THE HEAD OF ACCOUNTING, FINDS OUT, WE'LL BE IN *VERY* HOT WATER.
LET'S GO FOR IT.
AND ANOTHER COMPANY MYTH BITES THE DUST.
A FEW MINUTES LATER...
AL? IT'S JOHNNY JONS. BUCKY BURNSIDE'S COMPANY WANTS 1,000 MODEL 12'S. WE HAVE 50 ON INVENTORY. CAN YOU *DELIVER* 950 BY THE END OF THE MONTH?
THAT'S TWO WEEKS AWAY...

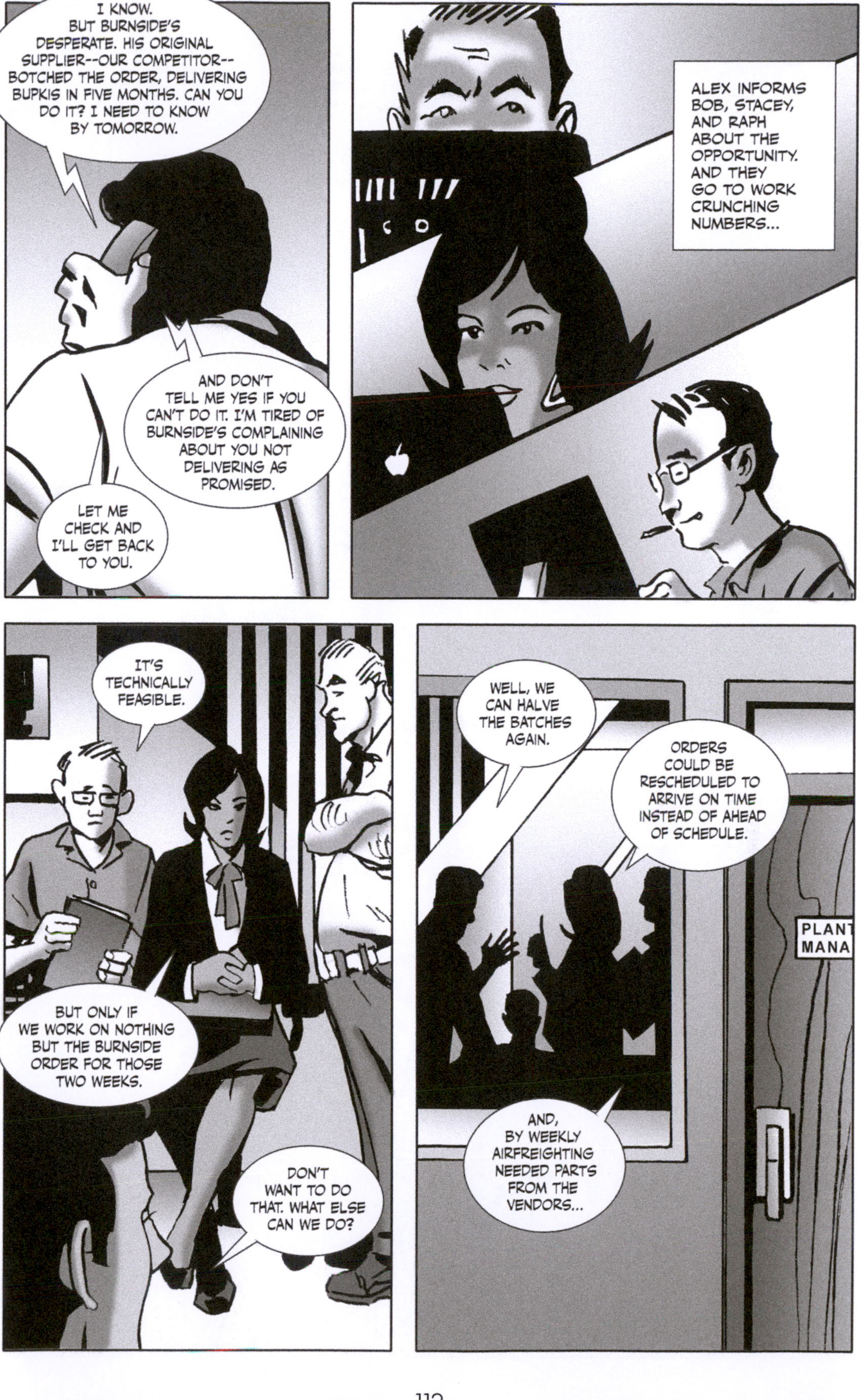
I KNOW. BUT BURNSIDE'S DESPERATE. HIS ORIGINAL SUPPLIER--OUR COMPETITOR--BOTCHED THE ORDER, DELIVERING BUPKIS IN FIVE MONTHS. CAN YOU DO IT? I NEED TO KNOW BY TOMORROW.
AND DON'T TELL ME YES IF YOU CAN'T DO IT. I'M TIRED OF BURNSIDE'S COMPLAINING ABOUT YOU NOT DELIVERING AS PROMISED.
LET ME CHECK AND I'LL GET BACK TO YOU.
ALEX INFORMS BOB, STACEY, AND RAPH ABOUT THE OPPORTUNITY. AND THEY GO TO WORK CRUNCHING NUMBERS...
IT'S TECHNICALLY FEASIBLE.
BUT ONLY IF WE WORK ON NOTHING BUT THE BURNSIDE ORDER FOR THOSE TWO WEEKS.
DON'T WANT TO DO THAT. WHAT ELSE CAN WE DO?
WELL, WE CAN HALVE THE BATCHES AGAIN.
ORDERS COULD BE RESCHEDULED TO ARRIVE ON TIME INSTEAD OF AHEAD OF SCHEDULE.
AND, BY WEEKLY AIRFREIGHTING NEEDED PARTS FROM THE VENDORS...
PLANT
MANA

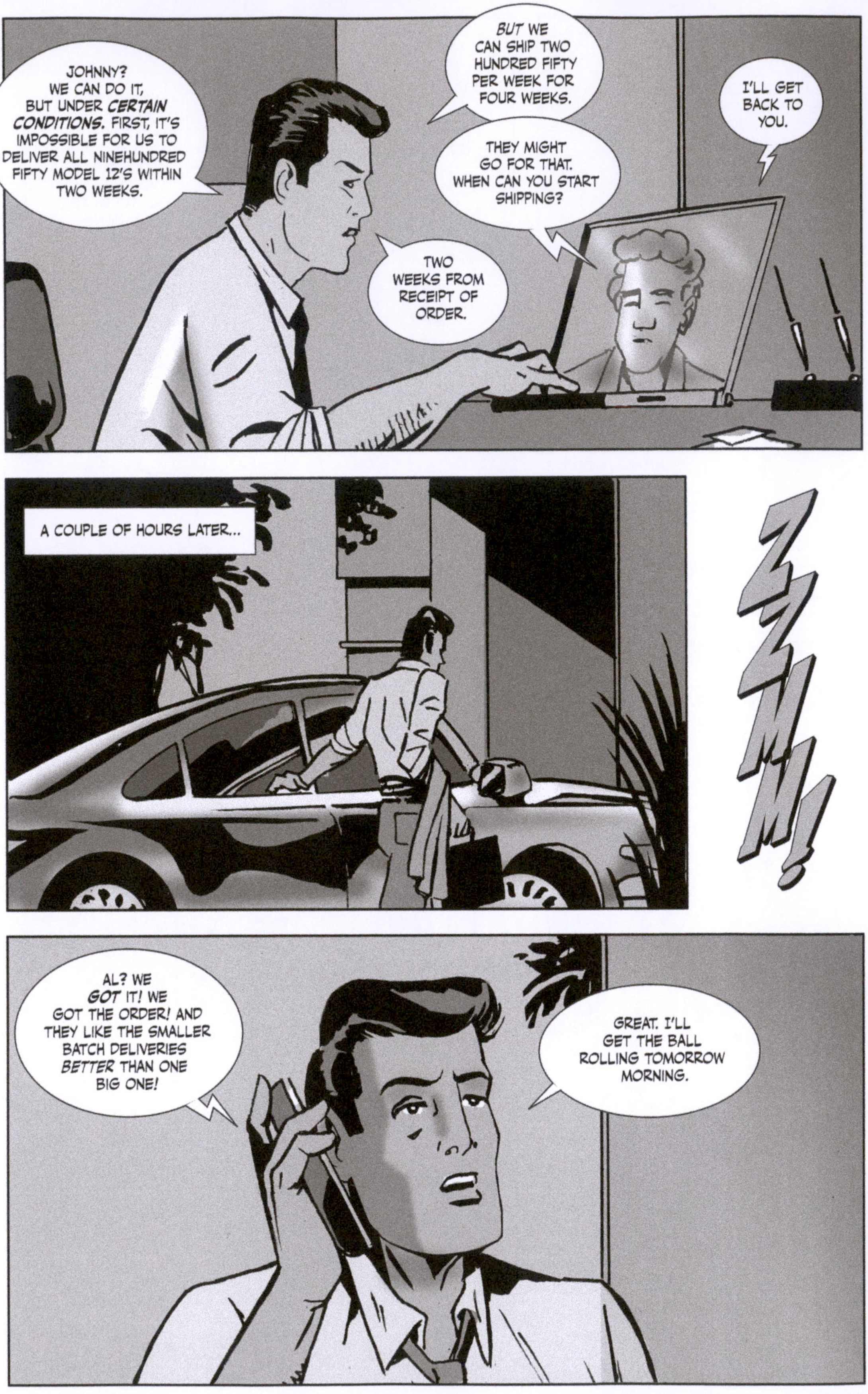
JOHNNY? WE CAN DO IT, BUT UNDER CERTAIN CONDITIONS. FIRST, IT'S IMPOSSIBLE FOR US TO DELIVER ALL NINEHUNDRED FIFTY MODEL 12'S WITHIN TWO WEEKS.
BUT WE CAN SHIP TWO HUNDRED FIFTY PER WEEK FOR FOUR WEEKS.
THEY MIGHT GO FOR THAT. WHEN CAN YOU START SHIPPING?
TWO WEEKS FROM RECEIPT OF ORDER.
I'LL GET BACK TO YOU.
A COUPLE OF HOURS LATER...
ZZMM!
AL? WE GOT IT! WE GOT THE ORDER! AND THEY LIKE THE SMALLER BATCH DELIVERIES BETTER THAN ONE BIG ONE!
GREAT. I'LL GET THE BALL ROLLING TOMORROW MORNING.

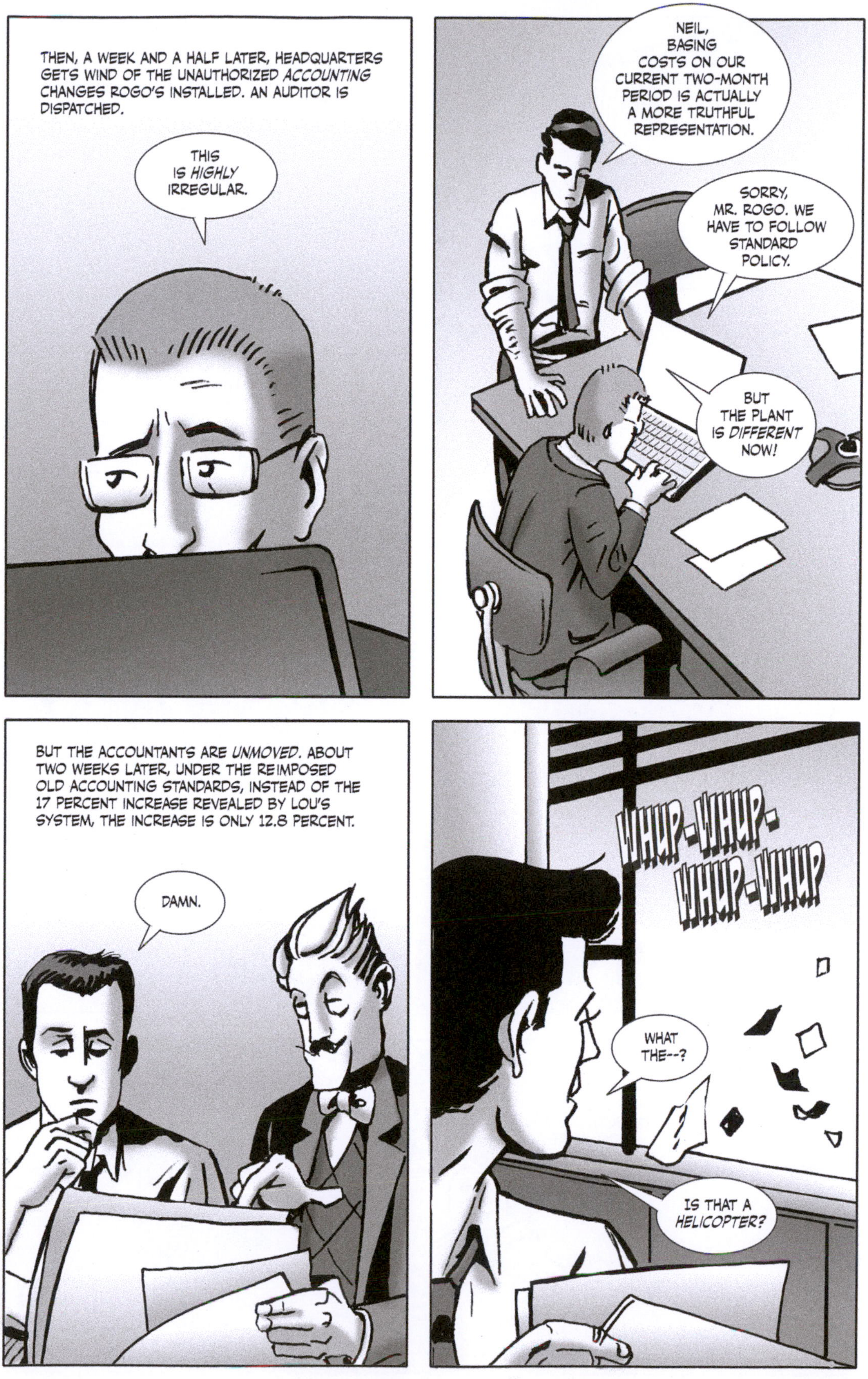
THEN, A WEEK AND A HALF LATER, HEADQUARTERS GETS WIND OF THE UNAUTHORIZED *ACCOUNTING* CHANGES ROGO'S INSTALLED. AN AUDITOR IS DISPATCHED.
THIS IS *HIGHLY* IRREGULAR.
NEIL, BASING COSTS ON OUR CURRENT TWO-MONTH PERIOD IS ACTUALLY A MORE TRUTHFUL REPRESENTATION.
SORRY, MR. ROGO. WE HAVE TO FOLLOW STANDARD POLICY.
BUT THE PLANT IS *DIFFERENT* NOW!
BUT THE ACCOUNTANTS ARE *UNMOVED*. ABOUT TWO WEEKS LATER, UNDER THE REIMPOSED OLD ACCOUNTING STANDARDS, INSTEAD OF THE 17 PERCENT INCREASE REVEALED BY LOU'S SYSTEM, THE INCREASE IS ONLY 12.8 PERCENT.
DAMN.
WHUP-WHUP-WHUP-WHUP
WHAT THE--?
IS THAT A *HELICOPTER?*

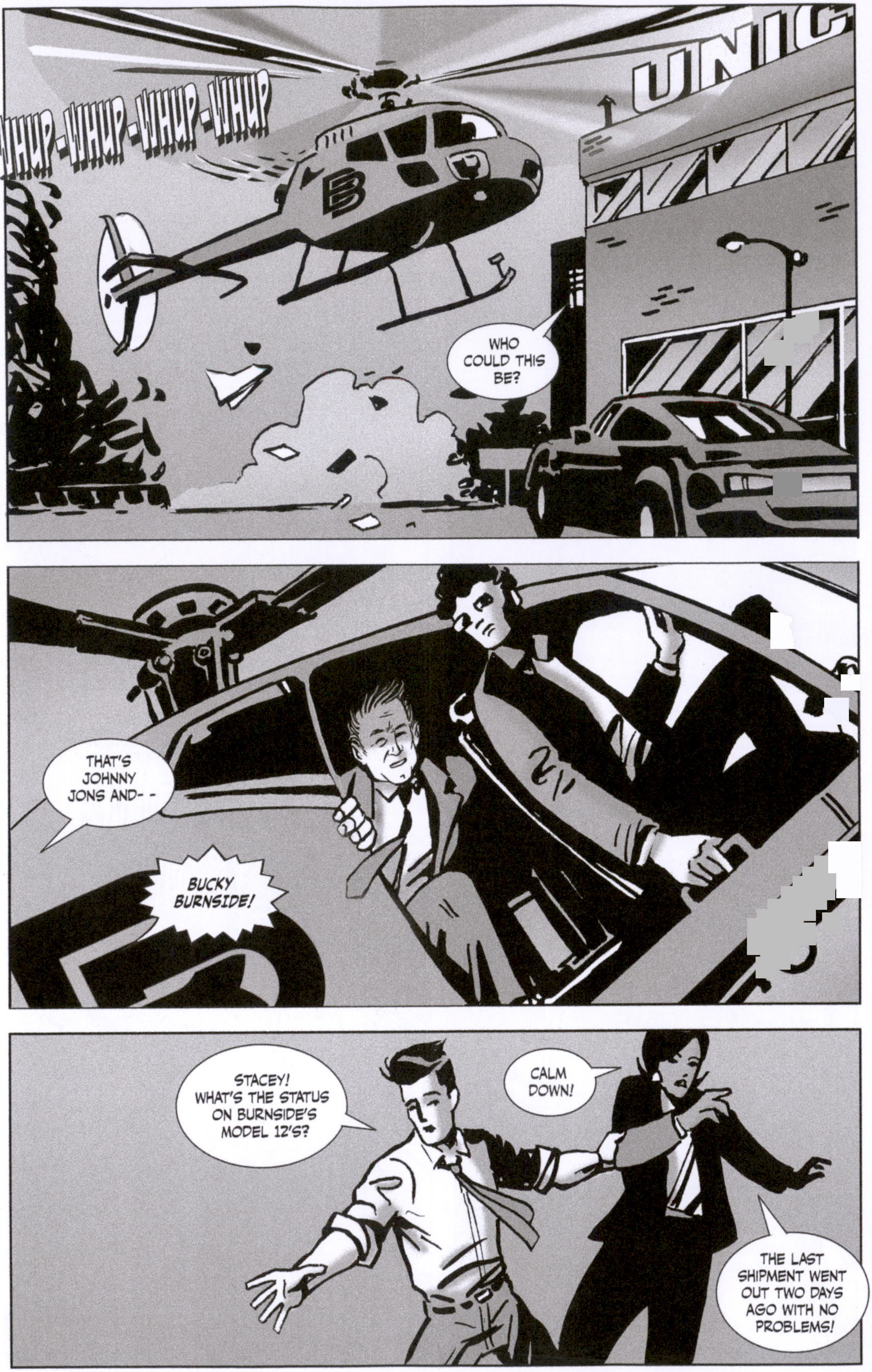
WHUP-WHUP-WHUP-WHUP
UNIC
WHO COULD THIS BE?
THAT'S JOHNNY JONS AND- -
BUCKY BURNSIDE!
STACEY! WHAT'S THE STATUS ON BURNSIDE'S MODEL 12'S?
CALM DOWN!
THE LAST SHIPMENT WENT OUT TWO DAYS AGO WITH NO PROBLEMS!

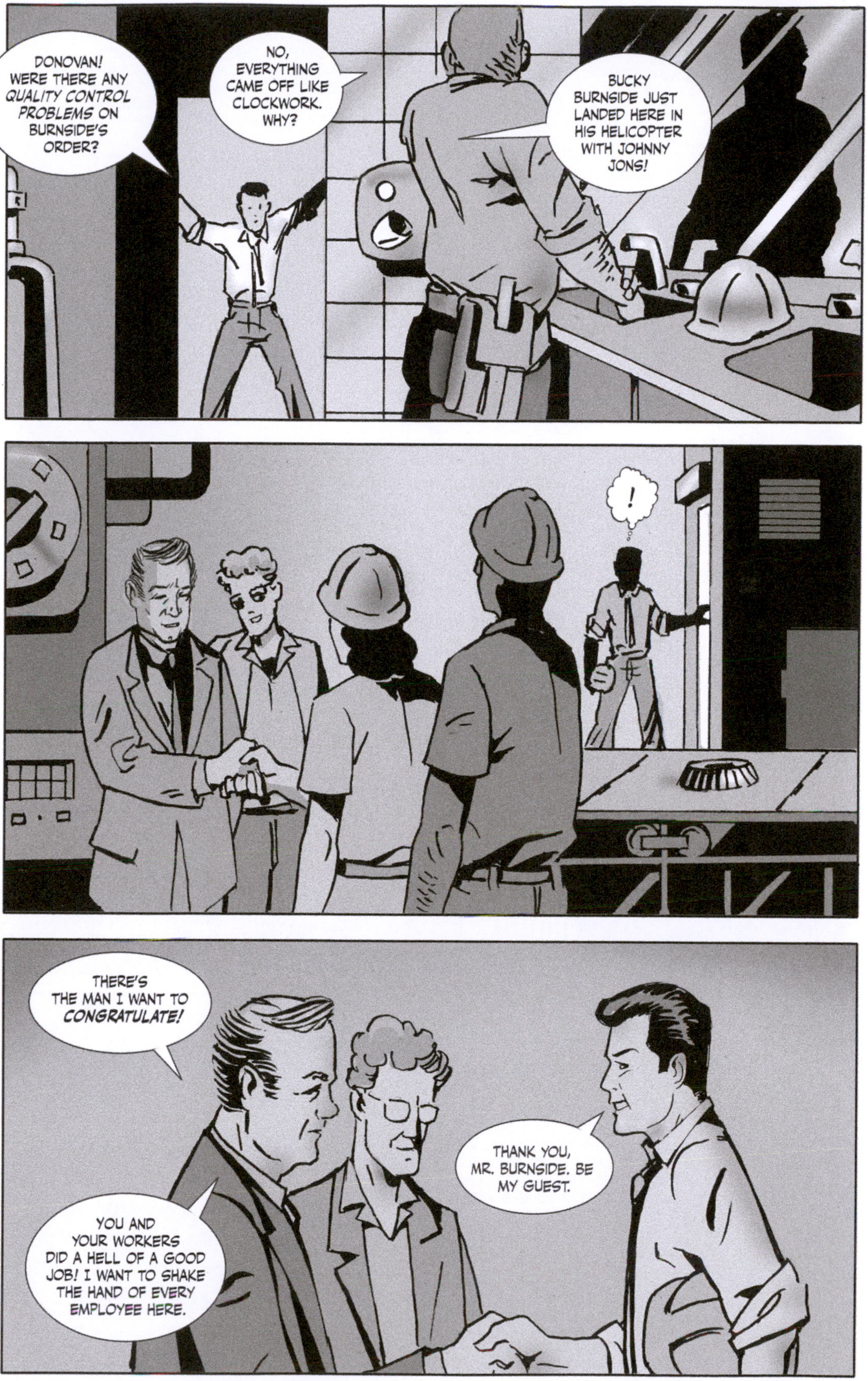
DONOVAN! WERE THERE ANY QUALITY CONTROL PROBLEMS ON BURNSIDE'S ORDER?
NO, EVERYTHING CAME OFF LIKE CLOCKWORK. WHY?
BUCKY BURNSIDE JUST LANDED HERE IN HIS HELICOPTER WITH JOHNNY JONS!
!
THERE'S THE MAN I WANT TO CONGRATULATE!
YOU AND YOUR WORKERS DID A HELL OF A GOOD JOB! I WANT TO SHAKE THE HAND OF EVERY EMPLOYEE HERE.
THANK YOU, MR. BURNSIDE. BE MY GUEST.

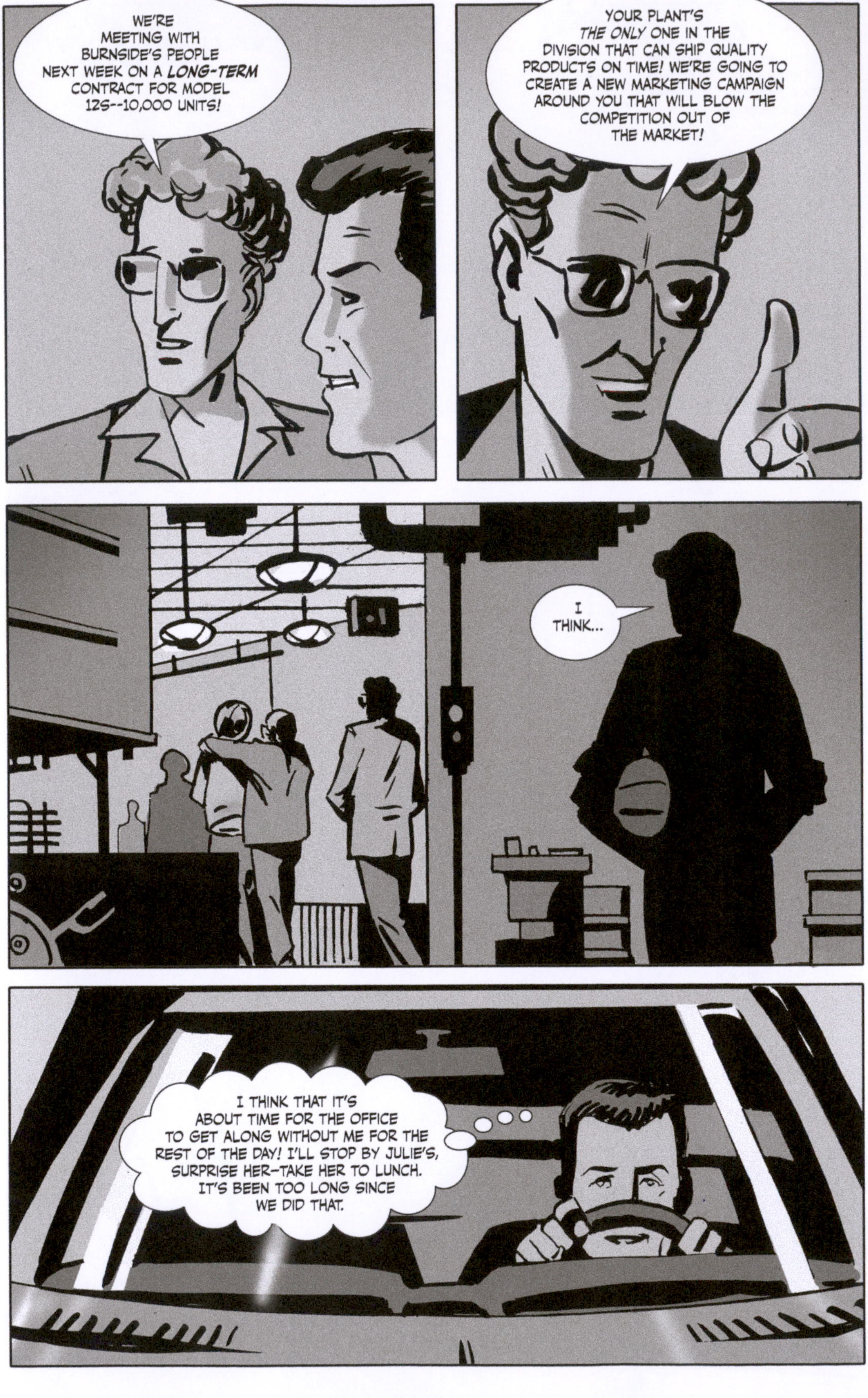
WE'RE MEETING WITH BURNSIDE'S PEOPLE NEXT WEEK ON A *LONG-TERM* CONTRACT FOR MODEL 12S--10,000 UNITS!
YOUR PLANT'S *THE ONLY* ONE IN THE DIVISION THAT CAN SHIP QUALITY PRODUCTS ON TIME! WE'RE GOING TO CREATE A NEW MARKETING CAMPAIGN AROUND YOU THAT WILL BLOW THE COMPETITION OUT OF THE MARKET!
I THINK...
I THINK THAT IT'S ABOUT TIME FOR THE OFFICE TO GET ALONG WITHOUT ME FOR THE REST OF THE DAY! I'LL STOP BY JULIE'S, SURPRISE HER–TAKE HER TO LUNCH. IT'S BEEN TOO LONG SINCE WE DID THAT.

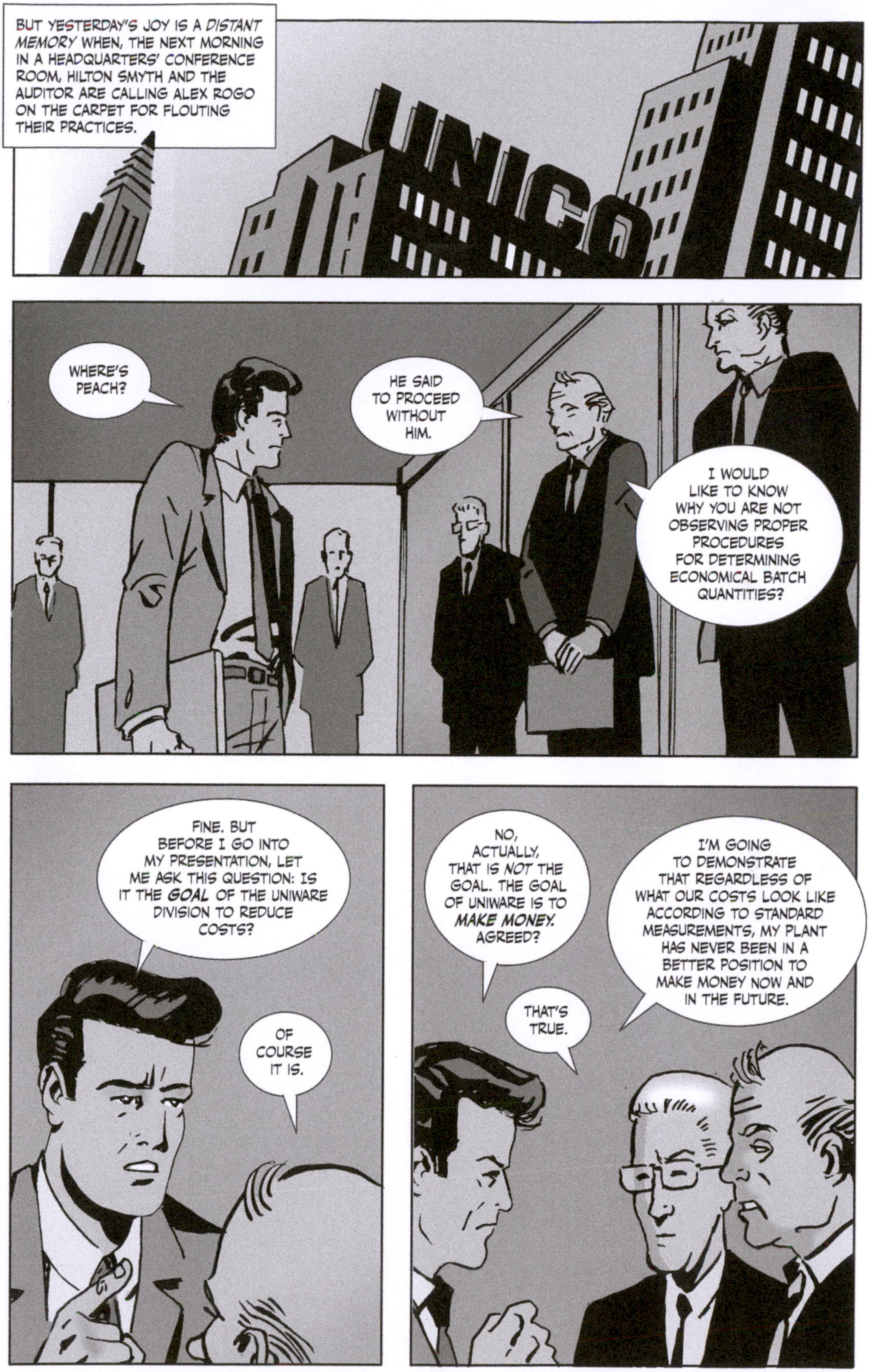
BUT YESTERDAY'S JOY IS A DISTANT MEMORY WHEN, THE NEXT MORNING IN A HEADQUARTERS' CONFERENCE ROOM, HILTON SMYTH AND THE AUDITOR ARE CALLING ALEX ROGO ON THE CARPET FOR FLOUTING THEIR PRACTICES.
UNICO
WHERE'S PEACH?
HE SAID TO PROCEED WITHOUT HIM.
I WOULD LIKE TO KNOW WHY YOU ARE NOT OBSERVING PROPER PROCEDURES FOR DETERMINING ECONOMICAL BATCH QUANTITIES?
FINE. BUT BEFORE I GO INTO MY PRESENTATION, LET ME ASK THIS QUESTION: IS IT THE GOAL OF THE UNIWARE DIVISION TO REDUCE COSTS?
OF COURSE IT IS.
NO, ACTUALLY, THAT IS NOT THE GOAL. THE GOAL OF UNIWARE IS TO MAKE MONEY. AGREED?
THAT'S TRUE.
I'M GOING TO DEMONSTRATE THAT REGARDLESS OF WHAT OUR COSTS LOOK LIKE ACCORDING TO STANDARD MEASUREMENTS, MY PLANT HAS NEVER BEEN IN A BETTER POSITION TO MAKE MONEY NOW AND IN THE FUTURE.

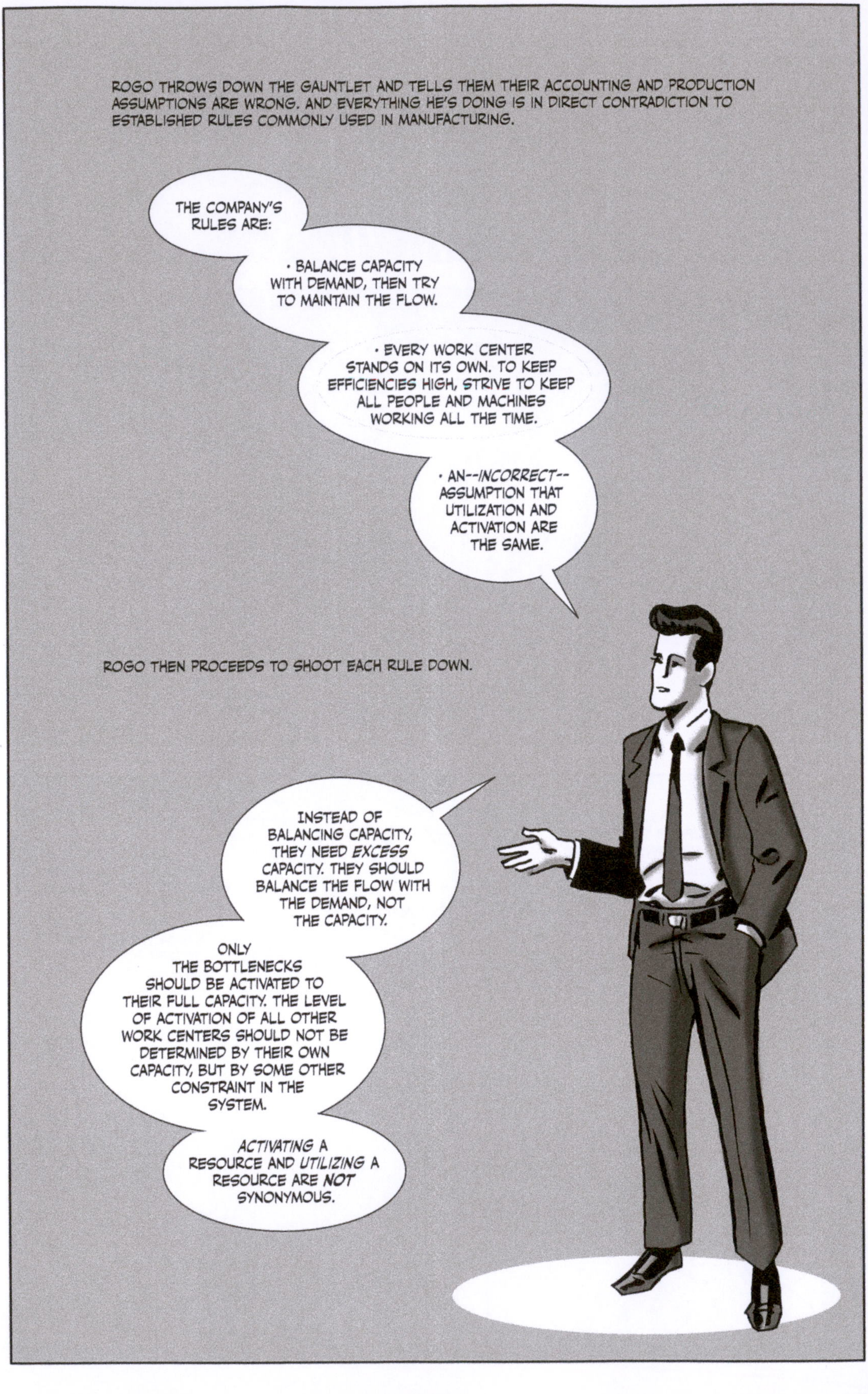

ROGO THROWS DOWN THE GAUNTLET AND TELLS THEM THEIR ACCOUNTING AND PRODUCTION ASSUMPTIONS ARE WRONG. AND EVERYTHING HE'S DOING IS IN DIRECT CONTRADICTION TO ESTABLISHED RULES COMMONLY USED IN MANUFACTURING.
THE COMPANY'S RULES ARE:
• BALANCE CAPACITY WITH DEMAND, THEN TRY TO MAINTAIN THE FLOW.
• EVERY WORK CENTER STANDS ON ITS OWN. TO KEEP EFFICIENCIES HIGH, STRIVE TO KEEP ALL PEOPLE AND MACHINES WORKING ALL THE TIME.
• AN--*INCORRECT*--ASSUMPTION THAT UTILIZATION AND ACTIVATION ARE THE SAME.
ROGO THEN PROCEEDS TO SHOOT EACH RULE DOWN.
INSTEAD OF BALANCING CAPACITY, THEY NEED *EXCESS* CAPACITY. THEY SHOULD BALANCE THE FLOW WITH THE DEMAND, NOT THE CAPACITY.
ONLY THE BOTTLENECKS SHOULD BE ACTIVATED TO THEIR FULL CAPACITY. THE LEVEL OF ACTIVATION OF ALL OTHER WORK CENTERS SHOULD NOT BE DETERMINED BY THEIR OWN CAPACITY, BUT BY SOME OTHER CONSTRAINT IN THE SYSTEM.
ACTIVATING A RESOURCE AND *UTILIZING* A RESOURCE ARE ***NOT*** SYNONYMOUS.

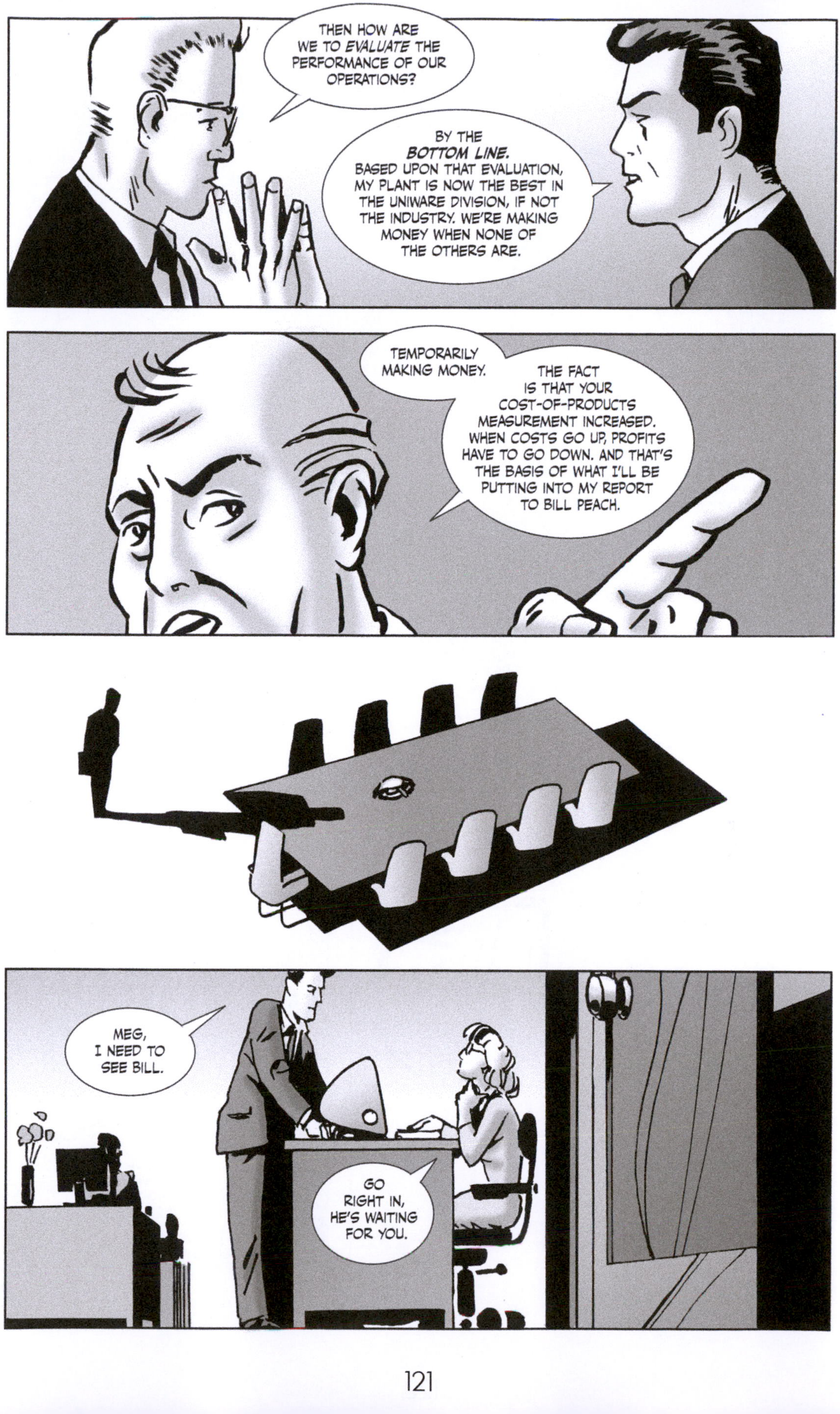
THEN HOW ARE WE TO *EVALUATE* THE PERFORMANCE OF OUR OPERATIONS?
BY THE **BOTTOM LINE.** BASED UPON THAT EVALUATION, MY PLANT IS NOW THE BEST IN THE UNIWARE DIVISION, IF NOT THE INDUSTRY. WE'RE MAKING MONEY WHEN NONE OF THE OTHERS ARE.
TEMPORARILY MAKING MONEY.
THE FACT IS THAT YOUR COST-OF-PRODUCTS MEASUREMENT INCREASED. WHEN COSTS GO UP, PROFITS HAVE TO GO DOWN. AND THAT'S THE BASIS OF WHAT I'LL BE PUTTING INTO MY REPORT TO BILL PEACH.
MEG, I NEED TO SEE BILL.
GO RIGHT IN, HE'S WAITING FOR YOU.

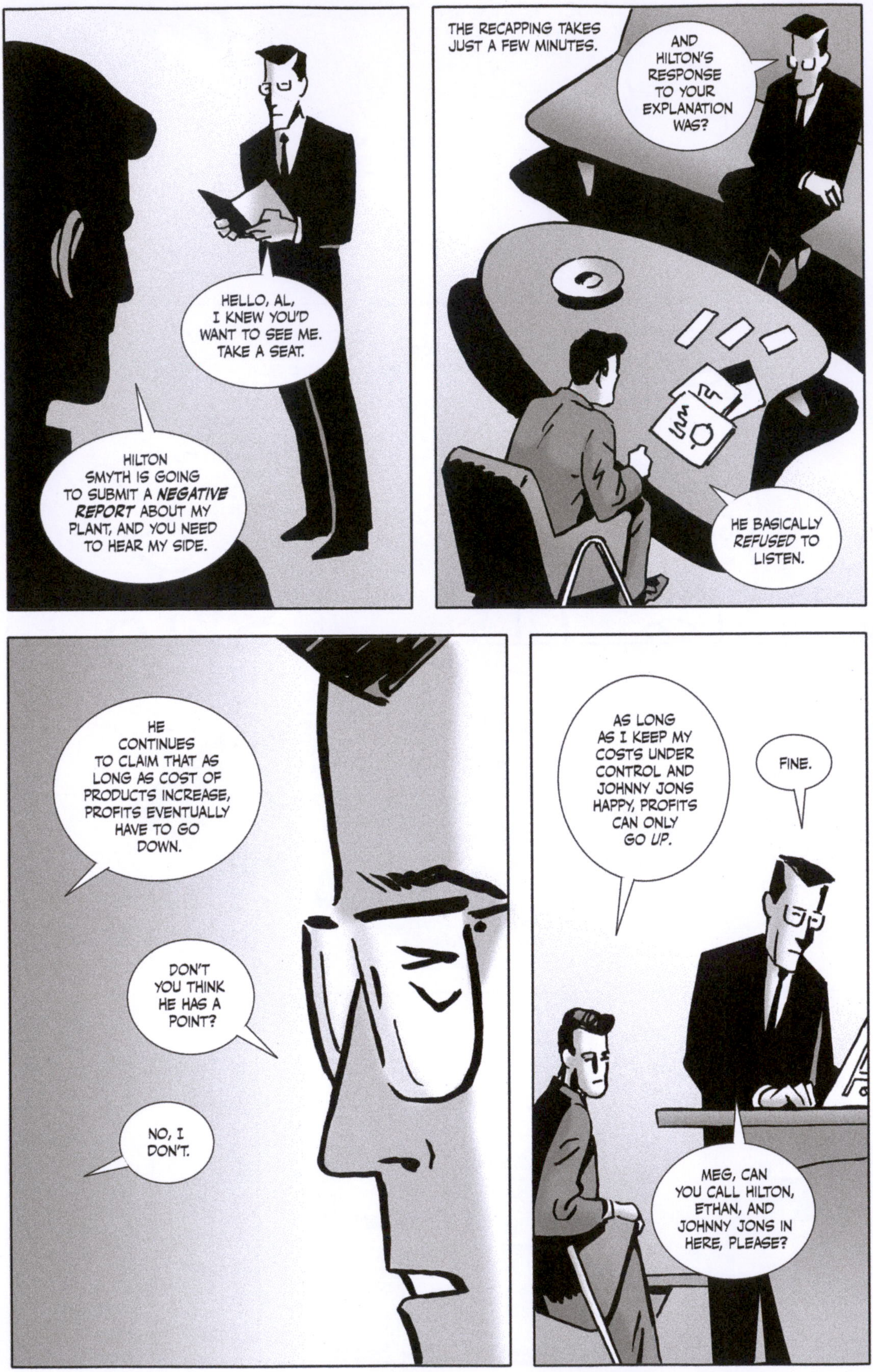
HELLO, AL, I KNEW YOU'D WANT TO SEE ME. TAKE A SEAT.
HILTON SMYTH IS GOING TO SUBMIT A *NEGATIVE REPORT* ABOUT MY PLANT, AND YOU NEED TO HEAR MY SIDE.
THE RECAPPING TAKES JUST A FEW MINUTES.
AND HILTON'S RESPONSE TO YOUR EXPLANATION WAS?
HE BASICALLY *REFUSED* TO LISTEN.
HE CONTINUES TO CLAIM THAT AS LONG AS COST OF PRODUCTS INCREASE, PROFITS EVENTUALLY HAVE TO GO DOWN.
DON'T YOU THINK HE HAS A POINT?
NO, I DON'T.
AS LONG AS I KEEP MY COSTS UNDER CONTROL AND JOHNNY JONS HAPPY, PROFITS CAN ONLY GO *UP*.
FINE.
MEG, CAN YOU CALL HILTON, ETHAN, AND JOHNNY JONS IN HERE, PLEASE?

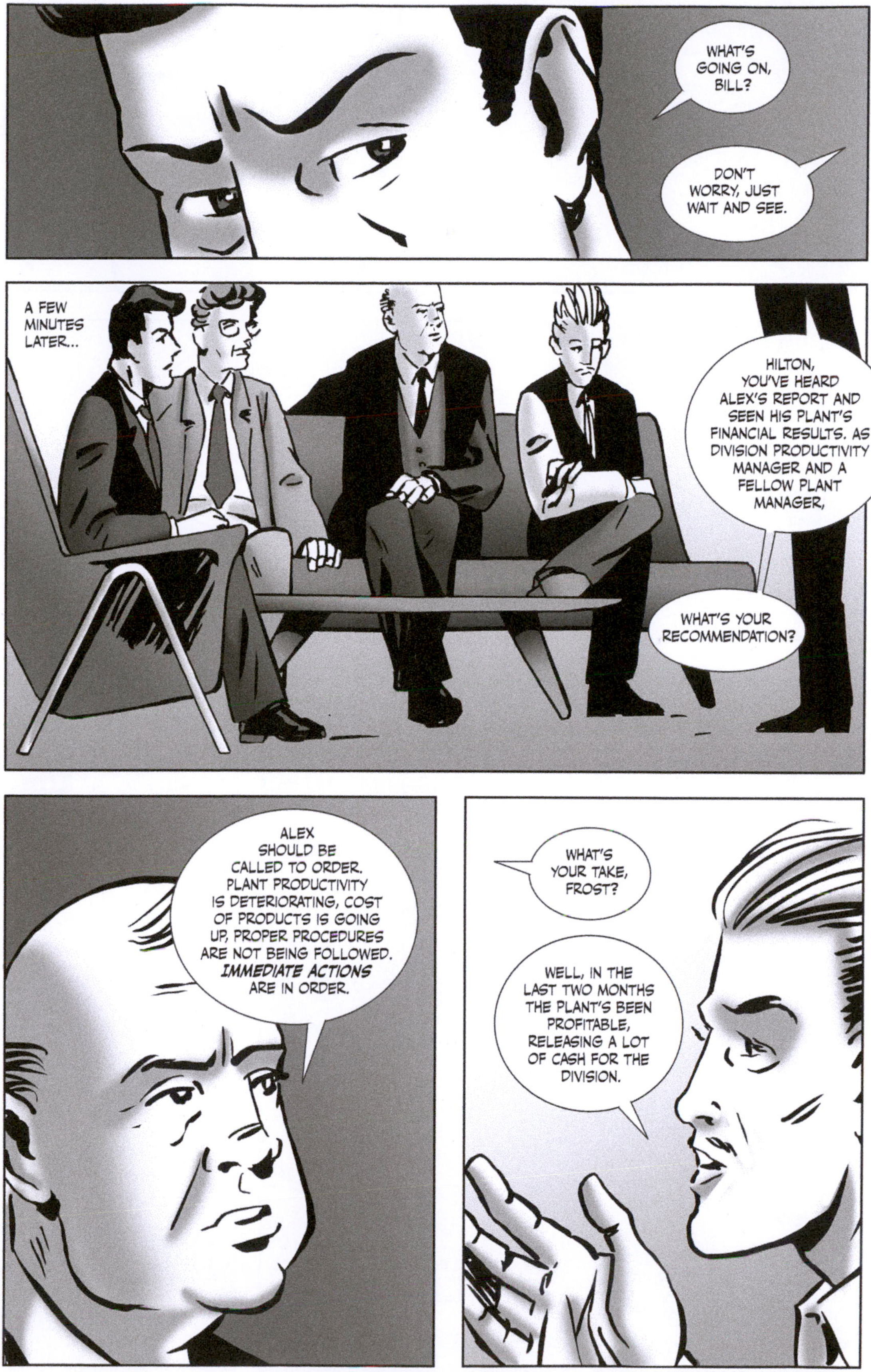

WHAT'S GOING ON, BILL?
DON'T WORRY, JUST WAIT AND SEE.
A FEW MINUTES LATER...
HILTON, YOU'VE HEARD ALEX'S REPORT AND SEEN HIS PLANT'S FINANCIAL RESULTS. AS DIVISION PRODUCTIVITY MANAGER AND A FELLOW PLANT MANAGER,
WHAT'S YOUR RECOMMENDATION?
ALEX SHOULD BE CALLED TO ORDER. PLANT PRODUCTIVITY IS DETERIORATING, COST OF PRODUCTS IS GOING UP, PROPER PROCEDURES ARE NOT BEING FOLLOWED. *IMMEDIATE ACTIONS* ARE IN ORDER.
WHAT'S YOUR TAKE, FROST?
WELL, IN THE LAST TWO MONTHS THE PLANT'S BEEN PROFITABLE, RELEASING A LOT OF CASH FOR THE DIVISION.

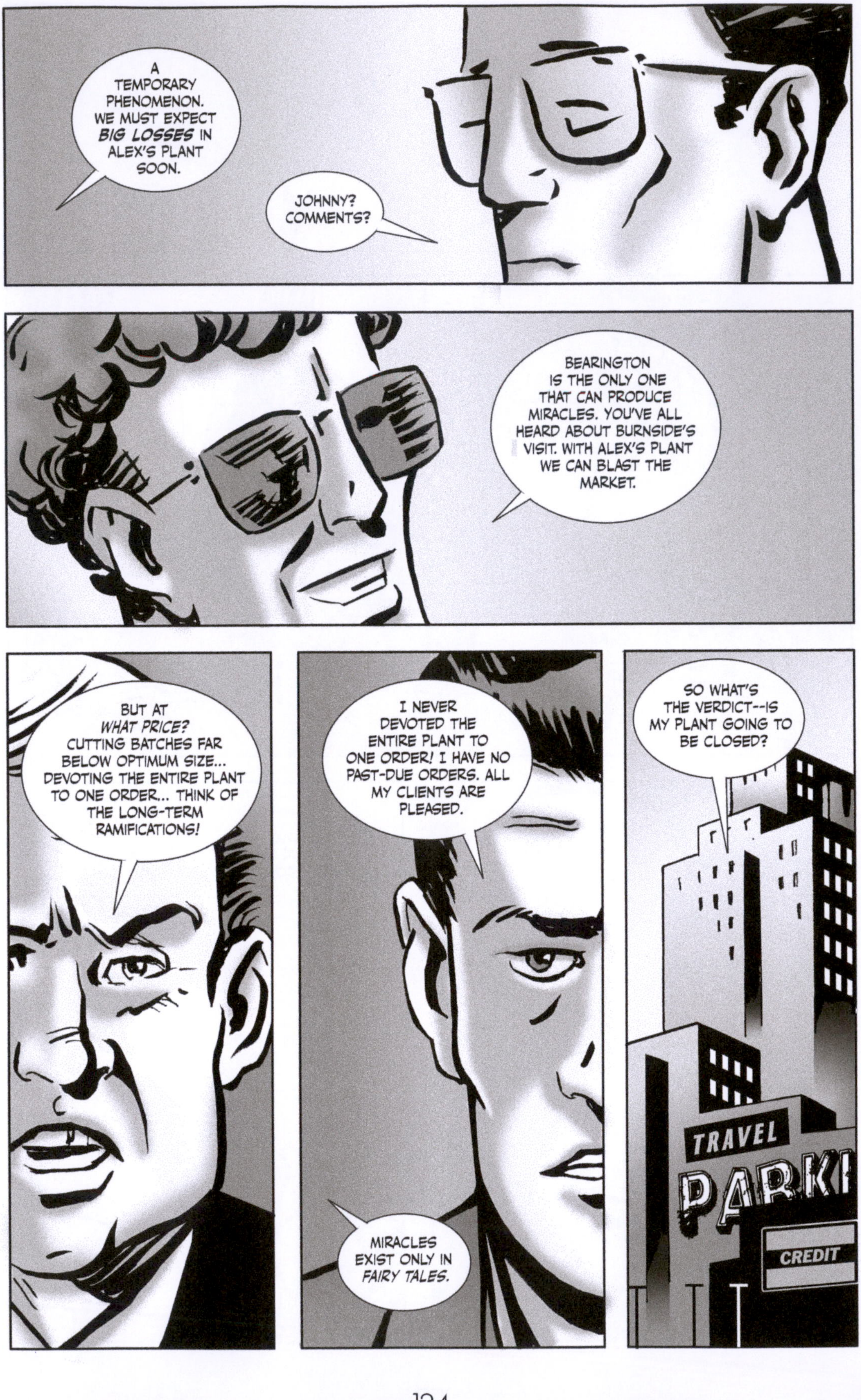
A TEMPORARY PHENOMENON. WE MUST EXPECT *BIG LOSSES* IN ALEX'S PLANT SOON.
JOHNNY? COMMENTS?
BEARINGTON IS THE ONLY ONE THAT CAN PRODUCE MIRACLES. YOU'VE ALL HEARD ABOUT BURNSIDE'S VISIT. WITH ALEX'S PLANT WE CAN BLAST THE MARKET.
BUT AT *WHAT PRICE?* CUTTING BATCHES FAR BELOW OPTIMUM SIZE... DEVOTING THE ENTIRE PLANT TO ONE ORDER... THINK OF THE LONG-TERM RAMIFICATIONS!
I NEVER DEVOTED THE ENTIRE PLANT TO ONE ORDER! I HAVE NO PAST-DUE ORDERS. ALL MY CLIENTS ARE PLEASED.
MIRACLES EXIST ONLY IN *FAIRY TALES.*
SO WHAT'S THE VERDICT--IS MY PLANT GOING TO BE CLOSED?
TRAVEL
PARKI
CREDIT

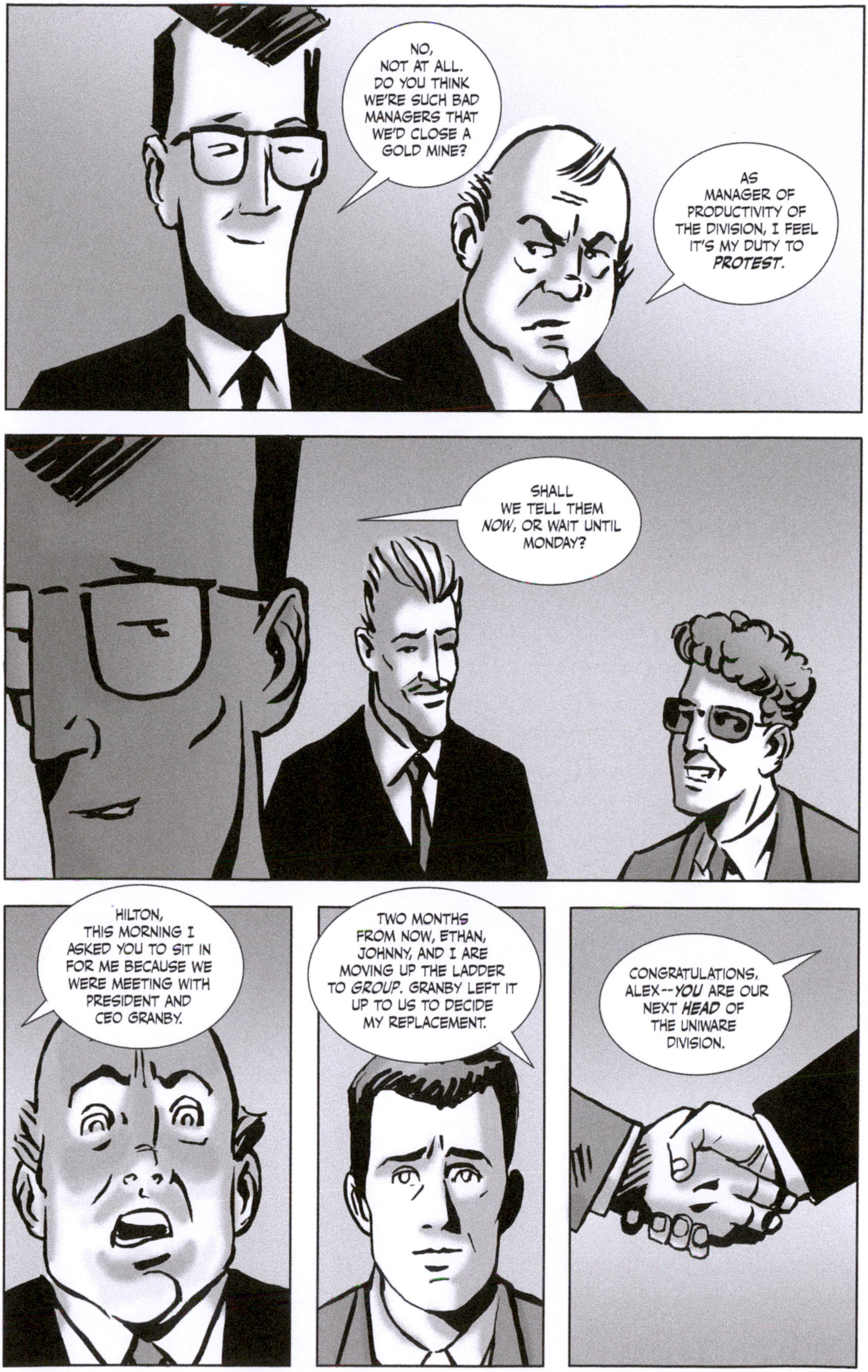
NO, NOT AT ALL. DO YOU THINK WE'RE SUCH BAD MANAGERS THAT WE'D CLOSE A GOLD MINE?
AS MANAGER OF PRODUCTIVITY OF THE DIVISION, I FEEL IT'S MY DUTY TO *PROTEST*.
SHALL WE TELL THEM *NOW*, OR WAIT UNTIL MONDAY?
HILTON, THIS MORNING I ASKED YOU TO SIT IN FOR ME BECAUSE WE WERE MEETING WITH PRESIDENT AND CEO GRANBY.
TWO MONTHS FROM NOW, ETHAN, JOHNNY, AND I ARE MOVING UP THE LADDER TO *GROUP*. GRANBY LEFT IT UP TO US TO DECIDE MY REPLACEMENT.
CONGRATULATIONS, ALEX--*YOU* ARE OUR NEXT *HEAD* OF THE UNIWARE DIVISION.

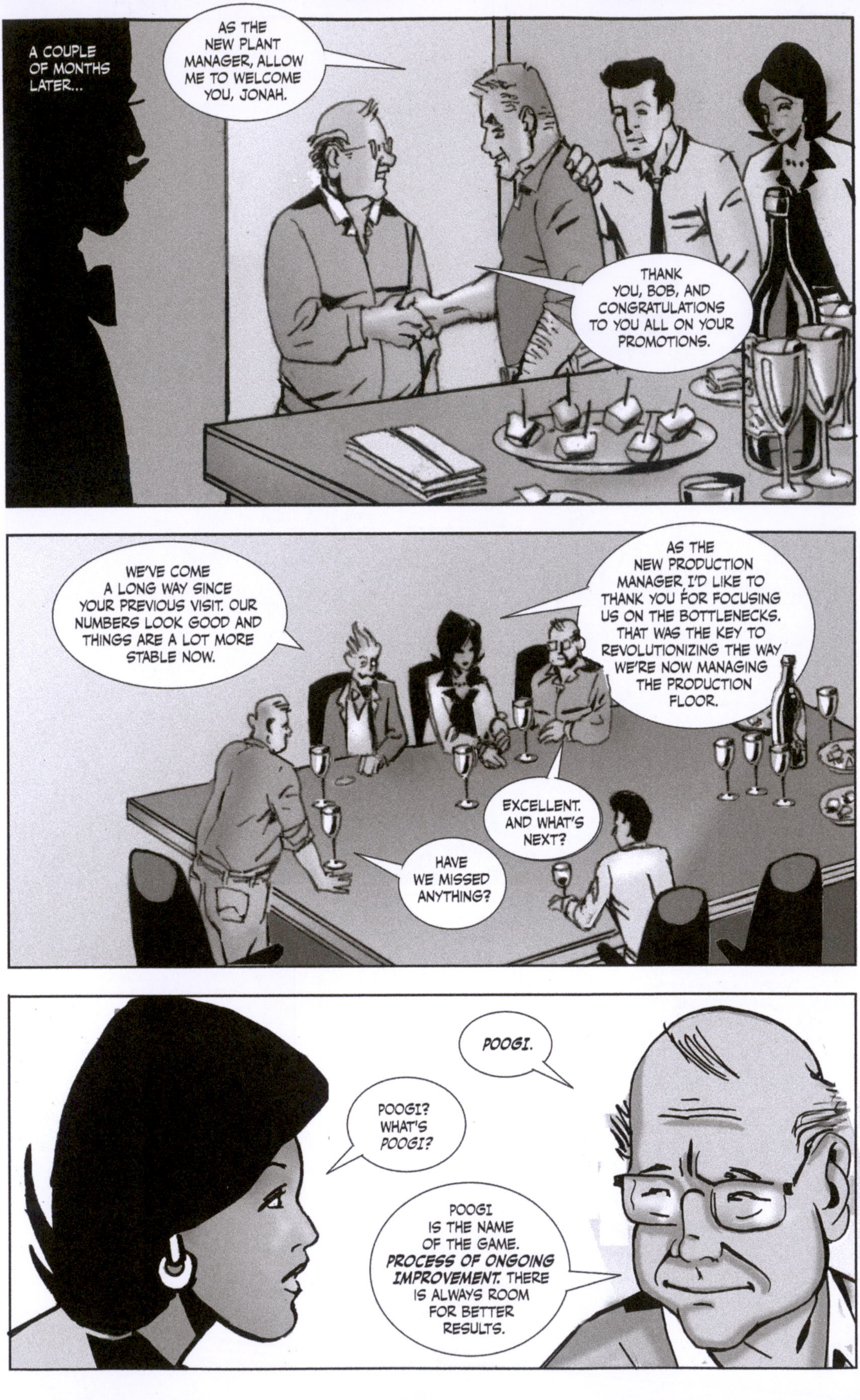
A COUPLE OF MONTHS LATER...
AS THE NEW PLANT MANAGER, ALLOW ME TO WELCOME YOU, JONAH.
THANK YOU, BOB, AND CONGRATULATIONS TO YOU ALL ON YOUR PROMOTIONS.
WE'VE COME A LONG WAY SINCE YOUR PREVIOUS VISIT. OUR NUMBERS LOOK GOOD AND THINGS ARE A LOT MORE STABLE NOW.
AS THE NEW PRODUCTION MANAGER I'D LIKE TO THANK YOU FOR FOCUSING US ON THE BOTTLENECKS. THAT WAS THE KEY TO REVOLUTIONIZING THE WAY WE'RE NOW MANAGING THE PRODUCTION FLOOR.
EXCELLENT. AND WHAT'S NEXT?
HAVE WE MISSED ANYTHING?
POOGI.
POOGI? WHAT'S *POOGI?*
POOGI IS THE NAME OF THE GAME. ***PROCESS OF ONGOING IMPROVEMENT.*** THERE IS ALWAYS ROOM FOR BETTER RESULTS.

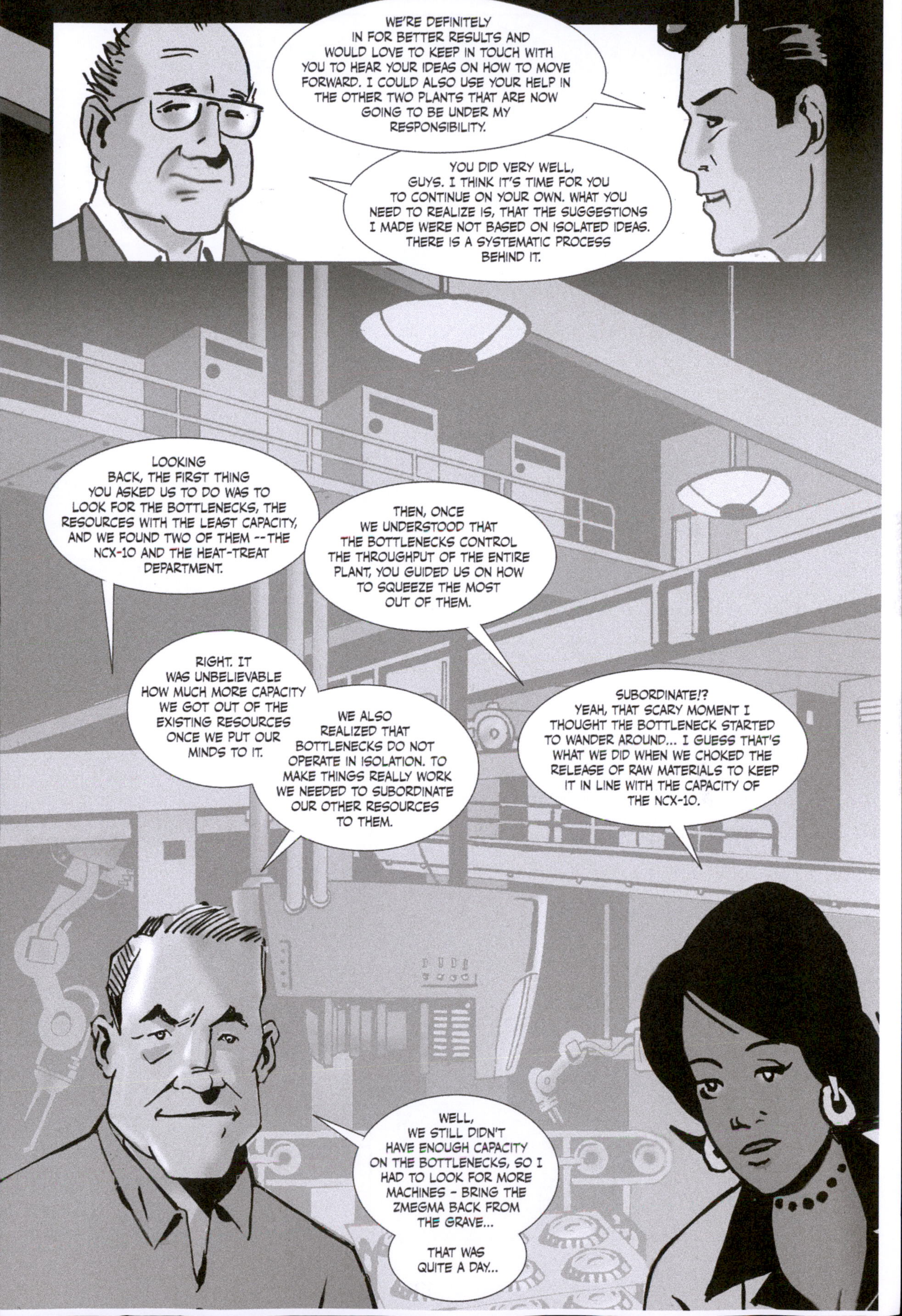
WE'RE DEFINITELY IN FOR BETTER RESULTS AND WOULD LOVE TO KEEP IN TOUCH WITH YOU TO HEAR YOUR IDEAS ON HOW TO MOVE FORWARD. I COULD ALSO USE YOUR HELP IN THE OTHER TWO PLANTS THAT ARE NOW GOING TO BE UNDER MY RESPONSIBILITY.
YOU DID VERY WELL, GUYS. I THINK IT'S TIME FOR YOU TO CONTINUE ON YOUR OWN. WHAT YOU NEED TO REALIZE IS, THAT THE SUGGESTIONS I MADE WERE NOT BASED ON ISOLATED IDEAS. THERE IS A SYSTEMATIC PROCESS BEHIND IT.
LOOKING BACK, THE FIRST THING YOU ASKED US TO DO WAS TO LOOK FOR THE BOTTLENECKS, THE RESOURCES WITH THE LEAST CAPACITY, AND WE FOUND TWO OF THEM --THE NCX-10 AND THE HEAT-TREAT DEPARTMENT.
THEN, ONCE WE UNDERSTOOD THAT THE BOTTLENECKS CONTROL THE THROUGHPUT OF THE ENTIRE PLANT, YOU GUIDED US ON HOW TO SQUEEZE THE MOST OUT OF THEM.
RIGHT. IT WAS UNBELIEVABLE HOW MUCH MORE CAPACITY WE GOT OUT OF THE EXISTING RESOURCES ONCE WE PUT OUR MINDS TO IT.
WE ALSO REALIZED THAT BOTTLENECKS DO NOT OPERATE IN ISOLATION. TO MAKE THINGS REALLY WORK WE NEEDED TO SUBORDINATE OUR OTHER RESOURCES TO THEM.
SUBORDINATE!? YEAH, THAT SCARY MOMENT I THOUGHT THE BOTTLENECK STARTED TO WANDER AROUND... I GUESS THAT'S WHAT WE DID WHEN WE CHOKED THE RELEASE OF RAW MATERIALS TO KEEP IT IN LINE WITH THE CAPACITY OF THE NCX-10.
WELL, WE STILL DIDN'T HAVE ENOUGH CAPACITY ON THE BOTTLENECKS, SO I HAD TO LOOK FOR MORE MACHINES - BRING THE ZMEGMA BACK FROM THE GRAVE...
THAT WAS QUITE A DAY...

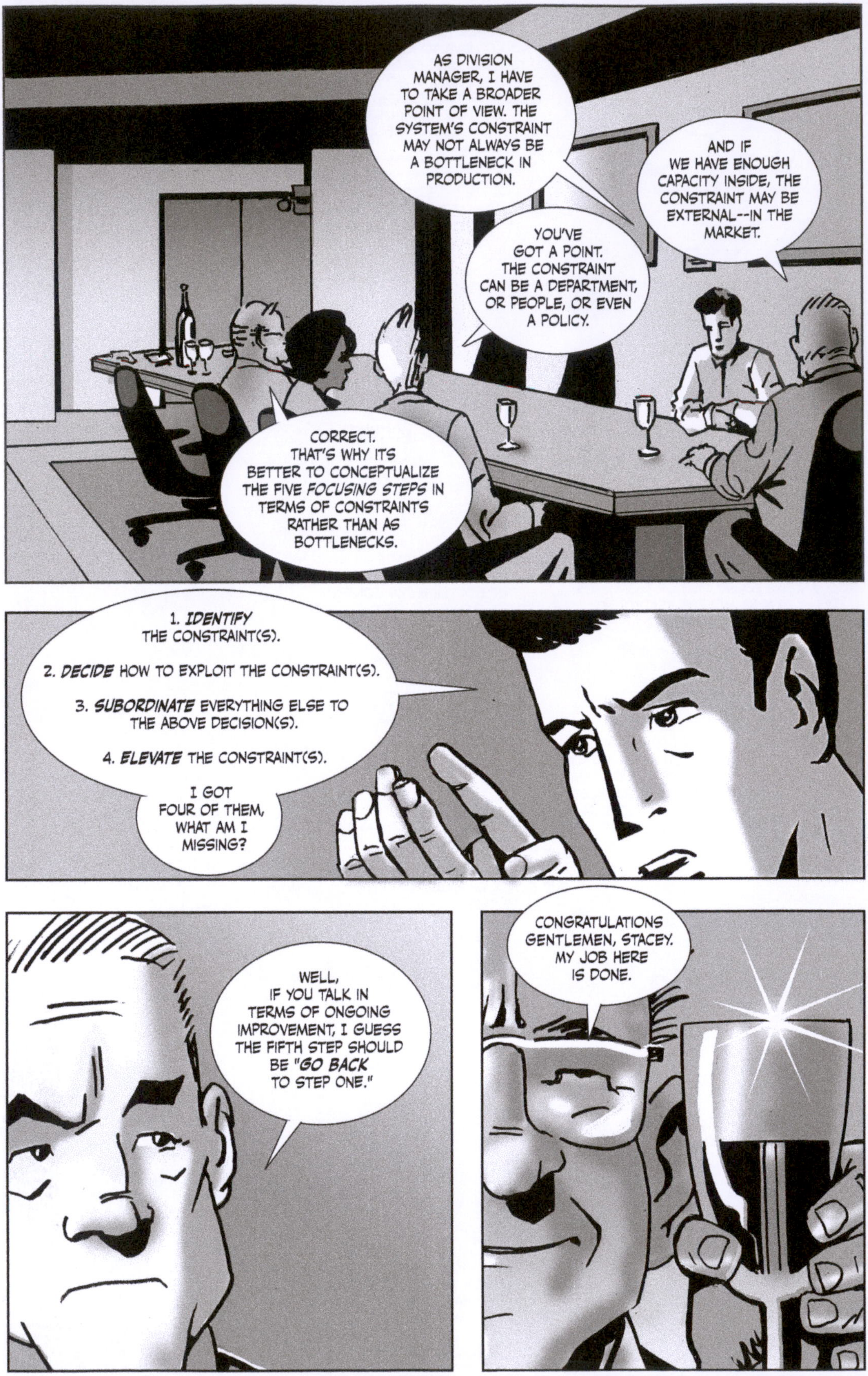

AS DIVISION MANAGER, I HAVE TO TAKE A BROADER POINT OF VIEW. THE SYSTEM'S CONSTRAINT MAY NOT ALWAYS BE A BOTTLENECK IN PRODUCTION.
YOU'VE GOT A POINT. THE CONSTRAINT CAN BE A DEPARTMENT, OR PEOPLE, OR EVEN A POLICY.
AND IF WE HAVE ENOUGH CAPACITY INSIDE, THE CONSTRAINT MAY BE EXTERNAL--IN THE MARKET.
CORRECT. THAT'S WHY ITS BETTER TO CONCEPTUALIZE THE FIVE *FOCUSING STEPS* IN TERMS OF CONSTRAINTS RATHER THAN AS BOTTLENECKS.
1. *IDENTIFY* THE CONSTRAINT(S).
2. *DECIDE* HOW TO EXPLOIT THE CONSTRAINT(S).
3. *SUBORDINATE* EVERYTHING ELSE TO THE ABOVE DECISION(S).
4. *ELEVATE* THE CONSTRAINT(S).
I GOT FOUR OF THEM, WHAT AM I MISSING?
WELL, IF YOU TALK IN TERMS OF ONGOING IMPROVEMENT, I GUESS THE FIFTH STEP SHOULD BE "*GO BACK* TO STEP ONE."
CONGRATULATIONS GENTLEMEN, STACEY. MY JOB HERE IS DONE.

THE 5 FOCUSING STEPS OF THE THEORY OF CONSTRAINTS

1. *IDENTIFY* THE SYSTEM'S CONSTRAINT(S).

2. DECIDE HOW TO *EXPLOIT* THE SYSTEM'S CONSTRAINT(S).

3. *SUBORDINATE* EVERYTHING ELSE TO THE ABOVE DECISION(S).

4. *ELEVATE* THE SYSTEM'S CONSTRAINT(S).

5. *GO BACK* TO STEP 1. WARNING: DO NOT ALLOW INERTIA TO CAUSE A SYSTEM'S CONSTRAINT.